# EUROGAMES

## The Design, Culture and Play of Modern European Board Games

### Stewart Woods

D1153557

McFarland & Company, Inc., Publishers
*Jefferson, North Carolina, and London*

Squad Leader (SL)/Advanced Squad Leader (ASL) are trademarks of Avalon Hill Games, Inc., a Hasbro affiliate. All rights reserved.
Wizards of the Coast and Magic: The Gathering are trademarks of Wizards of the Coast LLC in the U.S. and other countries. Images are used with permission of Wizards of the Coast LLC.

LIBRARY OF CONGRESS CATALOGUING-IN-PUBLICATION DATA

Woods, Stewart, 1967–
    Eurogames : the design, culture and play of modern European board games / by Stewart Woods.
        p.    cm.
    Includes bibliographical references and index.

    ISBN 978-0-7864-6797-6
    softcover : acid free paper ∞

    1. Board games — Europe — History.    2. Board games — Social aspects.    I. Title.
GV1312.W66  2012
794 — dc23                                              2012025613

BRITISH LIBRARY CATALOGUING DATA ARE AVAILABLE

Front cover image by Simon Holding (courtesy Amigo Spiel).

Manufactured in the United States of America

McFarland & Company, Inc., Publishers
    Box 611, Jefferson, North Carolina 28640
    www.mcfarlandpub.com

# Table of Contents

*When we discuss games, we are not discussing certain biologically inevitable occurrences, though they may be ethologically probable. Rather, we are discussing multidimensional phenomena, varied in the cultural purpose to which they are applied and inherently susceptible, for these varied reasons, to many possible systems of conceptual analysis.* — Sutton-Smith & Avedon, 1971a, p. 4

# *Preface*

Although I didn't know it at the time, the first table game I can remember playing could loosely be considered German in origin. My grandmother, a necessarily frugal woman, would collect the boxes from Lyon's individual fruit pies and carefully cut out the images on the front of the boxes. When my sister and I would visit her, these were used as the cards in a makeshift version of the matching game known in England as *Concentration*. Cleverly, my grandmother's design allowed for two variants — one where one simply matched identical pies, and another where the pies had to be matched with an image of the appropriate fruit. Of course, folk versions of this game had been around since at least the sixteenth century, but it was William Hurter's implementation, *Memory*, that cemented Ravensburger as the premier manufacturer of games at the 1959 Nuremberg toy fair. What I find so endearing is that my grandmother took the time to create her own version for us.

Like many adult gamers, I have played games in one form or another throughout my life. My father taught me to play chess at an early age — though I am still only a passable player — and some of the fondest memories of my childhood are of playing mainstream board games such as *Totopoly* (Palmer & Lee, 1938), *Bermuda Triangle* (1976), and *Buccaneer* (Bull, 1938). Later still, I vividly recall my father — who had an abiding interest in the Napoleonic Era — bringing home a copy of Waddington's *Campaign* (1971). The game was far more complex than those I was used to, and, to be honest, I don't know if we ever played a full game. But I do remember very clearly the words inscribed along the box-edge: "For adults and older children." This, along with the beautiful board, delicate pieces and luxurious rulebook, hinted at gaming that wasn't just for kids — board games, it seemed, were also something that grown-ups played.

As a teenager in the late 1970s a friend introduced me to *Dungeons and Dragons*.[1] Although like many I was initially baffled by the idea of a game with no board, it wasn't long before I fell under the spell of the game. By this time complexity had ceased to be an issue, and I derived boundless pleasure

1

from poring over the arcane charts and lists of magical items that made up the first Dungeon Master's Guide. I found a small group of school friends to play with, and for three years I was a passionate devotee. Through one particularly bleak English winter we completed the entirety of what are now known as the *Queen of the Spiders* modules.[2] We might even have completed the *Tomb of Horrors* successfully, but I doubt it. At the height of my enthusiasm, at an early UK convention I was even lucky enough to have the honor of playing across a table from the late Gary Gygax. Gaming had become a significant part of my life.

Like many gamers, however, the preoccupations of my later teenage years forced games to take a back seat for a period of time. I abandoned role-playing for the most part, but still continued to visit the Hammersmith Games Workshop, where I discovered hobbyist titles such as *Talisman*,[3] *Cosmic Encounter*[4] and many others that I foisted upon friends with varying degrees of success. Although I didn't attend university at that time, many of my friends did, and late night games of *Talisman* (with every expansion, of course), fuelled by a variety of intoxicants, were the stuff of legend. If you haven't played for five straight hours only to fall into the "horrible black void," then you haven't really played *Talisman*!

In later life I moved around a little but still managed to find a way to fit games into my life whenever possible. Shortly after moving to Australia I started a small gaming group. Being a little short of money, our source of games consisted of an old battered copy of *Risk*[5] and whatever we could find at local charity shops. One of the problems with acquiring games in this way was the tendency to come home with boxes of components that had, at some point, become separated from the actual rules to the game. It was while searching for rules to one particular game that I found the website *boardgamegeek*, and before long was exposed to the variety of modern titles that are collectively known as eurogames. Like many others, I was immediately taken by the design style and actively sought out more and more games to enjoy with the growing number of players who now found their way to the group. Before long my collection of games was growing exponentially, and I had helped to found the West Australian Boardgaming Association, a not-for-profit organization that aims to support gaming in the community and raise awareness of the benefits of playing games. Thus, when the time came for me to decide on a research topic for my doctorate, the direction was obvious. The result of that research is the book you now hold in your hands.

There is a reason for this lengthy preamble. I would like to think that this book is informed by every game I have ever played, from fruit pie *Memory* at my grandmother's table to the game of *Dominion*[6] I enjoyed with my son last night. To understand games one has to play them, and I have been lucky enough in my life to have played games with a host of wonderful people. Unfortunately, there is no way to thank them all individually. So if I've ever played a game with you and you don't find yourself in the following acknowledgments, thank you. I hope you had fun.

And so to those who have helped more directly in bringing this book to completion.

I would first like to thank my supervisor, Matthew Allen, for the academic rigor and repeated readings of my work while it was in thesis form. It is a role that only a fellow gamer could have performed with such enthusiasm. I am very much indebted to Mia Consalvo and Lewis Pulsipher, who were both extremely kind in their appraisal of the original thesis, and who both offered valuable feedback that I have endeavored to incorporate into this book.

I should like to thank those who agreed to be interviewed during this research: Greg Aleknevicus, Michael Barnes, Eric Burgess, Derek Carver, Ted Cheatham, Dominic Crapuchettes, Bruno Faidutti, Stephen Glenn, Joe Huber, Mark Jackson, W. Eric Martin, Nicholas Sauer, Greg Schloesser, Zev Shlasinger, Derk Solko, Ken Tidwell, Tom Vasel, Tom Werneck, and Steve Zamborsky. Thank you also to Rudolf Rühle, Seth Owen and Bruce and Sybille Whitehill for their correspondence and assistance. I would particularly like to express my gratitude to Stuart Dagger, who went the extra mile in furnishing me with details of early board gaming culture in the UK.

A general round of thanks goes out to all members of the *boardgamegeek* community, especially those who took the time to respond to my survey. Aldie and Derk have created a unique space for community to flourish on the Internet — we are all very lucky to have such a wonderful home for our curious little hobby.

Thanks to all the members of the West Australian Boardgaming Association with whom I have had the good fortune to play a game, in particular Warren Adams, Renato Bruno, Richard Cheng, Terry Chilvers, Michael O'Brien and Tim Tryhorn.

I would not have been able to write this book without the many people who have attended "Thursday Night Games" over the years. Thank you all for your company, camaraderie and competition. Extra thanks are due to the regulars for their perpetual willingness to play yet another new game: Warren Adams (again!), Tauel Harper, Monika Herold, Ulli Keck, Adrian McMillan, Peter Ramm, David Savat, Tiffany Scotney and particularly Naveena Roden, who was there from the start.

Throughout this process there have been many times when the last thing I have wanted to do is talk about games, when all I have wanted is company and a beer. In those moments I am indebted to the musketeers — John Boyle, Ameeta Doyle, Paul Featherstone and Paul Roberts. Good friends all.

Thank you to my family, who have tolerated the increasingly intrusive number of games that have found their way into our home. Thanks to Ali for keeping me up-to-date on all the latest video game news while I was temporarily sidetracked, to Louis for teaching me humility by beating me comfortably at any game I put between us, and to Julia, for keeping me sane and providing inspiration.

Finally, there is one person for whom thanks on a page are not nearly adequate. Barely a word of this book could have been written but for the constant and unwavering intellectual, practical and emotional support of my beautiful partner in the only game that really matters.

Thank you Helen.

# Introduction

*The research and study of board games could be seen as a "dead science" for many, especially now that a well-developed, digitally interactive media has found "videogames" to be a very prolific market. There has not been extensive research in the area of board games. Researchers have sporadically appeared and disappeared, leaving a legacy that few have systematically followed.*— Ortega-Grimaldo, 2008, p. 34

For many people, board games are an anachronism. The idea of gathering around a table to move pieces on a board conjures up visions of a bygone era, one in which a sense of community flourished, families played together and porch doors were always open. Although these same people will occasionally play board games, typically with their children or at family gatherings, for the most part these games are consigned to the same closet as typewriters and rotary dial telephones, all victims of the inevitable redundancy that accompanies technological progress. For some people, however, board games are far from being redundant. To them they are a hobby, a passion, even an obsession. It is these people, the games they play, and their experience of that play that is the subject of this book. Specifically, this book is a study of hobbyist gamers who play a form of board game commonly referred to as eurogames.

For the purposes of this book I use the term board game to refer to any game that requires a tabletop for play. However, many of the games described herein are not played on a board as such. In fact, a significant number are card games. Nevertheless, I have used the term board games to avoid the clumsiness of repeated reference to "board and table games." Where not indicated in the text, the specific form of a game is noted in the reference list that is found at the end of the book. The term "hobby games" is explained in detail in the second chapter of this book. Briefly, it refers to a number of specific game forms that have emerged over the last forty years and which appeal to a particular audience. Examples are wargames, role-playing games, collectible card games and the topic of this book—eurogames.

This book examines the form of eurogames, the hobbyist culture that surrounds them, and the way that hobbyists experience the play of such games. Aside from the personal involvement I have already described, my interest in this particular genre stems from two related observations. Firstly, eurogames are the most recent form of game to be taken up en masse by gaming hobbyists. Secondly, and this is perhaps the more interesting observation, eurogames have emerged and grown in popularity almost concurrently with the rise of digital games. While I am not suggesting that there is any causal relationship between the rise of these two forms, I cannot help but wonder what it is about eurogames that holds player interest at a time when the rich worlds of digital play have become the dominant form of gaming in the (developed) world. This is the first question that is central to this book — why do hobbyists play eurogames?

The second question that informs this book stems from my own play of games generally. As I approached this research, I found myself increasingly fascinated by an apparent contradiction in the play of social games. Ostensibly, a defining element of competitive play is the valorization of winning. Consequently, players play to win. Yet my experience of playing in a variety of contexts suggested to me that players were far more concerned with the social outcome of the game than with any status that could be gained by winning. Clearly then, there are two forces at work here — the desire to win and the desire to have fun with other people. The question that arises from this observation is this: How do players balance the structure of competitive play with the demands of an intimate social gathering?

The observation that eurogames are, by definition, a social experience leads to my final research question. In 1938 Johan Huizinga famously described play as "an act apart" (1950, p. 10), delimited by a "magic circle" that separates the activity from "ordinary life" (p. 13). Roger Caillois too describes games as "separate" (1958, p. 10), as does Chris Crawford when he proposes that games are a "closed formal system" (1982, p. 7). As Juul notes, however, the boundaries between the game world and the real are not perfect but rather are "fuzzy areas under constant negotiation" (2005, p. 36). My experience of game play has suggested to me that a particular game can offer a vastly different experience depending upon the context in which it is played. Players — and the interaction between them — can have a significant impact on the experience of social play in a way that suggests to me that board game systems are anything but closed. Thus, the final question I seek to answer in this book is this: To what extent does the social context of the game encounter shape the experience of game play?

Given the questions I have identified here, I hope it is apparent why the scope of this book is at once broad and highly specific. It is specific as it focuses on a particular type of game and a very particular type of player. Attempting to find answers to my questions in a way that could be broadly applied to any form of game and/or player would require multiple volumes and years of ethnographic and interdisciplinary research. By focusing on hobbyists and eurogames specifically, the answers to these questions, while limited in scope, are at least attainable.

At the same time, the ground covered by this book is broad. Looking at such a specific subset of play activities requires a multidisciplinary approach. For example, I cannot talk meaningfully about the eurogame form without considering its history and relation to other board game forms. Nor can I talk of hobbyists without considering the nature of subcultures and the performance of hobbyist culture. Thus, although the core focus of this book concerns play, nothing but broad generalizations can be expected without consideration of the specific game form, player identities and the culture of hobby gaming. In order to fully explore each of these elements, an eclectic range of disciplines and methods was required. In the course of this book I employ to some degree aspects of history, cultural and subcultural studies, leisure studies, ludology and play theory. It is only by adopting this multi-disciplinary approach that I can hope to adequately answer the questions at the heart of this research.

## The Study of Games

The last forty years or so have seen a significant change in the position of games within popular culture. The rise of video games has been swift and continual, to the point that the medium now rivals the commercial — and arguably artistic — status of motion pictures. As video games have grown in popularity among the broader population, they have also caught the attention of scholars. Viewing games with a critical eye, they have examined the aesthetic, narrative and systemic elements of video games, documenting the evolution of digital play and examining the nature of the game form with an enthusiasm that has typified the rise of new media. The discipline that has emerged from this interest has been termed ludology.

While modern ludology was originally imagined by Gonzalo Frasca as merely a "discipline that studies game and play activities" (1999), so far the emphasis has primarily been on video games. Nevertheless, a number of scholars have adopted a more inclusive approach in their work that acknowledges the commonalities between digital and non-digital games. Markku Eskelinen, for example, argues that video games are "remediated games ... one species among several within a general and transmedial game ecology" (2005, p. 93).[1] Jesper Juul, an early proponent of the study of games as an independent form, has described a "classic game model" that seeks to encompass "at least a 5,000 year history of games" (2005, p. 23). Aki Järvinen, in his book *Games Without Frontiers*, adopts a wide-ranging approach to the analysis of games that allows for all forms of games, digital or otherwise (2009). Salen and Zimmerman's textbook, *Rules of Play*, is similarly inclusive of all game types (2004). These are a few examples of writers and scholars whose analysis of games has embraced the entirety of the form.

Unfortunately, despite these proclamations of inclusiveness, board games appear to occupy the same position in the new ludology as they do in the broader culture — small primitive ancestors of an evolved form. It is true that a number of writers who acknowledge the commonality of game forms have argued for the value of examining non-digital games, most notably Eskelinen (2005, p. 10), designer Greg Costikyan (1998; 2011) and scholar Janet Murray (2003). However, while a few researchers have gone on to offer such analysis, they have typically discussed board games with a view to establishing connections and/or design features that relate to video games.[2] Thus, while the study of games has accelerated in recent years, academic attention to the specific area of board games remains relatively sparse.

The first serious research into sedentary games is that of ethnologist Stewart Culin, who embarked on a number of research projects that sought to collect and compare the wide variety of games that were found in disparate cultures (1891; 1894; 1899; 1900; 1907). In terms of tabletop games specifically, the first book that deals with a variety of examples is H. J. R. Murray's *A History of Board-Games Other Than Chess* (1952). Murray analyzed a number of abstract positional games, describing a schema by which they could be categorized. R. C. Bell adopted a similar approach, again limited to positional games, in his *Board and Table Games from Many Civilizations* (1979). David Parlett's *Oxford History of Board Games* (1999) adapts both Murray and Bell's taxonomies, again with a strong focus on abstract positional games. Gobet, de Voogt and Retschitzki's *Moves in Mind: The Psychology of Board Games* (2004) is another more recent addition to the literature, although its focus is the cognitive and psychological aspects in the play of traditional abstract games. This emphasis on traditional examples is also reflected in the work of the International Society for Board Game Studies. Established in the early 1990s, the society holds a yearly colloquium that has occasionally included papers on contemporary commercial games but is limited mostly to traditional examples.

In terms of mass-market board games, Bruce Whitehill has done much to document the evolution of games in the U.S. (1992; 2004). Most other writers have been content to focus on specific proprietary games and/or manufacturers, in many cases with a somewhat nostalgic tone.[3] David Pritchard's edited collection *The Games and Puzzles Book of Modern Board Games* (1975) is a notable exception, focusing as it does on a number of then-contemporary proprietary games, including mainstream titles such as *Monopoly* (Darrow and Magie, 1935) and *Cluedo* (Pratt, 1948), along with lesser known examples such as *Diplomacy* (Calhamer, 1959) and *Confrontation* (1974).

Hobby games have been of only sporadic interest to games scholars, with publications often arising from within the hobby rather than the academy. Wargames are a good example of this, with a number of titles devoted to discussing the form from the perspective of enthusiasts.[4] The more noteworthy of these include Nicholas Palmer's early *Comprehensive Guide to Board Wargaming* (1977) and *Best of Board Wargaming* (1980), Jon Freeman's *Complete Book of Wargames* (1980), and Jim Dunnigan's *Complete Wargames Handbook* (1980a). More recent critical analysis is found in the work of Matthew Kirshenbaum (2009) and Patrick Crogan (2003).

In contrast, role-playing games have been a site of interest for scholars since their inception. Undoubtedly the most well known work on the topic is Gary Fine's subcultural analysis of the early hobby, *Shared Fantasy: Role Playing Games as Social Worlds* (1983). Daniel Mackay's *The Fantasy Role Playing Game: A New Performance Art* (2001) provides a more up-to-date perspective on the performative aspects of the genre; while recent works by Jennifer Cover (2010) and Sarah Bowman (2010) address a variety of topics, including the creation of narrative and the construction of identity, respectively. The narrative aspects of role-playing games are also explored in a number of articles in Pat Harrigan and Noah Wardrup-Fruin's series of collections (2004; 2007; 2009).[5] A particularly strong scholarly community has developed around role-playing games in Scandinavia where the largest role-playing convention moves between four countries, producing a book on the topic each year.[6] Overall, the study of role-playing games has remained particularly active compared with other forms of hobby game.

One notable publication that manages to bridge the gap between video games and hobby games is the collection *Gaming as Culture: Essays on Reality, Identity and Experience in Fantasy Games* (Williams *et al.*, 2006). Taking as its theme fantasy games generally, the book contains a number of illuminating articles on the play and culture of collectible card games.[7] Other studies of collectible card games include Mark Bordenet's masters thesis on the identity of gamers (2000), and Lenarcic and Mackay-Scollay's (2005) discussion of the positive social impact of playing *Magic: The Gathering* (Garfield, 1993).

On the topic of eurogames specifically, critical writings are few and far between. Costikyan and Davidson *et al.*'s collection, *Tabletop: Analogue Game Design* (2011), includes an eclectic mix of essays, some of which address examples from within the genre.[8] Sybille Aminzadah examines the reasons for the popular success of *Die Siedler von Catan* (Teuber, 1995) through interviews with German players (2004); while Stöckmann and Jahnke have written on the general culture of gaming in Germany, as well as discussing the intersections between literature and German board games (2008a; 2008b).[9] Finally, Yehuda Berlinger's presentation at the 2009 Board Game Colloquium expressly addresses some of the identifying characteristics of the eurogame genre (2009b).

As is apparent from this brief review, to date there are no substantial critical works that address the topic of modern board games, much less eurogames. In the words of Francisco Ortega-Grimaldo, the study of board games has remained "a dead science" (2008, p. 34). Despite the resurgence of interest in games in general, there has been surprisingly little attention paid to board games and the play experiences they foster. This book aims in part to fill this gap, as well as to contribute to broader understandings of the adult play of games.

## Eurogames — Design, Culture and Play

This book consists of three parts, each of which seeks to address a particular element that contributes to the overall conclusions; these are the game form, the hobbyist player and the experience of play that emerges from the combination of these two.

### Understanding the Games

The first part of this book is given over to the evolution of tabletop hobby gaming, with a specific focus on the eurogame form. In order to discuss eurogames and their position as a core genre of hobby gaming, this part of the book examines the history and evolution of Anglo-American hobby games, the nature of the eurogame genre, the geo-cultural site from which eurogames emerged and the adoption of the form by hobbyists. To complement my own research, I conducted interviews with a number of designers, publishers and what might be termed "luminaries" within hobby gaming culture. My concern here is a deeper understanding of eurogames as games, and their positioning within the broader spectrum of hobby games. Of course, any examination of games as a participatory form also obligates the researcher to experience the play of them first hand (Aarseth, 2003; Lammes, 2007), and over the course of this research I played close to 300 different board and table games in both public and private venues. While the vast majority of these games fell within the confines of the eurogame genre, I also sought to play many titles that have directly or indirectly contributed to the evolution of hobby games. The experience of playing these games, together with the examination of the influences upon their design and a historical review of the tabletop game as a cultural activity, contribute to a situated understanding of the nature of eurogames.

## Understanding the Players

The second part of this book consists of a discussion of board game hobbyists and the broader culture of gaming that nurtures and sustains the hobby. In order to understand the nature of the hobby community, I analyzed texts produced by players as a meta-aspect of the hobby. Principle sources were discussions on the online forum *boardgamegeek*, as well as many other publications that focus on hobby gaming generally and eurogames specifically. Examples include amateur fanzines (e.g. *Sumo*, *Counter*), commercial print magazines (*Knucklebones*, *Games International*), Internet mailing lists and discussion groups (*rec.games.board*, *Spielfrieks*), along with personal websites, blogs and the occasional academic article that touches upon the topic. Coupled with this, I conducted interviews with a number of players and community figures.

In November 2007 I conducted an Internet-based survey that was made available through the *boardgamegeek* website. While response rates to individual questions varied, the average for the survey was approximately 650 responses. The first part of the survey consisted entirely of quantitative questions designed to extract demographic data along with basic information regarding playing habits (frequency, location, etc.). The marriage of this quantitative data with the analysis of discussion and commentary from within the hobby serves to establish a coherent picture of players, along with their understandings of, and performance within, hobby gaming culture.

## Understanding the Play

The third and final part of this book concerns the experience of playing games. As mentioned earlier, a number of key questions motivate this part of the enquiry:

- How do players derive enjoyment from the play of eurogames?
- How do players balance the structure of competitive play with the demands of an intimate social gathering?
- To what extent does the social context of the game encounter shape the experience of game play?

In pursuit of answers to these questions, the second part of my survey included a variety of open-ended questions designed to address the experience of play, with particular emphasis upon the issues outlined above. These survey responses are denoted in this book by the prefix R, followed by a number (e.g., R567). The format of the survey provided results that could not have been gathered through observation.[10] As a part of the overall enquiry, these responses informed the generation of a number of conclusions that were supported through informal participant observation.

## Tying It All Together — Informal Participant Observation

*Participant observation is of particular utility in disciplines like game studies where the object of study is emergent, incompletely understood, and thus unpredictable.*— Boellstorff, 2006, p. 32

Throughout this book my questions, research and analysis are informed by my own participation in the gaming hobby and my personal history of playing games. There is, of course, a lengthy history within the broader area of social sciences of ethnographic research by researchers who are "inside" the particular subculture they are examining.[11] In the case of some participatory cultures, it has been suggested that one can only appreciate the aesthetics and meanings of a particular activity if one is actively involved.[12] Participant observation as a research strategy has its origins in the work of anthropologists such as Bronislaw Malinowski and Franz Boas, who introduced the idea that the researcher must have daily and extended contact with the subjects of his research in order to grasp the situational knowledge that is held by a given culture (Nader, 1996). In the case of this particular book, participant observation has informed the enquiry on three levels: private, local and global.

For the last thirteen years I have been part of a weekly gaming gathering. In the last ten years this has been held primarily in my own home. The types of games played have varied and have included mass-market and hobbyist games. Since I embarked on the research for this book, there have been a far greater number of hobby games played, particularly eurogames. On a local community level, since 2007 I have been the chairperson of the *West Australian Boardgaming Association* (WABA), a non-profit organization that promotes hobby board games in the Western Australian community.[13] The organization has approximately 100 members, with meets regularly attracting upwards of fifty players. As well as providing regular monthly venues for hobby gamers, WABA has been involved with promoting gaming within the community via outreach programs in local libraries and schools. More recently, I have taken up a position on the committee of *Boardgames Australia*, a national organization that promotes the social benefits of board games.[14] The organization has also sought to recognize quality games through the establishment of national awards. Finally, on a global level, I have been an active member of the *boardgamegeek* online community since 2005.

Through these three avenues I have been able to gain a far greater insight into the topic of this research than I would have otherwise. However, it should be stressed that the nature of this participant observation has been entirely informal. Consequently, while there are very few explicit references to participant observation within this book, the experience of playing games with others and being a part of the hobby gaming community underlies many of the assertions and observations made here. Particularly in the later discussions of the social context of game play and the way players manage this, my personal observations could be said to inhabit the space between every line. Where I draw upon the anonymous qualitative data provided by surveying, at each turn the interpretation of the data is informed by these personal experiences. As I discuss later in this book, there is far more to understanding the gaming hobby than merely playing games. Immersion in this unique subculture is the only way to understand the hobbyist approach to games and the pleasure that participants derive from playing them. This is the most important goal of this book.

# 1

# A Brief Introduction
# to Hobby Games

*We might think of games as charming historical artifacts, but they are also telling reflections of social values and mores.* — Brown, 2004

Eurogames are the most recent variety of what have come to be termed "hobby games." While this term might seem to be self-explanatory, it has come to denote a variety of games that are differentiated from other forms by their appeal to a particular segment of the population over the last half-century. Leisure theorist Richard Stebbins describes the play of competitive games generally as one of four forms of "serious leisure," including in his description many sports, along with sedentary games such as *Bridge, Shuffleboard* and computer games (1992, pp. 13–14). Yet, while we might describe the active engagement with such pastimes as constituting a hobby, they are rarely, if ever, described as hobby games. Since the focus of this book is a particular form of hobby board game, a clear explanation of the games under discussion is necessary. Moreover, since the term hobby board game has emerged from within the hobby itself, the most effective way to clarify its meaning is to describe the various forms of hobby games that have appeared over the last fifty years.

To this end I begin here by discussing the principal ways in which traditional board games have been categorized in the past, identifying the limitations of these schemata in the context of contemporary board game designs. As an alternative, I propose that the contemporary board game market can be divided into three categories: traditional games, mass-market games and hobby games. Hobby games can be further delineated into four principal genres, those being wargames, role-playing games, collectible card games and eurogames. In discussing the first three of these genres in this chapter, I not only wish to document the nature and variety of hobby games that have emerged over the last fifty years, but also to provide a clearer idea of why it is that the term hobby games has been applied to these forms, and indeed why they are generally grouped together by members of the community and industry.

## Beyond the Abstract— Categorizing Board and Table Games

The typical approach to categorizing board games in the past has been to define game types by either the central mechanics of play or by the game goals (Murray, 1952; Bell, 1979; Parlett, 1999). Insofar as writers have tended to limit themselves to traditional board games such as *Chess*, *Mancala* and *Backgammon*, this approach has functioned well. The most recent example is found in David Parlett's authoritative study *The Oxford History of Board Games* (1999), wherein the analysis of games is largely restricted to what the author terms "positional games":

> The defining feature of these is not that they are played on boards, but that they are played on a pattern of significant markings, such as an array of chequered squares or a network of lines and points, whose purpose is to define the movements and positions of the pieces in relation to one another [p. 6].

While this restriction works adequately within the context of Parlett's work, it necessarily excludes a significant number of modern commercial games. Although Parlett suggests that such games might feature positional elements, he observes that contemporary proprietary games tend to involve play that is centered "above the board, in the minds of the players themselves" (p. 7). Perhaps as a consequence of this shift, Parlett devotes little space to the evolution of contemporary board games beyond a cursory mention of selected titles and thus, as hobbyist writer Mike Siggins notes, omits the significant developments in board game design that have occurred over the last forty years (2000).

One problem here is that where traditional abstract games can be effectively jostled into a framework through the examination of similar mechanics and/or goals, the increased complexity and variety of modern commercial games often sees them weaving several mechanics together in ways that defy such simple categorization. Indeed, a taxonomy based purely upon core mechanics and/or goals would almost certainly prove both unwieldy and unproductive in approaching the wide variety of games that have appeared in the marketplace over the last half-century. Moreover, it is important to recognize that, unlike traditional games, modern games are a manufactured commodity, designed and published at a specific time in history, and produced for a particular market and for essentially commercial reasons. The nature of such games is that they are played by particular groups of people and thus lend themselves to the development of cultural formations which reflect both the moment in which they are produced and the identity and recreational choices of the players. This historical, cultural and economic context cannot be ignored in considering any categorization. With this in mind, a more useful approach is a simple schema that distinguishes between three principal types of board game: the classical game, the mass-market game and the hobby game.

Broadly speaking, *classical games* refers to those non-proprietary games that have been passed down from antiquity and whose authorship is presumed to emerge from multiple iterative changes over time. *Mass-market games* refers to those commercial titles that are produced and sold in large numbers year after year, and which constitute the common perception of commercial board games. Finally, *hobby games* are those games that are not targeted towards the general mass market but to a specific group who can be termed hobby gamers. As I note above, many players of classic games, such as *Chess*, or proprietary mass market games, such as *Scrabble* (Butts, 1948), might describe themselves as participating in a hobby. However, in the sense that I use the term here, hobby games constitute a subsection of the broader market that tends to attract those with a specific interest in a particular form of commercial game. A brief discussion of each of these forms will serve to clarify these distinctions.

## Classical Games

Classical games are readily identifiable as those games to which no author is attributed and of which no company or organization claims ownership. Although some classical games have identifiable themes, they are most commonly abstract. In categorizing these public domain or "folk" games, Parlett (1999) draws on the work of H. J. R. Murray (1952) and R. C. Bell (1979) in describing four types of game, as identified by the game goals: race games, in which players traverse a track in an attempt to be first to finish (e.g., *Nyout*, *Pachisi*); space games, in which players manipulate the position of pieces to achieve prescribed alignments, make connections, or traverse the board (e.g., *Noughts and Crosses*, *Twixt*[1] and *Halma*, respectively); chase games, in which asymmetrical starting positions and goals cast players in the role of pursuer and pursued (e.g., *Hnefatafl*, *Fox & Geese*); and games of displacement, where symmetrically equipped players attempt to capture and eliminate each other's pieces (e.g., *Chess*, *Draughts*). While these games are not the focus of this book, it is worth noting that they are perhaps the closest relatives of the modern eurogames discussed here, in that it is the game system that holds the attention of the game player rather than the thematic elements that are so central to both mass-market games and many hobby game forms.

## Mass-Market Games

Mass-market games are those proprietary games that have come to dominate the shelves of large toy retailers and with which the activity of board gaming is commonly associated by the general public. Mass-market games tend to be one of three types. The first of these are the more successful of the numerous family games that were produced during the 19th and 20th century.[2] Examples such as *Scrabble*, *Monopoly* (Darrow and Magie, 1935), *The Game of Life* (Klamer, 1960), *Clue* (Pratt, 1948) and *Candyland* (Abbott, 1949) have continued to sell well long after their initial publication. Over time the rules to these games have become a part of the Western cultural lexicon and are easily transferred from one generation to the next. A result of this is that the shelves of large retail outlets are typically dominated by games that were, in many cases, designed more than half a century ago. While these games might be termed "classic" in the sense that they occupy a central position in cultural understandings of board and table games, they have, arguably, acquired this status largely through a combination of manufactured nostalgia and effective marketing.

The second form of mass-market board game is that of the "party game" whose popularity exploded following the success of *Trivial Pursuit* in the early 1980s (Haney and Abbot, 1981). Typically, such games are akin to Victorian-era parlor games in that they tend to focus on performance and social interaction as a primary goal in play. Thus they generally have simple rules and accommodate large groups of players. Examples of successful titles include *Pictionary* (Angel, 1985), *Outburst!* (Hersch, 1986), *Cranium* (Alexander and Tait, 1998) and *Taboo* (Hersch, 1989).

The final type of game that has become ubiquitous in the mass-market is the licensed game, whose origins can largely be traced to the emergence of television in the 1950s. The arrival of television had a significant impact on the way leisure time was spent in the average home. Games manufacturers were swift to embrace this new medium as a source of inspiration for a swathe of titles which Parlett terms "pulp games" (1999, p. 347). Although games manufacturers had often looked to current trends and fads for inspiration, the arrival of television had a far more dramatic impact on the games business than did earlier cultural trends, since each new television show brought with it another opportunity to repackage familiar mechanics with a new theme:

During the '50s, many game companies ... began to acquire more and more licenses to television shows. Businesses that once hoped to sell a game that would be a staple in the line for decades were now making products that would be obsolete as soon as the program on which they were based was no longer on the air. More attention was given to the name and character on the box than to the product inside [Whitehill, 1997].

Generally, these titles are of such socio-cultural specificity that they are usually forgotten as quickly as the shows, and later movies, which inspire them. Examples of these at the time of writing are *Dexter: The Board Game* (2010), *Glee Board Game* (2010), *Gossip Girl Never Have I Ever Game* (2009) and *Dancing with the Stars Board Game* (2008). The mechanics of these types of games are typically derivative and uninspired, prompting Parlett to evaluate them as "essentially trivial, ephemeral, mind-numbing, and ultimately [of a] soul destroying degree of worthlessness" (1999, p. 7).

A common and notable hybrid of these three forms stems from the growth in licensing and crossover branding. Where previously the larger game manufacturers might have commissioned new, if unoriginal, designs to accompany ephemeral trends, there is a tendency now to merely weave them together with existing game licenses. A quick survey of toy giant Hasbro's range of board games in 2010 reveals *Monopoly—Spiderman 3 Edition* (2007), *Monopoly—SpongeBob Squarepants Edition* (2005), *Monopoly—Transformers Collector's Edition* (2007), *The Game of Life—Pirates of the Caribbean* (2004), *The Game of Life—Simpson's Edition* (2004), *Candyland—Winnie the Pooh Edition* (2008) and *Candyland—Dora the Explorer Edition* (2005). In most cases the resulting hybrid retains all the same mechanical elements as the original game, the branding merely appearing as window-dressing in order to attract the targeted market.

The contemporary mass-market games industry is essentially built upon the repackaging of 20th century proprietary games, party games, and a few original titles that appear yearly to satisfy fans of particular media licenses. As designer and publisher Mike Petty notes, the larger game companies such as Hasbro and Mattel now have little motivation to explore the potential of new game styles (2006) and are reluctant to even consider game submissions from outside of a small pool of developers (Verbeten, 2007, p. 31). As industry commentator and designer Greg Costikyan eloquently affirms, "Hasbro is fat and happy and basically doesn't give a fuck about innovation" (1998).[3]

## Hobby Games

Where the rise of television was to prove a challenge for larger toy manufacturers that eventually resulted in a dearth of novel game play ideas, the hobby gaming industry and the culture surrounding it emerged and flourished in the latter half of the 20th century. Indeed, contrary to the impression that might be gathered from the shelves of large retailers, game design has experienced significant advances over the last five decades. Entirely new genres of game have emerged and evolved outside of the mass-market, so much so that the landscape of contemporary board and table games is radically different than it was in the 1950s when the larger companies seemingly decided that there were enough good games to satisfy the average consumer indefinitely.

In the final chapter of *The Oxford History of Board Games* Parlett briefly discusses contemporary commercial games, and in doing so, expands his taxonomy to describe the genre of "specialist games":

> These may be characterized as games of skill and strategy appealing to players broadly describable as adult, serious, educated, intelligent. Many of these share the associated features of classic games, from which category they are only excluded by their appeal to a specialist section of the market [1999, p. 347].

Parlett is referring here to a subsection of gaming enthusiasts that emerged in the latter half of the 20th century and whose interests lay largely outside of both classical abstract games and those that dominate the mass-market. The forms of games these enthusiasts play are more commonly referred to as hobby games.

## Hobby Game Genres

Although hobby games share a commonality in their appeal to particular segments of the market, there are a number of recognizable forms that have emerged over the last half-century that can be broadly considered genres. The use of the term genre can be problematic, as it is the source of much critical debate, particularly in the fields of literature and film studies. In the original sense, genre refers to the classification of texts into discrete types through an observation of similar traits within a type. However, as film theorist Robert Stam notes, discussion of genre tends to draw on a wide variety of criteria that often appear in conflict and/or intersect with one another (2000, p. 14). Furthermore, genre divisions, even when seemingly well established, are inherently subject to revision as new texts emerge and the boundaries between groups shift.

Defining genre boundaries has proven as problematic in game studies as it has in other areas, leading to a variety of approaches having been adopted to describe the similarities and differences between games. As described earlier, studies of classical games, such as those of Murray, Bell and Parlett, tend to favor a categorization based upon game goals. However, in his discussion of card games, Parlett refers to "game families"[4] with similarities based upon a combination of mechanics (2000). In *Dice Games Properly Explained,* designer Reiner Knizia breaks games down into those primarily determined by luck, those where luck can be mitigated, those of strategy and those of bluffing — a mix of mechanics and other shared traits (1999d).

Extending the discussion to video games, a number of scholars have attempted to establish a framework for understanding game genres, with varying degrees of success. David Myers, in his early discussion of genre in home computer games (1990), asks, "Upon what is a computer game's 'feel' based?" (p. 294), a question which leads him to conclude that the nature of the interactivity between the player and the game is a fundamental characteristic. Similarly, Mark J. P. Wolf argues that theme is unsuitable as a foundation for the classification of games, as a thematic similarity does not reflect the diversity of player experience (2002, p. 115).[5] Wolf's schema for genre in video games draws on a number of criteria, with an emphasis on the "dominant characteristics of the interactive experience and the games' goals and objective" (p. 260). The result is a list of genres that effectively replicates the confusion and cross-purposes that Stam observes in film studies.[6]

As game scholar Espen Aarseth observes, the problem with discussions of genre and video games lies in the fact that the video game is a widely divergent form (2004), an observation that is equally valid for other forms of game. Indeed, Myers recognizes the variety of influences that may affect the construction of genres within video games, citing, among other factors, a particular aesthetic appeal to designers and commercial patterns that see successful forms revisited (2003, p. 97).

In the case of hobby games, it is not surprising to find that even within this small area, informal categories have emerged based upon a variety of criteria. Gaming writer and hobbyist Greg Aleknevicus describes the current hobby gaming market as being composed of "four pillars": wargames, role-playing games, collectible card games and eurogames (2008). While collectible card games and role-playing games are loosely defined by a mechanic, in the case of wargames it is the theme that largely serves as nominator. However, the fact that a number of collectible card games utilize a theme of war reflects the intersections that are so common in discussion of genre boundaries.[7] Consequently, as with other media, it is more productive to think of genre as a series of conventions that provide a form of communicative shorthand, thus allowing authors to count on audiences having certain expectations and knowledge. In the context of game studies, players — who have a particular understanding of these conventions — formulate folksonomies that reflect their response to particular game forms (Myers, 1990, p. 289). For this reason

Aleknevicus' schema is useful in summarizing the principal forms of hobby games prior to the emergence of the eurogame.

## Wargaming

Wargaming, the earliest form of hobby gaming to emerge, has its origins in early simulation games employed by the military.[8] Evolving through the early 20th century largely through miniature-based games,[9] the hobby was experiencing a resurgence of interest in the 1950s when American Charles S. Roberts designed the first modern board wargame, *Tactics* (1954).[10] In 1958, after selling the initial 2000 copies, and with growing interest in the game, Roberts founded Avalon Hill, a company that went on to develop most of the dominant principles of pre-electronic wargaming in a successful series of games depicting specific conflicts.[11]

The success of Avalon Hill, and the enthusiastic response to the conflict simulations the company was producing, prompted other designers to follow its example. Along with Avalon Hill, companies such as Simulation Publications Incorporated (SPI), Game Designer's Workshop (GDW) and Simulations Design Corporation (SDC) ushered in "the golden age of wargaming" in the 1970s (Dunnigan, 2000). Of these companies, SPI was by far the most significant, producing the magazine *Strategy & Tactics*, a publication that set the benchmark for community contribution and feedback.[12] A typical board wargame of this period used a hexagonal grid representing a variety of terrain features, units represented by cardboard tokens printed with the abilities of each, and sophisticated probability-based tables for determining the outcomes of encounters based upon a combination of statistical data and designer's intuition. In contrast with mass-market games, the designer's name would often appear on the packaging; indeed, the term "game designer" was first coined by Redmond Simonsen at SPI (Costikyan, 2006).

At the same time as Roberts had been working on his fledgling designs, Alan Calhamer, a Harvard student of European history, was devising and refining a game based upon diplomatic machinations in Europe during the lead-up to the First World War. The game, *Diplomacy* (1959), was entirely different to Roberts' strategic simulations, relying on the interpersonal negotiating skills of multiple players in the resolution of relatively simplistic board-based conflict mechanics. Following unsuccessful approaches to major game companies, Calhamer initially produced a run of 500 copies of the game in 1959, and it has been in print near-continuously since then (Sharpe, 1978). Although not, strictly speaking, a wargame, *Diplomacy* has become a hobby unto itself, with postal play and later play-by-email proving particularly successful.

*Squad Leader*— the largest selling wargame to date (image by Wesley Williams, courtesy Multiman Publishing).

Avalon Hill's success continued throughout the 1970s. *PanzerBlitz* (Dunnigan, 1970), considered the first tactical-level wargame, introduced a geomorphic map that enabled players to reconfigure sections of the game board in order to play out a variety of scenarios. This innovation was later expanded and refined in the popular simulation *Squad Leader* (Hill, 1977), the best selling wargame to date (Costikyan, 1996) and one that spawned its own subculture of enthusiasts.[13] The period also saw the birth of "monster games," whose name reflected the epic scenarios they were intended to simulate (Palmer, 1980, p. 19). GDW's *Drang Nach Osten* (Chadwick and Banner, 1973) was among the first of this genre, requiring at least 50 hours for a complete campaign (Owen, 1990); while SPI's *War in Europe* (Dunnigan, 1976a), along with its siblings *War in the East* (Simonsen and Dunnigan, 1974) and *War in the West* (Dunnigan, 1976b), provided material for playing a campaign game lasting over 100 hours (Palmer, 1980, p. 171).

In 1975, Avalon Hill worked with a local wargaming club in Baltimore to establish the first Origins convention, which was later run in conjunction with SPI in order to promote the hobby. A time of prolific output, the late 1970s saw Avalon Hill producing five new wargames a year, with SPI managing a remarkable average of 27 titles a year (Owen, 1990).[14] Peaking in 1980, the combined sales of historical wargames for that year amounted to 2.2 million units (Dunnigan, 1997).

Within a few years, however, the growing popularity of role-playing games and the advent of the personal computer began to have a considerable impact on the wargaming hobby (Owen, 1990). A number of companies who had built their reputation on wargaming began to diversify into role-playing, while others failed to compete against the explosive growth of the new hobby. At the same time, the personal computer offered an attractive alternative to the complex manual bookkeeping required in many games. Although initially hampered by issues of platform compatibility and processing power, the rise of computer-based wargames increasingly saw players pursuing the hobby in a digital form.

In 1982, Tactical Studies Rules (TSR), now a sizeable company due to the success of the role-playing game *Dungeons and Dragons* (Gygax and Arneson, 1974a), purchased SPI. Although TSR re-released some of SPI's more successful games,[15] sales were unimpressive in comparison with the company's substantial line of role-playing publications (Owen, 1990). In the same year, toy giant Milton Bradley released *Broadsides and Boarding Parties* (Harris, 1982),[16] the first in a series of simplified wargames with high production values that, with the exception of Lawrence Harris' *Axis and Allies* (1981), failed to make any serious headway with mainstream audiences.[17] Following this trend, in the late 1980s TSR, Avalon Hill and GDW also began to produce simpler games, with mixed results.[18] Avalon Hill released *Advanced Squad Leader* (Greenwood, 1985) in 1985, which quickly gathered a significant following despite being a simpler game than the original.

Many reasons have been suggested for why the board wargaming hobby declined so dramatically throughout the 1980s and early 1990s. Greg Costikyan (1996) attributes the collapse to TSR, who, he claims, "shot wargaming in the head" by failing to honor subscriptions to SPI's *Strategy & Tactics*, which had become a lynchpin of the wargaming community. Dunnigan, however, suggests that it was largely computer gaming that was central to the collapse:

> One can make the case that wargame sales are better than ever, if one simply changes the definition of a wargame. That's what the market has done in response to market demands. But that's like saying that historical fiction should be reflagged as history books because few people will buy and read real history books anymore. No, the problem is that historical wargames were always a small market because they emphasized information and analysis at the expense of entertainment. Any gamer who was not a wargamer immediately saw that. Now that computers have made it possible for many more people to play wargames, you should not be surprised that most of them want to be entertained, not put through a training course [2000].

Although the conflict simulation branch of the hobby is still active today, wargaming has not again achieved the popularity of the 1960s and 1970s. While miniature gaming retains its attraction for younger hobbyists, principally through the efforts of Games Workshop and their *Warhammer* line of fantasy and science fiction games, the larger hobby has experienced a significant decline from its heyday.

As Dunnigan explains, wargame designers typically attempt to simulate specific moments in history, using detailed information to revisit pivotal conflicts. Although many forms of game are simulative to some degree, wargames took this to an extreme, utilizing complex rulesets and laboriously researched combat resolution tables (CRTs) to approximate the possible outcomes of any given event with a combination of dice and their associated probabilities. This element, which gamers refer to as "chrome." tends to result in extremely long and detailed rulesets. Indeed, the term "Avalon-ese" has become a way of describing rulesets that feature large numbers of exceptions in order to allow for every special circumstance that might arise during the game. In the 1970s and 1980s, when the wargame model expanded to encompass alternative futures, science fiction and fantasy, the notion that such games were simulations persisted, as did the attendant complexity. A consequence of this was that the play of such games was restricted to those who had both the patience and disposition to wade through lengthy rulebooks. The complexity of these systems meant that these were not games for the average person — these were "gamers' games." Players were not, generally speaking, casual participants but rather enthusiastic members of a growing hobby gaming culture.

## Role-Playing Games (RPGs)

In 1970 wargamer Gary Gygax was working on a medieval miniatures game based upon a rules system begun by a friend, Jeff Perren. The system, *Chainmail*, was published in 1971 by Guidon Games (Gygax and Perren, 1971) and included supplemental rules that covered "dragons, heroes, magic swords and spells" ("Gary Gygax Interview," 2000). One of the players of Gygax's system was Dave Arneson, a fellow wargaming enthusiast who had become somewhat bored with the conventions of the genre and was beginning to experiment with different styles of play in order to enliven the experience.[19] Initially, he introduced the notion of establishing an ongoing campaign in a medieval setting where each player controlled the leader of a small group. After further experimentation, Arneson introduced magic to his games and had his players each represent an individual adventurer in a collaborative attempt to infiltrate an enemy castle in what he has since described as the first fantasy role-playing game (Fine, 1983, p. 13). Before long, Gygax was exposed to Arneson's idea of one-player-per-character, and the pair spent the early 1970s working on a ruleset that would become *Dungeons and Dragons* (1974a), the first commercially produced role-playing game (RPG). Despite Gygax's feelings that the game would only appeal to a limited number of hobbyists,[20] the popularity of *Dungeons and Dragons* grew at an impressive rate, and the name of the game would become synonymous with the role-playing hobby.

Generally speaking, in role-playing games players take on the role of individual characters whose defining traits and abilities are specified by the ruleset, but whose goals and motivations are changeable and dependent upon the narrative of the game. A game master relates the unfolding events as they happen to players, describing the game world and conveying to the players the consequences of their actions. Typical of the game structure is the accumulation of experience in varying forms that affects the player character's statistics and therefore their relationship with the world as defined by the ruleset. Generally, early role-playing games were played in a series of ongoing sessions—a campaign—with individual play sessions forming a small part of a larger adventure.

During the late 1970s, the success of *Dungeons and Dragons* resulted in a flood of role-playing games that sought to emulate the success of the original.[21] Few literary or cinematic settings were not subject to the role-playing treatment.[22] Furthermore, as role-playing evolved, the early emphasis on combat inherited from the hobby's wargaming roots gave way to more imaginative and theatrical approaches.[23] Where previously game referees were content to build large, self-contained environments for players to explore and subjugate, emphasizing the combative elements of the game, the move away from this approach resulted in a focus on narrative as the principal player motivator (Mason, 2004, p. 6). Consequently, many games abandoned the dense rulesets that had characterized early games in favor of a more free-form approach.

By the mid–1980s it seemed that there were few fictional realms left untouched by role-playing. Steve Jackson's *Generic Universal Role Playing System* (GURPS) (1986) attempted to simplify the needs of players who wished to explore different environments by presenting a unified system that could theoretically be applied to any fictional setting. The approach was successful, spawning countless source books that covered a large variety of both generic and licensed properties.

Throughout the 1990s the implementation of role-playing games on the personal computer had a significant impact on the tabletop role-playing industry. Although arguably requiring little (if any) in the way of actual role-playing, the basic systems of character advancement and probability-based event outcomes proved ideal for the medium. Significantly, however, the solitary play also dispensed with the social element that was so integral to tabletop games:

> Paper RPGs, unlike electronic ones, are social affairs; players get together periodically to play, and spend at least as much time roleplaying for their friends as they do trying to maximize their character's effectiveness in a purely structural context. It's common for a group of friends to get together for years, playing the same characters in the game gameworld with the same gamemaster. In the process, they establish long character histories, flesh out the world background, and so on. For long term players, the stories they create can be as emotionally powerful and personally meaningful as anything you find in a novel or a movie — perhaps more so because the players are personally involved in their creation [Costikyan, 2007, p. 9].

Notably, as the popularity of computer role-playing grew, so too did the emphasis on collaborative and social storytelling in tabletop play.[24] In 1991, White Wolf, a U.S.–based gaming magazine/fanzine, merged with the small but influential games company Lion Rampant to form White Wolf Inc., a gaming company whose most significant contribution to the hobby was the "storyteller system," which would provide the foundation for a number of games. Most famously, *Vampire: The Masquerade* (Rein-Hagen, 1991), a modern gothic horror game that established a complex political background of fictional clans and bloodlines, pushed the genre even further towards the immersive storytelling model (Appelcline, 2007). Following the success of *Vampire*, White Wolf released a series of games set in the same universe,[25] "The World of Darkness," and expanded the series to incorporate perhaps the only commercially successful live action role-playing game, *Mind's Eye Theatre: The Masquerade* (Rein-Hagen *et al.*, 1993).[26]

The arrival of the collectible card game *Magic: The Gathering* (Garfield, 1993) had a significant impact on the role-playing industry, channeling many gamers away from the hobby (De Rosa, 1998). In response, many RPG companies turned their attentions to producing collectible card games in the hopes of emulating the success of *Magic* (Appelcline, 2006b). Consequently, by the turn of the century it was largely independent developers who were producing the most innovative role-playing games, with many capitalizing on the Internet as a medium for the distribution of pen and paper games. At the same time, critical interest in role-playing games contributed to the development of more sophisticated understandings of the genre, which in turn led to more nuanced designs. While familiar titles such as *Dungeons and Dragons* continued to be revised and updated for a new audience, the most interesting designs moved away from what Ron Edwards terms "gamism" and towards a narrative approach (2001).[27] Although role-playing had been the subject of serious academic attention as early as 1983 (Fine, 1983), works such as those of Edwards (2001) and Daniel Mackay (2001), along with a particularly vibrant Scandinavian community dedicated to the study of LARPs and role-playing games generally, have contributed to a deeper understanding of the nature of role-playing as both a game and a performative art.[28]

## Collectible Card Games (CCGs)

In 1993, game designer Richard Garfield was attempting to sell his latest design, a board game entitled *Roborally*,[29] to game companies in the U.S. Peter Adkison, founder of the relatively new role-playing company Wizards of the Coast, was interested but had concerns over the high production costs of a board game. While working with Garfield on development of *Roborally*, Adkison expressed his interest in a cheaper, more portable game; Garfield showed him *Manaclash*, a design he had been working on for a few years which combined elements of baseball card trading with a game (Appelcline, 2006b; Weisman, 2007). The concept itself was relatively simple: a two-player card game which could be infinitely expanded through the purchase of further packs, driven by an enormous variety of cards and a scaling of the rarity of individual cards. Evolving into *Magic: The Gathering*, the game was released in August 1993 and would transform hobby gaming almost overnight.

> There is no way to overstate how much CCGs changed the RPG industry back in 1993 and 1994. Gamers were lining up at stores on release day, purchasing the new sets by the $100 case. There was so much money in the fad that new game stores popped up just to get in on the booming industry. Print runs kept increasing, but pre-orders were locked in months ahead of each release, and Wizards couldn't afford to print much above them, so retailers and distributors were constantly limited in their purchases, as their desires typically had grown by release date [Appelcline, 2006b].

Role-playing and strategy gamers alike were drawn into the complex world that emerged from the ongoing release of expansion sets to the game. Most significantly, these ongoing releases and the collectability of cards led to a whole new metagame, that of deck-building. As players became experienced with differing play styles and new cards, the metagame of creating effective decks for play provided an extra level of enjoyment to the hobby. Although precise figures are not available, it is known that Wizards of the Coast sold over one billion magic cards within two years of the game's release (Giles, 1995). The company actively fostered a community of players through the provision of tournaments in hobby gaming stores and in 1994 they established a specialist magazine, *The Duellist*, to accompany the growth of the hobby.

In 1996 a professional competitive tour circuit, which offered prizes of up to $40,000, was established.

*Magic: The Gathering* was the first, and undoubtedly the most successful, of a genre that would come to be known as collectible card games (CCGs). As the phenomenal success of the game quickly became apparent, other publishers were quick to jump on the trend. Among the first wave of these were Decipher's *Star Trek: The Next Generation Customizable Card Game* (Braunlich *et al.*, 1994), TSR's *Spellfire* (1994), and Wizards of the Coast's follow up offering, also co-designed by Garfield, *Jyhad* (Garfield *et al.*, 1994).[30] By late 1995 the market was awash with CCGs, but ultimately none would surpass the popularity of *Magic*. Among the more notable of these early releases were the kung fu/science fiction–themed *Shadowfist* (Laws and Garcia, 1995),[31] the Tolkien-inspired *Middle Earth CCG* (Charlton, 1995) and arguably the most well-respected CCG after *Magic, Legend of the Five Rings* (Seay *et al.*, 1995). The year 1995 also saw the release of TSR's *Dragon Dice* (Smith, 1995), a collectible dice game that foreshadowed the emergence of collectible miniatures a few years later.

The stream of CCGs being released continued through the latter half of the 1990s. While some companies chose to follow the example of *Magic* and develop games based upon their own thematic mythos,[32] others licensed or

Richard Garfield's *Magic: The Gathering* spawned an entire genre of games (image by Simon Holding. © Wizards of the Coast LLC. Image used with permission).

expanded existing brands in attempts to leverage the popularity of the worlds they portrayed.[33] By the late 1990s the market was beginning to cool, with most attractive licenses having been subjected to the CCG treatment at some stage. The year 1999 brought the North American release of the first serious competitor to *Magic* in the unlikely form of a trading card game based upon a Japanese children's media franchise, *Pokémon* (1999). Although still a fully-fledged CCG, *Pokémon* was squarely aimed at a younger demographic, and its popularity was soon emulated by another Japanese entry to the market, *Yu-Gi-Oh!* (Takahashi, 2002).

New CCGs continue to be released, and although the market is certainly not as active as in the mid–1990s, notable and innovative titles do occasionally appear. More recently, collectible card games have made the leap into the virtual with the implementation of online versions. The first entirely online CCG was *Chron X* (Moromisato *et al.*, 1997), developed by Darkened Studios and released in 1997. Subsequently, many successful CCGs have been re-implemented in online versions, including *Magic* and out-of-print games such as Decipher's *Star Wars* (Darcy *et al.*, 1995). Another offshoot of collectible card games has been collectible miniatures. Blending the marketing model of CCGs with the physicality of miniature wargaming, the first to be released was *Mage Knight* (Weisman and Barrett, 2000). Subsequent successful releases include *Heroclix* (Weisman *et al.*, 2002), *Axis and Allies Miniatures* (Tweet *et al.*, 2005), *Heroscape* (Van Ness *et al.*, 2004) and *Star Wars Miniatures* (Grubb *et al.*, 2004). Perhaps the most inclusive of all these games is the *Dungeons and Dragons Miniatures* game (Elias *et al.*, 2003), which simultaneously aims to appeal to players of wargames, role-playing and collectible games.

## Communities of Play

James Lowder, editor of the essay collection *Hobby Games: The 100 Best* (2007a), describes a hobby game as one "that is designed in such a way that players can devote a lot of time to its strategy or the community surrounding it" (2007b). While many adults regularly play classical games, or occasionally mass-market games within a family environment, hobby games form a particular focus for a specific group, where discussion of the game form and participation in the community are often as important in a player's life as the play of the games themselves.

Whereas it has been suggested that adult play tends towards the normative in terms of its fixed rules (Paglieri, 2005), gaming hobbyists from the outset displayed a clear tendency to experiment with rulesets, expecting input into the kinds of games they wanted to play and experimenting with the form as a part of their involvement (Costikyan, 1996). Thus, as early wargaming created possibilities for adult recreational gaming, it also led to the formation of the first communities of hobby gamers (Dunnigan, 1997). Typically educated western males, those who were involved in the industry were enthusiastic participants in the hobby themselves, a characteristic reflected in the general culture of the community today, where the line between consumer and producer is blurred by the ongoing communication between the two groups and the proliferation of amateur content (Winkler, 2006, p. 14).

Situating the player as a character in an imagined environment with emergent, flexible goals, role-playing redefined understandings of games and their potential as a creative and expressive art. Role-playing brought large numbers of new participants into the gaming hobby, many of whom would go on to actively contribute to the evolution of the genre. In contrast to role-playing, collectible card games offered well-defined win and loss conditions, achieved through careful resource management and strategic play. At the same time, these games encouraged the formation of community through the metagames of deck-building and tournaments. Indeed, collectible card games that were discontinued by their original publishers remain the focus of active player communities (Bisz, 2009). Each of these genres has contributed to the shape of contemporary hobby gaming, influencing the growth of the culture — and the industry that supports it — prior to the emergence of eurogames.

# 2

# Anglo–American Hobby
# Board Games 1960–1995

The games that defined hobby gaming through the latter half of the 20th century typically focused on direct conflict as the key source of interaction within play. While wargames were explicitly modeled after historical or imagined armed conflicts, role-playing introduced the notion of the player versus an environment. Although later manifestations of role-playing shifted away from this adversarial relationship between the player and the game world, for a considerable period this model was the dominant form within the genre. Collectible card games, although largely abandoning the emphasis on verisimilitude that characterized wargames and early role-playing, typically pitted one player against another in a similar model of direct conflict. While these three genres were critical in establishing and nurturing a market for adult games, and, more significantly, an active community of gamers, in terms of design none can be considered a direct predecessor to modern eurogames.

Concurrent with the growth of these particular game forms, the broader field of board game design continued to evolve in ways that would later be reflected in the form of eurogames. Between 1960 and 1995 a wide variety of strategy board games aimed at the adult hobbyist market were published in the USA and Great Britain. Although none of these games fit comfortably into any of the hobby gaming genres described in the previous chapter, they were typically distributed through the same retail channels and played by a similar audience. As designers developed games outside the confines of the mass-market, innovative titles increasingly pushed the boundaries of board game design, and in doing so, laid some of the groundwork for the European-style designs that were to follow. In some cases the influence of these games on the eurogame genre is quite apparent, while in others it is perhaps only tenuous. Overall a significant number of the games published during this period display a tendency to de-emphasize positional mechanics in favor of play that draws on interpersonal skills and reasoning. More importantly, the titles discussed in this chapter are indicative of a gradual shift away from direct conflict in both mechanic and theme, a characteristic that would later serve to define modern eurogames.

## The Origins of Modern Eurogames—3M Games

In 1962 the Minnesota Mining and Manufacturing Company (3M) was exploring ways to increase revenues when employees hit upon the idea of producing a line of adult strategy games (Babinsack, 2007). Due to their popularity and subsequent influence on game designers in Germany, these games are particularly important in understanding the nature of eurogames. Among the designers whose work was recognized and published by the newly founded games division of 3M were Americans Alex Randolph and Sid Sackson. In the early 1960s Sackson was involved in a New York gaming group with a focus on designing and playtesting their own inventions (Sackson, 1969), while Randolph had recently abandoned the advertising industry in favor of a career as a game developer (Wolf, 1988). As well as producing a number of traditional abstract titles (e.g., *Backgammon*, *Chess*, *Go*), 3M enlisted Sackson and Randolph to create new games for their "bookshelf" series, so named because of the presentation method which fitted the components into a vertically-oriented book-sized box.[1]

The pair were among the first designers to be commissioned by 3M, and their work marked a significant turning point in the history of board games:

> All of the games published prior to this, and many more to follow, could be considered first generation board games. These first generation games followed a rigid format where turns alternated in a strict pattern, there was little player interaction, a minimal number of choices per turn and, with rare exceptions, no real need for players to remain at the table when it was not their turn to play [Shapiro, 2003].

Among the very first of these second-generation designs was Sackson's *Acquire* (1962), a business and investment–themed game of tile placement and speculation. Alongside *Acquire*, the 3M bookshelf range also included Randolph's abstract strategy game *Twixt* (1961), Rick Onanian's trivia game *Facts in Five* (1967), considered the precursor of category trivia games such as *Scattergories* (1988), and Sackson's game of supply and demand, *Executive Decision* (1971).[2] Beside the highly successful bookshelf series, 3M also went on to produce a series of "gametes" and a range of sports games and paper games until 1975 when the line was sold to Avalon Hill. Filis Frederick observes that at the peak of 3M's success the company was receiving between 400 and 600 game submissions a year (as cited in Babinsack, 2007).

3M began marketing games in Europe in 1966, employing Eugen Oker, an influential writer whose critiques of games had appeared in the respected national newspaper *Die Zeit* as its German editor (Oker, 2004; Whitehill, 2004). Although both Randolph and Sackson would go on to produce many more successful designs, their influence on game design in Germany would see their names far more recognized in that country than in the USA.[3] Recalling his first trip to the Essen games fair in the 1990s, gaming writer Stuart Dagger observed:

> One of the things that struck me was the esteem in which both Sid Sackson and Alex Randolph were held and the position in a place of honour on the second-hand games stalls of the 3M games from twenty years earlier. These were the games that clearly occupied pride of place in many collections. And of course the reverence for the designers went with that for the games, since most of those 3M titles were from one or other of those two [2008].

*Acquire* has since been recognized as the seed of the German style of game design (Shapiro, 2003; Eggert, 2005).[4] As Dave Shapiro writes:

> The significance and impact of *Acquire* cannot be overstated. It was the first of what 40 years later would be deemed German style games. An entire genre of gaming would grow from this seed. Sid Sackson was the founding father of the German style game [2003].

An early Schmidt Spiele edition of Sid Sackson's *Acquire* (image by Simon Holding, courtesy Amigo Spiele).

In essence, *Acquire* had most of the hallmarks that would later come to typify the eurogame: an emphasis on abstracted system over theme, a relatively short and clear ruleset, manageable playing time, and a lack of player elimination. The possible reasons for the strong influence of Sackson and Randolph's work will be discussed a little later. For the moment it is sufficient to acknowledge that at a point in the early 1970s designers in Germany began taking cues from their work that would eventually result in an identifiable game design style.

## *Board Game Design 1970–1980*[5]

In Britain an active board gaming community was forming in the early 1970s, aided in part by the first British magazine dedicated to gaming, *Games and Puzzles*. Founded in 1972 by South African Graeme Levin, the magazine covered traditional abstract games, proprietary games such as *Scrabble* and *Monopoly*, and wargaming. Importantly, *Games and Puzzles* was available in high-street newsagents and contributed to the growth of a healthy play-by-email *Diplomacy* community that established itself under the banner of the British Diplomacy Society. *Games and Puzzles* was also the principal avenue through which gamers in the U.K. could read reviews of recent releases. Generally, these reviews were of games from established British companies such as Waddingtons and Spears, along with wargame releases from the U.S.-based Avalon Hill and the occasional 3M game. Issue 4 of *Games and Puzzles* marked the first mention of the London shop and mail order business Games Guild (also owned by Levin), which, although only promoting British companies initially, would later feature 3M games prominently among their American offerings (Dagger, 2008). By 1976 the hobby had grown sufficiently to support the first annual games convention in Birmingham. The event was held annually, moving through a variety of locations before returning to Birmingham as ManorCon (Dagger, 2007). Both the existence of dedicated magazines and the establishment of regular conventions proved invaluable as building blocks for the hobby community.

Interestingly, at the same time as the hobby was expanding, innovation among the larger companies was declining:

> The two giants in the British board games industry were Waddington and Spears, and they no longer had the creative edge that they had had earlier. In Britain — and I think this is also true of America — the rise of television had seen a decline in the playing of board games. Families no longer played games together to anything like the extent they had in the fifties and before, and board games were now just things you bought as Christmas presents for the kids. Faced with this declining market, the two companies fell back on their

perennial best-sellers—*Monopoly*, *Cluedo* and *Scrabble*. There were new, not particularly inspired, games for the under 10s, but hardly anything of substance for an older market [Dagger, 2008].

The void left as the established companies neglected the adult market was soon filled by a number of smaller businesses offering strategy titles without the emphasis on conflict simulation that drove the American hobby. Among the first of these companies was Intellect Games whose early titles included the British political game *Election* (1972), the first edition of David Parlett's race game *Hare and Tortoise* (1973), and the two-player tile-placement abstract *Thoughtwave* (1974), designed by Eric Solomon.[6] Another Solomon design of the period, the innovative *Sigma File* (1973),[7] featured pieces representing spies that could be moved by any player but whose allegiance was secretly determined.

The U.K. games company Ariel published a number of successful games during the 1970s, of which the most significant was the War of the Roses simulation by Andrew McNeil, *Kingmaker* (1974).[8] Although ostensibly a game of military conflict, *Kingmaker* involved political machinations, a simulated parliament and random events that dramatically affected the course of play. The rights to the game were quickly acquired by Avalon Hill in the USA, where it was significantly revised by designers Don Greenwood and Mick Uhl in correspondence with McNeil (McNeil, 1979). In terms of wargaming, *Kingmaker* was "the first imported game to take the American hobby by storm" ("Avalon Hill General Index," 1980). Other notable games from Ariel included the Robert Abbott two-player abstract *Epaminondas* (1975), the nuclear war simulation *Confrontation* (1974), and the roll-and-move business game *Fortune* (Fenwick, 1979).

Perhaps the biggest influence on German board game design from the U.K. came from the games of Francis Tresham. Tresham's first game, *1829* (1974), offered players a simulation of railway expansion in southern England that simultaneously incorporated development and stock holding. A watershed in board game design, *1829* spawned an entire sub-genre of games known as the 18XX series, within which numerous designers have developed scores of scenarios and rulesets (often self-published) which see the development of railways in locations as diverse as Trinidad (Jacobi, 1996), Malaysia (Lau, 2006) and Namibia (Ohley and Romoth, 2004). The most successful iterations, however, have generally been produced by established companies and include the Avalon Hill–commissioned *1830* (Tresham, 1986) and Mayfair Games' *1870* (Dixon, 1994).

While signs of innovation were apparent in a number of U.K. games, developments in the USA also prefigured some of the features that would later appear in eurogames. In terms of American games of this period, one stands out as being remarkably innovative in terms of mechanics, James St. Laurent's *Crude: The Oil Game* (1974). A game of oil exploration and production, *Crude* was originally released in the U.S. in 1974, although the game failed to achieve success (Rossney, 1994). Interestingly, the game was subsequently re-issued without the designer's knowledge by German publisher Hexagames as *McMulti*. The principal innovation in the game is the mechanic whereby a single production die roll benefits all players, a mechanism that would appear to great acclaim some 20 years later in the highly successful *Die Siedler von Catan*. Other notable American non-wargames of the 1970s include James Koplow's game of negotiation and mob violence, *Organized Crime* (1974), and another game which draws on negotiation skills reminiscent of *Diplomacy*, Vincent Tsao's *Junta* (1978).

Innovation in board game design was not only the preserve of small independent publishers. Despite the company's reputation, Avalon Hill had never been solely concerned with wargames. Indeed, some of the company's earliest games included titles such as the courtroom simulation *Verdict* (Roberts *et al.*, 1959a) and the two-player railroad game *Dispatcher* (Roberts, 1958b). Along with the acquisition and re-issue of a number of 3M games and a large line of sports simulations, titles such as Dunnigan's *Outdoor Survival* (1972), one of the company's best-selling games,[9] and *Rail Baron* (Erickson and Erickson Jr., 1977), another early rail-themed game, established Avalon Hill more generally as a publisher of adult strategy games in the 1970s.

During this period several other American wargame companies, spurred on by the growing popularity of media science fiction and fantasy, began to produce games without the emphasis on verisimilitude that had given birth to the hobby. Writing in 1980, Nicholas Palmer discussed the emergence of these games:

> Unlike the boom in monster-sized games, which peaked in 1978 as prices began to outrun demand, the fashion in SF games looks quite durable, since players are quite happy with colorful but inexpensive designs which can be played in a few hours. Sooner or later we can expect to see a few monster SF games, but in general the preference seems to be for more light-hearted games than are usual in combat simulation [1980, p. 10].

SPI were among the first of the wargame companies to leverage the popularity of science fiction, with designs such as the galactic scale hex-and-counter game *Starforce* (Simonsen, 1974),[10] the *Star Wars*–derived *Freedom in the Galaxy* (Butterfield and Barasch, 1979) and Greg Costikyan's well-regarded *The Creature That Ate Sheboygan* (1979), which sees one player controlling a 1950s-inspired monster and the other the civilians, police and army in the eponymous town.[11] Fantasy too provided inspiration for SPI's designers, initially in a trilogy of games based upon Tolkein's *Lord of the*

*Rings*,[12] and later with titles such as *Swords and Sorcery* (Costikyan, 1978) and *Dragonslayer* (Simonsen and Hessel, 1981).

A similar shift at Avalon Hill also resulted in a number of notable games. The two most enduring titles of the period are the fantasy games *Titan* (McAllister and Trampier, 1980) and *Magic Realm* (Hamblen, 1978). *Titan*, essentially a multiplayer tactical wargame, deals with the mustering of an army of mythological creatures and their subsequent engagement in combat across varying terrains. Interestingly, the mustering of forces occurs on one shared master board, while combat takes place on a number of "battleland" boards. *Titan* remains popular and was reprinted by Valley Games in late 2008. *Magic Realm* was Avalon Hill's first foray into role-playing, albeit in a somewhat complex board game format. The game uses a modular hex board in the creation of a variable landscape, and, although initially hampered by poorly presented rules, it retains a small cult following.

Metagaming Concepts, another significant force in the gaming hobby during the late 1970s and early 1980s were most notable for the creation and popularization of microgames — small cheap games packaged in plastic bags (and, later, small boxes).[13] Of the many games released in this format, none was as successful as *Ogre* (Jackson, 1977b). An asymmetric simulation broadly reminiscent of the *Hnefatafl* family of abstract games, *Ogre* pitches an enormous armored vehicle against a small force of ground troops. *Ogre* was later reprinted by designer Steve Jackson's eponymous company and still garners respect among hobby gamers.[14] The concept of the microgame was later appropriated by a number of companies, including SPI, TSR and Task Force Games.

Although many of the titles of this era draw largely on the tropes of wargaming in their mechanics, a notable distinction in terms of gameplay was the increasing number of games that allowed more than two players, a trait that tends to lead to the presence of diplomatic negotiation within the game:

> These [multi-player games] seem to have a definite popularity edge in the SF contest, perhaps because the "fun" side of wargaming is dominant in both SF simulation and political skullduggery [Palmer, 1980, p. 18].

Exemplary of this development, and by far the most significant game of this period, is Eon's *Cosmic Encounter*.[15] Described by co-designer Peter Olotka as having been conceived as "the anti–*Risk*" (2010, p. 285), *Cosmic Encounter* begins with the simple premise of several players adopting the role of an alien race, each having control of a system of planets. Throughout the course of the game, each player attempts to establish bases on planets belonging to the other players through a series of randomly designated attacks. By enlisting the assistance of other players, both the attacker and defender are able to bolster forces to aid in their goals. What makes the game so unique, however, is the introduction of variable player powers, an element that dramatically overturned one of the principal tenets of game design:

> The impact of *Cosmic Encounter* simply cannot be ignored. The original concept it introduced has permeated every genre of gaming from war and card games to video games. It is a single, simple idea: every player is allowed to break a rule in a unique manner. Prior to *Cosmic Encounter* every player in every game played by the same rules set; equality was assured. With *Cosmic Encounter* every player began with an identical set up and a card that allowed them to "break" one of the rules of the game. This was revolutionary [Shapiro, 2003].

*Cosmic Encounter* has been cited by a number of designers as an early influence and has had a notable effect on the evolution of board games generally.[16] Beyond the innovation of player powers, the game brought to the fore diplomatic negotiations around and above the actual game board, with players jostling for the opportunity to be involved in individual battles. *Cosmic Encounter* has spawned no less than nine expansions and three English language reprints,[17] while numerous fan-created variants add still more replayability to the game.

Shortly after the initial success of *Cosmic Encounter*, Avalon Hill com-

**Fantasy Flight Games' 2008 re-issue of *Cosmic Encounter* (image by Simon Holding, courtesy Fantasy Flight Games).**

missioned the Eon team to develop a game set in the fictional world of Frank Herbert's *Dune* books. Like *Cosmic Encounter*, *Dune* (Eberle *et al.*, 1979) offered each player the opportunity to play as a unique faction in a fictional world, with each assigned variable powers, effectively reinforcing the relationship to the original novels. Eon's design team of Bill Eberle, Jack Kittredge and Peter Olotka have achieved a somewhat legendary status within the gaming community, further enhanced by later innovative titles such as the evolution-themed *Quirks* (1980) and *Borderlands* (1982), a complex mix of resource management, trade and diplomacy which introduced the idea of rotating the start player in each round, a mechanic borrowed from card games that remains commonplace in European designs (Levy, 1999).

## Board Game Design 1980–1995

The period preceding the widespread emergence of eurogames saw continuing innovation in terms of both the theme and mechanics of hobby board games. In 1980 Francis Tresham's company Hartland Trefoil released his most influential game, *Civilization*. Tracking 8,000 years of history and requiring at least six hours for a full game, *Civilization* was unique at the time of publication for many reasons. Most importantly, the thematic emphasis of this game tracing the development of ancient civilizations was not primarily upon conflict but cultural and technological advances. These advances were represented through a "technology tree," an innovative system that would subsequently appear in numerous computer and tabletop games. This is not to say that military conflicts were not present in the game, but that internal development, trade and diplomacy more often provided the keys to an effective victory. Even more so than Tresham's railroad development designs, *Civilization* is considered an iconic game among hobbyists. Infamously, a thematically identical computer game borrowed heavily from the original design and has gone on to spawn numerous sequels.[18] *Civilization* was reprinted by Avalon Hill in 1981, with expansions subsequently designed by Tresham (1982; 1988) and designers at Avalon Hill (Harper *et al.*, 1991).

Another noteworthy company of the 1980s in the U.K. was Gibson Games. Established in 1903 as The International Card Co., in 1911 Gibson Games had been responsible for a pre-cursor to *Stratego* (Mogendorff, 1959) called *Dover Patrol* (Gibson, 1911).[19] The company largely licensed designs from other companies in the 1970s, but in the early 1980s, following a change of management, it turned to publishing independent designs. The most notable of these was American Lewis Pulsipher's multiplayer game of civilization development and warfare, *Britannia* (1986). A highly influential design,

**Francis Tresham's *Civilization* (image by Simon Holding).**

*Britannia* spawned a number of derivative titles and was republished by Avalon Hill in 1987 and by Fantasy Flight Games in 2006.[20]

The popularity of role-playing also served, to a limited extent, as a foundation for the development of a variety of interesting board game titles. Various designers and publishers had been attempting to replicate some facets of the role-playing experience in the form of a board game since at least 1975, when TSR produced *Dungeon!* (Gray *et al.*, 1975), a highly simplified adaptation of a basic *Dungeons and Dragons* scenario that dispensed with a game master, pitting players against each other in a race to accumulate treasure.[21]

Steve Jackson and Ian Livingstone of Games Workshop produced a number of games by British and American designers, as well as working with other companies in reprinting existing games for the U.K. market. Among the first of the company's original titles was Pulsipher's *Valley of the Four Winds* (1980), a two-player fantasy wargame based upon a short story and a line of Games Workshop miniatures. Designer Derek Carver recalls his first steps into published game design with the company:

> Because there was a lack of new games coming onto the adult boardgaming market I started to invent and make my own. And because at the time Ian Livingstone and Steve Jackson ... used to join us at times they got to know these games. Games Workshop was a very small outfit in those days. However,

they then decided to publish their own games and being familiar with my games three of them got into the Games Workshop range [2008].

Carver's first game was originally a *Dungeons and Dragons*–inspired roll-and-move game which had players collecting gems, but since Games Workshop had recently acquired the rights to produce a game based upon the BBC television series *Doctor Who* (Carver, 2007), a theme change resulted in *Doctor Who: The Game of Time and Space* (Carver, 1980). It was Carver's *Warrior Knights* (1985b) and *Blood Royale* (1987), however, that were to have more long-lasting appeal. A game of negotiation and conflict in the medieval period, *Warrior Knights*' enduring popularity is evidenced by a 2006 re-implementation (Faidutti *et al.*, 2006).[22] *Blood Royale*[23] is a lengthy political negotiation game with elements of role-playing that Carver had intended to be a game system similar to that found in role-playing games.

The most successful of Games Workshop's forays into board game publishing, however, was another role-playing hybrid, *Talisman* (Harris, 1983). Designer Robert Harris originally conceived *Talisman* as a way of allowing players to enjoy the role-playing experience without the intensive preparation typically associated with the form:

> I had it in mind to come up with a way we could have all the excitement of a roleplaying adventure without all the hard work of creating characters and drawing maps. At the back of my mind was a game I had designed while still a pupil at Morgan Academy in Dundee. It was called "Rectocracy" and involved each player taking on the character of one of the teachers. You moved around the board, gradually working your way towards the centre, where you would try to make yourself Rector (headmaster/principal) of the school. I had a notion that I could use a similar layout to make a fantasy adventure game [Harris, 2007].

Essentially a simple roll-and-move game, many gamers both in the U.S. and the U.K. remember *Talisman* fondly, perhaps due to the way it blended the familiar themes of fantasy roleplay with mechanics reminiscent of mainstream family games. The first imprint of the game spawned six expansions[24] and three subsequent editions, the most recent by Fantasy Flight Games in 2008. As well as these original designs, Games Workshop also licensed the Swedish design *Drakborgen* (Bonds and Glimne, 1985), a competitive dungeon-delving game with superficial similarities to TSR's *Dungeon!*, retitled *DungeonQuest* for the English-speaking market.

The company also produced versions of *Cosmic Encounter* and *Quirks* in collaboration with U.S.–Based Eon, and a version of David Watts' 1973 design *Railways Rivals*. *Railway Rivals* is generally considered the first modern railway game and has spawned a number of similar titles in the U.S., most notably the Mayfair series of crayon rail games. Beginning in 1980 with *Empire Builder*

(Bromley and Fawcett, 1980), the Mayfair rails games, like *Railway Rivals,* allowed players to create their own train routes by drawing on a specially laminated board. Unlike the share-driven model of Tresham's *18XX* games, the emphasis in the crayon rails series is that of moving goods efficiently around a network. The series has seen numerous variations and new titles continue to be released.[25]

While companies such as Games Workshop were reprinting American designs, so too were American companies distributing the more successful European titles. The 1980s saw Avalon Hill reprint games such as Tresham's *Civilization* and *1829,*[26] along with the political negotiation game *Kremlin* (Hostettler, 1988), considered the first modern German language game to be reprinted in English (Scherer-Hoock, 2003).[27] Other notable Avalon Hill designs of the period include *Gunslinger* (Hamblen, 1982), a second-by-second simulation of gunfighting in the Old West, the chariot racing *Circus Maximus* (Greenwood and Matheny, 1979), and a 1990 reprint of Derek Carver's self-published auction game *Showbiz* (1985a).[28]

Smaller U.S. companies were also responsible for a growing number of

The fourth edition of *Talisman* by Fantasy Flight Games (image by David Dudley, courtesy Fantasy Flight Games).

games that introduced some innovative and memorable gameplay elements to the hobby. Designer Steve Jackson, who had left Metagaming to form his own company, produced *Illuminati* (1983), a satirical game of global conspiracy theories that took *Cosmic Encounter*'s rule-breaking exceptions to extreme lengths and added variable goals to the mix.[29] Tom Jolly's *Wiz War* (1983) was another title that gathered a sizeable cult following among gamers. Initially self-produced in a small Ziploc bag, the game, set in a typical dungeon-like maze, offered a simple rules system that effectively simulated the back and forth of dueling wizards in a chaotic battle via the use of card play.[30] Through a total of seven separate editions, *Wiz War* continued to be popular, and when the game finally went out of print it was not long before enterprising fans began making their own copies of this classic "beer and pretzels" game.[31]

In strong contrast to the confrontational style of gameplay found in games such as *Wiz War*, West End Games' *Tales of the Arabian Nights* (Goldberg, 1985) introduced elements of storytelling to a board game with a paragraph-based system that led players on an adventure through the world of 1001 nights. At the outset of the game, players choose their own victory conditions from a mix of story and destiny points. As the player moves around the board, increasing in status, his opponents read to him from the "Book of Tales," describing the encounters that occur and the results thereof. A clever mix of interactive narrative and board game play, *Tales of the Arabian Nights* was re-issued in a revised form by Z-Man games in 2009. Though not so explicit, similar narrative emphasis can be found in Richard Launius' *Arkham Horror* (1987), a cooperative game set in the Cthulhu mythos that sees players racing around the eponymous town in an effort to stop nightmare creatures from spilling over from an alternative dimension.[32]

## Light in the Blind Alley

The hobby board games described in this chapter demonstrate the gradual evolution of board game design alongside the more visible genres of hobby games. Although writer Richard Huzzey has dismissed American and British designers of this period as "flail[ing] about in a blind alley, with only the most fleeting and tenuous glimmers of quality" (2002), the recent reprinting of many of the titles discussed here is evidence of their enduring appeal among gamers. Developments in hobby board game design were almost certainly an influence on the European design style that subsequently emerged. As designer and publisher Morgan Dontanville observes:

> It's not like the Euro just magically appeared. In fact, an argument can be
> made that Euros spawned out of this proto-hybrid (that and every Sid Sack-

son and Alex Randolph game). To me, companies like 3M (*Feudal*) Avalon Hill (*Dune, Britannia, Gangsters, Merchant of Venus, Gunslinger*), Mayfair (*The Keep, Demo Derby*), Eon (*Cosmic Encounter, Borderlands, Quirks*), Hartland Trefoil Ltd. (*Civilization, Spanish Main*), and even Wizard Magazine (*King of the Table Top, The Awful Green Things from Outer Space*) had their finger on the pulse of streamlining and modernizing the conflict game [2006].

Sid Sackson and Alex Randolph were responsible for designing some of the first titles that would retrospectively be referred to as eurogames. Importantly, these designs were not focused on the simulation of armed conflict, having instead more abstract gameplay with an emphasis on the game system rather than the theme. Francis Tresham too produced deep engaging games that did not rely on direct conflict, spawning a myriad of imitators, both analogue and digital. Wargame designers, responding to the growth of the hobby, published multiplayer games that encouraged negotiation and diplomacy rather than statistical verisimilitude. As noted, a number of European designers have acknowledged the work of the team behind *Cosmic Encounter* as significant in their approach to design. Throughout the 1970s and 1980s, hobby board game designs shifted away from lengthy two-player games towards multiplayer games with an emphasis on sociability and playability over simulation. While Huzzey's assertion is perhaps correct in terms of mass-market games, hobby board game design left a lasting mark on the modern culture of board gaming. Perhaps more importantly, the popularity and diversity of the titles discussed here indicates a growing market for board games accompanying the general growth of the hobby gaming sector. This established community of adult gamers would provide an ideal environment for the dissemination of eurogames in the late 1990s.

# 3

# *Gesellschaftsspiele —*
# *Gaming in Germany*

*Like novels, games don't come out of the blue. They come from a given designer, at a given time, in a given social situation.* — Bruno Faidutti, in Appelcline, 2006a

Throughout the late 20th century Anglo-American board game design evolved largely subject to the influence of an expanding hobby game market. Concurrently, in what was at the time West Germany, a distinctive approach to game design was emerging that would later come to underpin the eurogame genre. Although the impact of this design style would not be felt in the broader hobby gaming market until the success of *Die Siedler von Catan* in 1995, the seeds of this approach can be found in games published in Germany as early as the late 1970s. The geo-cultural specificity of this design style, and the enthusiastic domestic reception to these game forms prior to 1995, suggests influences on game designers and players in Germany that were not present elsewhere.

Although clearly one cannot, even with the most diligent research, assign causal relationships between particular historical and cultural circumstances and the creation of specific artifacts, as designer Bruno Faidutti acknowledges above, games are not created in a cultural vacuum. Indeed, there can be little doubt that such influences played a part in the emergence of the eurogame form in Germany. A lengthy precedent for the production of high quality toys and games in Germany has resulted in the active preservation of these artifacts through the efforts of dedicated museums and archives. In turn, Germany has evolved a media ecology that reflects and reinforces the notion that sedentary games are a legitimate leisure pursuit. Indeed, a lively gaming culture within Germany actively encourages and rewards designers and publishers of original board and table games. Finally, the impact of post-war attitudes toward conflict arguably had a significant impact on the way that designers working in Germany approached the challenges of creating competitive games. These particular cultural and commercial considerations have influenced not only the growth of gaming in Germany, but also the form of the games that are produced. Together they provide an insight into why Germany has become the acknowledged center of board game design innovation worldwide.

## Toy Capital of the World

Germany has long been associated with the production of high-quality toys. Helmut Schwarz traces the beginnings of toy production (specifically clay dolls) in Nuremberg to the late fourteenth century (2003), and the city has long claimed the title of "toy capital of the world" (McCafferty, 1999). Taxation documents dated 1400 describe wooden doll makers, while illustrations from the mid–16th century depict craftsmen carving wooden figures. By the end of the 18th century a store catalogue lists 8,000 individual toys, all of which the owner claims originate from the city:

> The extensive range of Nuremberg toys and educational materials displayed in the document includes hobby-horses, wooden building bricks and figures, fully furnished doll's houses and kitchens, miniature shops, tin figures, children's crockery and musical instruments, *parlour games*, magnetic toys and optical and mechanical marvels [Schwarz, 2003, emphasis mine].

As Schwarz notes, such a large range of products in the pre-industrial period suggests the existence of significant international trade. As a cultural center of Europe, and under the protection of the Catholic Church, Nuremberg was renowned as the "birthplace of technology" within Germany. Extensive connections with cottage industries in surrounding areas contributed to the development of a sizeable wooden crafts industry, producing toys and other miniature items from wood. These goods, known as "Nuremberg wares," helped cement the city's worldwide reputation as a center of craft production. At the same time, in the realm of German domestic life, David Hamlin has suggested that the dominant ideals of the 18th and 19th century resulted in an increased desire by parents to separate children from the influences of the broader society (2003). This emphasis, which demanded control of the child's social environment, resulted in increased demand for toys. Moreover, the general trend towards industrialization during the 19th century resulted in Nuremberg becoming the principal industrial center in Bavaria. As a consequence of this shift, increasing numbers of toys were now constructed from tin, reflecting a society with a growing emphasis on technology. The city evolved to become the "undisputed centre of metal toy production" and was home to companies such as Gebrüder Bing and Schuco (Schwarz, 2003).

From the mid–19th century, the growth of the toy market was matched by a similar interest in board and table games. In 1883, Bavarian bookseller Otto Robert Maier established a publishing company specializing in the production of instruction pamphlets for architects and craftspeople (Hanson, 2006, p. 44). After early successes, Maier turned to the production of games, first commissioning a series of eight games for adults and then, in 1884, *A Trip Around the World*, a board game based upon the Jules Verne novel *Around the World in Eighty Days* (Hauser, 1993). The game quickly became popular on the German market, partly due to the high quality of the tin figurines and printed board that Maier commissioned from independent suppliers. By 1892, Maier had sold his bookstore and decided to focus exclusively on his thriving publishing business, which he registered under the name Ravensburger. Recognizing the growth of the games market in Germany, Maier registered a subsidiary company, Ravensburger Games, in 1900 (Hauser, 1993). By 1902 the Ravensburger catalogue featured approximately 100 games alongside the established line of books, and in 1912 the company began translating games into other European languages. Choosing not to compete with successful companies in the general toy industry, Maier focused on board games and puzzles.

By the time of the First World War, Germany dominated the worldwide production of toys (Burton, 1997, p. 9). The war brought production to a halt, as factories were turned over to arms production, and international markets were rendered inaccessible. Although Germany would recover somewhat, by the end of the war the domination of world toy markets was lost. Subsequently, and at the point of apparent recovery, the onset of the Great Depression and the rise to power of the National Socialist Party further damaged the industry, as racial policies forced a large number of Jewish manufacturers to leave the country. German toys were boycotted in many countries; and with the onset of the Second World War, those factories that remained were once again turned over to the production of arms, with a general ban on toy production issued in 1943 (Schwarz, 2003).

By the time the war came to a close in 1945, many of Germany's factories had been destroyed, and those that had previously made toys and games were no exception. However, recovery was relatively swift, and the West German toy industry increased exports from eight million to over 100 million DM between 1948 and 1953. In 1950 the International Toy Fair was held in Nuremberg for the first time, cementing the reputation of the region and the country as central to the world's toy industry ("Spielwarenmesse," 2008). Throughout the 1950s this successful growth continued, resulting in Schuco becoming the largest toy manufacturer in Europe over the course of the decade (Schwarz, 2003). In 1959, William Hurter's *Memory* was the hit of the Nuremberg Toy Fair, establishing Ravensburger as an international presence in family games

(Hanson, 2006, p. 45).[1] Although the 1970s saw sufficient competition from Asian and American toy producers to change Germany to a largely toy-importing country, German manufacturers continued to offer high quality products on the international market (Schwarz, 2003). The observation that German culture was seen as being a key to rapid economic recovery following the war (Carter, 1997, p. 22), and that the games industry recovered so quickly, suggests a perception of games as a vital part of the German national identity.

By the 1970s however, German game companies were presented with a problem. As Stuart Dagger notes, while the larger British and American companies were increasingly relying on tried and tested family games, German publishers did not have this option available:

> It is of significance that Ravensburger, the biggest of the German companies, did not own the German rights to *Monopoly, Cluedo, Scrabble* and so on. So for them the defensive business option of focusing just on these wasn't possible. In order to survive they had to go on being creative. This would also have made them willing listeners and supporters when the originators of the *Spiel des Jahres* and the *Essen Games Fair* began their efforts to improve and promote German board games [Dagger, 2008].

Ravensburger, principally a producer of family games, began to nurture an in-house design team to develop games that were German in origin. To retain a regional identity in an arena increasingly dominated by multinational corporations, it was clear that local ingenuity would be required. Fortunately, game companies were assisted in their efforts by a media that reflects the established cultural significance of games in Germany.

## Games and the German Media

Perhaps the greatest influence on contemporary gaming culture in Germany is the high media presence afforded games when compared with other nations. Games are reviewed on radio, designers appear on television shows with their latest creations, and many newspapers print regular board gaming columns (Kramer, 2000a; Heli, 2007). Additionally, a number of specialist magazines —*Spielezeitschrift*—are devoted exclusively to coverage of board and card games, and have wide circulation. The first of these, *Die Pöppel-Revue*, was established in 1977 and named after the iconic wooden pieces that were so commonplace in Ravensburger games of the time (Eggert, 2006a). Beginning as a vehicle for discussion of play-by-mail games, *Die Pöppel-Revue* was a simple fanzine that quickly grew to embrace many facets of German gaming culture. The final issue was published in December 2001. *Spielbox*, first published in 1981 by Reiner Müller, provides reviews of new games along with game commentary, news from game fairs, and, occasionally, original games and expansions by recognized designers such as Reiner Knizia, Sid Sackson and Alex Randolph. With a print run of approximately 13,000 (Galanti, 2005), the magazine publishes special almanac issues that focus upon a single designer and/or game.[2] Similar magazines include *Spielerei*, which organizes the annual Hippoodice game design competition (Werneck, 2004), and *Fairplay*, established in 1987, which, as well as taking over the voting for the *Deutscher Spiel Preis*, runs the Fairplay poll, an on-the-spot ballot held to gauge consumer interest in new releases at the Essen games fair.

## Game Awards

The most tangible outcome of the German media's support of gaming culture, however, is the *Spiel des Jahres* (Game of the Year), without doubt the most influential board and table game award in the world. Indeed, it has been suggested that a *Spiel des Jahres*–winning game can expect a tenfold increase in sales through its association with the award (Kramer, 2000b).[3] The prize was established in 1978 by a group of specialist journalists with the purpose of "promot[ing] the cultural asset games [sic], to stimulate the idea of playing games with family and friends and to give orientation within the large choice of games available" ("Spiel des Jahres," 2008). Active jury member and co-founder Tom Werneck describes the inception of the award:

> Our vision was to put such a strong pressure on the game industry that they struggle to bring the highest possible level of quality on a competitive market. When we look back now, 30 years later, we see that it worked out.... It worked out because the award *Spiel des Jahres* had such a strong influence on sales figures (factor 100!) that it worked like a sting in their flesh inflaming competition [2008].[4]

In addition to the awards process, the organization Spiel des Jahres e.V contributes to the gaming community in Germany through active promotion in the media, support of social institutions in adopting games, and the awarding of grants to game designers and scholars. The award jury is comprised of members of the German media who have "proven their competence and their power of judgment" in the assessment of games, with individuals who are directly involved in the gaming industry specifically excluded from participation ("Spiel des Jahres," 2008). Although the award offers no financial compensation, the publishers of the winning game are entitled to use the prestigious *Spiel des Jahres* emblem in promotion and packaging, for which they must pay the organization a licensing fee. This license fee is the primary source of revenue for the organization. A list of eligible games is produced shortly after the Nuremberg Toy Fair in February. The *Spiel des Jahres* jury then produces a shortlist of five games and a series of annotated recommendations (*Auswahlliste*), with the winner announced in June or July of the same year. Eligibility is restricted to games that have been published in Germany in the preceding year, though exceptions are occasionally made for reimplementations of older games. The judging criteria are identified as:

1. Game concept (originality, playability, game value)
2. Rule structure (composition, clearness, comprehensibility)
3. Layout (box, board, rules)
4. Design (functionality, workmanship)

Since 1991 the jury has also awarded the *Kinderspiel des Jahres* (Children's Game of the Year), which is decided upon via a separate selection process. Additionally, the jury often awards special prizes (*Sonderpreis*) which recognize particular elements of a game, such as the *Sonderpreis Schönes Spiel* (Most Beautiful Game), awarded frequently until 1997, *Sonderpreis Literatur im Spiel* (Best Use of Literature in a Game)[5] and *Sonderpreis Komplexes Spiel* (Best Complex Game). In 2011 a new award, *Kennerspiel des Jahres* (Connoissuer's Game of the Year), was introduced to "give guidance to those people who have already been playing games for a longer time and are experienced in learning new rules" ("Kennerspiel des Jahres," 2011).

In English-speaking countries it is difficult to appreciate the importance of the *Spiel des Jahres* in Germany. Although there are awards in the United States (e.g., International Gamers Award,[6] Origins Award),[7] these tend to be directed at hobby gamers, while the *Spiel des Jahres* has established a reputation for focusing on games that have a broader appeal to those outside the gaming hobby. Consequently, the jury tends to award those games that can be played within a family setting, eschewing overly complex games and those whose thematic appeal might restrict the audience. More complex hobbyist games are explicitly addressed by the *Deutscher Spiele Preis*, a separate award originated in 1990 by the German magazine *Die Pöppel-Revue*, whose votes are gathered from industry members and gaming clubs throughout Germany and, since 2001, via worldwide votes cast through the Internet and readers of *Fairplay* magazine.[8] The Essen Feather is awarded in the same ceremony as the *Deutscher Spiele Preis*, with an emphasis on the clarity and presentation of game rules ("Essen Feather," 2008).

Other countries have followed the German lead in creating awards similar to the *Spiel des Jahres* and the *Deutscher Spiel Preis*. As mentioned, the USA has the International Gamers Award, initiated by games writer Greg Schloesser, which has a similar focus to that of the *Deutscher Spiele Preis* and is judged, as the title implies, by an international panel of game writers. Austria's *Spiel der Spiele* was initiated in 2001 and avoids any potential redundancies attendant with the separate German awards by recommending games in a number of categories.[9] Two French awards, the *As d'Or*, awarded at the Cannes Games Festival since 1988, and the *Jeu de l'année*, initiated in 2003, were merged in 2005 and have a similar emphasis on family games as the *Spiel des Jahres*. Still, none of these awards has attained the prestige of the *Spiel des Jahres*.

## Nurturing a Culture of Game Design

In addition to a higher media profile and broader customer base, the very culture of German game design is arguably very different to that in the USA and U.K. In Germany, the creator of a given game is not generally described as an inventor, but as an author. This subtle difference in the way game designers are viewed, in comparison with most other cultures, reflects a different understanding of both the nature of the design process and the creativity involved in arriving at a genuinely innovative game system. Tom Werneck explains:

> The development of a game ... is in first line a creative process. Obviously it requires some systematic and hard work. Compared to the creative factor, however, diligence should be rather little. If games are "invented" based on pure analytics then you feel it. Such games mostly are bloodless and have only a poor playing appeal. They suffer from a lack of a creative momentum — just the flashover from mechanistic industriousness to a brilliant and ingenious idea [2004].

Over time, the recognition of the creativity involved in game design has led to the attribution of the author on virtually all German games.[10] Although initially the idea that the name of a game designer should appear on the box was given short shrift by game companies, Werneck suggests that a gradual shift can be attributed to a number of factors. As game companies began to see themselves increasingly as publishing houses, the attribution of an author seemed a natural progression. Smaller companies too began to realize that the name of an author served as a distinguishing element in a rapidly expanding marketplace. This distinguishing feature works not only for well-known designers but also for those who are producing their first game, since, if the first game by a given designer is successful, consumers are far more likely to gravitate towards subsequent releases (Werneck, 2004). Game publishers have also had to bow to pressure from individual designers. In 1988 a number of game designers attending the Nuremberg Toy Fair signed their names to the now-famous "Coaster Proclamation," a commitment not to sell games to companies who would not print the designer's name on the box ("The Coaster

Proclamation," 2010).[11] As a consequence of all these factors, by the 1990s it had become common practice to list the designer's name on the cover of a game.

Still, the commercial recognition of the designer as author is not enough in itself to create an active culture of game design. Since the 1970s and the establishment of the *Spiel des Jahres*, a community has developed which is highly supportive of game authors. In 1983 designer and artist Reinhold Wittig[12] introduced the term *"spieleautor"* (Game Author) with an invite to the inaugural *Spieleautorentreffen* (Game Author's Meeting) in Goettingen. Each year since then, new and experienced designers, publishers and game editors have met to discuss issues of significance within the game industry, to swap ideas and innovations, and to present prototypes to prospective publishers.

The Coaster Proclamation. Signatories are (top left, vertical) Reinhold Wittig, Helge Andersen, Hajo Bücken, Erwin Glonegger, Dirk Hanneforth, Knut Michael Wolf, Wolfgang Kramer, Joe Nikisch, Gilbert Obermeier, Alex Randolph, John Rüttinger, Roland Siegers and a not yet identified author (courtesy Christian Beiersdorf and the Spiele-Autoren-Zunft).

In 1991, responding to demand generated by the Goettingen events, the *Spieleautorenzunft* (SAZ)[13] was established as a guild for game authors. The goals of the guild are threefold:

- Promotion of games as cultural property
- Promotion of exchange of ideas among game authors and in the game industry
- Protection of the interests of game authors

The SAZ is currently the largest organization of game designers in the world and is now responsible for organizing workshops held at the *Goettingen Spieleautorentreffen*. Previous chairmen have included notable designers such as Wolfgang Kramer, Reiner Knizia and Marcel André Casasola Merkle. Members are permitted entry to the annual Nuremberg Toy Fair (an event only open to industry members) and the International Game Designer Conference in Haar, as well as to a large number of other organized events throughout the year ("Spieleautorenzunft," 2008). Since its inception, many successful games have been initially presented to publishers at Goettingen (Alden, 2008), along with a number of awards: *der Inno-Spatz* (innovation sparrow — awarded by the City of Goettingen), *der Förderpreis für Nachwuchsautoren* (prize for new authors awarded by *Spiel des Jahres e.V*) and der "Alex" (named after Alex Randolph and awarded by *die Spieleautorenzunft*, which recognizes promotion of gaming in the media).

Another highly regarded award is that for the *Hippodice Autorenwettbewerb* (Hippo Dice Authors Competition). Established in 1986, *Hippodice Autorenwettbewerb* was initially responsible for the fanzine *Speilerei*. In 1988, the club launched a game design competition that would subsequently become an important award within the game design community. Voted upon by a jury made up of industry figures, several winners and runners up have gone on to be successfully published, most notably the negotiation game *Chinatown* (Hartwig, 1999), Werner Hodel's *Spiel des Jahres*–winning *Mississippi Queen* (1998a),[14] Christwart Conrad's game of commodity speculation in the wine industry, *Vino*[15] (1999), and, more recently, Thomas Odenhoven's *Portobello Market* (2007), a short game of area movement and control that was initially themed around railways in East India (Aleknevicus, 2001a; "Hippodice Spieleclub," 2008).

## Game Shows

*For the lover of games, there is nothing quite like the spiel.* — Schloesser, 2008c

Another measure of both consumer attention and the design-oriented culture in Germany are the various gaming shows that occur throughout the year, the largest of which is the Essen Games Fair. Officially titled *Internationale Spieltage* but known to hobby gamers as simply "the spiel" or "Essen," the Essen Games Fair is the largest non-digital gaming convention in the world. Established in 1983, the fair was originally titled the German Games Con, with the objective of providing an event where people could "meet and play together and demonstrate that gaming was a vital part of the German culture" (Schloesser, 2008c). After initial skepticism over the level of public interest, the event grew considerably and eventually moved into the Essen Exhibition Centre (*Messe Essen*) in order to accommodate growing numbers. The spiel is traditionally held in late October and, along with the Nuremberg Toy Fair in February, is the principal showcase for newly released board games in the world. Unlike Nuremberg, the show is open to consumers and consequently attracts crowds of close to 150,000 people over four days ("Internationale Spieltage," 2008).

In gaming culture, the spiel has acquired something of a mythical reputation as the premiere board gaming event in the world. Drawing publishers from many countries, the event also plays host to the *Deutscher Spiel Preis*, the Essen Feather and, more recently, the International Gamers Awards. Following the success of Essen, several other fairs have appeared which offer an

Game stall at the Essen Games Fair, 2009.

opportunity for the consumer to sample games at various stages of development. The *Süddeutsche Spielemesse* in Stuttgart regularly attracts up to 100,000 visitors (Werneck, 2004; "Süddeutsche Spielemesse," 2008), with similar events taking place in München,[16] and Vienna in Austria.[17]

Importantly, games fairs are considered a place where budding board game designers can showcase new titles in the same venue as larger companies, and, unlike in the USA (where companies such as Hasbro generally eschew unsolicited submissions [Verbeten, 2007, p. 31]), the larger companies are actively looking for innovative designs. Designers such as Friedemann Friese, Andrea Meyer and Peter Prinz have all self-published games at Essen that were eventually picked up by larger companies. As much as the games fairs are commercial venues, the attitude of both publishers and designers retains a cultural pride in producing quality games, which is arguably as much a part of the German games industry as the quest for profit:

> The idea of the possibility of profit as the main reason to produce games would ring strange in German game companies' ears.... When I speak to American companies (like I did at this year's Essen) there always seems to be a kind of gleam in the eye when it comes to speaking of sales, whereas most German game companies I know seem to be more of an idealistic bunch. Of course they know that they have to sell games, but they also see a pride in the product itself, no matter how it sells. They know that the market is dominated by Trading Card Games and the like, but they find a certain pleasure in producing "their" game [Eggert, 2005].

The idealism that gaming writer Morritz Eggert describes here is further evidence of the particular value placed on games within German culture beyond that of commercial potential.

## *The Influence of Post-War Attitudes to Wargames*

> Germany is extremely critical towards war games. That comes from the history and the experiences of the Second World War. The majority of people, the family game culture, doesn't really like to play war games. It's modern fairy tales they want to play [Knizia in Glenn, 2002].

Approximately 300 to 400 new board and table game designs are published in Germany each year (Stöckmann and Jahnke, 2008a, p. 94). Over the last thirty years or so, German designers have consistently produced a high number of games that have been significantly different from those emerging in the rest of the world. Interviews with designers of the period, and commentary from those in the industry, suggest that the influence of post-war legislation and cultural taboo regarding conflict-themed play has been a factor in shaping the game designs that emerged during this period (Huzzey, 2002; Heli, 2007).

While in the USA wargames proved extremely successful in the latter half of the 20th century, in post-war West Germany the combination of public and governmental aversion to war-related products, along with strict laws prohibiting the depiction of Nazi symbology on entertainment products, meant that titles which were popular among hobbyists in other countries received scant attention in Germany. As gaming writer Moritz Eggert observes, "The generation that grew up in the bombed up remains of the 'Reich' didn't have 'Kriegsspiele'[18] on their mind when they became rebellious teenagers" (Eggert, 2006b). The most commonly cited example used to exemplify game manufacturers' response to this aversion is that of the mainstream wargame *Risk*. Whereas in the rest of the world the game was subtitled one of "global domination," the German version tasked the players with "liberat[ing] the world" (Freund, 2005).

Perhaps as influential as the cultural taboo surrounding conflict was the German law that prohibited the importation of war-related toys (Varney, 2000, p. 387). Although wargames were available in Germany, designers walked a fine line with regards to the depiction of historically accurate insignia, as evidenced by the case of game designers Harry Rowland and Greg Pinder. Copies of their game *Days of Decision III* (2004) were confiscated and destroyed due to the inclusion of a small swastika symbol on a counter depicting Hitler (Eggert, 2006b; Lanza, 2006, p. 20). This combination of cultural stigma and legal prohibition gave rise to the feeling that stores electing to carry American wargames were "teetering on the edge of doing something illegal," with some particularly controversial games being discussed on national television (Eggert, 2006b). British games writer Brian Walker describes this effect in a review of the 1988 Essen Spiel:

> Over to the Das Spiel stand now. This Hamburg based company is one of the best known games shops in Germany, though their stand is bereft of home grown products. Their speciality is importing and translating English and American games. A large selection of American wargames is kept discreetly under the counter, rather like the X-rated videos at your local newsagent [1988].

As Järvinen observes, any game with a war theme brings "a discourse of ethnic conflict into the game" (2009, p. 283). With the weight of recent history in Germany, it is understandable that both commercial and cultural considerations have played a part in shaping the work of aspiring designers who were raised in what political historian Thomas Berger describes as a broader "culture of anti-militarism" (1998).

Arguably, it is this aversion to themes and mechanics of direct conflict that led to the popularity of the 3M range of games when they were released in Germany. Although appealing to an adult market, few of the 3M games specifically called upon direct conflict in either theme or mechanism. Writer Rick Heli addresses the influence that these games might have had on aspiring designers:

> Taking Sackson's *Acquire* as their model, they [German publishers] created what they called *Gesellschaftspiele*, society games. The message was clear. The games are not about the lawlessness and disorder of war, but the normal operation of civilized society [2004].

In the light of the influences discussed here, game designers in Germany were implicitly tasked with the development of board games that avoided overt themes of war and conflict. This was not an easy undertaking, as designer Franz-Benno Delonge explains:

> If you want to move away from the idea of confrontation, which is classically at the core of nearly every game, then you have to come up with something really new as an alternative [in Freund, 2005].

The alternative that Delonge speaks of is evident in the design sensibilities that have come to typify the eurogame genre. The games that emerged from this time and place focused on individual development and comparative achievement rather than the direct conflict that typifies Anglo-American designs of the period. A number of designers have alluded to this tendency in their work. Wolfgang Kramer describes as one of the guiding principles in his work that

> players act constructive in order to improve their own results. They do not act destructive and destroy the playing of their opponents. In my games a player damages another player only then, when he makes a good move for himself. The sense of his move is to help himself and not to damage the game of the other player [in Yu, 2011b].

Klaus Teuber summarizes the appeal of his game, *Die Siedler von Catan*, thusly:

> I ... believe that most people in the world prefer to engage in constructive rather than destructive activities. The world of Catan is built on the philosophy of peaceful building, rather than war and violence. So the majority of people, who believe in constructive aspects in life, probably like playing Catan also for that reason ["Interview with Klaus Teuber," 2005].

Finally, designer Reiner Knizia is even more direct in discussing his own aversion to conflict:

> I don't like bloody games. I think we can get better missions out into the world of gaming for the youngsters and the old guys than motivating people to shoot each other [in Alden and Solko, 2009a].

As noted earlier, any claim of a direct causal relationship between particular cultural circumstances and a specific outcome must remain highly speculative. Yet the fact that German designers speak of their own aversion to themes of conflict within games hints at a broader design philosophy that eschews such subject matter. Particularly given the push among German companies to deliver games to the domestic family market, it is not surprising to find that the style of game design that emerged from Germany avoided culturally sensitive topics and explored different paths than elsewhere.[19]

## A Culture of Play

*The very size of the German game market alone witnesses to the fact that games are an important part of Germany's culture.* — Stöckmann and Jahnke, 2008a, p. 101

Although it would be a misnomer to imagine that the eurogames now played by hobbyists worldwide are to be found in every German home, Germans do purchase more board and table games per capita than residents of any other country (Curry, 2009). For the most part, these purchases mirror those in other countries in that the mass-market staples produced by Hasbro and Mattel dominate. Still, the broader awareness of games in Germany is reflected in the games aisle of the average toy store that typically stocks a variety of adult strategy games — games that would only find a home in specialist stores elsewhere in the world. Curator of the *Bayerische Spiele-Archiv* Tom Werneck compares the games market in Germany with that of the United States:

> The culture of board games in the U.S. is closely linked to marketing and trade. In Germany you find "Spielwarenhandel," shops where you can find all kind of toys and games. Furthermore you find well equipped departments with toys and games in all major department stores. Normally you will find sales staff who has at least a good basic knowledge about the games.... Therefore you find informed consumers or consumers who will get a good piece of advice if they ask for it. In the U.S. there is no culture of game critics and you will hardly find a game retailer who knows what's in the boxes. Market communication in the U.S. is done in a different way: TV. Since it is almost impossible to explain a complex board game between 12 (minimum time for a spot) and 30 seconds (whatever exceeds this timeframe costs a fortune) all major producers in the states focus on games which have either a very simple structure which can be demonstrated in a few seconds or they must include a sort of mechanic which can be shown on TV [2008].

The notion that German culture is more supportive of games is borne out by the observations of writers, designers and publishers within the industry. Gaming writer Mario Lanza notes that most Germans consider gaming a "good, healthy pastime" (2006, p. 20) while designer Reiner Knizia offers a similar perspective on the importance of games in the family environment:

> You need to understand that playing games in Germany is synonymous with "family values." It is good to play games and games are quite frequently bought as presents. It's seen as a very valuable way of spending time together as a family. Children grow up with a natural learning of games and as they grow up they see more and more games and become fascinated with them. I think that's a culture which is very valuable in Germany and creates a big market for many designers and many game companies [in Glenn, 1999a].

As a result of this attitude, the adult play of commercial board and table games does not suffer the kind of marginalization that is typically seen in other Western countries. Where in the USA and the U.K. board gaming is typically confined to small groups of hobbyists, in Germany the market is far more diverse. Games journalist Rick Thornquist describes the differences through his experience at U.S. and German conventions:

> If you go to Origins or GenCon [U.S. conventions] it is mainly a gamer type of convention and you do mainly see gamer geeks, but Essen[20] is not like that at all. It's very much regular people, families, teenagers, kids ... it's everybody, and it's amazing to see all these people playing the games that we play all the time.
> Because the Germans play games so much it's really a convention for everybody and not just for gaming geeks [in Alden and Solko, 2004a].

A variety of arguments have been put forward to explain the broader acceptance of gaming within German culture. GAMA[21] executive director Gordon Calleja points to the difficulties of surviving two world wars, suggesting economic motivations for pursuing inexpensive entertainment options (in Alden and Solko, 2009b). Games writer Moritz Eggert has suggested that the German predisposition towards gaming stems from a strong culture of hospitality:

> Why do Germans like games? I think there are several factors at work here. One is the German concept of Gemütlichkeit [difficult to translate, but, roughly, "hospitality, coziness"], which means that being invited over and spending an evening with your neighbours or your friends is seen as socially desirable [Heli, 2007].

Although such an emphasis on sociability is recognizable in any culture, it is only in Germany, claims Richard Huzzey, that "families savour the latest [game] designs" (2002). Whatever the reason for this sense of appreciation the result, Weiland Freund writes, is that "perhaps no other German cultural industry does as well, in relative terms, as board games" (2005).

It is clear that German culture has a unique relationship with board and table game play. Not only do Germans purchase more games per capita than any other nation, their cultural value is reflected in the game collections such as those held by the *Deutsches Spiele-Archiv*, the *Bayerische Spiele-Archiv* and the *Deutsches Spielemuseum*. Supported by *Spiel des Jahres e.V, Deutsches Spiele-Archiv* in Marburg was created in 1978 as a research center for the study and documentation of board and card games.[22] Housing one of the largest collections of non-digital games in the world (approximately 30,000), the archive also holds a vast library of related literature, including catalogues and brochures, primarily from the post-war era. The archive was established with the following goals:

- Documentation of games development in the German-speaking area after 1945
- Promotion of research and science in the field of games and gaming
- Promotion of the game within the family and in society
- Supporting the media in reporting about games ("Deutsches Spiele-Archiv," 2008)

From these goals it is evident that the organization places a special emphasis on the connection between gaming and the family, and the importance of promoting this aspect of games through the media. Alongside the *Deutsches Spiele-Archiv* is the smaller *Bayerische Spiele-Archiv* in Haar. Originally established to duplicate the functions of the larger archive to insure against loss, the two archives now function independently (Werneck, 2008). Closely related to the archives is the *Deutsches Spielemuseum* in Chemnitz. Housing 50,000 games from around the world, along with catalogues and documents dating back five centuries, the museum originated in 1986 in Hamburg, moving to its current location in 1994. The museum maintains traveling exhibits that have seen exposure throughout Europe, as well as hosting special events in the city ("Deutsches Spielemuseum," 2008).

## Family Games for Hobby Gamers

The particularity of the cultural context in which modern games developed in Germany goes some way towards explaining the reasons for the emergence of the eurogame as a distinct genre. The lengthy history of excellence in toy and game production, along with an established cultural disposition towards gaming, led to a perceived need for domestic innovation in the family game market. The drive towards originality in game design has been further enhanced and influenced by a broad level of institutionalized support for both the game design community and the hobby in general. Along with an active gaming community, the principal influences upon this positive perception have been the media, game awards, an active game design community, game shows and the presence of institutions which reflect the value of games as cultural artifacts (Kramer, 2000a; Werneck, 2004).

The German emphasis upon games that could be played by both children and adults alike cannot be overstated. From the outset, German game designers were mandated by cultural and commercial considerations with designing games that anyone could play—thus the need for short concise rules, manageable playing times and culturally acceptable themes. Where in the USA and the U.K. family games remained a fairly stagnant market in terms of originality, in Germany the fact that domestic companies were continuing to produce new titles resulted in a culture that was more accepting of innovation:

> The market for board games is immense in the German speaking countries, because consumers show a lot of interest, and there is a great demand for new (forms of) games. The current generation, which grew up with the intellectually-demanding board games, is selective and willing to deal with more sophisticated games [Stöckmann and Jahnke, 2008a, p. 100].

As quality games began to appear in increasing numbers, so the level of game design moved further in innovative directions to keep pace with the demands and expectations of a growing audience who have come to "appreciate systems innovation" (Costikyan, 2004).

While in the USA and the U.K. the family games market was largely a site of repetition and brand licensing, in Germany it was, in contrast, the site and impetus for innovation. The importance of the acceptance of more sophisticated titles lies in the fact that by the time German "family" games received attention within the USA and the U.K., it was small groups of hobby gamers who had sufficient experience and understanding to appreciate the quality of the games. Thus it was largely word of mouth within hobby game communities that led to the gradual emergence of German games upon the world stage. Moreover, it was not only game players who would come to embrace the form and elevate the genre to its current position, but designers working throughout the world who would take their cues from what would soon become known as eurogames.

# 4

# From German Games
# to Eurogames

*Every decade a new form of the hobby emerges and recruits the bulk of the
new gamers. In the 1960s the fad was wargames, in the 1970s, RPGs, computer
games exploded in the 1980s, the 1990s brought CCGs, and the new century
has seen the German game phenomenon.* — De Rosa, 1998

The state of the gaming hobby in Germany was not altogether dissimilar to that of the USA and the U.K. during the 1970s (Dagger, 2003). However, subject to the influences described in the previous chapter, between 1982
and 1994 the German game market experienced strong growth, often at a rate
of 10 percent or more (Kramer, 2000a). A number of newer imprints were
introduced by more established publishing houses,[1] while others came from
new companies entering the growing market.[2]

Throughout this period German designers produced a succession of
innovative and domestically successful titles. Although the broader English-speaking gaming community did not have ready access to these games
until 1996, small groups of game enthusiasts, firstly in the U.K. and later in
the USA, were following the development of German games long before
they became a staple of hobbyist culture. Importantly, as word of this movement spread through the hobby gaming community, the rise of the Internet in the late 1990s enabled the dissemination of information on a global
scale.

Rather than the result of a concerted marketing effort, the worldwide
popularity of German games principally arose through word of mouth, with
publishers rising to meet a demand generated by enthusiastic hobbyists. These
hobbyist communities were fundamental to the emergence of eurogames as a
mainstay of gaming culture.

## Early German Games (1980—1994)

The first few games to win the newly-founded *Spiel des Jahres* were not German in origin but rather foreign designs in their German edition. David Parlett, a British games historian and frequent writer for the U.K. magazine *Games and Puzzles*, was the inaugural winner with his strategic race game *Hase und Ingel* (1979). In 1980 the award was given to Ephraim Hertzano's *Rummikub* (1977), and the following year to Sid Sackson for the abstract Parker Brother's game *Focus* (1964). The year 1982 saw U.S. designer Alex Randolph and German Michel Matchoss win the *Spiel des Jahres* for the children's memory game *Sagaland* (1981); while in 1983 the award was given to an all–German team at Ravensburger for the deductive chase game *Scotland Yard* (Burggraf *et al.*, 1983), which was subsequently reprinted by Milton Bradley in the USA. The year 1983 also saw the first Essen Spiel event in a year that can be broadly identified as the beginnings of the new wave of German games. For the first time, the *Spiel des Jahres* shortlist was composed entirely of German designs. The popularity of *Scotland Yard*, at least within Germany, was evidence of this growth. Eggert recalls "*Scotland Yard* really was a common household item at one point — I knew no family who didn't own a copy and didn't play it from time to time" (in Heli, 2007).

*Dampfross* (Watts, 1984), a German variation of Englishman David Watt's *Railway Rivals*, secured the *Spiel des Jahres* in 1984, while the following year the award was given to *Sherlock Holmes Criminal-Cabinet* (Edwards *et al.*, 1981), a pseudo role-playing game of deduction. In 1985 the *Spiel des Jahres* was, for the first time, awarded to an individual German game designer, Wolfgang Kramer, for his bluffing and deduction game *Heimlich and Co.* (1984). Kramer had been designing games since 1974 — his *Niki Lauda's Formel 1* had been nominated in 1980 — but his securing of the award again in 1987 for the transportation game *Auf Achse*[3] led to his becoming the "first star" of German game design (Levy, 2001c).[4] Relatively unnoticed at the time, 1986 also marked the publication of Karl-Heinz Schmiel's game of German politics, *Die Macher*, a game that foreshadowed the deeper potential of the emerging German style, and which "gradually developed mythical status on both sides of the Atlantic, both for its game play and its scarcity" (Scherer-Hoock, 2003). In the meantime, 1988 saw the debut of another up and coming designer, Klaus Teuber, who won the award for his party game of clay modeling, *Barbarossa* (1988).

In Britain at this time, Mark Green, proprietor of the London retail store *Just Games*, was importing some of the more popular German titles and inserting his own translations into the box. The store rapidly became a mecca for British gamers who were seeking more adult-oriented games. Similarly, in the USA, Carol Monica of *Games People Play* in Cambridge, Massachusetts, had

Valley Games' 2006 re-issue of *Die Macher* (image by Simon Holding, courtesy Valley Games).

success importing European titles such as *1829*, *Civilization* and *Railway Rivals* (Scherer-Hoock, 2003). Close by, in Boston, ex–Avalon Hill designer Alan Moon had established the North Shore Gaming Club, largely through advertisements in *The General*.[5] Moon had become interested in German designs during his time at Avalon Hill and subsequently made contact with English gaming writer Brian Walker, who was familiar with the growing number of games now coming out of Germany. Throughout the late 1980s the North Shore Gaming Club continued to expand, and Moon's group increasingly played more German designs:

> German games were definitely there from the start. The club was sort of a third Avalon Hill games, a third *Axis and Allies* type games, and a third German games. By that point, I was mostly interested in German games; my interest in war games had been going down ever since playing my first game of *Kremlin* [Moon in Scherer-Hoock, 2003].

In 1988, Brian Walker launched *Games International*, the first British magazine whose coverage was broadly inclusive of German games. Walker produced sixteen editions of the magazine before commercial failure led to a name change in 1990 (*Strategy Plus*) and a decision to alter the coverage of the magazine to computer games. At the time of its inception, however, *Games International* was unique in its coverage of German games, borne largely out of Walker's interest in the genre:

I never really had a "marketing approach." German games seemed to me to be the best around at that time so I gave them some coverage. It was very exciting on a personal level to discover these games, so I figured that if they excited me then they would the reader [Walker in Haag, 2003].

Subtitled "The Journal of Fun and Games," the magazine was also the first to bring information about the annual Essen Spiel event to English speakers. In addition to reviews, the magazine featured interviews with designers, strategy articles and contributions from Moon, who had signed on as the American editor.[6] Peaking at approximately 400 subscribers, and generating print runs of 8000 copies (though Walker admits that perhaps 2000 of these were actually sold), *Games International* was available through British newsstands and specialty games stores, as well as a limited number of stores in the USA (Haag, 2003).

Following a brief period working for Parker Brothers, Alan Moon was now producing independent designs with the German market in mind.[7] Importantly for a designer, the German publishers' interest in the merits of individual game designs contrasted sharply with the license-driven character of the U.S. market:

> It was nice to be able to design a game and have somebody look at the game and play it and decide if they were going to publish it or not for that reason [Moon in Batty, 2006b].

One attendee of Moon's gaming club was designer Mike Gray, who began making frequent trips to the Essen fair on behalf of his employer, Milton Bradley. Gray brought a number of titles to his employer's attention during the 1990s, notably Kramer's *Niki Lauda Formel 1*, Reiner Knizia's *Flinke Pinke* (1994b), the dexterity game *Bausack* (Zoch, 1987) and the children's memory game *Zick Zacke Hühnerkacke* (Zoch, 1998), all of which were republished in the USA (Scherer-Hoock, 2003).[8]

In 1990 Klaus Teuber won his second *Spiel des Jahres* with *Adel Verpflichtet* (1990a). As well as winning the inaugural *Deutscher Spiele Preis* in the same year, *Adel Verpflichtet* is significant in that it was the first German game to receive widespread international publication[9]:

> Since many of these versions were by "hardcore" publishers (such as Avalon Hill and Gibson), more serious players were exposed to the game. And what they saw — short playing time, high player interaction, clever rules, attractive and functional components — was very influential in the initial opinion of what Germany could produce. To many players throughout the world, *Adel Verpflichtet* was the first "German game," and it served its industry very well [Levy, 2001a].

Meanwhile, in the U.K. one writer for the defunct *Games International*, Mike Siggins, began to formulate ideas for another magazine. Siggins had been introduced to German games in 1988 when Brian Walker had shown him the Walter Toncar bicycle racing game *6-Tage Rennen*[10] (1986) at a small games convention in the U.K. Siggins, a former wargamer, was immediately taken with the German design:

> From that point I never looked back, and I still cherish the feeling that this German Game, the very first of hundreds, imparted. Even now, it is hard to quantify the impact of the European game titles and but for them I might still be playing long, turgid stuff like *Civilization* [Siggins in Vasel, 2005c].

In October 1989 Siggins launched the most influential publication in the promotion of German style gaming in Britain, *Sumo*. The first issue, introduced at Essen Spiel that year, was a stapled-together fanzine photocopied onto A5 sheets of paper and distributed by mail. Siggins made *Sumo*'s raison d'être explicit in the first issue:

> For some time I have been thinking about publishing a newsletter to cover the recent influx of European games onto the U.K. games scene. There can be no doubt that quality games such as *Sechs Tage Rennen* and *Die Macher* have made a substantial impact on our game playing habits and expectations, yet there are very few people reviewing these games in-depth or providing associated services such as rules translations [1989].

Charles Vasey, Mike Clifford, Stuart Dagger, Derek Carver, David Farquhar and Alan How were regular contributors and reviewers in the magazine, which would eventually run for 44 issues over eight years.[11] Interestingly, Siggins notes that a quarter of the subscriptions were from Germany (1990). *Sumo* immediately gathered attention on both sides of the Atlantic, and the letters page attracted lively commentary from enthusiasts and active designers such as Americans Richard Berg, Don Greenwood and Alan Moon, and Englishmen Richard Breese[12] and Francis Tresham. Running alongside *Sumo* was Siggins' Rules Bank, a service he had started in 1989 to provide gamers with translated rules for imported games. He would seek out accurate translations and then make them available by request for the price of a stamped, addressed envelope. At its peak, Siggins was posting out 50 envelopes a week, supplementing translations provided by *Just Games*' Mark Green and others. A letter to *Sumo* suggests this was a badly needed service:

> Some of the English "translations" circulating with German games are, to be honest, rubbish. A number I've seen seem to have been written by people who couldn't read German but relied on writing down what they remembered from someone else who told them what they'd heard from ... etc. [Key, 1991].

Meanwhile, the growth of the Internet in the late 1980s offered another way for predominantly English-speaking gamers to discuss the hobby. Established in 1987, the newsgroup *rec.games.board* was the first dedicated forum

# SUMO

## GAME SYSTEMS • REVIEW • DESIGN

# MESSE ESSEN

ESSEN 96 - THE WATERSHED
PALMYRA - KNIZIA DOES IT AGAIN
X PASCH - FANFOR BACK FROM THE DEAD
CITY OF CHAOS - TABLE FOR FOUR
SAFE RETURN DOUBTFUL - EXCELLENT DESIGN
MATERIAL WORLD - REVISITED
AIR BARON - GOOD IN PARTS
DESIGN WORKSHOP - PREDICTABLE
PLUS REVIEWS, NOTEBOOK, 18XX AND LETTERS

ISSUE 33/34/35 NOVEMBER 1996          £7.00/$11.00/DM16,-

Mike Siggins' *Sumo* (courtesy Mike Siggins).

for hobbyists. Although sparsely populated for the first two years of its existence, by 1989 the group had begun to flourish, with a range of discussion topics mostly revolving around wargaming, abstract strategy games and play-by-email gaming (PBEM). The first mention of German games is found in a lengthy review of *Die Macher* by Avalon Hill designer Jennifer Schlickbernd, appearing on the newsgroup in October 1989. Although this review appears to have passed largely unnoticed, by 1992 a few enquiries began to appear regarding rules translations of European games, specifically *Die Macher, Full Metal Planète* (Delfanti *et al.*, 1988) and another Karl-Heinz Schmiel design, *Extrablatt* (1991).

In 1990, Alan Moon held the first Gathering of Friends, an informal invite-only convention for gamers interested in the new wave of European designs (Scherer-Hoock, 2003).[13] Taking place in Chicopee, Massachusetts, the convention continues to be held to this day, attracting a growing number of players, designers and, more recently, publishers, from the U.S. and Europe. In 1991 Moon also established White Wind as a vehicle for the production of his own games, 80 to 90 percent of which would be sold in Germany (Batty, 2006b):

> I wanted to publish limited editions of my own games, so I could actually get my games published without having to wait till someone else decided to publish them. I would then be able to send the published games to all the companies at once and avoid all the legal hassles of disclosures[14] since those rules don't apply to published games. I hoped other companies would then buy the rights to these games and republish them in much larger print-runs. Of course, this didn't happen, at least not right away [Moon in Tidwell, 1997].

In 1991 Klaus Teuber received his third *Spiel des Jahres* award — for *Drunter and Drüber*, a tile-laying game with a significant bluffing element. The *Deutscher Spiele Preis* was awarded to *Das Labyrinth der Meister* (Kobbert, 1991), a more advanced implementation of the earlier family game *Das Verrückte Labyrinth* (Kobbert, 1986). This innovative design incorporated a moveable maze that would lead to a series of successful games based upon the same mechanic.[15] The following year the award was given to Rob Bontenbal's cycle-racing game *Um Reifenbreite* (1991),[16] with Teuber claiming the *Deutscher Spiele Preis* for *Der Fliegende Holländer* (1992). Notably, 1992 marked the first recognition by the *Spiel des Jahres* jury of designer Reiner Knizia, whose name would soon become synonymous with German game design. An earlier card game, *Goldrausch* (1990), had placed in the voting for the 1990 *Deutscher Spiele Preis*, but it was the political negotiation game *Quo Vadis* (1992b) that found a place on the shortlist for that year.

Considered the "breakout year for [Reiner] Knizia" (Levy, 2001b), 1992 saw the release of the highly acclaimed auction game *Modern Art* (1992a), which would go on to claim the *Deutscher Spiele Preis* the following year. The winner of the *Spiel des Jahres* in 1993 was a reworking of an existing public domain dice game[17] by U.S. designer Richard Borg, entitled *Bluff* (1993). The 1994 list of contenders for the *Deutscher Spiele Preis* is a testament to the consistently high quality of the games that were beginning to appear at this time. Along with the winner, Wolfgang Kramer's card game *6-Nimmt* (1994), were the *Spiel des Jahres*–awarded *Manhattan* (1994), by Andreas Seyfarth; Stefan Dorra's game of deception, *Intrige* (1994) Ronald Wettering's exercise in social negotiation and survival on sinking lifeboats, *Rett Sich Wer Kann* (1993); and Knizia's mathematically-based game of tile placement, *Auf Heller und Pfennig* (1994a).

By 1993 a growing awareness of the emergent German design movement is evident on *rec.games.board*, bolstered largely by the Avalon Hill reprint of *Adel Verpflichtet*. Notably, the company had also published Karl Heinz Schmiel's *Tyranno Ex* in 1992, a game of conflict among dinosaurs that borrowed mechanisms from the designer's earlier title, *Die Macher*.[18] At the same time that these German titles were seeing their first English language impressions there was a growing sense of disillusionment with the current state of the hobby in the USA, as reflected in this post mourning the passing of the "golden age of board games":

> Now we have the anemic and predictable offerings by Avalon Hill — which produces games for people who love rules more than they love play — and repackaged Victorian parlor games (*Scattergories, Trivial Pursuit*), and brain-dead teach-your-child-where-Yugoslavia-used-to-be geography quizzes, and, surprisingly, games don't sell very well anymore.... It's a sad comment that the most interesting and original game produced by an American company in the last three years was *Set*,[19] which isn't a very interesting and original game [Rossney, 1993].

Although such complaints can be heard in hobby gaming circles at any given time, on *rec.games.board* there was subsequently an observable increase in the level of interest in German titles. Reviews of Knizia's *Quo Vadis* and *Modern Art* (1992a) in May 1993 were followed by a small flurry of enquiries over where to obtain these and other German games, the scarcity of which was highlighted by one poster excitedly announcing the discovery of a number of copies of Ravensburger's *Wildlife Adventure* (Kramer and Kramer, 1985) in a San Diego Animal Park (Pedlow, 1993). Adding to the wider exposure of German games in the USA, and promoted via the group, 1992 also saw the first issue of Peter Sarrett's *Game Report*, a U.S. based newsletter that echoed the style and content of *Games International* and *Sumo*. Additionally, in an August 1993 post to the newsgroup, Sarret listed and reviewed a large variety of games acquired on a trip to Europe (Sarrett, 1993).

In June of 1994 Californian Ken Tidwell established *The Game Cabinet* (2000) as an Internet-based monthly magazine and a repository for rules translations online. Following a visit to the U.K. and a trip to Mark Green's *Just Games*, Tidwell had become a contributor to *Sumo*. Remarkably, *The Game Cabinet* was one of the first 1000 web-sites on the then relatively unknown World Wide Web:

Two co-workers, Danfuzz Bornstein and Charlie Reiman, introduced me to the Mosaic and the nascent World Wide Web. I thought it was a great platform to get the word out about German games (there was no notion of Euro games in those days; we thought of them as German) [Tidwell, 2008].

The first issue of *The Game Cabinet* included reviews of Reiner Knizia's *Modern Art* and Klaus Tueber's early family game *Timberland* (1989), along with a rules translation of *Die Macher* and clarifications for Teuber's *Adel Verpflichtet* and Christian Beierer's game of pyramid construction *Tal Der Könige* (1992). *The Game Cabinet* quickly became the central repository among English-speaking gamers for information on European games.[20]

Throughout the early 1990s an increasing number of enthusiastic gamers in the USA had begun to acquire German games, generally from *Games People Play* in the USA, *Just Games* in the U.K. or through trading with personal contacts in Germany and Britain (Scherer-Hoock, 2003; Huber, 2008; Sauer, 2008). However, the issue of how to obtain German titles remained a difficult one. Ray Pfeifer, a Baltimore gamer inspired by a trip to Moon's Gathering of Friends, was one of those who had established a successful trading arrangement with Moon's business partner in White Wind, Peter Gehrmann. In 1994, thinking to capitalize on the success of *Magic: The Gathering* as a dealer, Pfiefer launched R&D Games as an importing mail-order business at the 1994 Gathering of Friends. The growing, but still small, number of European gaming enthusiasts in the U.S. now had a dedicated channel for acquiring German releases (Scherer-Hoock, 2003).

Meanwhile, the summer 1995 issue of *Sumo* contained the usual reviews of games and lively commentary from Siggins and other regulars. Given the benefit of hindsight, however, the dismissal of one *Spiel des Jahres* nominee stands out. Siggins was not overly impressed with Klaus Teuber's new game, *Die Siedler von Catan*, commenting that the game "has neither the depth, subtlety nor the tactical flexibility to make it a winner" (1995). Even though hobbyists such as Siggins were closely following the games emerging from Germany, none could foresee the impact that *Die Siedler von Catan* would have on hobby gaming. It was the release of this resource-gathering and development game that would change dramatically the perception of German games within the hobby and mark the coming-of-age of European game design.

## Die Siedler von Catan

*There is a branch of Mathematics that explores chaos theory. One of the tenants of the theory suggests that the flapping wings of a butterfly in China could result in a storm elsewhere in the world. In 1995 a "butterfly" in Germany flapped and unleashed a storm in the North American market that has expanded and continues to grow today.* — Shapiro, 2003

In 1995 Kosmos released Klaus Teuber's latest game, *Die Siedler von Catan*. The game combined development, trading and a dose of luck, casting players as explorers on the fictional island of Catan. Upon release, the game was an unqualified success in Germany, garnering the 1995 *Spiel des Jahres*, *Deutscher Spiele Preis* and *Essen Feather*, along with the U.S.-based Origins Award the following year. Five years after its release, in 2000, the game was still the best-selling game in Germany (Levy, 2001a). Subsequently it has inspired a variety of expansions and related games that have sold upwards of 15 million copies worldwide, becoming the best-selling and most widely known example of the eurogame to date (Curry, 2009).

The first copies of *Die Siedler von Catan* to enter the U.S. were imported by Ray Pfeifer's R&D Games in 1995 and sold at Alan Moon's Gathering of Friends that year. Pfiefer imported further copies for Avalon Hill's annual convention, Avaloncon, where the game met with an immediate and enthusiastic response:

> I remember that year the most played game at Avaloncon wasn't an Avalon Hill game; it was Settlers.[21] I sold them out of the trunk of my car in the parking lot at the convention. I remember at one point Jackson Dott came out to find out what was going on [Pfiefer in Scherer-Hoock, 2003].[22]

*Die Siedler von Catan* served as the introduction to German games for many English-speaking gamers (Levy, 2001a). Within weeks of the game's release, word was spreading on the Internet via *rec.games.board* and Ken Tidwell's *Game Cabinet*. The recognition of *Die Siedler von Catan* as the first German game to captivate English-speaking gamers en masse is echoed by the number of players who now fondly recall the game as their introduction to the genre. Retailer and gaming writer Michael Barnes describes this impact:

> We were blown away. It was the best board game we had ever played—it had dice, cardplay, trading, interaction, drama, a solid civilization building/development theme, and it was just a lot of fun to play in a reasonable amount of time. I did some research on the internet which lead me to discover that there was the beginnings of a subculture of eurogame enthusiasts ... of course, at the time, they were called "German games" [Barnes, 2008b].

Gaming writer Greg Schloesser echoes the sentiment:

> My life changed ... when I discovered *Settlers of Catan* at a local hobby store. We were captivated, and I began seeking out other "European" titles. *El Grande, Euphrat and Tigris* and other classics soon were added to my collection, and I was smitten [Schloesser, 2008a].

Almost concurrently with the release of *Die Siedler von Catan*, American game manufacturer Mayfair Games had decided to investigate the possibility of producing English language versions of some popular German titles. Game designer and owner Darwin Bromley had become enamored of German games and had been importing and selling these on the American market since 1991 (Scherer-Hoock, 2003). Reflecting Mayfair's association with railway games, Bromley had imported *1835* (Tresham and Meier-Backl, 1990)[23] and *Dampfross*, along with a range of games from Dutch company Flying Turtle. Prices were high due to the cost of import, and the games were simply sold on, without English rules translations, making for a rather limited market. Since these factors resulted in less than spectacular sales, Jay Tummelson, an employee with a history in the role-playing community, suggested including rules translations with the games, and later that the company consider publishing English versions (Glenn, 1999b). Subsequently, Tummelson was charged with obtaining licenses from German manufacturers. Traveling to Europe, he secured the rights to a variant of *Formel Eins* (Kramer, 1996a),[24] *Modern Art, Manhattan, Linie Eins* (Dorra, 1995)[25] and, somewhat fortuitously, the recent *Spiel des Jahres* winner *Die Siedler von Catan*. While Tummelson argued for the retention of the original German presentation, Bromley felt that the graphics were not suitable for the U.S. market and commissioned new artwork before releasing the games in 1996 (Alden and Solko, 2005).

## The Rise of German Games

Meanwhile, in Germany the success of *Die Siedler von Catan* provided yet more motivation for the games industry:

> The great success of *Die Siedler von Catan* showed the doubters the kind of financial rewards a good strategy game can produce. As a result, authors, publishers, and retailers who supported social strategy board games intensified their efforts [Kramer, 2000a].

The winner of the following year's *Spiel des Jahres* and *Deutscher Spiel Preis*, and a testament to this renewed effort, was the result of a collaboration between Kramer and Richard Ulrich, *El Grande* (1995). Themed around a quest for dominance in Renaissance-era Spain, and considered the first area majority board game, *El Grande* was a surprising winner of the *Spiel des Jahres*, since, compared to previous entries, the game was relatively complex. Nevertheless, the game marked the beginnings of a particularly prolific period in quality design that would last throughout the late 1990s:

> It's hard to overstate the significance of *El Grande*'s publication. It basically established a new kind of board game, one in which players strove to have the majority of pieces in different geographical areas of the board. It proved that "gamer's games" could be big sellers and initiated a trend toward such challenging games which continues to this day.... Finally, coming on the heels of

the fabulously successful *Settlers of Catan, El Grande* was the second part of the one-two punch that established once and for all that Germany was the source of the finest games in the world [Levy, 2001c].

Certainly the winners of the key German awards over the next few years continued to push the boundaries of board game systems and mechanics. The winners of the 1997 *Spiel des Jahres* and *Deutscher Spiele Preis* were Werner Hodel's game of paddleboat racing, *Mississippi Queen* (1998a) and Teuber's game of tile-laying and exploration, *Entdecker* (1996)[26] respectively. The list of nominations the following year for both awards provides ample evidence that game designers working in the German style were experiencing a period of rapid innovation. Alan Moon's *Elfenland* (1998), a simplified version of the earlier White Wind–published *Elfenroads* (1992), claimed the *Spiel des Jahres*; while Reiner Knizia's tile-laying game of development in the cradle of civilization, *Euphrat and Tigris* (1997a), was awarded the *Deutscher Spiel Preis*. Moreover, among those games nominated for the 1998 awards are Knizia's *Durch die Wüste* (1998a), a lightly-themed area enclosure game somewhat reminiscent of *Go*, Wolfgang Kramer and Horst-Rainer Rösner's area majority business game *Tycoon* (1998),[27] and the Hans im Glück reprint of Karl-Heinz Schmiel's 1986 game *Die Macher*.

Ironically, just as German games were about to make the leap to English-speaking markets, Mike Siggin's *Sumo* was coming to an end. With growing work commitments and a mounting disillusionment with playing games, Siggins was offered an opportunity to sell the rights to *Sumo* to fellow gamers Theo Clarke and Paul Evans. Clarke and Evans planned to take their own magazine, *Games, Games, Games*, to a more professional level, and Siggins, on the advice of friends, decided to accept (Dagger, 2008). The quirky fanzine that had alerted many British gamers to German games was no more:

> Overall, I think people liked it. They definitely liked the letters. They liked the hugeness of the average issue.... They liked the lack of computer games. They liked lists. They liked Mike Clifford. And generally it was popular because it was honest, interesting and there was nothing like it. Others reviewed the German games, but there was a mad level of enthusiasm in and for *Sumo*, like a bunch of 600 like-minded gamers meeting for a chat. It must have been responsible for much of the growth in German gamers in the early nineties, but who knows? [Siggins in Vasel, 2005c].

*Games, Games, Games* lasted two years before folding due to financial failure. Meanwhile, *Sumo* contributors Clifford, Dagger and How had hatched a plan for "son of *Sumo*" (Dagger, 2008). Consequently, with Dagger at the helm as editor, 1998 saw the first issue of *Counter*, a magazine with similar production values and content as *Sumo*. With a current subscription list of approximately 700 to 800 (the majority in the USA),[28] *Counter* continues to provide in-depth reviews and critical commentary, largely on the European games market, with a list of contributors that, not surprisingly, reads similarly to that of *Sumo*.

Meanwhile, in the USA former Mayfair employee Jay Tummelson, having seen the potential of German games in the U.S. market, decided to try his hand with his own company.[29] Tummelson's approach was to utilize contacts he had made in the German games industry and to partner with them in producing English-language versions of more popular titles. His company, Rio Grande, was the first to bring these games to English-speaking markets with components and artwork identical to that available in Europe. The first batch of six games was released in April 1998 with Klaus Palesch's *Fossil* (1998) meeting with early success and garnering the Games Magazine Game of the Year award in 1999.[30] At this point, Tummelson was negotiating an extended print run of existing games and contributing rules translations himself. By the end of 1999 Rio Grande had brought 20 games to market. In addition to then-current releases, Tummelson negotiated rights to games previously unavailable in English, adding successful titles such as *El Grande* and *Manhattan* to an expanding range. By 2000, 21 of the top 100 games listed by Games Magazine were produced by Rio Grande, including Best Memory Game,[31] Best Family Strategy Game[32] and Game of the Year.[33] Since 1998, Rio Grande games has released over 300 individual games, the majority with relatively low print runs that serve the growing number of gaming enthusiasts who have embraced German-style games.

With the availability of European games growing, so too was interest in the wider gaming community. Like many other interest groups, gamers were only now beginning to fully appreciate and utilize the Internet as a platform for information-sharing activities. In 1999 American designer Stephen Glenn was inspired by a private mailing list of game designers and industry figures to establish *Spielfrieks*, a public mailing list devoted exclusively to the discussion of German-style games. In July 2000 Canadian Greg Aleknevicus and American Frank Branham[34] established *The Games Journal*, an online journal with a similar focus to that of the print fanzines *Sumo* and *Counter*. The site attracted a number of articles from notable games writers such as Larry Levy and Greg Schloesser, along with contributions from designers such as Lewis Pulsipher, Wolfgang Kramer and Bruno Faidutti. With a letters section that read much like its analog forebears, *The Games Journal* provided gamers on the Internet with up-to-date reviews and opinions on the emerging German gaming scene.

Wolfgang Kramer and Michael Kiesling were awarded the *Spiel des Jahres* in both 1999 and 2000 with the action points–based games[35] *Tikal* (1999) and *Torres* (2000a). The year 2000 also saw the release of Kramer and Richard

Ulrich's highly regarded auction game, *Die Fürsten von Florenz*, Knizia's *Tadsch Mahal*, and Gerd Fenchel's intricate game of city development *La Città*. In 2001, however, Klaus-Jürgen Wrede's game of tile-placement and area majority, *Carcassonne* (2000), not only won both major German awards but also garnered enormous international success on a scale that came close to matching that of *Die Siedler von Catan*. *Carcassonne* has spawned numerous expansions[36] and a whole raft of associated games, some created by other well-known designers such as Leo Colovini and Knizia.[37] Like *Die Siedler von Catan*, *Carcassonne* has become regarded as a "gateway game," a particularly accessible game that can be used to introduce non-gamers to German-style games. The year 2001 is also notable for the release of Reiner Knizia's cooperative game *Der Herr der Ringe* (2000a). Published in the U.S. by Hasbro to capitalize on the success of the *Lord of the Rings* movie trilogy, the game was printed in large quantities, marking the first time that such a complex European-style design was given wide exposure in the English-speaking mass market.

Another result of the growing availability of eurogames in the USA and the increased visibility brought about by the Internet was the recognition by U.S.-based game designers that a distinctive style was emerging, and that the emulation of that style might be a worthwhile pursuit. In 2001 Americans Stephen Glenn, Dominic Crapuchettes, and Mike Petty organized the first *Protospiel*, a meeting where game designers could playtest games with an emphasis on German style designs:

> The goal was to get game designers together to workshop game ideas. The name of the convention was chosen because we want to emulate the high quality of board games that are coming out of Europe (mostly Germany). We made it very clear that we did not want people to come to the convention with their latest version of *Monopoly* or any other roll and move game. *Proto-Spiel* was created for game designers who wanted to create games for adults, not children [Crapuchettes, 2008].

Although the initial event was attended by only a small number of designers, *Protospiel* would subsequently provide the development base for a number of successful games including Glenn's *Spiel des Jahres*–nominated *Balloon Cup* (2003) and Crapuchettes' hugely successful party game *Wits and Wagers* (2005).

## From German Games to Eurogames

By the early 2000s it was becoming increasingly clear that German-style games were not merely a passing fad but had captured a sustainable portion of the global hobby gaming market. Although the genre had originated in

Germany, designers from other European countries had long been active in the design community.[38] As still more designers continued to adopt the general style, what were once "German games" were now commonly referred to as "eurogames."

As Rio Grande continued to leverage established business relationships to adopt a model of simultaneous publication (Alden and Solko, 2005), new companies began to spring up to cater to the growing demand for the genre. In 2002 U.S./French based Days of Wonder began publishing original European-style games simultaneously in English, French, German and Korean.[39] In 2004 the company was awarded the *Spiel des Jahres* for Alan Moon's *Ticket to Ride* (2004a), a rail-themed set collection and connection game that has subsequently seen enormous international success, spawning a number of sequels[40] and expansions.[41] In 2003 Utah-based Überplay Entertainment began publishing direct translations of popular European titles including *Ra* (Knizia, 1999a), *Alhambra* (Henn, 2003), *China*[42] and *Hoity Toity*, a re-issue of Teuber's *Adel Verpflichtet*.[43] Z-Man games, a U.S. company originally created to resurrect an out-of-print collectible card game, began publishing translations of successful German games in 2004,[44] later incorporating titles by U.S. designers that were heavily influenced by the European style.[45] Designers working in the USA increasingly opted to incorporate elements of both design approaches in the production of hybrid games that blended the Anglo-American taste for highly thematic gameplay with the perceived elegance of European mechanics.[46] Hobby games generally began to reflect the European design style as the influence of the genre spread through the gaming industry. Even mainstream U.S. manufacturers were not immune to this influence; in 2006 Mattel released two European-style designs,[47] while Hasbro revised the classic *Risk*, shortening the playing time and removing the emphasis on player elimination.[48]

As eurogames increased in popularity among gaming hobbyists, designs became increasingly more complex, straying from the family-oriented fare that had typified early German games. Exemplar of this is Andreas Seyfarth's game of colonization and development in the new world, *Puerto Rico* (2002). Although too complex to be awarded the 2002 *Spiel des Jahres*, which for the first time went to a dexterity game, *Villa Paletti* (Payne, 2001), *Puerto Rico* easily claimed the *Deutscher Spiele Preis* and, surprisingly, proved more popular with the international gaming community than that in Germany (Alden and Solko, 2009b). The *Spiel des Jahres* continues to award those games that are at the lighter end of the complexity scale, with winners such as the family-friendly *Niagara* (Liesching, 2005); Karen and Andreas Seyfarth's *Thurn und Taxis* (2006), a set collection and connection game themed on the early German Post Office; and Michael Schacht's *Zooloretto* (2007), a board game expanding on the mechanics of his earlier card game, *Coloretto* (2003a). Although the jury has always favored less complex games, more involved games were recognized through a separate award for best complex game (*Sonderpreis Komplexes Spiel*), awarded in 2006 and 2008 to William Attia's *Caylus* (2005) and Uwe Rosenberg's *Agricola* (2007), respectively. The need for a permanent award that acknowledges the increasing complexity of emerging eurogames was met in 2011 with the establishment of the *Kennerspiel des Jahres*.

In 2009 the influence of European designs came full circle, with the *Spiel des Jahres* awarded to the American-designed and published *Dominion* (Vaccarino, 2008), a game that draws heavily on the deck-building mechanics of collectible card games while also incorporating the broader aesthetics of eurogame design.[49] At the same time, popular eurogames such as *Die Siedler von Catan* and *Carcassonne* began to make substantial in-roads into the mainstream U.S. board gaming market (Muller, 2009). The most popular of eurogames, *The Settlers of Catan*, received coverage in *The Washington Post* (Eskin, 2010), *The Wall Street Journal* (Tam, 2009), *The Atlantic* (Keys, 2011) and *Wired Magazine* (Curry, 2009). In June 2011, versions of the game occupied two out of the top ten spots on Amazon's list of top selling board games — a list that was notably devoid of staples such as *Monopoly* or *Risk* (Keys, 2011). Throughout the late 2000s, a number of eurogame titles were successfully ported to video game consoles. More recently, the rise of touch-enabled mobile devices, and the concurrent industry shift towards socially-oriented games, has proven an ideal match for a wide variety of European-style games. In the space of fifteen years, games that had initially only been of interest to a small number of hobbyists now seem set to enter the mainstream.

As dedicated gaming hobbyists became aware of the design style emerging in Germany, it was largely through word of mouth, community uptake and small start-up companies that these games spread to the broader gaming community. The fact that awareness of these games was spread in such a way suggests a revolution inspired by the games themselves rather than by the companies who produced them. Emerging from a cultural context and market that was geared to produce innovative games for the family demographic, the aesthetic that originated in Germany has spread to become a significant force in the niche hobby of board gaming. Not only is this manifest in the genre now commonly referred to as eurogames, but more generally in the broader field of tabletop game design. While many hobbyists continue to look to Europe for the latest releases, the extent of the genre's influence is seen in the way it has transformed hobby board and table gaming globally.

# 5

# *The Eurogame Genre*

*There exists in the world today a game design movement called eurogame design. Its roots run back to the 1960s, it began flourishing in the 1980s, and it spread worldwide in the 1990s.* — Berlinger, 2009a

The games that began to appear in Germany in the early 1980s, which were to subsequently influence the world of tabletop game design and play, bear a number of recognizable traits that distinguish them from other hobby games and those in the mass-market. Anecdotally speaking, eurogames tend to be accessible games that privilege the role of mechanics over theme in gameplay. They typically facilitate indirect rather than direct conflict, de-emphasize the role of chance, offer predictable playing times, and are usually of a high standard in terms of component quality and presentation.

In this chapter I wish to step beyond this anecdotal summary to delimit the type of game classified as eurogames by analyzing a selection of 139 representative titles. This list of games is drawn from the winners and the nomination shortlist of the *Spiel des Jahres* award from 1995, the year in which *Die Siedler von Catan* was first published, through to ten years later in 2005, a time when eurogames had made strong inroads into global gaming culture. This selection reflects not only the variety of games that fall under the eurogame banner, but also those that are considered outstanding examples by a judging panel that oversaw the rise in popularity of the genre.[1] Players perceive eurogames as constituting a genre typified by common conventions, although they may display a wide variety of traits. Consequently, much of the analysis presented here consists of the type of necessary generalizations that are common in any discussion of genre. This chapter will highlight the way in which eurogames typically emphasize accessibility and individual accomplishment in mechanics, goals and themes. The intent of this chapter, then, is to develop a clear description of the type of games to which hobby gamers can point and say "that is a eurogame."[2]

## Game Elements in Applied Ludology

For the purposes of identifying the various game traits that might serve as genre identifiers in eurogames, I will first use elements of game scholar Aki Järvinen's framework, as put forward in his 2009 book *Games Without Frontiers: Theories and Methods for Game Studies and Design*. My principle reason for adopting this model is the way in which it can be utilized to analyze any form of game. The systemic model that Järvinen describes is highly developed and broad in scope, addressing game rhetoric, psychology, emotion categories and player experience. In this chapter I utilize a subset of these ideas that is most appropriate for this type of formal analysis.

At the heart of Järvinen's work is the identification of various elements that can be found within games, providing a framework by which games, reduced to their constitutive elements, can be analyzed and understood. Importantly, Järvinen does not claim that these elements are found in every game, merely that their nature and presence (or lack of) in a particular example offers an insight into the structure and form of the game. Järvinen approaches his analysis from the center of the game system outwards to the periphery of the play experience and identifies nine such elements, dividing them into three types: systemic, behavioral and compound. These constitutive elements are outlined in figure 5.1.

| | |
|---|---|
| Systemic Elements | Components |
| | Environment |
| Compound Elements | Ruleset |
| | Mechanics |
| | Theme |
| | Interface |
| | Information |
| Behavioral Elements | Player |
| | Context |

Figure 5.1: Game Elements from Järvinen (2009).

In Järvinen's terms, systemic elements are those that constitute the game world in terms of spatial characteristics and elements to be utilized and configured. Compound elements, including the ruleset, mechanics, interface, information and theme, are those that link the systemic elements with the behavioral ones and bring about the dynamic play of the game. Behavioral elements refer to the player and the context of the game that "make games essentially a human phenomenon" (p. 29). The examination of these human elements forms a large part of the latter half of this book, and, as such, I will set these aside for the moment.

## Systemic Elements in Eurogames

Järvinen defines systemic elements as those that make up the game world. In terms of board games, these are the *components* that constitute the objects the player can manipulate through the course of play and the *environment* that defines the spatial arrangement of the game. In terms of components, eurogames typically employ a board, cards, currency and/or various tokens that can be controlled through the course of play. In this regard, these games do not differ significantly from other forms of table game. Nor are play environments in eurogames functionally dissimilar to those of other board and table games. Games can be categorized as those with no environment, those with a miniaturized representation as environment, and those with an entirely abstracted environment. Games with no environment are typically card or dice games that have no need of table-based environmental components.[3] Closely related to these are games that utilize abstracted boards in order to assist in play of the game either through visual indicators of key mechanics[4] or as a reference for the consistent positioning of other elements.[5]

The majority of eurogames, however, take place on a miniaturized representation of a real-world geographical location[6] or a stylized rendering of an imagined setting.[7] In most cases these games employ a map purposely as a positional reference where spatial relations play a significant role in the game. Most commonly the game world is accessible to players throughout the game, though in many tile-laying games it emerges through the course of play.[8] Although the environments in these eurogames echo the spatial emphasis of wargames and Anglo-American hobby board games, they are typically abstracted and/or stylized to a far greater degree, often falling closer to traditional abstract games in terms of fidelity to the represented environment. Noticeably, a number of games utilize spatiality through entirely abstracted boards with no representation of real or imagined geographical location.[9]

Although the type of components and the nature of the game environment in eurogames differ little from other forms of table game, in their aesthetics they have come to hold an almost iconic status within the hobby (Eskin, 2008). Game components in eurogames are typically of a far higher quality than those commonly found in other commercial games (Sigman, 2007). The use of wood rather than plastic in key components imbues the games with a sense of quality that has become a design hallmark of the eurogame. Similarly, the graphical presentation that ties the game's theme back to the components is typically of a very high standard. This attention to quality in the graphic design of packaging and components is reflected in the recognition of particular artists who work within the field of game illustration.[10] Although one can argue that this emphasis on aesthetic appeal does not constitute a part of the game's formal system, the application of high production values is one of the defining traits of eurogames, and one that has had a strong influence on subsequent Anglo-American productions (Sauer, 2008).

## Compound Elements in Eurogames

Compound elements create a link between the systemic and behavioral elements of the game. However, for the purposes of this analysis they can be discussed in relative isolation. Following Järvinen's model, the compound elements of a game consist of the *ruleset, mechanics, information, interface* and *theme*. In the remainder of this chapter I discuss each of these elements, with the exception of the interface. While acknowledging that it is possible to perceive game components themselves as constituting an interface, like Järvinen I consider access to these components to be more or less direct; thus I have elected to exclude them from this discussion (2009, p. 79).

## Rulesets in Eurogames

Rules are what games are made from, the abstract raw materials that separate the contrivance of games from more spontaneous forms of play. In a broader sense, the rules *are* the game (Parlett, 1999, p. 3). Like Salen and Zimmerman (2004, p. 126), Järvinen identifies a number of different rule forms. While some rules define the initial set-up of the game (the environment), others describe the ways that players can interact with the system (the mechanics), the way the system logic functions internally (in the case of board games, procedures governing component behavior in the environment), and the over-arching goals of the game. As can be seen from these descriptions, each of these types of rules is embedded into another element of the game, an observation that leads Järvinen to conclude that "all different types of rules have to do with a particular game element" (2009, p. 66). Following this assertion, while individual rules are not game elements themselves, the ruleset constitutes an element, as it describes and constrains the behaviors of other elements within the system.

Before discussing the embodiment of the rules through other elements, it is important to note a general characteristic of rulesets in eurogames: the relative simplicity of rules when compared with earlier hobby game designs. When describing or defining eurogames, writers almost invariably emphasize the fact that they typically have succinct rules that can be learned in a relatively short space of time (Pulsipher, 2006; Berlinger, 2009b). This distinction is particularly evident when eurogames are compared with other forms of hobby game. Since wargames are, for the most part, founded upon the idea that games can effectively simulate real or imagined conflicts, they typically involve numerous complex rules to govern particular situations and influences upon the conflict to be simulated.[11] Role-playing games, although they have in some cases become increasingly less rule-bound as they have matured, were originally based upon similar ideas — while characters in early iterations of *Dungeons and Dragons* might be fighting mythical beasts in a fantastic realm, the simulative roots of the genre can be seen in the need to monitor encumbrance and the logistics of maneuvering a ten-foot pole around a dungeon corner. Although not derived from this simulative approach to design, collectible card games rely almost entirely on the implementation of rule exceptions in that most cards modify the basic rules of the game in some way. Each of these genres is distinctly marketed towards a core group of players who are content to absorb the complexities of the rules in order to enjoy the play of the game.

In contrast to these examples, eurogames tend to have relatively simple and approachable rulesets. As Nick Sauer describes:

> The designers of eurogames I felt had moved farther in the art of taking a complex rule concept and massaging it down to a much simpler rule set. The reason I would say that the American designs were so fiddly was again the wargaming heritage. The view was still strongly held that games were supposed to be simulations first and games second. The German game designers had that order reversed in their heads and, I would argue, thus forced them to make a rule more elegant and fit better into the game's flow if they felt the rule absolutely needed to be present [2008].

This emphasis on the game as a *game* rather than a simulation is often called upon in discussions of Anglo-American designs when compared with the European style. Gaming blogger Mr. Bistro describes this shift as one towards a "new aesthetic":

> The New Aesthetic rejected the indulgences of older designs, and instead focused on the mechanics of a game. Rules were streamlined to enhance playability and to reduce playing time. Now a game's theme was built around its rules, and no longer burdened by a need to create levels of simulation the games of the New Aesthetic felt sleeker. Players took notice and soon terms like "elegant" were being used to describe game rules [2009].

While there certainly exist some complex titles, a typical eurogame has a ruleset that is of equivalent complexity to games such as *Monopoly*. This is not to suggest that the genre lacks depth. Indeed, it is a trait of many classical abstract games that they involve the emergence of deep and engaging play through a small number of rules. It does, however, draw attention to two factors that are significant in understanding the nature of eurogames in comparison to other types of hobby game. Firstly, they are far more accessible than games that have previously attracted the interest of hobbyists. Secondly, the designers are generally far less concerned with the relationship between theme and mechanics in terms of modeling the behavior of referent systems. As we shall see, this latter point is particularly significant as it affects the relationship between the mechanics and themes of the eurogame.

## Mechanics in Eurogames

As Järvinen notes, there is a degree of semantic confusion within game research and design as to the use of the word mechanic (2009, pp. 247–250). Designers and game scholars generally use the word mechanic to describe, in a vague sense, what it is that players *do* during the play of a game. Salen and Zimmerman describe the core mechanic of a game as "the essential play activity players perform again and again in a game" (2004, p. 316). In these terms the game mechanic describes the principal *functional* interaction form with either the game system or other players. In multiplayer competitive games, this interaction is primarily concerned with the achievement of the game goal, leading Järvinen to conclude that

> Game mechanics is a functional game feature that describes one possible or preferred or encouraged means with which the player can interact with game elements as she is trying to influence the game state at hand towards attainment of a goal [pp. 251–252].

In the sense that it is defined here, all games involve one or more mechanics by which the player can influence the outcome of the game. Through a process of iterative analysis, Järvinen constructs a list of 40 mechanics that are commonly found in games, further delineating between primary mechanics (those that are available to the player at all times), sub-mechanics (those that are supportive of the primary mechanics) and modifier mechanics (those that are available to the player either conditionally or at specific times) (p. 260–263).

One of the distinctive traits of eurogames is the way in which mechanics are layered in such a way as to create relatively complex systems from a variety of sub-mechanics. Consequently, and for the sake of clarity, in this analysis I have chosen to focus on the principal game-defining mechanics and sub-mechanics that are employed in pursuit of the game goal. Using Järvinen's list of 40 mechanics, I have selected the one that best characterizes the primary mechanics and sub-mechanics of each of the games under examination. Figures 5.2 and 5.3, then, provide an overview of the principle mechanics employed in eurogames.

The immediate observation that arises from these results is the degree to

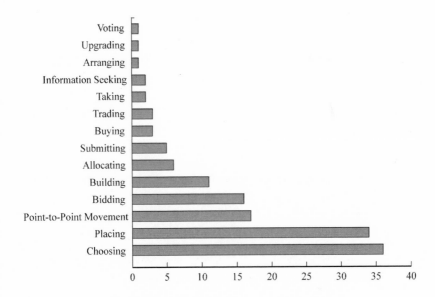

**Figure 5.2: Primary mechanics in eurogames.**

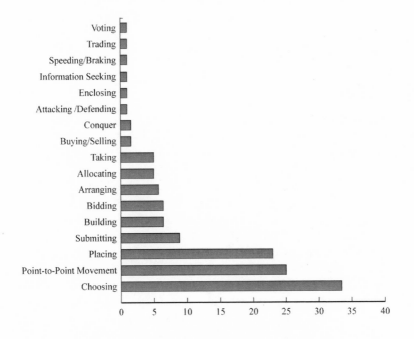

**Figure 5.3: Primary sub-mechanics in eurogames.**

which certain mechanics are dominant within the games analyzed, most notably choosing, placing and point-to-point movement. Indeed, choosing is both the most common mechanic and sub-mechanic in this sample. While placement and point-to-point movement are common in most styles of board games, the identification of choice as the primary mechanic in eurogames provides an insight into the way in which these games can be differentiated from other genres. Eurogames typically offer the player a relatively small number of actions to take on a given turn, balancing each such that these types of decisions are considered a defining element of the genre (Saari, 2003; Pulsipher, 2006; Berlinger, 2009b).

Clearly, most sedentary games involve meaningful choices that impact upon the game state. However, I use the term here to describe a specific game mechanic. As an example, *Chess* involves the player choosing a move from a large number of possibilities. However, it would be misleading to consider choosing as the central mechanic of *Chess*, even if this is, in effect, what the player spends the majority of time doing. *Chess* is a game of displacement, a goal that is achieved primarily through the mechanics of point-to-point movement and capture (Parlett, 1999, p. 12). While choosing from a large number of possible moves is implied by the rules of the game, these choices stem from the possibilities enabled by the principal mechanics. In Järvinen's terms, the identification of choice as a mechanic stems from the way in which choice is explicitly embodied in the rules (2009, p. 385). This distinction is particularly important, as it highlights restricted choice as one of the key elements of eurogame designs.

As an example of this, in the game *Tikal* players explore a region of jungle in Central America, uncovering temples, locating treasure and attempting to retain that treasure for themselves in order to score points.[12] Within the game a number of different mechanics are utilized (e.g., placing, point-to-point movement, exploration, exchanging, controlling and bidding).[13] On a player's turn they may select from a subset of these mechanics; however, the choice of actions to employ is restricted by a corresponding cost in "action points," of which the player only has 10 per turn. The choice of which actions to perform in a given turn is the core mechanic of the game, explicitly presented to the player as a restricted choice. Thus, the decision is not one of how to employ a particular mechanic but rather which mechanic to employ.

The nature of eurogames can also be understood by considering the mechanics that are largely absent. Indeed, it is particularly noteworthy that of the 139 games analyzed here, only two involve conquering[14] and one attacking/defending.[15] Although it would be misleading to suggest that direct conflict is entirely absent from eurogames,[16] it is a defining trait of the genre that conflict is characteristically afforded by mechanics that only indirectly affect

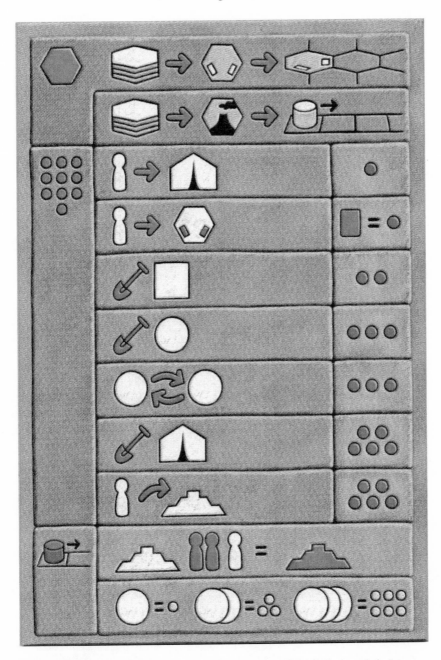

Figure 5.4: *Tikal* quick reference card showing possible choices and their attendant cost in "action points" (courtesy Wolfgang Kramer, Michael Kiesling, Ravensburger and Rio Grande Games. © Franz Vohwinkel).

other players. Conversely, a typical Anglo-American hobby game of the 1980s and 1990s relied heavily on the possibility of directly affecting the position of other players.

The advent of eurogames marked a shift in hobby gaming from directly conflicting play to a style that is more broadly identifiable as competitive. Gaming podcaster Eric Burgess and hobbyist Nick Sauer, speaking of the mid–1990s, identify this change explicitly:

> We were playing *Wiz-War, Diplomacy, Machiavelli, Up Front, Magic the Gathering, TV Wars, Family Business, Man-to-Man, Nuclear War, Naval War, Dungeonquest, Talisman, Kings and Things,* and *Illuminati* in those days. Yes, we had *Outpost, Acquire, Can't Stop* and some other games (including *Shark*) that felt more competitive than confrontational but most of them still had the "take that" mentality [Burgess, 2008b].

> One of the transitions that I distinctly remember going on in my head was the jump from "how can you do a game on anything that doesn't involve conflict?" to "how can you ONLY do games that involve conflict?" [Sauer, 2008].

While this breakdown of typical core mechanics based upon Järvinen's work is interesting in the way it highlights the move away from direct conflict, as a schema broadly applicable to all types of game it can only go so far in revealing the more specific forms of interaction that typify the genre in comparison with other board and table games. As game players who are familiar with the nuances of various games utilize the term mechanic, they have tended to establish their own vocabulary to label specific interaction forms. While these informally agreed-upon categorizations might not fit neatly into a predefined schema, they can shed far more light on the specifics of eurogame dynamics as they are experienced and understood by players. It would be helpful then to describe some of the more common "mechanics" as they are described by players in order to establish a clearer picture of the typical eurogame.

## Common Mechanics in Eurogames

Writer and game designer Yehuda Berlinger lists six examples of game mechanics that have come to be associated with eurogames — Tile Placement, Auctions, Trading/Negotiation, Worker Placement/Role Selection, Set Collection and Area Control (2009b). Given that these descriptions arise from within the hobby rather than from an academic perspective, it is not surprising to find that some of these mechanics do not have a direct correlation with those identified within Järvinen's framework. Auctions can be directly linked to bidding; tile placement and worker placement to choosing/placing; and trading/negotiation with trading and conversing. Area control and set collection are, in terms of Järvinen's systemic elements, goals rather than mechanics. Still, these inconsistencies point to the way in which gamers develop their own descriptions of game systems without the constraints that underpin more formalist approaches. In this way they serve to tell us more about the style of game design and the play they encourage than do strictly taxonomical approaches to analysis. I will briefly clarify what is typically meant by these terms as they are understood within the hobby gaming community.

## Tile Placement

The term tile placement is used to describe the spatial placement of particular game components as they are constrained by their relationship to the board or to other components. While the specific components are most commonly tiles, the term has come to be used to describe a number of game components that are placed in certain configurations.[17] Tile placement itself is not a particularly innovative game mechanic, with records of Chinese domino play dating back to at least the tenth century (Kelley and Lugo, 2003, p. 10). Occasional examples surfaced in the mid–20th century, with the most obvious and successful example being the word-game *Scrabble*.

In terms of modern hobby games, Sackson's *Acquire* stands out for its innovative use of tile placement to simulate the merging of corporations. Given the influence of Sackson's work on eurogame designers, it is not surprising to find this mechanic employed frequently within the genre. *Acquire* is an example of tile placement constrained by the relationship between the shared board and individual tiles. Each tile is assigned a grid reference that defines where on the central board it can be played.[18] The restriction of a pre-existing board is seen in titles such as *Euphrat and Tigris* (Knizia, 1997a), *Metro* (Henn, 1997), and *Chinatown* (Hartwig, 1999). In each of these examples other rules govern or inform the placement of tiles in particular configurations. In *Euphrat and Tigris*, players develop groups of orthogonally placed tiles that, subject to the positioning of their player tokens, reward the player with points. In *Metro*, tiles are played to establish connections between pre-designated points on the board.[19] Finally, in *Chinatown*, placement is constrained by the simultaneous play of cards that indicate spaces where tiles can be played. Numerous other examples of this type of spatially bounded tile placement exist within the genre.

Another form of tile placement is one where the players' tiles form the game environment itself through the course of play, unconstrained by a pre-existing board. The most well known example of this type of game is *Carcassonne*. In *Carcassonne*, player tiles form a geographical representation of a

**Figure 5.5:** Tile placement in *Euphrat & Tigris* (image by Simon Holding, courtesy Hans im Glück).

medieval landscape, with placement constrained by matching the abutting edges of connected tiles. Other examples that take this mechanic a step further include *Taluva* (Casasola Merkle, 2006) and *Gheos* (Wiersma, 2006), wherein tiles can be placed over existing tiles to develop a three dimensional landscape, and *Lost Valley* (Goslar and Goslar, 2004), where the evolving landscape can subsequently be traversed and exploited by all players. Klaus Teuber's *Entdecker* (1996) and Kramer and Kiesling's *Java* (2000b) are examples of games that blend both of these forms, in that players draw tiles to place on a constrained board and in doing so create a representation of a geographical environment. A final, and increasingly common, form of tile placement game is that in which players place tiles on their own individual playing space. As is the case with a shared board, the space may be bounded[20] or unbounded.[21]

## Auctions

Auctions are a mainstay of the eurogame genre and are present in a wide variety of forms.[22] In some cases auctions are the core mechanic of the game,[23] while more commonly they are implemented as one in a number of interlocking mechanisms.[24] Auctions may involve purchasing resources from the game system itself[25] or from other players.[26] They may also involve the procurement of a variety of in-game advantages or actions,[27] with those affecting turn order being common.[28] In some cases, both actions and resources are made available through the auction process.[29] While most auctions are for an individual resource, some are for groups where the value of bids determine the order of selection of the items.[30] Finally, players may be bidding to *not* receive the item that is being auctioned due to the negative impact of the resource under auction.[31]

The most commonly used form of auction is a variation of the English auction wherein players bid until such time as only one player is prepared to pay the accumulated price. However, unlike a classic open-ascending auction, players typically take ordered turns to bid.[32] This form of auction is also common in a limited form where players only have the opportunity of a single bid, commonly referred to as a "once-around" auction.[33] While in a typical English auction bids are open, games such as Faidutti and Schacht's *Fist of Dragonstones* (2002), and Alex Randolph's *Hol's der Geier* (1988), employ a sealed auction where bids are revealed simultaneously. A number of games employ a Dutch (or reverse) auction, with the price decreasing until such time as a player elects to purchase it. In the case of Cathala and Faidutti's *Queen's Necklace* (2003), cards drop in price each turn until players elect to buy, while in Knizia's *Die Kaufleute von Amsterdam* (2000b) a mechanical timer with price increments ticks down until one player stops it and wins the auction.[34]

The sheer variety of auction mechanics found in eurogames is quite overwhelming, and the mechanic could almost be considered a genre nominator itself. The use of auctions combines interpersonal interaction with indirect player conflict and also serves as an in-game balancing mechanism, as prices are determined by the amount players are prepared to pay.

## Trading / Negotiation

Although trading and negotiation have long been a part of business-themed games, both within mass-market and hobby gaming, a number of eurogames implement the mechanic in innovative ways. When discussing trading in terms of the eurogame genre, this mechanic does not refer to merely exchanging items of equivalent value with the game system itself, but rather to the combination of negotiation and trade between players that gives rise to a living market within the game.

In eurogames trading is typically limited to specific game resources that, through other design features of the game, are generally of a different value to individual players. For example, in *Die Siedler von Catan* players are able to trade with others on their own turn in an attempt to gather the core resources required for specific buildings and actions. Dependant upon player position and strategy, the specific resources will hold different values. Similarly, in the card game *Bohnanza* (Rosenberg, 1997), players trade types of bean seed on their turn and are often driven to negotiate unfavorable trades or even give away resources due to the constrained mechanics of the game, which make some cards near-worthless to them yet of value to others. In games such as these, although trading can be considered one of the core mechanics, it is typically limited to particular game resources. Thus a player need evaluate whether a particular trade is beneficial, given a reasonable idea of the worth of the item to each player.

More interesting, perhaps, is the type of negotiation seen in games such as *Die Händler von Genua* (Dorn, 2001a) and *Quo Vadis*, where the actions of other players are negotiable. In a sense, players are not only offering goods for trade, but also services. In these cases, players must not only determine the worth of different types of resource for individual players, but also the value of particular actions. *Quo Vadis* is an archetypal example of this type of game where actions on a player's turn are traded for the promise of a reciprocal action on a subsequent turn.

Like auctions, trading and negotiation bring to the table a degree of competitive interpersonal interaction. They also allow all players to be actively involved in the game when it is not their own turn to play, reducing the time spent waiting for other players.[35] Finally, by allowing players themselves to determine the terms of a particular trade, negotiation acts as a game-balancing feature inasmuch as players who are perceived to be ahead can be constrained by the nature of the trades imposed by other players.[36]

## Set Collection

Following Järvinen's schema, set collection more accurately describes a goal rather than a mechanic, referring as it does to the *objective* of collecting related game resources in groups determined by the rules. Still, within the gaming community it is commonly referred to as a mechanic, perhaps since its implementation may be many steps removed from the overall goals of the game. Of games that utilize set collection as a core mechanic/goal, examples such as *Coloretto* and *Bohnanza* focus almost entirely upon the acquisition of sets that generate points or in-game currency. As with other mechanics, however, set collection typically forms only one part of a more complex design. Of the games that feature set collection as one of the central mechanics, Knizia's *Ra* blends the mechanism with auctions, Brunnhofer and Tummelhofer's *Stone Age* (2008) with worker placement, and Dirk Henn's *Alhambra* (2003) with tile placement. In each of these games the accumulation of specific sets constitutes the principal criterion for scoring.

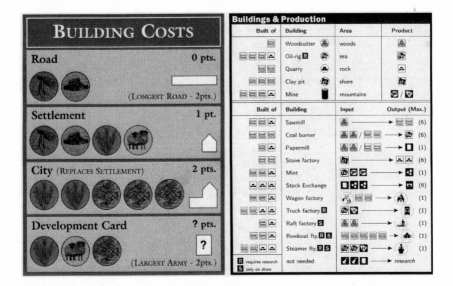

Figure 5.6: Player aids showing set collection requirements in *Die Siedler von Catan* (left) and *Roads and Boats* (right) (courtesy Catan GmbH and Splotter).

Many eurogames are built around a model of economic and technological development wherein basic resources are accumulated in specified sets, with the objective of converting them to more valuable ones. Although the method of acquiring these resources varies widely, the general principle remains — players pursue particular development paths through the acquisition of resources that enable them to manufacture further resources. In some examples this process consists of only one degree of separation between the base resources and the item to be acquired.[37] In more complex examples, however, the development process is extended, with the acquired resources accumulated in sets to produce still further resources.[38]

## Area Control

Also described as area majority, area influence and majority control, area control refers to gaining control of a specific game element through the allocation of resources to that element. The entity to be controlled, the resources to be allocated and the method of allocation vary from game to game. As with set collection, area control might more accurately be considered a sub-goal. Designer Shannon Appelcline identifies three types of majority control game based upon the element to be controlled: share-based, area-based and tile-based (2005b). Arguably the latter two of these can be considered varia-

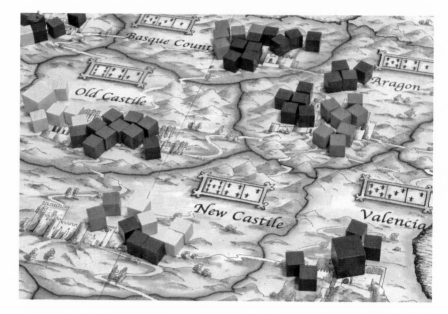

**Figure 5.7: Area control in *El Grande* (image by Simon Holding, courtesy Hans im Glück).**

tions of the same form, as tile-based refers to the fact that the areas to be controlled are evolving through game play. In cases where control is established through the allocation of resources over time, the area majority can be considered an evolution of the auction mechanism.

Share-based majority control games describe those in which control of game elements is determined by the allocation of funds to accumulate shares in a given game entity. This model has long been popular in Anglo-American game designs, most obviously in the *18XX* series of games, and eurogames too have employed share-based majority in rail-themed games.[39] However, while it has occasionally been implemented in eurogames, the mechanic is not strongly associated with the genre.[40]

Within eurogames, straightforward area-based control games are far more common than the share-based model. Although examples are seen in earlier designs,[41] Wolfgang Kramer and Richard Ulrich's *El Grande* is typically identified as the first successful game to utilize the area-based majority mechanic. In *El Grande*, players seek to gain control of areas of the board through the placement of pieces representing caballeros in medieval Spain. The options for placing these pieces are governed by an auction phase that precedes placement, with players able to score during specific rounds through the course of play.

Undoubtedly the most successful game to utilize area-based majority is

*Carcassonne.* The game is an example of tile-based area majority in that tiles are progressively added to the playing surface to construct an evolving board. As players place these tiles, they subsequently have the option to play tokens to assert control over specific areas of the game board as it is created. When these areas are completed or the game ends, they are scored in a similar way to *El Grande.* Other examples of area-based control games include *Kardinal and König* (Schacht, 2000), *Tikal,* and *Louis XIV* (Dorn, 2005).

## Role Selection / Worker Placement

If there is one variety of game mechanic that can lay claim to having been a direct result of the emergence of eurogames, it is that of role selection and worker placement. Appearing first as role selection and in later games as worker placement, this term refers to the mechanic of choosing a particular type of action during a turn. Importantly, this selection is not made simultaneously[42] but rather in a progressive manner, with player choice affecting the options available to subsequent players.

The idea of individual players having distinctive roles within a game can be traced back to the *Hnefatafl* family of abstract strategy games and is commonly seen in other forms of hobby game.[43] However, the first effective implementation of role selection, where players choose a specific role as a part of

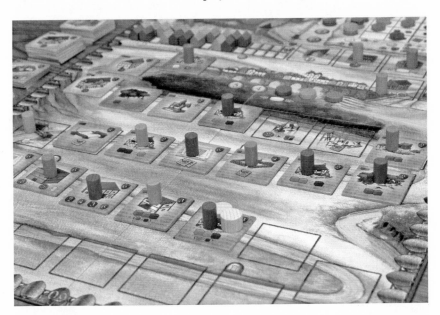

Figure 5.8: Worker placement in *Caylus* (image by Simon Holding, courtesy Ystari Games).

their turn, is generally attributed to Marcel-André Casasola Merkle's card game *Verräter* (1998).[44] In this game, players take turns in selecting a role from a stack of five cards, with each card providing a benefit during a particular phase of the turn.[45] Importantly, and unlike other games that had come before, since roles are selected in turn, once a given role has been chosen it is unavailable to other players. Bruno Faidutti's highly successful *Ohne Furcht und Adel* (2000b) employs the mechanic in an almost identical fashion.[46] Role selection has subsequently been manifest in a variety of ways, most notably in *Puerto Rico*[47] and its card game adaptation *San Juan* (Seyfarth, 2004). In both of these examples the role selected by the player will be performed by all players, with the active player receiving an additional benefit.

Worker placement refers to the mechanic of having a number of tokens that can be allocated to specific places that provide defined actions on the game board. Although it is commonly perceived as an evolution of the role selection mechanic, worker placement first appeared at around the same time in Richard Breese's *Keydom* (1998).[48] In *Keydom*, players allocate a number of worker tokens to areas of the board that provide a variety of resources and actions. While any player may place as many tokens as they wish on most of these spaces, hidden values on the underside of the tokens are subsequently used to determine who receives benefits from the space.[49] In later manifestations of the mechanic, such as the highly successful *Caylus*, once a particular location has been claimed, no other player may place there. Combining the two most common eurogame mechanics, choice and placing, worker placement has quickly become a staple of the genre in the wake of *Caylus'* success, as evidenced by titles such as *Stone Age*, *Die Säulen der Erde* (Rieneck and Stadler, 2006) and *Agricola* (Rosenberg, 2007).

## Weaving Mechanics

In describing these six mechanics that are frequently used in eurogames, I have not sought to make definitive statements but to suggest some common design elements that typify the genre. Although particular games are used to highlight a specific mechanic, in the majority of cases they employ combinations of multiple mechanics in their designs. As noted, mechanics such as tile placement and set collection are hardly original. However, it is the use of these mechanics in combination and the variety of ways in which they are implemented that leads writers to point to the innovative nature of eurogames. As designer Larry Levy notes:

> The genius of the Euro designers is their ability to add subsystems to the basic mechanics-heavy base of their games. This gives them added depth and color,

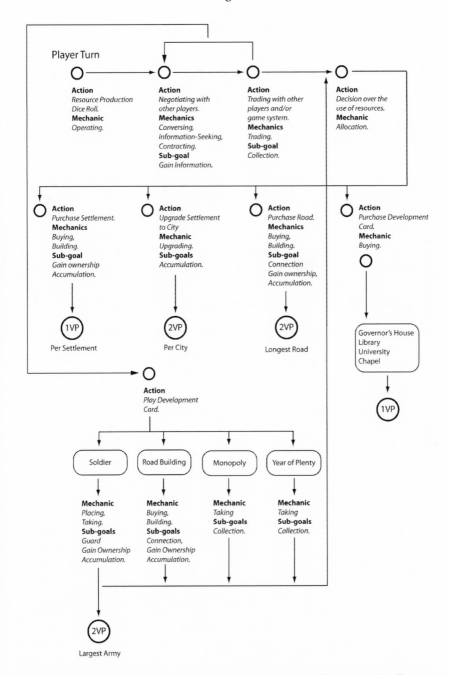

**Figure 5.9: Simplified diagram of mechanics and sub-goals in *Die Siedler von Catan*.**

**Figure 5.10:** *Die Siedler von Catan* board during play (image by Simon Holding, courtesy Catan GmbH).

making them, in my mind at least, considerably more interesting than pure abstracts [2007].

As an example of this layering of mechanics we can refer back to Järvinen's model in analyzing a relatively simple (yet archetypal) eurogame such as *Die Siedler von Catan*. *Die Siedler von Catan* is a 3 to 4–player game in which players attempt to settle and develop the fictional island of Catan. The overarching goal of the game is to be the first player to accumulate 10 victory points, which, in Järvinen's terms, constitutes a race goal. The accumulation of victory points can be achieved in a variety of ways: the construction and upgrading of buildings, the collecting of soldier cards, the development of an extensive road network, and the possession of specific cards that provide points.

Figure 5.9 details the various mechanics that are employed and the sub-goals present in a typical turn of the game. As can be seen, players perform a wide variety of mechanics in pursuit of the sub-goals that contribute to the eventual overarching goal. On any given turn a player will perform the operation of dice-rolling, conversing, information-seeking and contracting in the form of negotiation, trading with both other players and the game system and allocating resources to either purchase or build game elements. Coupled with this is the random determination of resource production that establishes a fluctuating resource market within the game. The result is a combination of interlocking mechanisms that combine to produce a particular gestalt experience. As gaming writer Jonathan Degann notes:

> Games such as *Puerto Rico*, *Power Grid*, *Goa*, and *Settlers of Catan* cannot readily be understood in terms of their component mechanisms nor summarized by a central mechanism that drives all others. The cogs of each mechanism are too tightly meshed [2008].

The principal reason for deconstructing this game is to point out both the variety of mechanisms and the complex relationship between mechanics and goals. To re-emphasize an earlier point, what makes this observation so significant is that *Die Siedler von Catan* is, from a player perspective, a relatively simple game with a few key choices that disguise the complexity of the game system. While many eurogames employ this interweaving of mechanics in innovative ways, their designers typically bury these multipart systems in such a way as to keep the gameplay itself relatively simple. This emphasis on accessibility is a defining trait of the eurogame genre.

## Goals in Eurogames

*A game's goal is a central feature of its formal structure. When players come together to play a game, the goal is at the centre of the magic circle, the pole that holds aloft the circular tent of the game while the players are inside the structure, at play with one another. The goal sustains their interest, their engagement and their desire.*— Salen and Zimmerman, 2004, p. 258

If there is one element that is the most useful in both understanding and playing a game, it is the goal. The goal, as it is prescribed by the ruleset, provides the sense of challenge that drives the movement of the game forward. As a motivating force, it constitutes the principal intrinsic reason to engage with the mechanics of the game. Whether players achieve this over-arching goal or not results in the quantifiable outcome that separates casual play from a structured game.[50]

Typically when discussing the goal of a given game it is the endgame goal that is being considered. While the over-arching goal of all competitive games is, ostensibly, to achieve the winning condition through employment of the game mechanics, during the course of the game many sub-goals are established, either by the rules (implicitly or explicitly) or internally by players themselves. As an example, while the over-arching goal of a chess game is to capture the king (or render it immovable), a player may adopt numerous sub-goals on their way to this (e.g., capture the opponent's queen, protect their own king, etc.). Throughout the course of play, players are given the opportunity to work towards the game goals through the application of the various game mechanics. Thus the game goals shape the way players experience the game inasmuch as they emphasize a particular use of those mechanics. Building on the work of Staffan Björk and Jussi Holopainen (2005), Järvinen describes 32 goal categories that are commonly encountered in games. Applying these categories to this sample of eurogames demonstrates the ubiquity of accumulation as a quantifying endgame goal within the genre.

As is clear from figure 6.11, the over-arching goal of a large proportion of eurogames is the accumulation of a particular game element, typically victory points and/or game currency. Notably, this accumulation is not quantified in the sense that the attainment of a specific amount grants the player victory — in Järvinen's terms this would be considered a race goal — but by a comparative measure at the game's conclusion. Eurogames commonly feature combinations of sub-goals that together contribute towards an accumulation of a particular game element, commonly abstracted to a points system. Indeed, the ubiquity of this design approach within the genre is reflected in the commonly used term "*kramerleiste*" to describe a scoring track that often encircles the board.[51] Thus this distinction marks the outcomes of most eurogames as being measured by comparative performance rather than qualified accomplishment.

To say that accumulation, rather than accomplishment, is the typical overarching goal for a eurogame is to overlook the sub-goals of the game. As Björk and Holopainen note, goals in games constitute a hierarchy, with the highest order goal supported by a variety of sub-goals that are either explicitly identified within the game rules or are implicit in the strategic possibilities

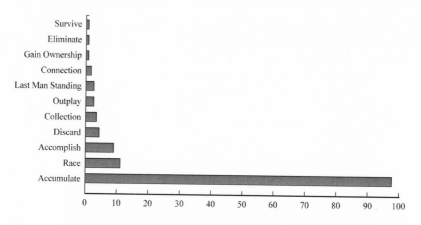

Figure 5.11: Quantifying (endgame) goals in eurogames.

encountered during play (2005, p. 321). So while it may be accurate to suggest that the goal of most eurogames is accumulation, this reveals little about the underlying sub-goals and mechanisms that characterize the genre, and thus the variety of games and play experience that are afforded.

Although games typically employ a variety of sub-goals, the identification of the principal sub-goal can be described as the goal implicitly expressed through the possibilities made available by the core mechanics. In figure 6.12 Järvinen's goal categories are employed in the identification of the principal sub-goal that is afforded by the core game mechanics.

The observation that can be made from this analysis is that there exist a wider variety of sub-goals underlying the overarching goals of accumulation previously identified. The diversity of these goals is further highlighted by the fact that they incorporate no less than 19 of the 32 goal categories that Järvinen describes as commonly occurring in games. Notably, the goal of gaining ownership of in-game elements is the most common of these sub-goals. It is also interesting to note the degree to which the majority of the goal verbs identified here describe achievements in relation to the game system rather than the other players. Sub-goals such as gaining ownership, configuration, connection and traversal, in combination with overarching goals of accumu-

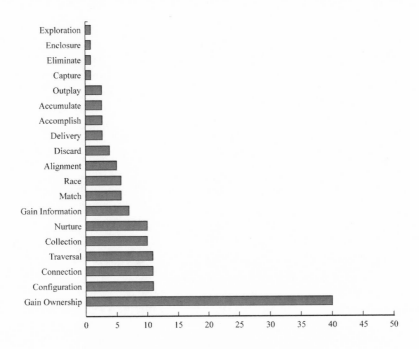

Figure 5.12: Principal sub-goals in eurogames.

lation, emphasize competition rather than conflict. That is to say that player sub-goals are typically not in direct conflict with each other. This distinction has important ramifications for the nature of the game as the players experience it and is another significant characteristic that typifies the eurogame genre.

## Multiplayer Solitaire — Players and Goals

Björk and Holopainen's examination of the way that specific types of goal formulation shape the relations between players in a game differentiates between a number of goal structures (2005, pp. 277–338). As I have shown, goals in eurogames are differentiated by a focus on performance within the context of the game system itself rather than through direct conflict with other players. Generally speaking, the overarching goals of most eurogames are symmetrical. They can be described as "goals that several different players have that can be generalized to fit the same definition without changing the structure of the individual goal definitions" (p. 333). In the case of the typical eurogame, this goal might be "accumulate the largest amount of resource X by the end of the game." Clearly in this situation player goals are not only symmetrical but also incompatible; it is not possible for all players to achieve the goal.

However, as players progress through the game, they are called upon to establish their own sub-goals in pursuit of the overarching goal. Since there is typically significant freedom of choice over how to achieve the overarching goal, the strategies and tactics that can be employed tend towards the asymmetrical (Björk and Holopainen, 2005, pp. 334–335). Notably, while these goals may be conflicting, the paucity of mechanics available that directly impact upon the position of competitors means that players can concentrate on their own performance within the game. As Järvinen notes, using the example of *Ticket to Ride*, there is a tendency then for the conflicting higher-order goals to be set aside in the player pursuit of individual optimization (2009, p. 131).

As an example, consider the popular game *Carcassonne*. As mentioned previously, *Carcassonne* is a game of tile laying and majority control. In the game, players take turns placing a square tile on the table according to specific rules of configuration. As these tiles are placed, they form regions of fields, cities, roads and priories. When a tile is placed, a player has the option to also place one of their limited number of tokens on the tile to claim ownership of the region. Over subsequent turns they can build upon these individual regions, with the eventual endgame scoring dependent upon their size. Importantly, players cannot place tokens in a region that is already controlled by

**Figure 5.13:** *Carcassonne* (image by Simon Holding, courtesy Hans im Glück).

another player (though they may at a later stage attempt to connect two regions and share control with another player).

In this case the principal sub-goal of the game is the ownership and expansion of regions to increase the eventual comparative score that is the overarching goal of the game. As play of the game unfolds, the emergent sub-goals for each individual player become increasingly differentiated from those of their opponents. It is from these asymmetrical sub-goals that the tactics and strategies of the game emerge. A player may adopt a longer-term strategy that focuses on joining regions such that both are awarded the associated points; however, there is no opportunity to directly reduce the number of points scored by another player. Although player sub-goals can potentially come into conflict with those of other players — indeed, *Carcassonne* can be played in an extremely cutthroat manner by limiting an opponent's scoring opportunities — they are not inherently bound to the zero-sum model of direct conflict. It is common in games with more than two participants for players to work together to expand regions in order to share the associated points.

Interestingly, while this type of emergent non-conflicting goal asymmetry is one of the hallmarks of eurogame design, it is also associated with one of the principal criticisms of the genre. In extreme examples, such as *Die Fürsten von Florenz* and *Goa* (Dorn, 2004), the mechanics that do allow interaction with other players[52] comprise such a small part of the game when compared with the core system of individual optimization that many in the hobby gaming community have suggested these games could be described as a multiplayer form of solitaire.

While these examples are somewhat extreme, the combination of overarching goals of comparative performance and mechanics of indirect influence is one that is seen in the majority of eurogames to some degree. Clearly it is important to recognize that these observations are by necessity somewhat generalized, but together they serve to establish an overall sensibility of creative endeavor rather than destructive confrontation. Not surprisingly, this sensibility is typically carried through into the theme of most eurogames.

## Theme in Eurogames

*In eurogames, the mechanics are the heart of the game; the theme is icing to help market the game.* — Berlinger, 2009b

There exists an ongoing debate within the board gaming hobby over the relative importance of theme and mechanic. The debate mirrors a theoretical clash that emerged within the academic field of game studies in the early 21st century. The so-called narratology/ludology debate initially emerged from two differing perspectives on how digital games — and games more generally — should be studied. To summarize this extensive and far-reaching discussion, the narratological[53] position proposed that games might be studied as a form of narrative, focusing on the theme and stories produced during play. Conversely, the ludologist claim was a formalist one, which argued that games needed to be analyzed on their own terms — that is, through the abstract systems they encompass.[54] Dismissing the study of games through the lens of literary theory, so-called "radical" ludologist Markku Eskelinen argues:

> Stories are just uninteresting ornaments or gift-wrappings to games, and laying any emphasis on studying these kinds of marketing tools is just a waste of time and energy [2001].[55]

As Eskelinen suggests, theme and story are clearly not constitutive elements of a game, as evidenced by sports and the myriad of abstract table games that remain playable and enjoyable despite the omission of an explicit theme. However, as Järvinen argues, the ornamental nature of game themes *do* have consequences for player experience (2009, p. 21).[56] Describing the theme as a "metaphor for the ruleset," he proposes that in creating such a metaphor, an extra level of meaning is created "for everything that happens in the game" (p. 74). Furthermore, the existence of this metaphor has implications for the player themselves since they are positioned as actors within the metaphor, typically charged with a thematic goal which overlays the functional one:

> In practice, thematization consists of a set of communicative techniques with which the ruleset and the elements it governs is framed towards the meanings ... that are pursued [p. 76].

In the earlier discussion of goals, I noted that the functional goal of many eurogames is the accumulation of game elements, typically currency or points. The accumulation of these in-game elements is a measurement of the comparative success or failure of the player in performing the game mechanics in the context of the game system. The application of theme to these mechanics and goals, while not strictly necessary, serves not only to make the game more readily understandable, but also provides the player with a role around which their actions within the game can be contextualized. In short, it imbues in the player a sense of meaning for all actions taken in the game and, more importantly, frames those actions in terms of another system. Consequently, the referent system around which the theme is based, and the thematic goals pursued by the players, are important elements of any particular game design.

Theme, when present in board games, is relayed through a number of game elements, primarily the contextual backstory offered on the box and rules, and the graphic design of packaging and components.[57] In addition to graphic presentation, the game box will usually introduce the player to the backstory of the game through a description of the theme and the player's role and goals. For example, from the English translation of the game *Die Händler von Genua*:

> Genoa, in the middle of the 16th century, is the largest trading city in the Mediterranean. The many trading houses compete to be the richest and most profitable. But to be successful, they must sometimes cooperate.
>
> The players take the roles of traders in Genoa. They fulfill orders, deliver messages, and take ownership of important buildings in the city. Of course, this is not possible without the help of the other traders. And that can cost money ... and other valuable goods! [Dorn, 2001b].

In terms of the actual gameplay, *Die Händler von Genua* reflects the theming of the game relatively closely. Players travel around a board that bears a stylized top-down representation of the city of Genoa,[58] delivering goods and messages to specific buildings, which they may also purchase. Throughout the game a series of negotiation rules allow players to influence the actions of other players by bribing them to visit specific locations. In this sense the theme serves to support the mechanical aspects of the game, and it is difficult to imagine one without the other.

Although the example of *Die Händler von Genua* is useful in describing

Figure 5.14: Delivering goods and messages in *Die Händler von Genua* (image by Simon Holding, courtesy Alea and Rüdiger Dorn).

the way that theme serves to complement game mechanics and goals, the close marriage described here is somewhat atypical for a eurogame. The abstraction of accumulation as an overarching goal appears to free designers from such close adherence to theme — to the degree that many have classified eurogames as being largely abstract games with themes that are applied late in the design process (Aleknevicus, 2004; Faidutti, 2005b; Pulsipher, 2006). Indeed, Greg Aleknevicus goes so far as to describe the loose application of themes in eurogames as fraudulent[59]:

> The wholesale grafting of a theme onto a set of mechanics is dishonest if those mechanics have no real world connection to that theme. Can a game really be about exploring the Amazon if it can easily be re-themed to the terror of the French Revolution? Is it realistic to simply add floors to an existing skyscraper? Did ancient explorers really decide the orientation of the islands they discovered? [2004].

Often referred to as an exemplar of this approach is mathematician turned designer Reiner Knizia, whose games commonly appear as abstract exercises with only a circumstantial relationship to the theme proposed by the artwork and background. One of many examples to be found in Knizia's ludography is that of *Ra*. The box cover of the English translation describes the game and the players' roles:

The game spans 1500 years of Egyptian history. Seek to expand your power and fame by influencing Pharoahs, building monuments, farming on the Nile, paying homage to the gods and advancing the technology and culture of the people [Knizia, 2005].

Despite the suggestion of a sweeping historical saga, *Ra* is a relatively straight-forward game of bidding and set collection, with the various achievements described in the backstory referring to sets of tiles that players seek to collect through a series of auctions. Evidence of this somewhat tangential relationship between theme and mechanics is found in the game *Razzia!* (2004a), another Knizia game published five years after *Ra*. In *Razzia!* players are cast as the heads of mafia families who seek to accumulate wealth before the arrival of police, who terminate the game round. Notwithstanding these seemingly incompatible themes, *Ra* and *Razzia* are, with some small changes, essentially the same game in terms of mechanics.[60] A similarly loose relationship between game mechanics and theme in eurogames can be seen in many games that have been re-issued with new themes.[61]

Given the broad range of mechanics in eurogames, one might expect that this variety would be reflected in the range of themes that are applied to them. For the purposes of identifying the dominant themes in eurogames, I have broken the analysis of theme down into two elements. Firstly, there is the broader thematic context through which the ruleset is framed, which I term the *thematic model*. Secondly, there is the motivation implied by this theme, the implicit role that draws the player into the world of the game and provides their actions with a context. This I term the *thematic goal*. In other words, the thematic model is the world into which the player is transported, while the thematic goal provides the fictional motivation to pursue the goals

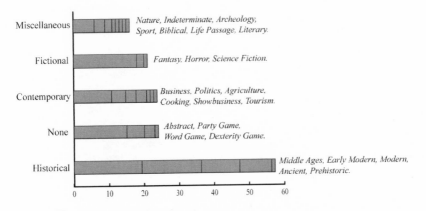

Figure 5.15: Thematic models in eurogames.

of the game. In concert, these elements reveal much about the nature of the eurogame genre.

Figure 5.15 provides a diagram of the various thematic models that can be observed in the games under analysis here. For the purposes of this analysis, these models were largely derived from the contextual backstory and graphic design of the game. If we are to consider theme, at least partly, as a constituent element of the eurogame genre, an immediate observation that can be made from this sampling is the degree to which history provides a thematic backdrop for many titles.[62] Setting aside those games that are not themed in any way, historical themes constitute 65 percent of all remaining games. In comparison with Anglo-American forms of hobby game, while fantasy themes are present in a significant number of titles,[63] science fiction is notably under-represented.[64] Still, despite the dominance of historical titles, the thematic frames presented here constitute an eclectic mix.

Figure 5.16 indicates the thematic goals as they are presented to the player

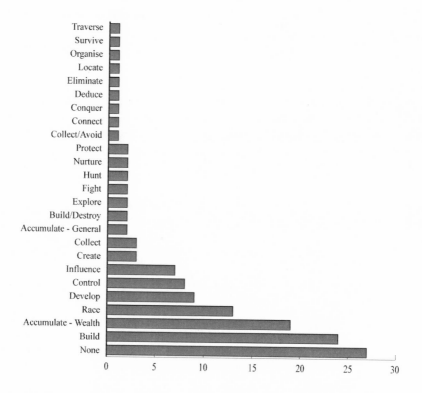

**Figure 5.16: Thematic goals in eurogames (goals as presented to the player through backstory).**

through the contextual backstory and the thematic aim as proposed by the rules. This is not information taken from the goals as they are presented within the game rules themselves, but by the description of play typically offered on the game's box and/or as an introduction to the ruleset. Immediately apparent from this data is the number of titles that do not explicitly describe a goal in the context of the game's thematic model. Once again setting aside those games that are entirely abstract, a number of the games analyzed are overlaid with a theme that has no coherent relationship with the game's mechanics, and thus no thematic goal is presented. In these cases the theme does simply serve as "gift wrapping," and the game system itself bears a largely arbitrary relationship to the suggested theme. In examples such as *Hol's der Geier*, *6 Nimmt!* and *Coloretto*, animals appear on the packaging and cards, but the application of theme essentially ends there.[65] As Bruno Faidutti has noted, these games tend to lie at the simpler end of the design spectrum:

> Some games, mostly those based on a single and simple mechanism, can easily have their setting changed, because it's just a setting and not a real theme, and they don't need it to work.... When games are more complex, and involve many game systems, the theme becomes much more than a background setting. It becomes what gives a meaning to the game's action, what makes the game coherent — and this is true not only for the games that were designed starting from the theme [2005a].

Following Faidutti's assertion, it is not surprising to find that theme is consistently present in the more complex games analyzed. Among those games that do offer a thematic goal, the emphasis upon individual achievement that was identified in the functional goal rules is reinforced. Thematic goals that emphasize goals-of-self, such as building, development and the accumulation of wealth, are commonplace. Furthermore, as with the functional goals and the mechanics underlying them, there is a distinct paucity of goals that suggest direct conflict.[66] While a theme is often only loosely woven into the overall fabric of the typical eurogame, in the vast majority of cases the emphasis upon comparative achievement is carried through from the mechanics to the thematic goals. As varied and eclectic as their themes are, the central essence of games that charge players with goals-of-self and resolve through comparative performance remains.

Although theme might be considered arbitrary in analyzing the behavior of a game system, it is an important element in terms of both marketing and player experience. For a publisher, theme is an important factor in attracting the target audience to purchase a particular title, while for players it can function to draw them into the fictional world of the game and thus enhance the player's experience. As with mechanics, the most notable observation concerning the presence of theme in eurogames is the degree to which particular subject matter is not present. Direct conflict particularly is rarely called upon to motivate players as a thematic goal. Instead, the emphasis is typically upon individual achievement, with thematic goals such as building, development and the accumulation of wealth being prevalent. While eurogames commonly employ history as a thematic backdrop, they tend to focus on political and economic aspects of the period they draw upon, rather than the ideological and political clashes. It is also notable that eurogames tend not to draw on the fictional settings of science fiction and fantasy as commonly as Anglo-American hobby games do.

The emphasis on historical and economic themes is a significant trait of eurogames, as it affects their positioning in the marketplace. Unlike Anglo-American games that often focus on niche interests (historical conflict, science fiction, etc.), eurogame themes are arguably more accessible to a broader market. While a sustained interest in fictional genres, such as science fiction and fantasy, is perhaps a requirement for enjoying a game tightly themed around these settings, the loose application of generic subject matter, such as history, business and the natural world, requires little player investment in the thematic background in order to engage with the game. As discussed above, this approach to theme is one of the key criticisms of the genre, though given the roots of eurogames in family gaming, this emphasis on accessible themes is not surprising.

## Information in Eurogames

The vast majority of eurogames are sequential in nature, meaning that players make decisions in turn, based upon information they receive from the actions of other players and the current game state as it is represented by the environment and components.[67] As such, from the perspective of each individual player, new information is added to the game system on each turn, an iterative pattern that simulation designer Richard Duke describes as "pulses" (1974, p. 40). In the context of Järvinen's framework, these pulses establish an evolving relationship between game information and other game elements that constitutes the "fuel of meaning" distributed between the self, others and the game system (2009, p. 71).

In discussing the nature of games, writers commonly refer to the distinction between perfect and imperfect information, terms borrowed from mathematical game theory. Games of perfect information are those in which the player not only has access to all information regarding the game state, but also all the previous and potential actions taken by other players, along with the related consequences.[68] Examples of games of perfect information include traditional abstracts such as *Chess* and *Go*. Within the genre of eurogames, perfect information games are rare, although examples do exist.[69] Most eurogames are games of imperfect information, although the type of information and the way it is hidden varies a great deal.

In games where information is hidden by the game system, a random element is introduced to increase variety while simultaneously rendering the game less susceptible to any conclusive analysis. A deck of hidden cards or tiles is a common example. In *Carcassonne* players draw from a stack of face down tiles which are placed to form the environment of the game; while in *Puerto Rico* the plantation tiles that are available for purchase each turn are initially randomized and hidden, only being revealed at the beginning of each turn. In *Agricola* a series of actions are progressively made available to players from round to round. Although the nature of these actions is known, the exact order in which they will be made available is not, thus adding unpredictability to an otherwise relatively procedural game.

When individual players hold specific information, a game is far less susceptible to logical analysis, since a player is not aware of every possibility and consequence of other players' actions. Game elements that are distributed to individual players can then shape the strategic and tactical possibilities available to them as they progress through the game. Many eurogames employ a privately held hand of resource cards or tiles,[70] while others employ such hidden elements as currency,[71] points[72] and bonus cards.[73] In some cases player sub-goals are also held privately.[74] As Appelcline notes, the nature of privately held information is such that it tends to add a level of meta-communicative interpretation to the gameplay, as players may attempt to deduce or infer certain information through careful observation of another player's behavior and/or actions within the game (2003). Significantly, when particular information is held by the game system it introduces purely random elements to the game, and luck enters the system.

## The Role of Chance

The relationship between luck and skill is one that has long been of interest to game scholars. Roger Caillois, in classifying differing types of games, refers to games of skilled competition as *agôn*, noting that games infused with this quality have as their raison d'etre "for each player to have his superiority in a given area recognised" (1958, p. 15). To games of chance he ascribes the term *alea*, appropriating the Latin term for dice games. Caillois acknowledges that most games offer up a combination of these two forms, and for the most part eurogames employ an element of both skill and chance.

Skill, of course, is called upon by the various mechanics discussed earlier, allowing players to affect their position within the game. The way that random elements are implemented when compared with other forms of hobby gaming bears a little closer examination.

Greg Costikyan has discussed the attitude within western culture that tends to devalue games the more that they employ chance in determining the outcome of the game (2009). Games of pure chance are often only considered interesting inasmuch as they offer an opportunity for wagers or serve to introduce young children to the practice of formal game play.[75] Costikyan specifically describes eurogames as a genre that "prizes strategy and planning," yet, perhaps surprisingly, it is rare to find examples of eurogames that do not contain some element of chance. Notably it is the particular way in which chance is implemented that offers a potential distinction between the eurogame and other forms.

The role of chance in eurogames is typically mitigated through a shift in the chronology of random events that are presented to a player. Writer Greg Aleknevicus identifies this approach with an explicit comparison to American-style games:

> In American hobby games, a player will perform an action and then random chance will determine the outcome. For example, in *Risk*, I decide to attack the Ukraine from Northern Europe, then I roll dice to see who wins. In European games, random chance will determine the options and the player then decides which to choose. For example, in *Settlers of Catan*, I roll the dice to see what resources I receive, then I decide how I will trade/spend these resources. To my mind, this is a far better way to differentiate the two styles of games [2008].

Although the distinction Aleknevicus makes here is useful, it is problematic in that, despite its iconic status as the most well known eurogame, *Die Siedler von Catan* is a relatively rare example of the genre because it employs dice as a randomizer — an inclusion that has up until quite recently not been favored in typical eurogame designs (Pulsipher, 2006).[76] While the comparison to *Risk* is valid, and indeed can be expanded to include the typical structure of many hobby wargames and early role-playing games, Aleknevicus fails to take into account collectible card games that offer a similar chronology. Still, these small issues notwithstanding, Aleknevicus' observations do ring true for the vast majority of eurogames, in that luck is typically mitigated by having random factors presented in the game before the player makes decisions. As Berlinger describes:

> Many eurogames randomize the resources available during each round or each game. Note that you usually know the available terrain and resources BEFORE you take an action, and so can use this information to plan your strategies, rather than the dice, cards, or spinners occurring AFTER or AS you take an action to determine if you have succeeded [2009b].

Once again, the reasons for this differing approach lie in the simulative roots of Anglo-American hobby gaming. The nature of armed conflict, at least on a strategic or operational level, is such that the outcome of individual actions cannot be predicted with any degree of certainty. In order to accurately simulate a particular battle or operation, a wargame must account for this lack of unpredictability. Of course, this is not to suggest that the outcome of a wargame is randomly determined, since players are at least notionally aware of the statistical probabilities underlying a particular decision. However, the short-term outcome of any given decision cannot be completely certain. As hobby gaming evolved and role-playing games appeared, this model of combat — a decision followed by a randomly determined outcome — became the dominant model.[77]

The designers of early eurogames, on the other hand, were not designing simulations, they were designing games for the family market. Consequently, random factors are employed to heighten variability and to embellish the decision-making process. As long as these random factors are balanced, their overall effect can ideally be mitigated through skilful play. Costikyan uses the example of *Torres* to highlight how the random drawing of cards adds color to decision-making without unduly influencing the eventual outcome:

> The action cards in *Torres* allow players to do different things but, at least a priori, none of the actions they permit is obviously better or worse than the others. In addition, to draw a new action card, a player must forgo taking some other action in the game, so the question of whether or not to draw a card becomes a strategic concern. Chance is not entirely eliminated through this scheme, however; in a particular strategic situation, drawing a new action card might provide you with an ability that is precisely what you need at this moment, or something that is of no immediate benefit — and so luck continues to play a role [2009].

Luck is present in most games, and those being discussed here are no exception. In eurogames, where particular emphasis is placed upon the mechanics of choosing, the ability to review the result of a random process before making a decision ensures that players have a sense of control over their own progression within the game. Importantly, it is not necessarily the case that this design element has any direct correlation with the role that skill plays in a particular game,[78] but, as Salen and Zimmerman point out, player perception of random elements is defined not so much by the mathematics of probability that underlie them, but by the way these events are implemented (2004, p. 175). In the case of eurogames, the perception of control brought about by shifting the chronology and structure of random elements can be seen as a defining trait of the genre.

## *Maintaining Player Involvement*

In many eurogames, designers appear to have deliberately set out to remedy problems associated with players being removed from, or losing interest in, a game due to their poor performance. In the case of the former, it is very rare within the genre to find games that include player elimination, a common feature in many hobby and mainstream designs. In the vast majority of eurogames, all players are involved with the play of the game until the end of the game, as designers of eurogames have adopted a number of techniques for maintaining player involvement in a game until the closing moments.

In games that focus upon accomplishment of a specific goal it is often the case that the eventual winner is readily identifiable long before the cessation of play. The designers of eurogames, despite shifting the goal focus to that of accumulation, face a similar problem in that any openly scored game will see some players leaping ahead while others trail behind. The simplest solution to this problem is that the element to be accumulated (e.g., points, currency) be held in secret. The obvious problem with this is that since the distribution of these resources is typically public they are susceptible to tracking, introducing a cumbersome memory element to the game. A number of games do feature this solution,[79] while others partially solve the problem by having some of the scoring commodity distributed in secret so that players can develop a rough idea of the position of their competitors without being entirely certain of the outcome.[80] Finally, a significant number of games delay scoring until the cessation of play. In cases such as these, the points can be calculated from careful observation of other players' positions, but the required calculations make the task tiresome for all but the most determined players.[81]

Another solution to this issue lies in what Berlinger terms "cascading points" (2009b). This practice is that of distributing smaller numbers of points at the beginning of the game and escalating either the quantity or frequency of distribution as the game progresses. A simple example of increasing the availability of points as the game goes on is found in games such as *Union Pacific* and *Alhambra* where a draw card pile is seeded with cards that bring about a scoring round. In both of these games the cards are added to the draw pile in such a way that scoring rounds occur more frequently towards the end of the game.

A number of eurogames require players to build what might be termed a "point-scoring engine," whereby it is only possible to score small amounts in the beginning of the game, with these increasing as the game comes to a climax. In examples such as *Puerto Rico* and *Age of Steam* (Wallace, 2002), players are developing systems for the shipping of goods. At the outset of the game the quantities of goods that can be moved are relatively small. As the game moves forward, a player's ability to move goods increases, with tension at the endgame emerging from the large scoring opportunities afforded by larger shipments. One of the perceived issues with this type of game system is the tendency for those who have developed the more efficient engine to pull further and further ahead from the other players, a problem referred to as having a "runaway leader." To combat this, a number of games deliberately employ systems that benefit the player in the losing position (or hinder the leader) in order to maintain tension. For example, in *Funkenschlag (Second Edition)* (Friese, 2004) the player who has the lowest number of points at the beginning of each round is granted the first opportunity to purchase resources and build connections, an advantage in terms of resource pricing and route availability. Similarly, in Teuber's *Die Sternenfahrer von Catan* (1999), players below a certain point threshold receive a bonus resource that can be used towards construction in the game.[82]

The variety and frequency of these design elements suggest that the issue of keeping all players actively involved with the game throughout the course of play is one that has caught the attention of eurogame designers. Through the implementation of a wide range of design techniques, the overall experience is commonly that the outcome of a particular game cannot be predicted until quite close to the game end. This notion, that players should always be actively engaged with the game, is carried through to another trait of the genre — that of constrained playing times.

## Constrained Playing Times

When describing eurogames, another commonly cited attribute of the genre is that they are normally playable within a maximum of two hours. There are, of course, exceptions to this generalization — more complex examples such as *Die Macher* and *Roads and Boats* may often take in excess of three hours — yet overall, eurogames tend to fall within a shorter time frame. Moreover, it is generally the case that the playing time of a particular game is predictable given the number of players.

The game of *Chess*, on the other hand, is an example of a game of unpredictable duration. Were a novice to play against a Grandmaster, it is likely that the game would be over in no more than a few minutes, while games between two equally matched players have been known to take as long as 24 hours.[83] In most games where the goal conditions involve a particular accomplishment, unpredictable play times are common. In games of score accumulation, particularly in sports, the most common way to restrict the playing time is to apply an arbitrary time limit, such as that in *Soccer* or *Test Cricket*.

In eurogames the duration of the game is typically constrained either by the implementation of a set number of rounds or, more commonly, by having the endgame conditions attached to the depletion of a particular game element. Examples of the former, such as *Tadsch Mahal* and *Im Jahr des Drachen* (Feld, 2007a), take place over a set number of rounds.[84] The tension in these games arises from the fact that players have a limited amount of turns, known from the outset, in which to accumulate points.[85] Depletion of a particular game resource is a very common way of bringing about the ending of a game, yet in some cases it is arguably the case that the implementation is functionally identical to using a set number of rounds. For example, *Carcassonne* has players randomly draw a tile to play on the table. Since it is generally quite rare for a tile to be unplayable, should a player take the time to count the number of tiles and then divide this by the number of players, a reasonable estimate of how many rounds will be in the game can be achieved.

In most cases the amount of an element used varies from turn to turn. If the remaining quantity is open information, as it is being depleted, players can develop a rough estimation of the remaining turns, a system that leads to increasing tension as the particular element dwindles. Examples of this type of endgame condition are plentiful within the genre.[86] Finally, a number of games blend these two approaches. The auction game *Ra* takes place over three "epochs" (a theme-inspired euphemism for rounds), with each of these being brought to a close when there are no more spaces available on a track on the board. The moment the available spaces are depleted, scoring for that epoch is calculated and the next round commences.

Although these techniques for constricting the playing time of a game are not particularly innovative or unique — all manner of card games employ rounds and depletion — the fact that they are so common in eurogames is notable. As it is found in the vast majority of titles, a relatively short and predictable duration is an identifiable trait of the eurogame genre.

## The Subjectivity of Genre

*Anytime you want to start a good argument just ask a group of people to come to an agreement as to what eurogame means.* — Steve Jackson in Burgess, 2008a

I have highlighted here a series of traits and qualities that have become identified with the eurogame genre. As I mentioned in the opening paragraphs, however, this analysis is littered with the types of generalizations that make genre identification so subjective. For all of the qualities cited in this chapter, there are counter-examples. There are examples of eurogames with mechanics of direct conflict, examples with war themes, and those with poor components, lengthy playing times and high doses of luck. However, the qualities listed here together form a point of reference by which hobbyists are able to identify a particular game as falling within the genre. Figure 5.17 provides a summary of these traits.

| | |
|---|---|
| Components | Typically high quality but otherwise similar to other genres of board and table game. |
| Environment | Typically representational when present. |
| Ruleset | Typically short and relatively simple. |
| Rules (Goals) | Typically goals of comparative accumulation layered over a wide variety of sub-goals. |
| Mechanics | Typically non-confrontational, with choosing, placement and point-to-point movement common. |
| Information | Typically games of imperfect information. |
| Theme | Typically an emphasis on the historical, with thematic goals that stress individual achievement. |
| Random Elements | Typically present but mitigated. |
| Duration | Typically 1–2 Hours |

**Figure 5.17: Traits of Eurogames (Summary).**

Inasmuch as eurogames can be compared to other genres of board and table game (both proprietary and non-proprietary), similarities exist in the common utilization of mechanics, such as point-to-point movement and placement. Having said that, the emphasis upon choice from a limited subset of potential actions, and the absence of mechanics that facilitate direct conflict, can be considered defining traits of the eurogame genre. Coupled with the employment of comparative accumulation as an overarching goal, this shift away from direct conflict gives the eurogame design movement a distinct and recognizable sensibility that highlights construction, development and comparative achievement over conflict.

It is clear that among the designers of eurogames there is a strong tendency to prioritize the development of innovative and interesting mechanics over that of theme. This shift in perspective is the factor most commonly cited in comparing mass-market and Anglo-American hobby designs with the European style (Hardin, 2001). On the one hand, the emphasis on theme in Anglo-American designs is commonly considered upon as enhancing the sense of immersion in a game, a claim that brings to mind the narrativist argument in video game studies. On the other hand, mechanics are seen as the defining element of a game, with theme merely a trapping to contextualize and simplify player understanding of the underlying mechanics, a strongly ludological approach.

French game designer Bruno Faidutti explicitly refers to a geo-cultural split in identifying these two aesthetics:

> The German school of game design in which you can count some American designers such as Sid Sackson or Alan R. Moon, clearly attach more importance to the system. They feel like the theme is only a practical tool to describe the rules in a clearer and more efficient way — better talk of wheat and wood than of yellow and green cards. This means that the theme is often chosen after the game has been entirely designed, and sometimes doesn't fit very well, when some rules feel like "out of theme." This doesn't prevent such games from being great ... the game systems are good enough to make for a great game experience, but very different from the one you can have with baroque games dripping with theme, like most CCGs or American style war games [2008].

German designer Reiner Knizia perceives the difference in design philosophy as being founded upon a similar division:

> In America, the theme is seen as the game where as in the European [sic] the game mechanics and the game system are seen as the game [Knizia in Batty, 2006a].

The emphasis on theme that Faidutti and Knizia draw attention to here is amply evident in the evolution of Anglo-American wargames. Following the popularity of media science fiction during the late 1970s, wargame companies were quick to begin publishing games with science fiction and fantasy themes, without significant innovations in the underlying mechanics. The heritage of these games lay within the wargaming hobby, where simulation constitutes "a major part of the aesthetic" (Costikyan, 2009). The principles of conflict simulation that were laid down relatively early in the history of the hobby demanded little mechanical innovation in the shift to new contexts. As *boardgamegeek* user Leo Zappa describes, there is a reason why innovative mechanics in wargames are not a design priority:

> Wargamers, by and large, do not play a game to experience a unique set of mechanics, but rather play a game to experience a unique take on a historical battle or campaign. In fact, use of commonly understood, tried-and-true mechanics (hex map, zones of control, stacking limits, ... etc.) in new games is often considered a virtue by wargamers, as it means they don't have to waste time learning the fundamentals of how to play the game system, and can focus instead on the unique strategic and tactical aspects of the situation being modeled [2007].

Although not tied to a simulative design model, collectible card games are another example of the thematic emphasis to which Faidutti and Knizia refer. These games typically draw heavily on the core mechanics of *Magic: The Gathering*, relying on market differentiation through the application of themes drawn from popular media licenses. Consequently, theme can be seen to play a significant role in the decision to play one particular game over another. Mark Bordenet (2000, pp. 38–39) identifies the strong attraction of the fantasy theme in *Magic: The Gathering* and the importance of thematic familiarity in players choosing to play the *Star Wars CCG* (Darcy *et al.*, 1995).

While designers of eurogames develop mechanical systems, perhaps with specific themes in mind, it is often the publishers of these games who decide upon the eventual themes.[87] Games are brought to market within a particular cultural context in which both the theme and mechanics may play a role in the success of a given title. As gaming writer Andrew Hardin points out, most hobby gamers consider both the theme *and* the quality of the underlying mechanics important (2001). The majority of eurogames do have a theme, even if it is not uppermost in the minds of designers. So, despite the apparent prioritization of mechanics over theme in these designs, the latter cannot be dismissed as merely window dressing, especially considering the close relationship between thematic and mechanical goals identified here.

Both the thematic and mechanical goals of the typical eurogame are imbued with the sensibilities of construction, development and accumulation, a sharp contrast to the conflict-driven simulations that form the basis of Anglo-American hobby gaming. This emphasis on individual accomplishment through collaborative competition rather than achievement through direct conflict and elimination arguably implies a more sociably oriented design philosophy. The combination of simple rulesets, predictable playing times and loosely applied generic themes of development that typify eurogames are evidence of a game form with a particular focus on accessibility. Still, at the time of this writing, eurogames remain a niche genre familiar for the most part only to a dedicated hobbyist audience. It is to this audience, the players, that I turn my attention in the next chapter.

# 6

# *Hobby Gamers*

*Hobby gaming of any variety adds an aesthetic framework, an ethical panorama and a structured sense of social dynamism to a player's life. The consequences of this are the provision of outlets for personal expression and exploration as well as scope for community involvement and spiritual growth.* — Lenarcic and Mackay-Scollay, 2005

In previous chapters I have focused primarily upon the history of hobby gaming and the specific forms of games that have contributed to the evolution of hobby gaming culture. As I have noted, the emergence of eurogames as a distinct genre within the broader hobby gaming culture was driven largely by word of mouth within the culture rather than from a concerted commercial effort on the part of publishers. An important question then, is why have these games, essentially evolved from the European family market, proven so popular among hobby gamers? In order to answer this we need firstly to have a clear understanding of who hobby gamers are and secondly what participation in board gaming culture typically entails.

Consequently, in this chapter I will examine the motivations and activities of players for whom the board gaming hobby occupies a central role in their leisure pursuits. In identifying members of the website *boardgamegeek* as a particularly active and easily accessible gaming community, my analysis of players and play behavior is based upon a large-scale survey of site members. Following a review of the basic demographics of site members, I argue that the degree of enthusiasm for board games that is evident positions members as a particular type of board game player — the gaming hobbyist. This enthusiasm is manifest in a variety of ways, most notably through active participation within the hobbyist culture, the acquisition and accumulation of games, and a degree of evangelism for the hobby. This level of engagement with the gaming hobby marks these players as atypical of the broader range of people who, on occasion, play hobby games. This distinction has important ramifications for the discussions of play that occur later in this book.

# Boardgamegeek

The rapid growth of the Internet over the last two decades has resulted in the emergence of virtual "communities of interest" centered on particular topics and a shared enthusiasm for specific cultural products and/or activities (Armstrong and Hagel, 1996). The result is that such communities offer an ideal space for the exploration of both the nature of specific communities and the subject of their interest. *Boardgamegeek*, a website devoted to the cataloguing and discussion of board and table games, is such a community of interest whose members can be seen as broadly representative of players with a strong interest in hobby board games, particularly modern eurogames. The enthusiasm for this particular form is reflected in the active discussion of not only the games themselves, but on many elements of the culture surrounding the hobby and the nature of play as it is experienced by gamers.

Launched in 2000 by American gamers Scott Alden and Derk Solko, *boardgamegeek* has become a nexus for board game hobbyists on the Internet. As of mid–2011 the site boasts 400,000 members and a database containing over 50,000 individual games. *Boardgamegeek* is among the top 7,000 most frequently visited websites on the Internet according to Alexa.com ("boardgamegeek.com," 2010).[1] Gaming hobbyists use the site to discuss all aspects of games and gaming culture. Features of the site include individual listings for games, game rankings, discussion boards, collection management tools, facilities for storing game-related files, a messaging service and trading functionality. In 2010 the site was awarded the *Inno-Spatz* for "outstanding achievements in the world of games" at the game designer's convention in Goettingen (Drude, 2010). Founded upon a shared interest in the emerging eurogame genre and a desire to provide a platform for sharing information and discussion (Alden and Solko, 2004b; Vasel, 2005e), *boardgamegeek* is exemplary of the way in which communities of interest have found new life on the Internet, becoming what cultural scholar Henry Jenkins describes as "expansive self-organizing groups focused around the collective production, debate, and circulation of meanings, interpretations, and fantasies in response to various artefacts of contemporary popular culture" (2002b, p. 159).

# Boardgamegeek Demographics

In 2007 I undertook an extensive online survey designed to draw out basic demographic information about *boardgamegeek* members, along with more qualitative information about the nature of their play experiences. In order to situate the responses that are discussed in this book, I here review the basic demographic data that was collected through this survey. This data provides demographic information on the *boardgamegeek* community, based on an average response rate for each question of approximately 650. As these respondents are a self-selecting group, they can be considered representative of frequent visitors and contributors to the site. Given the central role of *boardgamegeek* within the broader hobby community, these respondents constitute a sample with a particularly strong interest in board games.

## Age, Gender and Relationship Status

The level of female participation in the *boardgamegeek* community is extremely low (about seven percent) with males accounting for about 96 percent of respondents. The average age of respondents is approximately 36 years, with a significant proportion over 40 (28 percent). A different survey revealed that 62 percent of respondents are married, with a further 16 percent in a "serious relationship." Only 17 percent identify themselves as being single. 48 percent have children.[2]

## Education

Respondents were questioned as to the highest level of education they had achieved. 68 percent of respondents indicated that they had achieved an undergraduate degree or higher, with slightly more than 10 percent holding a doctoral degree.

## Nationality

Although *boardgamegeek* is based in the United States and the majority of users are North American (68 percent), community members are drawn from throughout the world, with a significant number from Europe (25 percent).

## Profession/Income

Member professions were not captured in this survey; however, user LankyEngineer conducted an informal poll in 2008 through the site's forum pages that addressed this question specifically (2008b).[3] 38 percent of users work in IT or engineering related fields. Other notably represented fields of employment are education (9 percent) and business management (6 percent). Average income of site members is approximately U.S. $50,000 per year, 10 percent higher than the median in the United States at the time of the survey ("U.S. Census Bureau," 2006).

## Play Habits — Frequency and Style

Not surprisingly, *boardgamegeek* members play board games more commonly than might be deemed "normal" in mainstream culture. The games most commonly played by survey respondents are eurogames, with 47 percent playing at least weekly and 85 percent playing at least once a month. Since *boardgamegeek* was chosen for precisely the reason that it is a nexus for eurogame players, this result was entirely expected. Video games in various forms are also played with some frequency, particularly those that can be played at home in isolation (single-player PC games, MMORPGs and console games). While other forms of hobby gaming are not well represented in the survey, they are undoubtedly played with more frequency than among the general population.[4] Of other forms of hobby game, American style board games are best represented — 33 percent play at least once a month — although they are generally played with far less frequency than eurogames.

## Play Habits — Environment

Like most gaming hobbies, strategy gaming is one that takes place largely in the domestic sphere of the players' own homes. 85 percent of players indicated that they frequently play with friends at home, while 70 percent play with their families. 36 percent of players participate in organized gaming groups that are based in private homes. Not surprisingly, then, the most common play environment for most respondents is the home (76 percent). As Richard Butsch observes, the increased commercialization of leisure in the 20th century also marked a period where leisure activities were increasingly focused in the privacy of the home (1990). Regional gaming groups operating in public locations are another common venue for players, with 47 percent indicating that they attended an organized group at a separate venue, although only 21 percent indicated that this was the most common location for play. 34 percent of respondents indicated that they engaged in open gaming at conventions, while only 12 percent of respondents attest to participating in organized tournaments.[5]

## Summary — The Aging Male Gamer

The picture that emerges of the typical *boardgamegeek* member, then, is one of an educated and relatively affluent married American male in his midthirties. Interestingly, in his 1983 study of role-playing gamers, Gary Fine makes the observation that participants in role-playing games are "almost entirely male," and that "the typical gamer is in his late teens or early twenties," suggesting that "like the participants in many leisure 'scenes,' most fantasy gamers are young" (1983, pp. 39–41).[6] Fine attributes this younger demographic, most of whom he notes are students, to the higher proportion of leisure time that is available to younger adults:

> Adolescents and young adults have free time, few social responsibilities, and are relatively open to fantasy. Players cite marriages, full-time jobs, and graduate school as reasons for disengaging from the hobby, indicating that social responsibilities affect the free time necessary for participating in these games [p. 40].

Bordenet identifies a similar age group in his 2000 study of collectible card game players.[7] However, although demographic data concerning hobby gamers is relatively sparse, or at least closely guarded by the industry, a 2000 survey by Wizards of the Coast found that the age of gamers was rising steadily, with over 50 percent of gamers over the age of nineteen (Dancey, 2000).[8] Furthermore, while the survey indicates that those players who take up gaming during high school continue the pastime, there is also the suggestion that "the existing group of players is aging and not being refreshed by younger players at the same rate as in previous years." My responses suggest that *boardgamegeek* members constitute a significantly older demographic than did those who responded to Fine's and Bordenet's surveys. While there is no firm evidence that the two groups are linked, the notion that gamers constitute an aging demographic generally is borne out by research into video games that has seen the average age of players rising over the last two decades ("2008 Sales," 2008; Juul, 2010). A similar shift has been observed in comic book readership, another staple of geek culture (Deppey, 2004).[9]

It is interesting that Fine partially attributes the age demographics of role-playing gamers to the high proportion of leisure time that is available to younger adults. Jesper Juul, in appraising the shifting demographics of video gamers and the rise in popularity of "casual games," suggests that one explanation is to be found in the changing life circumstances of gamers (2010, p. 10). The idea that game playing habits are, in part, shaped by the shifting responsibilities of age is a key focus of his book on the topic. The notion that time constraints and other age-related responsibilities play a part in shaping the gaming habits of players is reflected in discussions on *boardgamegeek*, in particular where players attest to having played other forms of hobby game earlier in their lives. Board games generally, and eurogames specifically, are often identified as fitting far more comfortably into players' lives as they grow older:

> I know from my experience that shorter games have gotten me back into the hobby. As a young adult (college and shortly post-college), I used to play a lot of longer games- *1830, Axis and Allies, Civilization, Stellar Conquest, Junta,*

and others. With a few exceptions, like *Acquire*, that's pretty much what was available at the time if you wanted something better than what they sold at Toys 'R Us. I loved these games (and still do love *1830* and *Civilization*), but once I had a demanding job, a wife, a home to take care of (home ownership is much more work than an apartment), and a child, it really got to the point where I could only play a 5+ hour game once or twice a year. The other guys in my group were all in the same boat — we really wanted to play more, but getting everyone together for a long game was just too hard with our schedules [Hamburg, 2005].

The comparatively small time investment required by modern European board games when compared with earlier Anglo-American designs and other forms of hobby game can be attributed to the relative simplicity of rules and shorter playing times. The result are games that are far easier to fit into a player's life.

## *"The Hobby of the Over Educated"*

Survey data from the U.S. indicates that 1 percent of the total population have achieved a doctoral degree, while 28 percent have completed undergraduate studies (Bergman, 2006; Nettles and Millett, 2006). A comparison with survey respondents here indicates that *boardgamegeek* members constitute a highly educated segment of the population. That no less than 78 percent have attained at least an undergraduate degree, and 10 percent a doctoral degree, appears remarkable. However, earlier research into other hobby gaming forms suggests that these results are not as extraordinary as they initially seem. Fine's study of role-playing gamers also points to a high level of education among players (1983, p. 41),[10] as does Bordenet in his analysis of collectible card game players (2000).[11] A series of surveys conducted via SPI's *Strategy and Tactics* magazine throughout the 1970s and 1980s identifies a similar, if not higher, level of education among wargamers, leading Jim Dunnigan to describe the hobby as that of "the over educated" (1997).

The idea that hobby gamers represent, on the whole, a highly educated segment of society is borne out by the data concerning profession and income. As noted earlier, survey respondents on average earn 10 percent more than the median in the U.S. More revealing, perhaps, are the vocations that supply this income. 45 percent of *boardgamegeek* members earn their living in fields related to IT, engineering or education. Of particular interest are those working in computer or mathematics-related fields. Site co-owner Solko has suggested that those working with computers make up a sizeable proportion of members. Indeed, the relationship between strategy gaming and computing culture is occasionally discussed on the website:

I think you are going to find computer folks drawn to the hobby because of the nature of the underlying system design. There is going to be a respect for a well designed, elegant system in a game just like a well designed, elegant computer process. Games are procedural in nature and exercise the same thought processes as designing and writing code. In some senses, it's just like writing code, but you are using people and cardboard to execute the logic [Beyer, 2005].

The comparison of games and computer programming as procedural processes highlights an affinity between board gaming and other interests. Perhaps not surprisingly, these interests tend towards the intellectual. After all, the name of the website is *boardgamegeek*, a title with particular socio-cultural connotations.

## Gamer Geeks

The basic demographics of *boardgamegeek* that are presented here — highly educated males with an exaggerated interest in a particular form of intellectual recreation — serve to highlight the appropriateness of the site's appellation, and its common abbreviation: the geek. Hobby games are a part of a broader range of related hobbies and interests that together constitute what might be loosely termed "geek culture." In a general sense, the term geek refers to an individual who is "fascinated, perhaps obsessively, by obscure areas of knowledge and imagination" (Konzack, 2006). However, as Lars Konzack observes, the objects of this fascination tend towards those with an emphasis on individual fulfillment through the construction of fictional worlds. Science fiction, fantasy, games (both digital and non-digital), comic books and the broader culture of computing fall under this umbrella.

Although use of the term geek has somewhat pejorative origins (Smith, 1995, p. 12), as William Svitavsky notes, the rise of information technology and the attendant cultural shifts have seen the label "subverted ... into proud self-identification" (2001, p. 101). Konzack refers to the introspective pursuit of consistent alternative realities as "the third counter-culture" (2006). Citing longer periods of education, increased leisure time and the nature of Internet communities in facilitating the sharing of specialized knowledge, Konzack highlights the affinity between geeks and gaming culture generally:

From classic role-playing games, LARP, and strategic board games to trading card games and highly developed videogames, the geek culture is mixing fun with substance, rapidly changing how culture and aesthetics are perceived in our culture [2006].

Clearly the correlation between gaming and geek culture is apparent in the naming of *boardgamegeek*. Moreover, among members there is evidence of a degree of pride in identifying as geeks — a label that suggests perhaps an obsessive focus on games. The self-selecting sample that participated in this survey constitutes a devoted group of enthusiasts whose interest in games extends far beyond that of a casual player. Indeed, there is a marked difference between those who would, on occasion, sit down to play a modern board game and those who would identify themselves as being involved with "the hobby." This observation is also important in the context of gender among site members. While women constitute a very small proportion of the respondents to this survey, this should not be taken as indicative of the level of female participation in the play of board games generally, but rather of a focused engagement with all aspects of the hobby. As gaming writer Greg Aleknevicus comments of *boardgamegeek* members in general:

> I think this is a small percentage of the people who actually play European-style games. It's hard to imagine a more useful and interesting website than the *boardgamegeek* and yet the majority of people I game with do not visit it often, if at all. They're perfectly content to get their information from other players or the local game shop. The net's greatest influence is seeding information to the "super fans" who pass it along through more conventional means: word of mouth [2008].

*Boardgamegeek* user Tim Kilgore describes the role of these "super fans" in terms of how they shape the playing habits of more casual players:

> There are people that buy games and people that play them. Most gaming groups tend to have only one or two alpha-geeks (the guys that buy more than half of the games). These are the guys that tend to be the evangelists [2005].

The identification made here of "alpha geeks" and "super fans" is one that confirms my own experience of board gaming groups. Typically, one or two members who align themselves closely with the hobby pursue information on releases, make purchasing decisions and, ultimately, determine the games that more casual hobbyists play. These alpha geeks are almost invariably male.

Aleknevicus' use of the term "fans" in this context is also a particularly fitting one. Gordon Bruner and Scott Thorne have undertaken an extensive review of literature concerning the nature of fans and fandom, describing a fan as:

> A person with an overwhelming liking or interest in a particular person, group, trend, artwork or idea. Behavior is typically viewed by others as unusual or unconventional but does not violate prevailing social norms [2006, p. 53].

An interesting observation here is that the notion of fan culture does not necessarily suggest a counter-cultural stance that challenges societal norms. Although fans characteristically pursue the object of their fandom with considerable zeal, they rarely threaten or offer disruptive alternatives to the dominant ideologies of the society in which they are found. In the past, however, fan communities have typically been marginalized due to their apparent strangeness. Typically this has not been a result of the level of devotion (which is surely shared by enthusiasts of more mainstream activities such as sports), but by the perceived lack of "worthiness" of the specific subject (Jensen, 1992). Reflecting this, gaming writer Rick Heli tellingly compares board gaming culture in the U.S. with science fiction fandom:

> These games have mostly been a counterculture thing here. Those who are thoughtful, precise and analytical have often been ignored in this country, which gave rise to science fiction, the literature of the smarter who long to have their due — see A.E. van Vogt's Slan which features big brain aliens secretly masquerading as ordinary humans.... Games have had the very same sort of appeal in many cases [Heli in Eggert, 2005].[12]

The sense of community within gaming culture is comparable to that of science fiction fandom as they both share the heritage of an intellectual geek culture (Konzack, 2006) and are both outside of the mainstream.[13] More significantly, as David Hartwell notes, participation in science fiction fandom involves far more than the consumption of texts. Hartwell distinguishes fans not by the fact that they read science fiction, but by their participation in related activities such as conventions, collecting and the production of amateur content (1984, pp. 158–159). In the context of the gaming hobby, designer Rick Holzgrafe describes a similar level of involvement:

> Actually playing the durned things is only a small part of the hobby. There's collecting, searching for bargains and rare games, discussions of strategy, reading reviews, writing reviews, written session reports and verbal post-mortems, rule-lawyering, designing and discussing variations, deconstructing designs to see how the masters go about their craft, anticipating new releases, going to cons to talk with designers and see the latest stuff, making player aids and travel kits, making homemade copies of hard-to-find games, even creating your own games. There are a hundred ways to play with games when you can't actually play the games themselves [2006]

As Holzgrafe indicates here, hobby gaming not only involves the dedicated play of games but also the acquisition of specialized knowledge that can then be applied to discussion and critique of the form. This specialized knowledge, coupled with the relatively small size of the hobby gaming industry, tends to lead to a blurring of the line between consumer and producer, particularly when hobbyists circulate knowledge and texts back into the community. As dedicated gamers who actively engage with the hobby and each other in ways that surpass casual interest, hobbyists are comparable to many other fan communities in that they constitute a unique segment of the audience whose enthusiasm marks them as notable yet atypical.

The board gaming hobby is best described as a leisure subculture. I use this term, borrowed from Gary Fine's work on role-playing gamers (1983, p. 237), for two reasons. Firstly, the term neatly sidesteps the political connotations that are so often associated with more counter-cultural forms of subculture. In the case of hobbyists, there is no shared political dimension that accompanies engagement with the hobby. Hobby gamers are individuals who, attracted to a particular leisure pursuit, seek each other out and form loose aggregations around a shared interest. As cultural studies scholar Lawrence Grossberg observes:

> The fact that a group of people share a taste for some texts does not in fact guarantee that their common taste describes a common relationship. Taste merely describes people's different abilities to find pleasure in a particular body of texts rather than others [1992, p. 42].

The second reason for using this term is to highlight the fact that since the focus of the culture is a leisure pursuit, any attachments to other, more politicized groupings are unlikely to be eclipsed by participation in the hobby. Leisure subcultures rarely hold sway over individuals in the same way as do more counter-cultural examples, such as youth subcultures (Fine, 1983, p. 237).

Having distanced game hobbyists from more politicized and cohesive notions of subculture, it is important to note that leisure activities are not chosen on an ad hoc basis. Typically generalized preferences exist in which individuals "develop broader systems of leisure behavior consisting of a number of interdependent elements" (Roberts, 1978, p. 37). As I noted above, one of the "broader systems" that contributes to an interest in hobby gaming is that of geek culture. The embrace of particular board games as a legitimate and laudable cultural product is, as Konzack argues, typical of this:

> The geek (or at least the well-educated geek) marvels not just at anything, but seeks the quality in these cultural products. Not all games are equally good. The same goes for movies, comics, literature, etc. In that sense it's actually anti-post-modern, because they are not saying "anything goes." On the contrary, they are saying that these aesthetic contributions need to be taken seriously, demanding meticulous criticism and genuine research [2006].

Evidence of this type of "meticulous criticism" is abundant on *boardgamegeek*. Reviews and comparisons of games, debates over the merits of particular designers, discussions of the nuances of mechanics and the relative importance of theme — these are among the core activities that define the content of the website. As a community of interest, *boardgamegeek* provides a forum for hobbyists to thoroughly analyze every facet of board game design, production and play, an environment ideally suited to the geek tendency to focus tightly on one specific topic.[14]

Although not necessarily politicized, like many subcultures, gaming positions itself against a more conventional counterpart — in this case the mainstream board game market. The majority of respondents indicate that they rarely, if ever, play mainstream games (59 percent), while a further 35 percent play only occasionally.[15] This dismissal of mass-market board games is readily identifiable in discussions on the website, with the ubiquitous *Monopoly* often held up as a prime example of everything that gamers perceive is "wrong" with mainstream games:

> It's dismissed for several things which combine to a poor game design in today's terms — runaway leader, large luck which "scales up" the more the trading is done (and trading is very close to the only meaningful decision), player elimination, and a long play time for the amount of decisions made [Van Zandt, 2009].

> The distribution of properties is the most important determinate of who will win, and they are distributed randomly by rolling dice and moving onto them. A game in which the most important way to win is rolling the right number on a set of dice can never be terribly interesting [Spencer, 2008].

As suggested here, the principal reason cited for the dismissal of mainstream board games is that they rarely offer players meaningful decisions through which they might affect the outcome of the game. This esoteric criticism reflects the way in which hobbyists think critically about games as vehicles for entertainment. While for the non-gamer a board game might be seen as a way to pass a few idle hours without too much thought, for the hobbyist games are often only valued to the degree they allow players to engage with a system that produces meaningful decisions and outcomes. Through experience of a wide variety of games, players develop what might cynically be termed an elitist stance against mainstream games, precisely because they do not provide the kinds of pleasures that hobby gamers pursue in game experiences. Given the breadth of gaming experience of the typical hobbyist, the development of this perspective can be largely attributed to active and sustained engagement. Although a popular perspective in sociology attributes aesthetic taste to social origin[16] — certainly a factor in the broader development of geek leisure preferences — it is important to acknowledge the way in which enthusiasts operate as a "competing educational elite" (Jenkins, 1992, p. 86), recognizing the value and quality in particular cultural products. French sociologist Antoine Hennion describes this reflexive relationship between the individual and taste:

Tastes are not given or determined, and their objects are not either; one has to make them appear together, through repeated experiments, progressively adjusted.... Through comparison, repetition and so on, things that are less inert than they appear are made more present [2007, p. 101].

Of course, this is not to say that there are not other factors at work in developing a preference for a particular form of game over another. The opinions of friends and colleagues may have a significant impact on perceptions, an effect that is only magnified within a community of interest such as *boardgamegeek*. The various game awards also serve to shape preferences and guide purchasing decisions. Additionally, as writer and reviewer Michael Barnes suggests, the unique origins of eurogames may play a role in their current popularity:

> There's this cache of perceived exoticism and esotericism that comes with being into "German Games" that has created this mindset among the current generation of gamers that someone "foreign" equals "superior" and there's this whole new set of aesthetics founded largely on that concept [Barnes, 2006].

All of these factors — social origin, the opinions of friends, the views of peers in the community, and the accumulation of social capital — doubtless contribute to a propensity for playing a particular kind of game. Still, the fact remains that board game hobbyists tend to be passionate about their hobby, and, in their devotion to the pastime, analyze, critique and discuss games with a dedication that is comparable to fans of many other cultural products. Of course, in order to develop this level of specialist knowledge, hobbyists must play, and consequently buy, many games.

## Acquisition, Accumulation and Collection

> *In some ways I think we're more like beer, wine, or scotch enthusiasts. It's fun to know about a lot of different games: how they're alike or different, how a game reflects its designer, publisher, and the era or country in which it was published. How well a game works with different ages, or with different numbers of players.* — Dubin, 2008

Hobby gamers typically purchase many games through their participation in the hobby. The acquisition and accumulation of games is, for some, a significant part of their enjoyment of the pastime. Unlike classical abstract games, a specific game rarely becomes the focus of a player's attention to the exclusion of all others (Aleknevicus, 2001b). Although there are exceptions (such as those players who focus exclusively on the *18XX* series of railroad games), for the most part board game hobbyists move between different games with a particularly strong emphasis on new releases. Although lacking the focused dedication that is often seen with "lifestyle" games, such as *Chess* or *Go*, this diversification can, perhaps, offer a more general understanding of games:

> In a mono-gaming culture (where you played the same game over and over again), you'd become an expert on strategies for playing that game. In the more diverse gaming environment, you start thinking about game design more generally as you compare how different rules/mechanics shape the feel of different games. Individual games may be quicker, but you're still developing a cumulative knowledge of gaming which is a result of many hours of play/study/experience/thought [Hemberger, 2005].

The trend towards diversification and accumulation is reflected in an informal poll of active *boardgamegeek* members conducted in 2009, indicating that approximately 57 percent purchase one or more games a month, with over one-third purchasing two or more (Williams, 2008).[17] In part, the drive towards accumulation may be a result of there being far more games available in the marketplace than was previously the case:

> There are far too many good books to read them all in one lifetime. I think the "problem" is that good games are now almost like good books. There was a period of time where gamers had relatively little choice of what good games to play. Now we're spoiled for choice. That can lead to the tendency to jump around [Witt, 2005].

The aging player demographic and the associated rise in income is also a relevant factor. As gamer Ken Mixon notes, "nowadays, we're all grown up, have varying degrees of disposable income, and are able to succumb to our material wants more easily" (2005).

For many players it is the desire to experience new games that drives their acquisition of new titles, a focus that has come to be known as "the cult of the new." Often this may be a part of an ongoing quest for an optimal assortment of games that represents particular mechanics or themes, can accommodate a particular number of players, or, more generally, provide a game for every social setting. There is also a sense that some players are pursuing an indefinable "ideal" game experience:

> Ideally, I'd like to own just one game—and I'd like it to be a game that everybody I know (including me) absolutely loves and can never get enough of and will never tire of or outgrow. A game that brings back all the wondrous magic of childhood and excitement of good game play for everyone involved, every time. Anytime I buy a new game, it's in hopes of it turning out to be that one ultimate game [Carroll, 2008b].

Although it is possible to view this habitual acquisition of games as merely an example of unnecessarily conspicuous consumption, another perspective is that modern games are not suitable for repeated play. Arguably, eurogames lack the strategic depth that is attributed to classical abstracts and older, more complex hobby games. A common criticism is that new publications are often variations on previous titles, merely remixing and adapting familiar mechanics. Consequently, when original designs do appear there is a sense that the focus upon innovative mechanics in European designs does not lend itself to repeated plays:

> I think most new eurogames are disposable, something you expect to play maybe 5 to 7 times, are priced to match, and that's OK. Every so often you get a great one you play again and again, but you expect the numbers of those to be small. At some level, a chunk of the enjoyment of a game for me is just in the experience of playing it, of seeing how it works — experiencing the game as one might experience art or a movie — and that is obviously something that's not going to be as impressive the second (or third or whatever) time through…. They [German games] simply aren't designed to be played endlessly [Farrell, 2005].

In an early *Sumo* article, Charles Vasey questioned the reasons for accumulating games and in doing so, challenged readers to examine how many of their games had been played five or ten times (Dagger, 2006b). The resultant "five and ten" lists served as an indicator of how few games were being played repeatedly.[18] Nevertheless, discussion of the value of games is common on *boardgamegeek*, with users often drawing comparisons with other forms of consumer goods and activities[19]:

> With a board game what you're really talking about is bang for your economic buck. Even a $50+ board game compares favorably with the cost of an evening out, and it's going to have a much longer lifespan of enjoyment than a night at dinner and the movies — and a not unappreciable lifespan in comparison with video games [Jenkins, 2008].

The fact that hobby gamers have a tendency to purchase large numbers of games is most commonly a result of the desire to engage in new gaming experiences. Viewed in this light, the hobbyist is what marketing theorists term an "accumulator" (Belk *et al.*, 1988, p. 548) — that is, one who acquires significant quantities of related items for their utilitarian and/or aesthetic value. However, as Lawrence Belk observes, the accumulator is closely related to another role, that of the collector (1995, p. 67). In the acquisition of games, slippage between these two roles may often be unconscious:

> I have a suspicion that a lot of gamers periodically give in to a "collecting" urge even though they're not collectors. They only buy games to play, and they already have more than enough games to play, but when something shiny and new comes along, they still want it. And then at some point, they end up like me — looking at a closet full of unplayed games and wondering, What was I thinking? [Carroll, 2008a].

In a poll conducted by *boardgamegeek* user LankyEngineer in August 2008, close to half (48.7 percent) of respondents report owning more than 100 games (2008a).[20] More telling of the "cult of the new," however, is a similar survey conducted in 2009 indicating that over a quarter of *boardgamegeek* members have more than fifty unplayed games in their collections (Seldner, 2009).[21]

Although most hobbyists on *boardgamegeek* refer to their accumulated games as a "collection," there are some members for whom the acquisition of games is driven by factors beyond their functional or aesthetic value. For these hobbyists, the accumulation of games is not merely a side effect of their interest in play — it constitutes another form of engagement with the hobby. The distinction between the accumulator and the collector is an important one, since it grants the objects collected a value beyond the utilitarian, typically through the way that an object forms a part of a set (Belk *et al.*, 1988; Baudrillard, 1994, pp. 7–8). As collecting is a voluntary and organizational activity, it can also be considered a form of play itself (Katriel and Danet, 1994, p. 222).

J. Patrick Williams identifies the way in which consumption operates within hobby gaming subcultures (2006). Following the work of Fine (1989), he identifies the organizational level by which manufacturers nurture subculture through the constant provision of new products. Although the collectibility of board games is not nearly so overtly realized as it is with the collectible strategy games that Williams discusses, some game publishers do cater to the collecting urge in hobbyists. Series of games are numbered,[22] or, more often, are linked by similar packaging and presentation, thus increasing the perception that a range of games constitutes a "set."[23] More explicitly, it is extremely rare that a successful game does not result in at least one expansion. Indeed, many hobbyists attest to an urge towards completism in the accumulation of expansions related to a favored game.

A more nuanced way that this consumption operates is found in the way that a game collection contributes to identity and cultural capital within the community (Williams, 2006). Theorists interested in cultural understandings of consumption argue that the acquisition of goods acts as a way by which individuals can establish a sense of identity (Featherstone, 1991; Friedman, 1994; Mackay, 1997). For these writers, the value of consumer goods is not only found in their utility but in their capacity to define a sense of self and to express that identity to others. As gamer Gabe Alvaro observes:

> One could ... question whether the acquisition of more games is an activity wrapped in one's identity as viewed by others. For example, are you the "guy who is always bringing out the cool new games?" If you are, and you like the attention of being recognized as such, it's possible you might also be buying more new games to keep up that reputation [2008].

In the case of board game hobbyists, such identification can play an important role in establishing cultural capital within the community. The possession of a large number of games and the continual acquisition of newer titles implicitly suggests a greater degree of immersion in, and understanding of, the hobby. Additionally, the ownership of specific highly valued and/or rare games can indicate to other hobbyists a commitment to the culture that can bestow a degree of authenticity upon the individual.

The accumulation of games not only serves as a way by which players can establish capital within the culture, but it also identifies them to the broader society as a gamer. Large game collections demand a conspicuous amount of space in the home and can alter the domestic space significantly. Some players have dedicated gaming rooms to accommodate both play and storage, the display of which on the Internet site is generally greeted with enthusiastic appreciation.[24] As Belk and Wallendorf observe, the identity of a collector is often revealed through their collection:

> A collection is closely linked to the collector's identity; someone cannot excuse a collection by saying, "Well, I just happened to pick that up from some-where," or "someone gave that to me." Because a collection results from pur-poseful acquisition and retention, it announces identity traits with far greater clarity and certainty than the many other objects owned [1994, p. 240].

The existence and popularity of collection management tools on *boardgamegeek* are clear evidence of the relationship between game playing and game collecting among hobbyists. Discussions on the site regarding meth-ods of game storage and collection management are common, while images of large game collections are referred to as "game pr0n"—a clear allusion to the desirability of owning numerous games.[25]

While most hobbyists can be considered accumulators of games, there is a crossover with those who might be considered "real" collectors. In both of these roles the interest is expanded beyond that of merely playing games to other related activities, the reporting of which on *boardgamegeek* serves as cultural "glue" within the community. Collection and accumulation, activities found within many fan cultures, contribute to the development of specialized knowledge that can then be circulated back into the community.

## *A Shared Culture—Designers/Publishers/Players*

Henry Jenkins explores the relationship between media fans and content creators in his influential work *Textual Poachers*, describing how particular media texts are reworked and remediated by fans to create new meanings, often resulting in derivative works that are then re-circulated back into fan culture (1992). Media theorist John Fiske describes this process as "textual productivity," pointing to motivation and circulation as key differentiators between these products and "legitimate" texts:

> Fans produce and circulate among themselves texts which are often created with production values as high as any in the official culture. The key differences between the two are economic rather than ones of competence, for fans do not write or produce their texts for money; indeed, their productivity typically costs them money.
>
> There is also a difference in circulation; because fan texts are not produced for profit, they do not need to be mass-marketed, so unlike official culture, fan culture makes no attempt to circulate its texts outside its own community [1992, p. 39].[26]

In discussing the ways in which some leisure subcultures can be perceived as "copyrighted," Fine pays particular attention to games as a consumer good that are manufactured and purchased by members of a specific culture, with the entrepreneur providing the rules by which games are played (1989). However, as Fine notes, the communal nature of gaming subcultures often complicates understandings of authority, such that players perceive themselves as having ownership of the game, and thus the freedom to manipulate the rules and engage creatively with texts. Reflecting this, the history of hobby gaming culture is replete with examples of creative textual productivity that date back to long before the rise of the Internet. Early wargame magazines are filled with suggested rule variants — a tradition that is continued in fanzines such as *Sumo* and *Counter*— while many hobby games have inspired enthusiasts to develop alternative rules, maps, and scenarios that modify the base game. Role-playing games in particular encourage creativity through the provision of a rules system that is adaptable to a wide variety of scenarios and player-created narratives.

While the existence of an active participatory culture is not predicated upon the presence of digital communication technologies (Jenkins, 2002b; Merrick, 2004), the avenues of communication provided by the Internet have helped to foster a community of gamers who are able to circulate fan products to a large and geographically dispersed audience. The wide availability of digital design tools and the simplicity of downloading and printing graphic files have resulted in a wide variety of supplementary documents being available via the files section of *boardgamegeek*.

The most common form of downloadable fan-created content on the site arises from a perceived shortcoming of published games. Player aids, at-a-glance summaries of the process of play, are available for a large number of games. While some are simple text documents intended merely as a handy reference tool, others elaborately incorporate graphics from the original game in order to provide a document that not only assists in play but also augments the published game. In some cases, where the rulebook published with the game is considered inadequate, enthusiasts have entirely rewritten the rules in order to make the game more accessible for others.[27] Given the European origins of many games, rules translations too are common.

While these forms of content creation are undertaken out of perceived necessity, more elaborate examples of textual productivity can be seen in the many fan-produced expansions for games. Examples include numerous expansions for *Carcassonne*,[28] fan-created maps for rail games such as *Age of Steam* and *Railroad Tycoon* (Drover and Wallace, 2005), and the development of new cards for games such as *Dominion* and *Race for the Galaxy* (Lehmann, 2007).

Interestingly, perhaps due to the often-tenuous relationship between theme and mechanics in many eurogames, another common form of fan-created content involves re-theming games with other icons of geek culture. Days of Wonder's popular cooperative game *Shadows over Camelot* (Cathala and Laget, 2005), has been re-imagined in the realm of *Monty Python's Holy Grail*, while Reiner Knizia's Egyptian-themed auction game *Ra* is transposed to a world of surreal horror inspired by H. P. Lovecraft in *Rathulhu*. The ancient war-themed card game *Battle Line* (Knizia, 2000c) — itself a re-theming of the original *Schotten Totten* (Knizia, 1999e)[29] — can be downloaded from the site in a file that replaces all of the cards with characters from the television series *The Simpsons*. In cases where games have long been out of print, some fans have taken it upon themselves to produce freely available downloads of entire games, with graphical components either rendered specifically for this purpose or appropriated from copyright-free sources.[30]

The fact that this type of fan activity occurs largely unhindered speaks to the relationship between game hobbyists and the small industry that caters to them. As Richard Busch observes, a consequence of the 20th century shift towards the domestic sphere in the practice of leisure was that pastimes became less subject to the hegemonic values of society (1990). Hobby businesses particularly tend to grow out of small entrepreneurial foundations that are commonly the work of hobbyists themselves. Thus, the micro-industries that sprang from this shift are not entirely "impositions of monolithic capital" (p. 19) but have come to embody a negotiated relationship between the consumer and the producer. Due to the fact that the majority of individuals working within the hobby gaming industry are themselves members of the culture, the industry operates, for the most part, in a manner quite dissimilar to that of the prototypical capitalist business (Winkler, 2006).

Since hobby board gaming occupies such a niche in English-speaking countries, significant value is placed on word-of-mouth marketing. A game that becomes successful will rarely, if ever, do so due to intense advertising campaigns or carefully considered corporate marketing techniques. Thus, business owners are aware that gamers can have a significant role in the success of individual titles. Consequently, companies have a particularly strong need to communicate effectively with those hobbyists who tend to make purchasing decisions and act as "tastemakers" for the hobby. To this end, many designers and publishers utilize *boardgamegeek* as a point of intersection with the broader gaming community, and a large number maintain active accounts on the website.[31] In the case of designers, many have posted to the site to clarify rule queries and answer specific questions concerning games they have designed, with some contributing essays and anecdotes explaining the origin of games and the nature of the design process. On occasion designers have been known to incorporate feedback from the website into re-issues of a game.[32]

One especially useful aspect of the relationship between gamers and the individuals and companies who make games is the ability to gauge the potential demand for a product before committing to publication. The ability of publishers to effectively measure consumer interest is useful in deciding to translate successful European titles into English, as with Z-Man Games' reprint of the 2008 *Spiel des Jahres* special prize winner *Agricola*. A number of game companies have reprinted games specifically due to their venerated status among hobby gamers. A good example of this model is found in the small publisher Valley Games who have successfully reprinted Karl Heinz Schmiel's *Die Macher* and the long-out-of-print Avalon Hill titles *Hannibal: Rome vs. Carthage* (Simonitch, 1996) and *Titan*.

The close ties between the hobby gaming industry and its customers can often result in hobbyists having a more formal relationship with publishers. Play-testing, the process of development and refinement through iterative play sessions, is often outsourced to gaming groups where in-house resources are limited. Translation is another area where enthusiasts can, and do, contribute. While amateur translations are common on *boardgamegeek*, on occasion these texts are used in the published versions of the game.[33] At conventions it is often hobbyists who are enrolled to demonstrate games to prospective customers.

Given the insights into game design and the industry generally that hobbyists typically acquire, it is not surprising to find that many decide to take their interest further by designing and/or publishing their own games. At the simplest level this typically involves the development of "print and play games" that can be downloaded from *boardgamegeek* at no cost. Some designers have had games picked up by existing publishers, while others have self-published their games. Although the most popular site for the discussion of game design on the Internet is the *Boardgame Designers Forum* (2009), an active game design community does exist on *boardgamegeek*. The most important role that the site plays for prospective designers and publishers lies in the ability to disseminate information to hobbyists. Jeremiah Lee, the designer of *Zombies in my Pocket* (2009a), highlights the importance of the community in raising awareness of what was originally a free print and play game:

> The Geek was a big influence on my process, as I hadn't heard of PnP games until I came here, and without all the people that printed, played, loved, and rated ZimP, it wouldn't have found a publisher [Lee, 2009b].

Jackson Pope of Reiver Games is an example of an independent publisher for whom the *boardgamegeek* community has been significant in raising awareness of his games:

> I designed *Border Reivers*[34] a couple of years before I found the Geek, but coming here definitely gave me the impetus to self-publish. I made 100 copies by hand and they sold out within 11 months, largely due to the Geek. So then I published 300 copies of Yehuda's *It's Alive!*[35] ... again by hand, and again it sold out within a year. Since then I've gone into it full-time and got a re-print of *It's Alive!* manufactured for me and a third game, *Carpe Astra*,[36] by Ted Cheatham and I [2009].

A wonderful example of the relationship between the hobbyist community and the industry can be found in Steve Zamborsky's game *Cleopatra's Caboose* (Zamborsky, 2010). In 2005, *boardgamegeek* user Chuck Uherske created a tongue-in-cheek geeklist entitled *Things I'm Sick Of!*, which lampooned particularly overused tropes within the gaming hobby (2005).[37] Listed among these were Egyptian-themed games, auction games and train games. In a response to the list, amateur designer Zamborsky commented that he was currently working on "a game that auctions off trains. In Ancient Egypt." Another user chimed in with the (again, tongue-in-cheek) suggestion that the game should be titled "Cleopatra's Caboose." Zamborsky describes how the game came to be:

> When I read that Geeklist, I thought it would be pretty funny to comment that I was working on a game that combined several of those elements, even though I wasn't. Apparently, my subconscious thought otherwise and my mind had been processing some things that I wasn't aware of, because next thing I know I'm writing down notes for Caboose after waking up one day. Some more notes later, I realized I had to create the prototype to test the ideas and make sure that what I came up with worked. The rest, as they say, is history [2009].

History, in this case, saw the game picked up for development by Z-Man Games, with characters whose names are derived partly from historic railroad barons and partly from Egyptian gods.[38] Released in late 2010, *Cleopatra's Caboose* is an elaborate in-joke, an inspired parody of modern strategy games that reflects the close relationship between hobbyists and game publishers.

*Cleopatra's Caboose*— developing train networks in ancient Egypt! (image by Gary James, courtesy Z-Man Games).

As is common within niche hobbies, the line between consumer and creator within the board gaming hobby is frequently blurred by the activities of enthusiasts, whether this is in the form of developing supplementary materials for existing products or through more formal participation in the industry. Board game hobbyists are not passive consumers, detached from the industry that supports their interests; they share a "sense of identity and feeling of inclusiveness" engendered by a mutual enthusiasm for the activity of gaming (Winkler, 2006, p. 148). Not surprisingly, then, there is a tendency to share this enthusiasm with those outside of the hobby.

## The Gaming Evangelist

> *Our hobby grows by word of mouth. Get one person in, and they bring in one more. They bring in a family, their children bring their friends, their friends bring their parents. I got my manager to play* Take It Easy. *Her boy loved it. She got all her friends to play it, their kids loved it, bought it, and even after leaving the dept, she's still asking me where to get it.*— EYE of NiGHT, 2005

Perhaps the most interesting trait of hobby board gaming culture in terms of its relationship to the mainstream lies in the belief shared by many members that hobby games — particularly eurogames — have the potential for far broader appeal. While a degree of enthusiasm for sharing is to be expected in any hobby, there is a perception that unlike other forms of hobby gaming, which require a degree of involvement with a marginalized subculture, eurogames could achieve considerable popularity given sufficient exposure. After all, since the roots of eurogames lie in titles that are designed to be played by the family rather than by dedicated hobbyists, it seems natural to some hobbyists that these should supplant mainstream American games. As a result, many players see themselves in an evangelical role, with every person a potential recruit to the hobby.

*Boardgamegeek* members commonly talk about the successes and failures they have experienced in attracting new players, and discuss ways in which they might be more effective in drawing in friends and family to share the perceived pleasures of the hobby. Frequent discussions as to which games are most effective in introducing newcomers have led to the adoption of the term "gateway games" to describe aesthetically attractive and relatively accessible games. A common belief is that many non-gamers view board games in a negative light due to their previous exposure to mainstream games:

> I will keep trying to introduce TGOO[39] to people who haven't seen them for the sheer satisfaction that I get from watching someone's face when they ask which piece can they move and be told, "Any of them!" Which direction? "Any." Etc. There are people out there that really believe (because they've never seen another type of game) that you roll dice, count spaces and do what the new space says [Russell, 2008].

As hobbyist Scott Russell suggests here, there is more to introducing players to the hobby than sitting them down in front of an unfamiliar game. In the USA the image persists that board games are the domain of children. Although modern hobbyists might see their choice of games as being a world apart from other styles of games, this perception is not commonly shared. As one hobbyist comments:

> Board games just aren't as social[ly] acceptable in the U.S. That's what it boils down to. On the other hand, it's not as bad to have DVD collection of movies, TV shows, documentaries, and concerts that fill up an entire wall. It's not as "socially awkward" to put on face paint, scream at referees, and easily spend hundreds to thousands of $$ for season tickets for sports games [Yao, 2008].

From another perspective, it is not so much that board games themselves are perceived as problematic, but the degree of enthusiasm and interest shown by hobbyists. Negative stereotypes that have historically been attached to the enthusiastic pursuit of gaming and other "geek" interests persist. As a consequence of this perceived stereotyping, some members attest to not mentioning their hobby for fear of such connotations, while others describe creative ways in which to distance themselves from this image:

> I always stress that I play German import games. It makes it sound really exotic, and thus makes you sound less obsessive and geeky. The response is always, "Huh, that's interesting." and then I can give the spiel about the differences between American and German games. Something like, "German games have been refined so that they emphasize a wonderful and dynamic social experience ... blah blah blah." The key is to try and talk about them as if you were talking about fine wine or antiques [Carr, 2005].

The idea that the play of games by adults is not socially acceptable in the U.S. is complicated by the huge rise in popularity of video games over the last three decades. Particularly in the last ten years it has become far more acceptable for adults to not only engage with games, but to incorporate them into their lives on a level comparable with other recreational media. Strangely, while the millions who play these games regularly attest to the popularity of games in general, it would seem that there still remains something a little too "geeky" about gathering with friends to play with physical components.

One explanation commonly offered for the dismissal of board gaming as a legitimate leisure pursuit draws on the perceived intellectualism of geek culture generally and board games specifically. This line of thought among hobbyists runs that since board gaming draws such a relatively well-educated audience, it is predictable that the majority would not enjoy them:

> I can't speak for the world, here in the U S of A, a vast majority of people really don't want to think. Not deep down. Either because they are tired or busy or stressed or simply uninformed, they don't seek out anything but "normal." Look at popular music, popular television, popular news channels, popular political commentators, popular books, popular anything, and you'll see a preponderance of "please don't make me think." ... People (for the most part) want to be spoon-fed their entertainment. Occasionally they will enter a thought-provoking discourse or activity, but it's usually the exception and rarely the norm. Even gateway games make you think. And as a nice diversion, they are a nice diversion. But that's what they will remain. A momentary diversion in between spoon-feedings [Winter, 2008].

This attitude bears comparison to the notion of "slans" in science fiction fandom — those who consider themselves in possession of an unspoken truth bestowed by superior intelligence and familiarity with particular texts. However, where slans perceived their authority to be grounded in a tacit understanding of science and the world-changing potential of technology (James, 1994, p. 136), the evangelist gamer occupies a far more conservative position. Here, the "truth" that is celebrated is the benefit of active participation in an intellectually challenging and social hobby as set against a society where mainstream entertainment media are viewed as passive and undemanding. As gamer Nikodemus Solitander observes, if modern board games are ever to be accepted into the mainstream, perhaps what is required is a fundamental shift in the values of society:

> I see ... the question to be similar to "How can we make gay erotica mainstream within the book industry?" You'll have your occasional gay erotica book breaking over — but it'll be hard to make the whole genre mainstream without a societal change in values. A societal change in values would within board games convert into people leaving the computer game ideal of fast setups, no rule books, pick-up and deliver, and instead opt for regular quality family time and meeting up with friends, developing patience (to read a rule book) and a will to learn (and teach) rules. I'd love for this to happen but I don't think it will — not for a long time [2008].

Not surprisingly, others share Solitander's appraisal that it is not so much a lack of intelligence or education but a predisposition towards learning new game rules that is lacking:

> I think a lot of us take the patience and concentration required to understand most of the popular games on this site for granted.... I've sat down (more than once) with well-educated, intelligent (but non-gaming) people, who have sat there getting exasperated as I've tried to explain the rules of something as "simple" as *Carcassonne* to them [King, 2008].

> Almost every game that I like to play (except for some party games) have rules that are too detailed and too difficult for most non-gamers to bother to understand. It's not that they're dumb. Far from it. But would a person watch TV if it came with an instruction manual that made you read carefully for 20 minutes or so before you can activate it? And if you had to do that every time you changed the channels (new show = new game), don't you think most people would skip it? [Cox, 2008].

The conviction that eurogames might gain mainstream popularity given sufficient exposure is one of the most interesting qualities of modern board gaming culture. Although some hobbyists are dismissive of the potential appeal of board games, it has been my experience that most are, to some degree, actively involved in evangelizing the hobby to others. In part this can be attributed to the fact that the play of board games requires a consistent supply of opponents, but it is more commonly inspired by a genuine desire to share the pleasures of the hobby.

Ironically perhaps, the one area where eurogames are making significant inroads into mainstream gaming culture is through the adaptation of popular titles for a variety of video game platforms. As mentioned earlier, titles such as *The Settlers of Catan* and *Carcassonne* have been successfully deployed on Microsoft's Xbox console, while an increasing number of lesser-known games are finding a new home on smart phones and tablet devices. Whether these implementations can still be considered board games is a matter for debate. Certainly in cases where players are not co-located there are likely significant ramifications for the way that play unfolds as a social activity. Still, the success of these titles points to the resilience of European-style designs in crossing media boundaries. While the chances of *The Settlers of Catan* replacing *Monopoly* as a family staple are perhaps small, all indications are that games that were previously only known to a niche audience are beginning to gain some visibility outside hobbyist circles.

## The Gaming Hobbyist

> Involvement in a leisure world presumes a store of knowledge — information that enables the competent doing of that activity. — Fine, 1989

While hobbyists involved with a site like *boardgamegeek* may be seen as a new phenomenon enabled by the Internet, the existence of gaming communities centered on a particular field of interest is not exclusive to digital environments. Gaming conventions and dedicated fanzines were in existence long before the advent of the Internet and served to create what Benedict Anderson terms an "imagined community"— that is, a sense of community which arises not from geographic location but from a mental image held by members which affirms their affinity (Anderson, 1983). For a long time there have been people who call themselves "gamers." Yet, as Bruner and Thorne note, for the isolated fan with no social outlet for discussion of his fanaticism, online spaces offer a very convenient medium through which to engage with others and actively participate in a shared culture (2006). As gamer Marshall Miller observes:

> I think that the percent of the population playing games has likely not changed in the last 30 years (I say thirty because video games have irrevocably stolen a portion of game players). However, I believe that, via the internet, gamers are no longer isolated. Before, gamers were limited to the portion of the population they knew personally. Now, we are seeing a new degree of gamer interconnectivity. Simply put, we are now just more aware of each other and it only seems like there are more of us [Miller, 2008].

The interconnectivity that Miller refers to here is manifest on *boardgamegeek* through the discussion, evaluation, critique and comparison of games and play that dominates the site. Moreover, discussion is not limited to the games themselves, but branches out into reflection upon the industry, the relationship between hobbyists and the broader community, and a plethora of related interests.

As active participants on a website devoted to board and table games, survey respondents in this book can be considered representative of hobbyist board gamers generally. Their familiarity with a broad range of games, and their active participation in the hobby, differentiates them from the occasional player and is manifest in a variety of ways. Active participation in the hobby involves the accumulation of specialist knowledge about game forms. Consequently, there is a tendency to eschew mainstream games for their perceived lack of meaningful decision-making in play. Although enthusiasm is typically marked by the ongoing acquisition of new games, as is common in other forms of hobby gaming, players have a relationship with the industry that is far more involved than that of a mere consumer. Hobbyists may develop their own game variants, participate in the creation of content that augments existing games, and, in some cases, contribute to the hobby through the creation of their own games. Reflecting this blurring of the line between producer and consumer, members of the hobby gaming industry are, more often than not, members of the gaming subculture themselves. Not surprisingly, the shared enthusiasm for board gaming — particularly eurogames — is not only manifest within the culture, but is also actively evangelized within the broader community.

My reason for emphasizing the degree of involvement with gaming culture in this chapter is that, as Fine notes, active participation in a leisure world involves the accumulation of specialized knowledge, not only *about* the activity but also concerning how that activity is competently performed (1989). Of course, the idea that there is a "right way" to play a particular game or that there exists a formal set of guidelines that shape play is disingenuous. Hobbyist board gamers are a specific subset of the broader population whose attitudes to and experience of game play should be understood within this context. With the understanding that hobby gamers are not typical board game players, the following analysis of player motivations, expectations and experience provides insight into the way this particular group understands competitive social play.

# 7

# *The Pleasures of Play*

*Gaming isn't about rolling dice and moving your piece around a track. Gaming is about interactions, decisions and social skills.* — Alan Moon, in Aleknevicus, 2002

In previous chapters I have outlined the demographics of board game hobbyists, providing an overview of who they are, the games they play and a variety of ways in which they actively participate in the culture of hobby gaming. In identifying survey respondents as particularly active participants within hobby gaming culture, I have sought to differentiate this group from those who merely play board games as an occasional distraction. Although many people play hobby games, only a small percentage of this number are what might be considered "hobbyists." For these people, hobby games have a particularly strong attraction — broadly speaking, they constitute a significant part of the individual's leisure habits. It is clear that activities other than the playing of games constitute an important part of these players' enjoyment of the hobby. With this important distinction in mind, I now turn my attention to the specific question of how players derive enjoyment from the play of modern board games.

To this end, in this chapter I examine those elements of board games and the experience of play from which players derive enjoyment. Firstly, I review previous theories of motivation and enjoyment as they pertain to games generally. This provides a context for a discussion of specific mechanics that are commonly employed in modern board games and their relationship to player enjoyment. I then identify and discuss broader features that are commonly found in board games and the degree to which these elements contribute to enjoyment in games. Drawing on survey responses, I focus particularly on player preferences in terms of the way that games elicit in-game interaction. Finally, I discuss the general experience of board game play and how players view facets of this experience as significant in the overall pleasure they derive from the play of modern board games.

## Play, Games and Motivation

It has long been understood that play is, in itself, intrinsically self-motivating (Verenikina *et al.*, 2003). In the play of children — a topic that preoccupied early theorists — the inherent attraction of play led many scholars to theorize its purpose as instinctive and functional. Not surprisingly, these early ideas were largely founded upon the physical play of young children who, it was imagined, had an excess of energy that was not available to adults engaged in work activities.[1] Subsequent theories have retained this functional purpose in attributing to play an important role in the psychological,[2] cognitive,[3] and social development of children.[4]

In discussing the propensity for play in human beings more generally, Johan Huizinga dismisses this emphasis on function, instead proposing that play — and, more specifically, higher forms of play, such as the contest — operate in the realm of ritual (1950, pp. 46–75). Huizinga argues that no benefit need necessarily be gained from play activities since they are entirely intrinsically motivating: "[Play] interpolates itself as a temporary activity satisfying in itself and ending there" (p. 9). Thus, the social, cognitive or physical benefits that might arise from play are not seen as essential ingredients in the motivation to play, rather the activity is entered into purely for the experience it provides (Rodriguez, 2006).

The idea that certain activities are entered into solely for the experience they offer has been elaborated upon by psychologist Mihaly Csikszentmihalyi in his seminal work *Flow: The Psychology of Optimal Experience* (1990). Originally advanced in the 1970s, Csikszentmihalyi's work identifies flow as a state of "optimal experience" that is brought about by a challenging task with clear goals that requires a focus of attention:

> For an event to offer the potential for flow experience it must be perceived by actors as intrinsically rewarding, satisfying in its own right.... In flow experiences, self-consciousness is eliminated. Action and awareness are tightly and reflexively intertwined, merging together [Mitchell, 1988, p. 55].

A number of writers have argued that flow is a state also associated with the play of video games (Holt and Mitterer, 2000; Sherry, 2004; Cowley *et al.*, 2008) and of games generally (Koster, 2005, p. 98; Salen and Zimmerman, 2004, pp. 336–339). This pursuit of optimal experience — "satisfying in its own right" — reflects Huizinga's assertion regarding the intrinsic motivations of play. Although games are widely understood to be intrinsically motivating, the reasons for enjoyment are myriad and may vary widely from game to game and from player to player. Generally speaking, however, we can assume that the anticipation of some form of enjoyment is a contributing factor to the reasons that people engage in particular leisure activities. While it is not the only factor, it is certainly an important element in the motivation to play.

Game designer Raph Koster attributes the inherent fun in all games to the act of cognitive problem solving, suggesting that the pleasure of game play can be summarized as "the act of mastering a problem mentally" (2005, p. 90). Nicole Lazzaro focuses on emotion as the central source of player enjoyment in games (2004). In doing so, she identifies "four keys" that, she proposes, unlock emotions within players: the "hard fun" that is found in problem solving; the "easy fun" derived from immersion; the "altered states" produced by internal experience; and the "people factor" that comes from viewing games as mechanisms for social experiences. In a more generalized framework, Marc LeBlanc proposes "eight kinds of fun" that are commonly derived from video games: sensation, fantasy, narrative, challenge, fellowship, discovery, expression and submission (2005).

These are just a few examples of the models that have been proposed to explain player enjoyment of games.[5] In reviewing these models, it is clear that pleasure is derived from a wide variety of emotions and experiences that arise from the play of games. Why then, given the variety of game forms available within a society, does an individual choose to play a particular game or style of game?

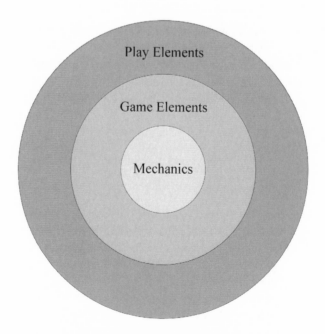

Figure 7.1: Three levels of player enjoyment.

As a means of identifying possible reasons in relation to modern board games, survey respondents were asked a number of questions concerning the enjoyment of play. Firstly, players were surveyed as to which common board game mechanics they particularly enjoyed. Secondly, players were asked to indicate the degree to which a number of specific game elements contribute to their enjoyment. Finally, players were questioned as to the pleasures they derived from the experience of board game play generally. This series of increasingly broader questions forms the basis for a model of player enjoyment in this chapter (see Figure 7.1). The answers to these questions offer a clear picture as to why it is that hobbyists choose to play one game over another, and why they choose to play board games generally.

## Player Enjoyment— Mechanics

As I have discussed, eurogames — and board games generally — tend to draw on a common pool of core mechanics. In this section I wish to explore the extent to which players associate their enjoyment with the implementation of specific mechanics. Jesper Juul describes the experience of being a gamer as "the simple feeling of a pull, of looking at a game and wanting to play it," noting that "the [video] game's pull is a subjective experience that depends on what games you have played, your personal tastes, and whether you are willing to give the game the time it asks for" (2010, p. 2). Although the description of a "pull" is somewhat vague, the idea that play preferences are dependent upon previous experiences with other games and subjective notions of taste applies equally to board games.[6] Hence, as a starting point for the discussion of what it is that attracts players to eurogames, my survey included a question that asked respondents to indicate the degree to which they enjoy particular mechanics within games. The description of mechanics was taken from categories on *boardgamegeek* in order that the terms used would be familiar to respondents. Figure 7.2 summarizes the responses to this question, reducing the data to a binary distinction between mechanics that are "rarely if ever enjoyed" and those that are "usually or always enjoyed."[7]

An immediate observation that arises from this figure is the degree to which no particular mechanic stands out as being markedly more popular than others. Rather, there is a gradual scale that highlights an aversion to luck-based mechanics. Not surprisingly, the most commonly enjoyed mechanics are those that are closely associated with the eurogame genre (e.g., variable phase order,[8] area control, tile placement and action points).[9] In contrast, the least popular mechanics are those that limit the player's ability to make mean-

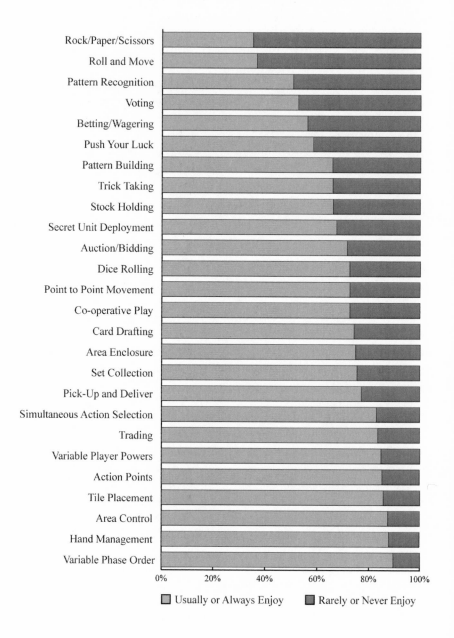

Figure 7.2: To what degree do you generally enjoy the following mechanics/game styles in board and table games? (summarized for clarity).

ingful decisions (e.g., roll and move, rock/paper/scissors, pattern recognition), a concern that is reflected in the eschewal of mainstream games discussed earlier.

## *Player Enjoyment— Game Traits/Elements*

The overall impression from the responses above is that players do not generally favor a particular mechanic but rather the gestalt experience provided by their implementation. As one player describes:

> Game mechanics are not as important as the way in which they are implemented. Depending on the circumstances, I like drinking coffee or a soda or a beer. But a coffee must be a good coffee, and the beer must be a good beer [R330].

As discussed earlier, eurogames typically involve a mix of mechanics that combine to produce an overall game experience. An alternative approach, then, is to ask respondents which elements of this overall experience contribute to enjoyment. As a part of preparing my survey I constructed a list of elements and/or traits that are commonly found in modern board games in order to

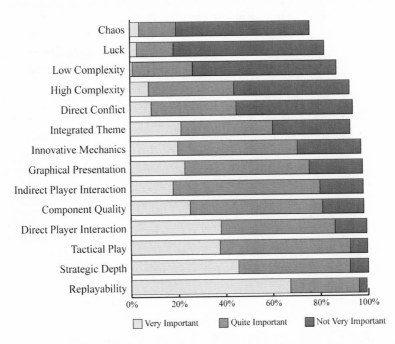

Figure 7.3: To what degree is the presence of the following elements important to your enjoyment of board and table games?

gauge their importance for hobbyists. This list of constitutive elements was developed through my own observations and through analysis of critical commentary on the hobby from various sources. While the meanings of these are mostly transparent, some have more domain-specific denotations within the board gaming hobby and are explained in more depth in the sections where I discuss their importance for players. Survey respondents were asked to what degree the presence of these elements was important in their enjoyment of board and table games. The responses to this question are detailed in Figure 7.3.

## Replayability

*The more the game gets played, the more you discover its depth.* — R512

The first observation to be gathered from these results is that respondents consider the potential for replayability as the most important factor in their enjoyment of games.[10] While in theory all games are replayable inasmuch as the rules are repeatable (Salen and Zimmerman, 2004, p. 123), different forms of game lend themselves more readily to repeat plays. Highlighting this variability, Juul identifies a basic distinction between what he terms "games of progression" and "games of emergence" (2005, pp. 67–83). The former describes those games in which the linear and consecutive nature of the challenges presented results in a "predefined sequence of events" that a player must traverse. The most obvious example in hobby gaming is the role-playing game, which first introduced progression and an explicit narrative as structural traits of games in the early 1970s.

The nature of games of progression is that, although the rules are repeatable, there is rarely any motivation to repeat a sequence of events once the designed challenge of the game has been overcome. In the case of role-playing games — which provide a framework for play rather than an explicit sequence of challenges — the players will complete one quest and embark on another. In the case of progressive video games, however, when the challenges have been surpassed, players rarely have a strong motivation to re-attempt them.[11] The result is that such games have a limited potential for play and are "purchased, used and eventually cast away like most other consumable goods" (Hunicke *et al.*, 2004).

Generally speaking, board games are what Juul terms games of emergence[12]:

Emergence is the primordial game structure, where a game is specified as a small number of rules that combine and yield large numbers of game variations for which the players then design strategies for dealing with [Juul, 2002].

Derived from systems theory, science and philosophy, emergence describes the way that complex patterns arise from a relatively simple set of rules. As Juul notes, most multiplayer games are emergent in that they are comprised of a relatively simple ruleset (in comparison with games of progression) that reveals complex patterns through play (2005, pp. 73–75). The opportunity that emergence offers for repeated plays is considered of primary importance for survey respondents when discussing their enjoyment of games:

> I like to play a game often enough to have some real insight about options and paths to victory [R404].

> [I enjoy] innovative mechanics that invite a lot of replay until you feel you have grasped the strategy and tactics [R130].

> I like the familiarity of a game I know rather than constantly trying new games, so a game has to have a lot of replay value, but ideally also not be too intimidating to beginners, as I play a lot with friends who aren't experienced gamers [R744].

> I like a game to have layers, to grow and master more components the longer you play it, rather than be too simple to enjoy after the first few times [R469].

Given the observations made earlier regarding the propensity for gaming hobbyists to amass a large collection of games, the emphasis upon replayability here is somewhat ironic. Yet, clearly, survey respondents do appreciate the opportunity that a game offers for repeated play.

## Intellectual Challenge — Strategy and Tactics

> *Intellectual challenge — this is why I strive to win, but don't mind losing. It is the challenge that is important.* — R735

Hobbyists commonly discuss the importance of replayability in terms of the opportunity for the exploration of tactics and strategy that familiarity with a particular game provides. Not surprisingly, then, survey respondents cited the presence of strategic depth and opportunities for tactical play as highly significant in their enjoyment of particular games. In the context of games, strategy is broadly understood as the devising and implementation of longer-term plans in the pursuit of a given goal, while tactics refers to the momentary decisions by which short-term (lower order) goals are achieved (Järvinen, 2009, p. 146). Strategic depth and the opportunity for tactical play offer players decisions with either long- or short-term consequences. That players enjoy the presence of these elements is reflective of the way in which they value the intellectual challenge that is derived from meaningful decisions within a game.

The presence of strategic depth in a given game is directly connected with the emergent traits of the abstract game system. For a game to offer players meaningful decisions, it should have sufficient complexity to afford a variety of strategies by which players can pursue the game goals without being so unpredictable that the development of long-terms plans is impossible. The possibility of anticipating the behavior of a game system is fundamental to the development of longer-term strategies. This opportunity for the formulation and execution of long-term plans is considered by survey respondents to be an important factor in their enjoyment of games. 92 percent of respondents indicate that strategic depth is either quite important (47 percent) or very important (45 percent) to their enjoyment of games:

> Strategic depth and meaningful choices are the most important. My favorite games provide depth while using simple rules [R111].

> I really enjoy when a game promotes creativity in strategy and allows the chance for big moves that catch everyone off guard [R742].

> Strategy games that have high levels of social interaction are the type of game I derive the most pleasure from. They need not be overly complex, but they should have enough depth that it makes them difficult to master [R180].

> I enjoy games which have multiple strategies that can achieve a win. I enjoy trying the different strategies. A game also has to be challenging enough. I usually enjoy the games I lose on the first play more on later plays than the games I win right away [R280].

In the context of board games, tactics can be understood as the implementation of specific actions that further a player's immediate position and/or limit the possibilities for another player to further their position. 92 percent of respondents consider the opportunity for tactical play as either quite important (55 percent) or very important (37 percent) in their enjoyment of a game. A tactical play may form a part of a broader strategy or it may be an isolated action — a move of opportunity. Tactics are typically prompted by the behavior of the game system or by that of other players. The opportunity for this type of reactive play is considered by survey respondents to be a significant contributor in their enjoyment of specific games:

> [I enjoy] developing a plan and then implementing it on the board and making the necessary adjustments in response to your opponents' movements and strategies [R500].

> [I enjoy] Trying to make the best of the situation presented to me by my opponents' play and the luck of the game [R642].

> I enjoy solving the tactical problems, either complex or simple, presented by a real opponent [R667].

Eurogames can be largely tactical and/or highly strategic. Although the term "strategy games" is often used to describe the genre, in actuality they typically offer a mix of strategy and tactics in much the same way as do classical abstract games. The common feature in describing these two elements is the way in which their implementation in a specific game affords meaningful choices to the player. Strategic and tactical choices are only significant inasmuch as the decision itself is a difficult one. Where one strategy is obviously more successful than all others, the play of a game becomes predictable and uninteresting (Juul, 2005, p. 59). Similarly, if one tactical play is obviously more beneficial than any alternative, a game can come to feel "scripted"— that is, the play of the game does not require any decision-making on the part of the player.

Given the mix of strategic and tactical play that is encompassed by a typical eurogame, it is interesting to note that survey respondents generally consider the *degree of complexity* of a given game to be relatively unimportant. The suggestion here is that players evaluate games in terms of the framework for decision-making they present rather than the inherent complexity (or lack thereof) of the game system. Thus, a deeply strategic game such as *Caylus* is situated within the same genre as a tactical exercise such as *Carcassonne*; when implemented effectively, both strategy and tactics offer players intellectually challenging choices that provide meaningful play. However, since the roots of eurogames in family gaming generally tends to result in games with a relatively simple ruleset, this challenge is rarely engendered by the operation of the game system itself, but rather by the decisions that arise from the way that the game shapes interaction between the players.

## *The Importance of In-Game Interaction*[13]

> *When we play, we don't play the game, we play our opponent. The game just happens to be the agreed upon arena of play.* — Hermosa, 2007

The way that eurogames stimulate decision-making through particular forms of interpersonal interaction is a distinguishing feature of their play. The preponderance of goals that focus upon accumulation and mechanics that afford ownership of game elements results in games where the principal conflict arises when players seek to gain ownership of the same game element. Although this observation can be extended to other forms of game, it is the way in which these conflicts are resolved asynchronously that leads to the description of interaction in eurogames as indirect.

In eurogames, mastery of the abstract game system rarely constitutes a particularly complex challenge. Given the roots of the genre in family gaming and the associated emphasis on approachability, it is not surprising to find that the operational rules of the game system are usually relatively intuitive. In contrast with examples such as wargames and collectible card games, where comprehensive knowledge of the operational rules commonly requires a degree of dedication to the game, Lewis Pulsipher has suggested that the systems of most eurogames can be understood after only one play (2009b). Thus, the designs of eurogames assume that the core intellectual challenge arises from the interaction between players. While all multiplayer games draw on this element to some degree, the predominance of eurogames designed for more than two players tends to elevate the significance of player interaction as a determinant of the game outcome. *Boardgamegeek* founder Derk Solko explains the impact of multiple players when compared with two-player games:

> In any multi-player situation, every move every player takes has effects beyond the player's action. In a two-player game, this facet is referred to as "zero-sum": every action which is good for me, is bad for you. However, the existence of other players muddles the equation. Which is why players often just say, "I'm playing to better my situation." But as much as players deny it ... what other players do during the game has more effect on your performance than what you do [2005].

The importance of player interaction in eurogames stems from the way that particular mechanics draw on the psychology of competitive play to challenge players. Unlike single-player games of progression, where mastery of the underlying game system is the path to completion, in multi-player games the system generally acts as a framework within which players implement strategies and tactics in competition with other participants. Pulsipher describes this characteristic in his discussion of the systemic and psychological elements of games:

> The second part to playing games is understanding how the players interact with the system, learning how to recognize what the players are trying to do, and finally figuring out how to forecast and to manipulate the other players. We might call this knowing the psychology of the game, as opposed to knowing the system [2009b].

Pulsipher here is making a distinction that, on the surface, appears quite obvious. However, it is one that has significant ramifications for understanding the distinction between social and solitary play. In multi-player games the ability to read player intent, to anticipate the play of opponents and to manipulate the perceptions of other players is a critical component in successful play. While understanding a game system allows a player to play the game competently, it is the interpersonal psychology that the game provokes which provides the principal challenge. As one respondent observes:

All games have an element of the unknown, as each player will use different paths to get to the victory conditions. It is that implied chaos that makes games interesting and so replayable. Games are as much about strategy and tactics as they are about social interaction and the ability to "read" people [R77].

Given the preponderance in modern eurogames of mechanics that offer indirect interaction, it is interesting to note that both indirect and direct player interaction are considered important, though the latter finds slightly more favor.[14] Notably, this does not indicate a preference for direct conflict, a form of interaction considered relatively unimportant in player enjoyment.[15] Rather, players clearly enjoy being able to interact with each other within the context of a game, either directly or indirectly:

> I value interaction in board games. Just as I far prefer multi-player computer games to single-player ones, I wouldn't sit down and play a solitaire board game by myself, but I seek out opportunities to play with others [R93].

> The opportunity to interact with others is my most basic pleasure. Another rewarding aspect is to develop a plan and successfully execute the plan when all others involved are trying to do the same thing. Challenging and beating a computer opponent in a game is one thing; to win against other thinking beings that have the same goal of defeating others is exciting [R722].

> I enjoy games with high interaction, either cooperative or competitive. I love the social aspect that lacks in computer games, even multi-player ones [R352].

> [I enjoy] the interaction with the choices other people make in the game and how the players play off of each other [R371].

As discussed earlier, interaction in eurogames is often indirect, as the mechanics of the game rarely facilitate the kinds of direct conflict that are associated with many classical abstract games and Anglo-American hobby games. Pulsipher notes that eurogame designers are increasingly developing games in which player interaction is limited and the focus is on players developing an economic "engine" in relative isolation through the course of the game. In this style, Pulsipher argues, "the psychological component does not exist, or barely exists, and the game only has a system component as though it was a traditional video game" (2009b).[16] Given that the majority of survey respondents indicate a preference for eurogames yet also place a great deal of emphasis on the interaction derived from game play, a question arises as to how, if not through direct interaction, eurogames facilitate this psychological dimension of play in their mechanics.

## Interaction in Eurogames

I have previously described a number of informally defined "mechanics" that are commonly found in eurogames. I also pointed to the fact that, of these, set collection and area control were more accurately defined as goal-types rather than mechanics. If for this reason we omit these two forms, we are left with the common interaction forms of tile placement, auctions, role selection/worker placement and trading/negotiation. Each of these forms of interaction is concerned with gaining ownership of some in-game element, be they a part of the environment, resources or actions. Interesting is the fact that of these four, the mechanic of trading/negotiation stands out as one that is the most direct form of interaction yet is also the only one that is largely collaborative in nature. For this reason I will discuss this mechanic separately, following consideration of the other three forms of interaction.

Tile placement is most commonly concerned with gaining ownership of parts of the game environment. Conflict arises when more than one player seeks ownership of a particular area. Thus, the conflict is decided asynchronously through a player's choice to place a particular tile. This choice may be restricted by the opportunities presented through the game system (e.g., random elements), but the onus on the player is to evaluate his or her own priorities and simultaneously evaluate any other player's intentions to shape the environment. This evaluative process informs the decision to place a given tile at any specific moment or in a particular location.

Role selection and worker placement operate in a similar manner to tile placement, as players seek to gain ownership of the rights to a particular in-game action. Again, the decision to select an action is simultaneously informed by the player's own priorities and the evaluation of the intent of other players. In both role selection/worker placement and tile placement, the decisions faced by the players revolve around prioritization and the evaluation of intent. Since role selection and worker placement are typically procedural in nature, as Pulsipher notes, this type of interaction can be characterized as "make the right choice before the other person does" (2009a).

Auctions in games are used as a mechanism for gaining ownership of a wide assortment of in-game elements. In examples where the auction is of the simple "once-around" variety, there is a clear similarity to tile placement and role selection/worker placement in terms of the nature of the decision. Here the player is called upon to assess the worth of a particular in-game element without necessarily having any explicit information concerning how much other players value it. In the more common form of English auctions, a player may have more informed knowledge of an object's worth through the evaluation of other players' bids but must still balance their own valuation with that of others.

The interactions arising from each of these mechanics are indirect, as any conflict between players is resolved asynchronously. Following this observation, it is now clear why players regard area control as a mechanic rather than a goal, and, furthermore, why Appelcline considers the form very close to auctions (2005a). The procedural placement of game elements to an area on the board is similar to the three mechanics discussed here since it calls upon players to evaluate the worth of particular areas and, as such, draws on the need for players to read their opponents' intentions for placement.

Importantly, the mechanics of trading and negotiation typically operate in a distinctly different fashion than do tile placement, auctions, role selection/worker placement and area control. Firstly, trading and negotiation are typically synchronous in that players are simultaneously engaged in the pursuit of an outcome. Secondly, unlike the mechanics discussed above, the performance of negotiation with other players is a collaborative one in which multiple players seek optimal results. Thus, eurogames commonly use indirect interaction to resolve conflict and direct interaction to facilitate collaboration.

*Die Siedler von Catan* can be used to highlight this distinction between forms of conflict and collaboration. Through the course of the game players build settlements, cities and roads on a hex-based map of limited size. Since players may not encroach on another player's buildings, there is conflict between players to establish roads and settlements quickly — to gain ownership of the game environment — before the available space is used up. As players take their turns, this conflict is resolved asynchronously with each player seeking to "make the right choice before the other person does." However, since the construction of these game elements requires resources that are unevenly distributed between players, they must negotiate trades in order to build. Here the interaction is synchronous and therefore direct, but is not a source of conflict but rather an opportunity for collaboration.

In each of the mechanics described above, it is clear that competent gameplay requires the ongoing evaluation of player intent. The ability to assess the importance of in-game elements to another player requires the formation of a mental model of that player's intention for future actions within the game. Similarly, evaluating the worth of a particular element in the context of an auction or a trade is dependent upon making assumptions about the value others place upon that item. These skills are some of those to which Pulsipher refers when he describes the psychology of a game. They are certainly an element of player interaction that survey respondents enjoy:

> [I enjoy] the ability to distinguish what other players are doing, and why. Seeing different strategies in action is a lot of fun [R190].

> [I enjoy] setting up a strategy; guessing other players strategys [sic]; surprising and misleading other players [R1].

> [I enjoy] trying new strategies and coming up with a really good one that wins the game. It usually gets quickly adapted to, forcing you to try more new

strategies or to disguise your intentions. I love the move/countermove thinking in many games. It is very satisfying to correctly predict what your opponent will do while deceiving them as to your own intentions [R395].

In part, the ability to perform this type of assessment is dependent upon
familiarity with the game system. Players use their knowledge of the game
system and strategies that can be employed to infer the possible intentions of
other players. Since the number of choices presented to players in eurogames
is typically limited, and the complexity of the game system relatively low
(inasmuch as it can be performed by analysis of the game state), this prediction
of intent is far easier than in games such as *Chess*.

Given Pulsipher's observation that board games — particularly those in
the eurogame genre — have become increasingly less interactive and more
focused on individual achievement, it is interesting to note that enthusiasts
of the genre place such a great degree of importance on the presence of in-
game interaction. The suggestion here is that players simply value the presence
of interaction more than the amount of interaction a game offers. While titles
such as *Puerto Rico*, *Die Fürsten von Florenz* and *Goa* are exemplary of this
design style, none are entirely devoid of interaction. As Greg Aleknevicus
observes, board games without any interaction are extremely rare (2002).[17] As
a number of survey respondents observe, without some degree of interaction
there really is very little game:

> I'm not adverse to multi-player solitaire; however, it can get boring when
> completely unmitigated — I would say that being able to affect each other is
> what makes a game truly fun and dynamic [R640].

> I enjoy an intellectual competition against another person, or multiple people.
> The puzzle-solving aspect is key, so while I enjoy games with high player
> interaction, I can also be happy with low-interaction games. But some interac-
> tion is required, or else one is playing against a set of rules and not a person
> [R447].

While the importance of some form of interaction is held to be a constitutive element of games in many scholarly definitions,[18] it is important to
note that players here are referring specifically to interaction *with other players*
rather than with the game system:

> I like games with lots of interaction between the players (whether direct or
> indirect). You want to play versus your friends, and not just versus the system.
> I don't want to be playing solo in a multi-player affair [R35].

> I enjoy games where I get to directly interact with other players. Games with
> auctions, negotiations, trading, bargaining are my favorites [R192].

> [I enjoy] player interaction. Whether we are working together or against each
> other having everyone involved through as many phases of play as possible is
> most important to me [R262].

The best games are ones that require a good amount of discussion and interaction among players but not in excess.... If I wanted to play a game without talking to people I'd have stayed home and played it online [R145].

While eurogames typically offer little opportunity for direct conflict, they operate to promote social interaction between players on two levels. Firstly, the asynchronous mechanics that focus on gaining ownership call upon players to carefully evaluate their opponents' intent. This form of interaction shifts the focus of play away from the game space and towards other players. As Parlett describes of modern games generally, the play is centered "above the board, in the minds of the players themselves" (1999, p. 7). Secondly, through synchronous interactions, such as trade, players collaborate in the pursuit of mutually beneficial outcomes. It is clear that for survey respondents this kind of stimulated and mediated interaction remains an important factor in their enjoyment of specific titles.

## Components and Graphics

Players place a high value on the physical and aesthetic properties of board games. Graphical presentation was deemed very important (23 percent) or quite important (53 percent) by 76 percent of respondents. Component quality was considered to be very important (25 percent) or quite important (56 percent) by 81 percent of respondents. For the most part, players indicated that the general production quality of a game contributes significantly to their enjoyment:

I love the beautiful boards and components, and opening the new box and punching out the pieces [R50].

I do like an attractive, well laid out board, with lovely pieces [R377].

I love a beautiful gameboard, beautiful pieces and quality in general [R517].

Games which are well produced are visually uplifting [R97].

The elements of both graphical presentation and high-quality components contribute towards what Hunicke *et al.* term the "game as sense-pleasure" (2004). In particular, as designer Jesse Schell notes, the tactile nature of physical game play is closely related to the pleasure of playing with a toy (2008, p. 109). Reflecting this association, a number of survey respondents referred explicitly to the tactile aesthetics of board and table games as a contributing factor in their enjoyment:

For some games, Days of Wonder titles or dexterity games or the GIPF series I just love the bits. It's a pleasure to handle them, and the great bits can make up for inadequacies in gameplay [R369].

> I appreciate that the games I play are tactile and physical objects that can be manipulated within a system of simple rules [R120].

> I also take a great amount of pleasure from simply handling the pieces and moving them around [R79].

While the importance of game play is apparent in the comparative weight respondents place upon replayability and interaction, it is clear that the visual aesthetics and component tactility of board games are highly valued. Greg Costikyan has attested to the significant impact that presentation and component quality can have on the experience of a game:

> As an example of the difference that mere sensation can make, consider the boardgame *Axis and Allies*. I first bought it when it was published by Nova Games, an obscure publisher of hobby games. It had an extremely garish board, and ugly cardboard counters to represent the military units. I played it once, thought it was pretty dumb, and put it away. Some years later, it was bought and republished by Milton Bradley, with an elegant new board, and with hundreds of plastic pieces in the shapes of aircraft, ships, tanks, and infantrymen — I've played it many times since. It's the sheer tactile joy of pushing around little military figures on the board that makes the game fun to play [2002, pp. 26–27].

Board games draw upon the tactile pleasures associated with toys. The description Costikyan provides of "pushing around little military figures" brings to mind the pleasures of childhood play with miniature worlds that Chaim Gingold posits as a source of gratification in the play of video games (2003).[19] Notably, the tactility of board games and the opportunity they provide to interact directly with the game world were explicitly compared with the intangibility of video games by a number of respondents:

> I like the physical nature of board games compared to computer/video games — rolling dice, holding cards, collecting wooden cubes [R580].

> I love the "unplugged" nature of board games. Everything else in my life seems to be digital, it is really nice to sit down at a table with some friends and have a good time with just some simple bits of wood and paper [R735].

Graphical presentation and component quality clearly contribute to player enjoyment in eurogames, as they provide aesthetic pleasures while also introducing tactile sense-pleasure through the opportunity to interact physically with the game. The fact that respondents cite this trait as more significant in their enjoyment than the presence of an integrated theme or innovative mechanics is perhaps surprising, given the emphasis on game play that is commonly the focus of hobbyist discussion and critique. Clearly this aesthetic dimension is an important one, a fact that has not escaped notice in other areas of the hobby game industry where the quality of eurogames has prompted a rise in production values generally.

## *Theme and Mechanics*

The contribution of integrated theme and innovative mechanics to player enjoyment is not as significant as might be anticipated given the amount of discussion that these two elements generate among hobbyists. While these elements are important to a sizeable number of players, as noted, they are both considered less important than the production quality of a given game.

Given the emphasis within the eurogame genre upon the novel implementation of mechanics, it is surprising to find that only 20 percent of respondents consider this trait as very important, with 51 percent describing it as quite important. Respondents who do value the implementation of innovative mechanics are generally those for whom the exploration of the emergent properties of the game is an important source of pleasure:

> I really like innovative mechanics. The novelty factor of exploring a new game and seeing something new is really engaging [R404].

> I like to look how rules and mechanics of the game work. I'm always excited when I find a new way to use the mechanic, be it legal in the game or not. Of course, if it's illegal in the game, I won't do it, unless we house-rule it to be legal. I'm just interested in the mechanics and their possibilities and interactions [R576].

As discussed previously, theme in eurogames is often only circumstantially related to the mechanics of the game. Nevertheless, it is clear from this survey that the thematic premise remains an important element in player enjoyment. Indeed, several respondents explicitly referred to the sense of narrative and story that is created by weaving theme and mechanics together:

> Looking top-down, the best gaming experiences are those which have a fluid connection between their "narrative" on the high end down into the game's "mechanisms" on the low end. My definition of integrated theme would be a context which allows for the mechanisms of gameplay to easily create different story arcs when playing that same game multiple times [R56].

> I love integrated, very interesting and immersive themes combined with very nice, theme-integrated mechanics with some competition and sense of narrative [R212].

This "sense of narrative" is typically not something that eurogames are renowned for. However, it is important to recognize that the relationship between theme and mechanics is largely a subjective one. That is, what to one person may seem a well-integrated theme may to another appear merely loosely connected with the mechanics. A good example of this subjectivity can be found in discussions of Knizia's *Euphrat and Tigris*, which is seen by some players as a richly thematic game of development in the cradle of civilization and by others as a dry, abstract game of tile placement.

Where players do discuss specific themes and mechanics, there is often a reference to the kinds of constructive endeavors that are typically emphasized in the design of eurogames:

> I prefer themes that relate to building and improving. Games that involve building a point generating "engine" are favourites of mine [R177].

> I like games that are not so much about hurting other players as making moves that help them less than they help you (e.g., role selection in *Puerto Rico*.) I enjoy "building something" over the course of the game — managing resources in order to most efficiently convert them into points by the game's end. I like conflict where other players can interfere in this process (e.g., in *Caylus*, claiming a building that you need or beating you to the castle), but not where they can somehow take away or tear down what you've already done (e.g., in *Settlers*, by stealing a resource from you using the robber or a Monopoly card) [R176].

In eurogames, where the subject matter is often an afterthought or is only loosely applicable to the core mechanics, players are invited by the thematic presentation of the game's rules to view the mechanics through the lens of this theme, and thus it is inevitable that their experience of the game be shaped by it, however loosely applied. Where in other forms of hobby game the accuracy of simulation might be considered a measure of a game's worth, the popularity and preponderance of eurogames without a tightly integrated theme suggests a shift away from this model in hobby game design. Certainly this survey suggests that while a significant number of players appreciate the effective implementation of mechanics that reflect a theme, such verisimilitude is typically not foremost in the minds of players as a source of enjoyment.

## Luck and Chaos

The presence of random elements in a game contributes to unpredictability by ensuring that the initial game state and/or flow of the game are different during each iteration of play. Respondents did not consider the presence of luck in a game to be particularly significant in their enjoyment, perhaps since the introduction of random elements into a game system reduces the possibility for strategy formation, a trait of games that is considered important by players. For the most part, survey respondents did not seem to object to the presence of luck, but rather considered it unimportant in their enjoyment. Most commonly, randomness was considered acceptable as long as it was not perceived as pivotal in determining the outcome of the game:

> [I don't enjoy] too much randomness or luck which can't be mitigated or augmented by strategic/tactical play [R680].

> I enjoy an element of luck in games because I like the excitement it brings, but it shouldn't dominate [R456].

> I have no problem with luck as long as it does not directly influence the winner of the game (for example, *Risk* is fine, the luck is predictable and, if planned for, avoidable) [R697].

The presence of chaos is also considered by players to be unimportant in their enjoyment. In common parlance, chaos refers to events that are either unpredictable or random. In gaming terms, chaos describes elements that are determined by the actions of other players but sufficiently unpredictable as to be perceived as random events.[20] Chaos is closely tied to two factors: player numbers and the degree to which they can alter the game state. In a game of *Chess* one does not perceive the actions of the opponent as random events. Yet when the number of players is increased — as is often the case with eurogames — there is often a rise in the perception that the sum of player actions is random. Salen and Zimmermen refer to this element as a "feeling of randomness" and describe the experience in the game of *Chinese Checkers*:

> If you closed your eyes and opened them only when it is your turn to move, it might seem like the board is merely reshuffling itself, particularly in the middle period of the game, when the center area is most crowded. This feeling of randomness is only an illusion, however, as there is no formal chance mechanism in the game. Perfectly logical players (who only exist in hypothetical examples) wouldn't feel any randomness: they could look at the board and immediately trace every move back to a series of strategic decisions [2004, p. 176].

While the hypothetical players that Salen and Zimmerman describe might be able to distinguish the pattern of plays that occur in an open-information abstract game, the prevalence of imperfect information and the implementation of truly random elements in eurogames contributes to the perception of such events as being beyond player discernability. Given the importance players place upon strategic planning, it is not surprising to find that the presence of chaos is not a significant contributor to player enjoyment.

## Summary— Player Enjoyment of Game Traits/Mechanics

So far this chapter has focused upon the traits of specific games as a source of player enjoyment. In the case of individual mechanics, there is a general preference for those mechanics that are associated with the eurogame genre, and a relative aversion to those that are perceived as being overly dependent on randomness. In terms of the general framework for play that a specific game provides, players value the opportunity for meaningful decision-making and in-game interaction. Together, these two elements contribute to the replayability that is seen as crucial in player enjoyment of a particular game.

The importance of graphical presentation and component quality is valued, as it contributes to the overall aesthetic pleasure derived from the game. Similarly, elements such as the presence of innovative mechanics, integrated theme and random factors are valued only as they contribute to the overall experience of game play. Although these elements contribute to player enjoyment, their presence is typically viewed as unimportant in comparison with the opportunities for meaningful decision-making and in-game interaction that a game provides.

Taken together, these results indicate a clear preference among hobbyists for games that afford strategic and tactical play while also offering in-game interaction. The preference for both of these elements bears comparison with other forms of game. Were strategy and tactics alone of primary importance, then one could argue that traditional two-player abstract games such as *Chess* and *Go* would be far more suitable. Conversely, were the opportunities for in-game interaction the defining attraction, party games such as *Pictionary* (Angel, 1985) and *Charades* would better fit player preferences. From these survey responses it is clear that it is the combination of interpersonal interaction and intellectual challenge commonly found within this genre that are the most valued elements of particular games. Given this preference for intellectually challenging and socially interactive games, I now turn my attention away from specific game elements to the general experience of play and the pleasure that hobbyists derive from it.

## Player Enjoyment— General Experience of Play

*I think the reason that I enjoy games so much is because it gives people another venue in which to interact with one another; a venue that is often overlooked that stimulates both the intellect and the social side of your personality simultaneously. There are very few, if any other, activities that do this.* — R419

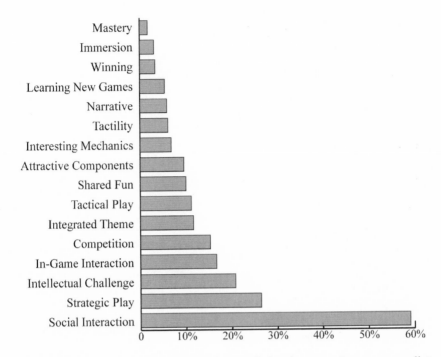

**Figure 7.4: From what aspects of play do you derive the most pleasure generally? (open-ended).**

As a final question focused upon player enjoyment, respondents were asked which elements of board game play generally they found enjoyable. Unlike the previous questions where respondents were presented with a pre-defined range of options, this question was open-ended. Thus, respondents were able to express in their own words the principal pleasures they derive from play.[21] The results of this analysis, displayed in Figure 7.4, reveal the degree to which the constitutive elements of games are considered secondary to the overall social experience of play.

For the most part, the ordering of in-game elements as they contribute to player enjoyment is similar to the findings detailed earlier. Most obviously, strategic play and in-game interaction are again cited as important elements in player enjoyment. Similarly, theme, mechanics and production quality occupy comparable relative positions as when specific game elements were identified. Undoubtedly, these results suggest that the most important factor in player enjoyment of eurogames is the general quality of the social experience that they foster.

In proposing a model of social interaction within multiplayer games, José Zagal offers a distinction between interaction that is stimulated by the game and that which is spontaneous and voluntary (2000). Zagal cites games such as *Tag* and *Disease* (Stevens, 1998) as those wherein the mechanics of the game specifically call upon players to interact socially. As identified earlier, a number of mechanics commonly implemented in eurogames are used to generate this kind of social interaction (e.g., auctions, negotiations, etc.) However, it is not this form of in-game interaction that players are describing when they cite the pleasure of social interaction as principle in their enjoyment, but rather the spontaneous interaction that occurs as a by-product of game play.

As Zagal observes, the presence of this kind of spontaneous interaction within a specific instance of a game is completely independent from the nature of the game itself, but is rather a product of player composition (2000, p. 452). Theoretically, it is possible to play all multiplayer games without any spontaneous interaction whatsoever. Yet as Zagal also notes, "It is hard to imagine playing a board game of any sort without engaging in idle talk with other players" (p. 451). Where we might envisage a multi-player game played over the Internet without such spontaneous interaction, the shared physical space and components have a profound effect on the nature of the game encounter. Indeed, in co-located play, participation typically involves far more than the performance of game mechanics.

In understanding this relationship between games and interaction, the work of sociologist Erving Goffman is particularly relevant. In his essay "Fun in Games," Goffman describes the play of co-located games as a type of "focused gathering":

> For the participants, this involves: a single visual and cognitive focus of attention, a mutual and preferential openness to verbal communication; a heightened mutual relevance of acts; an eye-to-eye ecological huddle that maximizes each participant's opportunity to perceive the other participant's monitoring of him [1961, pp. 17–18].

Goffman perceives a clear distinction between what he terms "gaming," a gathering of players who "are face-to-face with the avowed purpose of carrying on a game," and a "gaming encounter," a focused gathering that includes the play of games. The difference here, as Goffman describes, is that "the first kind of subject matter is codifiable and clean, the second is very sticky."

The distinction that Goffman describes has obvious similarities with that made by Zagal between required in-game interaction and the informal social interaction that surrounds the play of games. Respondents appear to demonstrate an understanding that co-located play not only involves interactions derived from the play of the game but also from the context of the social environment. Goffman uses the term "spontaneous involvement" to describe the way in which a participant in a gaming encounter is caught up in the social moment as much as in the game itself (p. 37). He describes three reasons why such involvement is significant. Firstly, the acknowledgment of shared focus provides a sense of security for all players. Secondly, it increases relatedness through mutual involvement. Finally, it confirms the reality of the shared world of play (1961, p. 40).

Significantly, Goffman suggests that it is only in face-to-face play that this spontaneous involvement can be communicated to other players. Although he writes before the emergence of computer-mediated play, Goffman's observations regarding games played at a distance are equally applicable to these forms[22]:

> Multi-situated games and game-like activities can define the situation for their participants and create a world for them. But this is a loose world for the individual, allowing for periods of lack of interest and for wide variation in attitude and feelings.... The world of a multi-situated game can be lightly invested in, so that while the game defines the situation it does not bring the situation into lively existence [1961, p. 41].

It is this "lively existence" that defines the play of co-located games as social experiences. Where we might talk about "social games" and incorporate into this definition any game played by multiple players, the experience of co-located play is circumscribed by the spontaneous interactions from which players derive pleasure and from which they indicate their involvement to other participants. As respondents indicate in this survey, it is not so much the in-game interactions that provide the pleasure of play, but the shared involvement and the social interactions that arise from the gaming encounter.

Researcher Nicole Lazzaro describes the pleasure engendered by this rich social interaction as "people fun" (2004). Board and table games bring players together within a shared social space — typically a domestic one — and thus require a capacity for informal sociability. The process of coming together and engaging in conversation within an informal environment necessarily provides context for the more formal experience of playing a game. As Lazzaro describes, the attractiveness of this form of interaction is evident in those players who say "it's the people that are addictive not the game" (2004).

## The Play and Not the Game

*Gaming unplugged is all about social interaction.* — R509

At the beginning of this chapter I cited designer Alan Moon's description of board games wherein he claims that games are not "about rolling dice and moving your piece around a track" (in Aleknevicus, 2002). As a professional game designer, it is particularly telling that Moon dismisses the idea that board games are about the mechanics that define play. Instead, claims Moon, "Gaming is about interactions, decisions and social skills." The survey responses that I have summarized here go a long way to confirming Moon's observation.

Of the pleasures derived from games specifically, it is the opportunities for decision-making and interaction that players value most highly. Elements such as immersion and narrative that have such a significant place in the study of video games are considered comparatively unimportant when set against the possibilities for meaningful interaction with other players within the context of the game. The importance of this decision-making as intellectual challenge, and the dependency upon interaction with other players, is highlighted by a number of player responses:

> I derive most pleasure from working out my brain, in a socially interactive setting. I can do either (work out my brain or interact socially) on its own, but there is a synergy between the two that gets my whole brain abuzz that isn't really achieved by much else [R7].

> I prefer involved games in a social environment. I prefer a social environment for play, however don't really enjoy "party games." I like involved games, where you have to think about the game, but lots of people who play these can get too serious and don't have a chat while in the game. Any game that can combine social environment but be fairly involved works well for me [R195].

> I enjoy challenging games that force me to use different strategies. I also like to be able to experience these games with others in a fun, social atmosphere [R305].

> I love to play for the play and for the social interaction between friends that a boardgame originates. It's much better than playing a console or computer game, and it really exercises your intellect and imagination. It's a good intellectual exercise that I love to do and is not rivaled by anything [R672].

Above all other constitutive elements of particular games, respondents valued the pleasure of the game encounter and the spontaneous interaction brought about by participation in the social event of the game. When asked to describe in their own words what it is that they enjoy about play, the proportion of respondents who cite the social interaction afforded by face-to-face gaming is far higher than those citing any in-game element:

> Social interaction is very important, as the entire reason I play is to get with a group of people to have fun. If I wanted to do something by myself I'd do something else [R13].

I play games as a way to relax, spend time with family and friends. These are social games [R143].

I enjoy the social interaction. I have a regular weekly game group that will try any game. We can experiment struggling through something new, or play an old favorite, it doesn't matter, the conversations, in-jokes, and fun remain no matter what. If the social interaction wasn't there, there is not a point to play [R164].

What I like most about playing boardgames is that it gives me a good social outlet. It's "play," with all that suggests, and it allows social interaction over a particular event [R608].

I think I play games at this point more as a social medium than to find a specific in-game experience. The eurogame model of design has allowed for people to get together for an evening of play, with some chit chat and snacks, to enjoy the games and interacting with each other. I wouldn't characterize the games themselves as the most enjoyable for what I want out of a game, as they tend to be a little too abstract and themeless; however, I bend to the reality of time and other obligations and get what I can out of the games that work for the group [R361].

The comments listed here are just a few of the many that emphasized the social experience of play as paramount in the enjoyment of board games generally. Such responses indicate why enthusiasts have a tendency to evangelize the hobby — it is not so much the games that are being evangelized, but the sense of sociability and security that must necessarily accompany them. That is, it is not the game, but the game encounter, that provides this. The particular form of semi-structured social interaction that spontaneously occurs through co-located play provides an intrinsic motivation to engage with the hobby.

The importance placed by players on social interaction stands in contrast to a number of the pleasures that were earlier identified as being associated with video game play. While Csikszentmihalyi's model of flow may be applicable to the focused play of a game, as Sweetster and Wyeth note, social interaction often serves to disrupt immersion and thus the flow state (2005). Koster's suggestion that cognitive problem solving provides the fun in games is reflected here to a degree; yet when Koster describes the "social fun" that can be derived from play, it is framed largely in terms of *schadenfreude*,[23] a focus on achievement that was largely absent in responses. Lazzaro too mentions *schadenfreude*, although her estimation of social pleasure is closer to the findings of this survey, as she discusses the camaraderie that is brought about by shared goals. Finally, Hunicke *et al.*'s notion of fellowship, which sees games as a "social framework," falls closest to the types of pleasure described by participants in emphasizing the playful social interaction engendered by games as a principal source of enjoyment. As Goffman notes, "While it is as players that we can win a play, it is only as participants [in the gaming encounter] that we can get fun out of this winning" (1961, p. 37).

Despite the emphasis I have placed here upon the social aspect of gaming, it must nevertheless be acknowledged that the specific avenue for interaction remains the games that are played — in this case eurogames. The interaction that occurs through play is situated within a specific semi-structured environment that emphasizes competition. While the design of eurogames tends towards indirect or asynchronous interaction, the fact remains that the intellectual challenge to which players attribute so much of their enjoyment is focused specifically upon engaging in competition with others. Thus, as much as the formal game structure prescribes the pursuit of goals, players are simultaneously called upon to engage in competition while at the same time maintaining the sociability that is at the heart of the encounter.

Yet as Goffman notes, the participant in a gaming encounter is far removed from an ideally rational player whose focus lies purely on the game (1961, p. 38). Although the game rules, both explicit and implicit, describe a structure for interaction that constitutes a world apart from the real, "The character and stability of this world is intimately related to its subjective relationship to the wider one" (p. 80). As players are caught up in spontaneous involvement with the gaming encounter, the world apart that is ideally created by participation in the game cannot be entirely separated from the context in which the encounter occurs. As has been seen through these survey responses, to set aside this spontaneous sociability would be to ignore what makes the activity so enjoyable. Thus the question arises as to how it is that players are able to maintain the competitive drive mandated by the game within such an environment. It is to these ostensibly incompatible motivations — competition and sociability — that I turn my attention in the next chapter.

# 8

# *Goals and Outcomes in Social Play*

*The true gamer doesn't play for winning, but he knows that trying to win creates the "plot" in a game. Therefore s/he adheres to the plot "everybody tries to win" easily, but can immediate [sic] forget the failure as the enjoyment of the game moved on by the plot is bigger than the disappointment of not winning.* — Eggert in Heli, 2007

In the previous chapter I identified the key aspects of board game play that appeal to hobbyists, noting that while certain game elements may contribute to player enjoyment, generally speaking it is the social aspect of play that provides the principal form of pleasure. While intellectual challenge, in-game interaction and a variety of other elements are considered significant as traits of specific games, the overall pleasure derived from games is found in the sociability that accompanies play. Given that the vast majority of modern board games are ostensibly framed around competition, a question arises as to how players negotiate competitive play within the social context that surrounds the gaming encounter. In short, how do players manage the apparent opposition between sociability and competition in order to maintain the convivial atmosphere from which pleasure is derived? In order to examine this question, it is important firstly to understand what game goals mean to players.

## *Goals, Outcomes and the Predictable Player*

In his book *Half-Real: Video Games Between Real Rules and Fictional Worlds*, Jesper Juul develops what he terms a "classic game model," criteria by which an activity can be defined as a game. Building upon the work of other scholars, Juul describes six elements that together constitute "an abstract platform upon which games are built" (2005, p. 54):

> A game is a rule-based system with a variable and quantifiable outcome, where different outcomes are assigned different values, the player exerts effort in order to influence the outcome, the player feels emotionally attached to the outcome, and the consequences of the activity are negotiable [p. 36].

Although Juul uses this model to highlight the way that understandings of games have been altered by role-playing and digital games (p. 53), he describes how all of the games contained within David Parlett's *The Oxford History of Board Games* (1999) and *The Penguin Encyclopedia of Card Games* (2000) fall within this model. Essentially, Juul's claim is that, until recently, all forms of game could be defined using these criteria.

Following Juul's model, a "classic" game proceeds towards an outcome that is largely indeterminable at the outset of play. Of the potential and variable outcomes, some are valorized and can be considered "better than others" (2005, p. 40). In the case of multiplayer games, it is reasonable to assume that here Juul is referring to the achievement of the winning condition as being preferable to not achieving it — it is *better* to win than to lose. The final assertion that Juul makes with regard to the potential outcomes is that "the player is emotionally attached to the outcome of the game in the sense that a player will be winner and 'happy' in the case of a positive outcome, but a loser and 'unhappy' in the case of a negative outcome" (p. 36). In making this claim, Juul's focus shifts from the game as an *object* to the game as *subjective experience*. In claiming that "the emotional attachment of the player to the outcome is a psychological feature of the game activity" (p. 40), he moves from the realm of formalist game studies into that of play theory, and in doing so raises a number of questions about the limitations of a structuralist perspective in dealing with the complex nature of play and motivation. As Markku Eskelinen notes, the assumption that player motivation is always related to the outcome of the game "runs the risk of reducing the range of the player's personal attachments, motivations, styles, and reasons for playing into the mere outcome or preferring one type of attachment to all the others" (2005, pp. 15–16).

The outcomes of modern board games are variable, quantifiable and valorized, at least by the formal rules describing winning conditions. These rules explain the mechanics through which a player may influence the outcome of the game, implicitly or explicitly describe the hierarchy of goals, and conclude with the higher-order goal that prescribes the winning conditions.[1] As discussed previously, the importance of the game goals lies in the way that they shape player actions. Yet despite the critical position goals hold in defining and understanding games, in terms of behavior within a play environment, the notion that player actions are oriented towards goals is one that is "curiously understudied" (Heide Smith, 2005). Game scholars and designers often take this understanding of player motivation as an a priori assumption. Video game scholar Jonas Heide Smith has undertaken significant research into the assumed goal-orientedness of players in his doctoral dissertation. His research is concerned with analyzing the "common folk theory" that players want to win a game (2006, p. 6). He identifies four player models which contribute to understandings of player behavior. Of these, only two, the rational and the active player, are actually concerned with player actions during play (pp. 23–24).[2]

As Heide Smith observes, the idealized model of the rational player is the one inherent in texts that focus upon the process of game design and mathematical game theory (p. 257).[3] Consequently, the model is predicated on a very computational model of player behavior. The rational player's behaviors are motivated entirely by the goals of the game and form an ordered set of preferences based upon information received exclusively from the game state and rules. As a model, the rational player provides a baseline from which deviance can illuminate aspects of the relationship between game and player. In observing physically co-located players of video games,[4] Heide Smith's results demonstrate the utility of the rational player in that the model "neatly predicts in-game behaviour" in terms of general goal-orientedness (p. 239). Importantly however, he acknowledges that these behaviors are "subjugated by social norms defining appropriate play" (p. 242). In practical terms, Heide Smith observed that player behavior within the game space was largely goal-oriented, while the social context was seen as an opportunity to share helpful information about the game being played. As one possible motivation for these differing behaviors, Heide Smith suggests that players are attempting to introduce a degree of fairness to the gaming encounter. In describing this incongruence between goal-orientedness during play and the contents of interpersonal communication, Heide Smith introduces a distinction between the "game circle," wherein the rational player pursues his or her goals with commitment, and the "gaming circle" wherein the social expectations of the game in context are met (p. 228).

In making this distinction, Heide Smith highlights the existence of the active player — that is, the player who engages in complex practices and social interactions in ways "often not predicted or prescribed by the game designers" (p. 24).[5] Derived from semiotics and reader-response theory, the active player is imagined as a participatory agent in the interpretation and configuration of the game rather than a product of the game's rules, slavishly bound to the prescribed goals. Consequently, as Espen Aarseth notes, the active player has proven a particularly attractive model for those who study digital games. Examples of transgressive and subversive play, although perhaps "statistically marginal," are "nevertheless a crucial aspect of, and key to understanding all kinds of play and game culture" (2007, p. 131).

In terms of goal-orientedness, Heide Smith's study is of particular relevance to this discussion in that he identifies a clear incongruity between formal understandings of games and the play of the game as a social experience. In his research into video game players, Heide Smith observes that players limit their pursuit of fairness to information sharing:

> The players display a willingness to help others by giving advice and sharing information. This indicates that the players find strongly competitive behaviour legitimate as long as it is accompanied by a desire to share relevant information with other players. Put differently, *concerns about fairness do not extend to gamespace behaviour* but clearly mean that performance in the game should not be a consequence of superior or inferior knowledge about how the game works [2006, p. 242, emphasis mine].

This sharing of information between players about how the game is played ensures that each player is conversant with the rules and mechanics of the game, and that a level playing field is retained. Although Heide Smith refers to this phenomenon as "self-handicapping," this is a misnomer. Self-handicapping is generally defined within studies of play behavior as "the deliberate attenuation of the force or intensity of an action by one or other play partner in order to give the other a better chance of 'winning' or at least to allow more evenly matched encounters" (Boulton and Smith, 1992, p. 436). As indicated above, Heide Smith finds no evidence of such attenuation in his research.

Nevertheless, it is apparent that the players in Heide Smith's research are communicating in order to maintain fairness and a sense of social cohesion. In the case of video games, however, the division between the game space and the social space is artificially clear. The video game takes place behind the screen, while the social interactions surrounding it are located in the "real world." This distinction is made apparent when Heide Smith suggests that

> While game playing may be one of the few spheres of life where people are in fact expected and entitled to care only for their own objective interests ... close-proximity verbal interaction in a couch is not [p. 228].

This distinction that Heide Smith makes between the game circle and the gaming circle is not only imagined, but also actualized in the separation of the player environment and the game world as displayed on screen.

The reason I raise this distinction is to contrast this with the nature of board game play. In a board game, players not only share close physical proximity, but also intimate involvement with the physical components of the game. They are also engaged with the many mechanics employed in modern board games that explicitly invoke social interaction between players. Given the degree to which interpersonal psychology and social negotiations are often embedded in the ruleset of a board game, the division between play of the game and the social interactions brought about by that play is blurred. Where the screen space of video games allows a clear delineation between the goal-oriented play of the game and the social expectations that accompany it, no such boundary exists within the play of a board game other than that constructed by the player through the social context and degree of engagement.

## The Facilitative Nature of Goals

Clearly, in order to maintain the play of a typical board game, a position of goal-orientation must ostensibly be maintained, lest the activity ceases to operate as a competitive game. Reflecting this, the attitudes of survey respondents initially appear to align with the model of the rational player. In reply to the question of whether they are generally pursuing victory, 79 percent of players were in general or unequivocal agreement that victory is the goal towards which they are typically working. Not surprisingly, the most common reason offered by respondents for this goal-orientedness is that it is essential in order that the integrity of the competitive game be maintained. Many respondents demonstrated an explicit awareness of the level of cooperation required in order to maintain an instance of competitive play. Without each player working towards the prescribed game goals, the game system becomes untenable. Indeed, in some cases players viewed the pursuit of goals and the nature of games as being inseparable:

> "Pursuing victory" and "playing a game" are synonymous, so this question is a tautology [R355].

> That's what makes a game: everybody trying to win. There wouldn't be a game if none would want to win [R213].

> I believe that playing a game involves an implicit contract between the players that, among other aspects, requires a mindset that tends towards the pursuit of victory [R738].

> Regardless of the enjoyment derived from socializing with friends and family, and even as a tool to facilitate that, games are built around victory conditions, and playing to win is appropriate within that context [R158].

As Linda Hughes notes in the context of children's play, "a great deal of cooperation is required to sustain a competitive exchange" (1999, p. 108). The importance of this complicity is clearly identified by philosopher Bernard Suits in his discussion of the nature of games. Suits identifies the "trifler" as the player who, in *Chess*, is "a quasi-player of the game who conforms to the rules of the game but whose moves, though all legal, are not directed to achieving checkmate" (1978, p. 58). However, when Suits suggests that such a player lacks the necessary zeal for play and, in abandoning goals, is not actually engaged in the game (p. 59), he is not drawing on the notion of the individual rational player. Rather he is explicitly foregrounding the necessity of goal-orientedness as it serves to facilitate the particular experience that is a game. Suits' definition of games clearly acknowledges the arbitrary nature of game structures, including goals:

> To play a game is to attempt to achieve a specific state of affairs, using only means permitted by the rules, where the rules prohibit use of more efficient means, and where the rules are accepted just because they make possible such activity [1978, pp. 54–55].

Here Suits is proposing that the *purpose* of a game is the *process* of the game. The rules, goals and limitations placed upon players are there merely to facilitate the experience of play. Reflecting this, a number of respondents explicitly referred to the pursuit of the victory goal as being facilitative rather than prescriptive in the process of play:

> Victory gives you a goal to guide you through the game to its conclusion, but the getting there is much more interesting to me than the end result [R140].

This notion, which sees the goals of the game merely as a means to an end, is one that was immediately called upon by many players in their responses concerning the pursuit of victory. Despite the fact that the vast majority of players conform to a rational model of goal-oriented play (in that they actively seek victory), it is significant that a sizeable number felt the need to include some type of qualification in their responses, typically highlighting the experience of play as the primary goal of a gaming encounter.

Although these respondents share a similar attitude in nominating the experience of play as the primary goal, the experiences to which they referred varied. In some cases the experience was the challenge presented in mastering the game:

> I tend to enjoy the games where I tend to lose more than the games where I succeed. It would seem that I enjoy the challenge a game puts in front of me. In order to improve, I must learn how the game is best played. A perfect example for me of just such a game is *Power Grid*. I have played many times (almost always with our games group) and yet, I have never won.... The game forces me to learn, to be adaptive and to watch how others succeed where I have failed. This process is fabulous. I know that I am alive and a social being when I play a game like *Power Grid* [R163].

In others, the fantasy element of play is foregrounded:

> Winning is not as important as the process of playing, and particularly experiencing the theme of the game — in "*Tikal*," for instance, I enjoy the fantasy of being part of an archaeological expedition more than I enjoy winning [R396].

Common to these responses, once again, was an explicit understanding that game goals were facilitative rather than prescriptive. The most common qualification offered in terms of contextualizing goal-orientedness was found in those responses that focused on the social elements of the game. Understandably, given the social motivations for play identified earlier, many players recognized the social aspect of the game as holding far greater weight than the attainment of goals:

> The primary portion is actually on trying to establish communications among players. I enjoy when a game encourages players to talk and discuss among one another, with cussing allowed if it means making the game more enjoyable [R418].

> Winning is nice, but the interaction is reason for playing [R224].

> I generally enjoy the process of the game. I like doing the game. Victory is tertiary to socializing [R695].

These responses are typical of players more interested in the social context of play than the achievement of the prescribed game goals. These players share an understanding that the principal pleasure of games is to be found in the sociability they promote. For them, the game itself is largely corollary to the interactions that stem from play. While such players do not constitute the majority, the importance of context in the pursuit of goal-orientedness further highlights the significance of this social element.

## Social Context and the Pursuit of Goals

> *Once while I was still in my twenties my partner in bridge made a stupid misplay. When I frowned she said that three of them were playing for fun and she would keep making the same stupid play until I understood that. From that day I understood the difference.* — R603

The importance of the social context in which play occurs can have a strong influence on the general goal-orientedness of players. The degree of commitment to the pursuit of the game goals is subject to a variety of contextual social influences that shape player behavior. As one player observes:

> There is a clear axis here ranging from "decisive result" through to "experiential outcome." And, as with many of the other axes, people will disagree about where exactly a particular game should be positioned — and, indeed some games' positions depend entirely upon the context in which you are playing. *Carcassonne* can be played extremely cut-throat, with players who know exactly what tiles are available and how to mess things up. Or it can be played socially, with discussions about the best moves for other players. In one environment you play for victory. In another you play for the experience [R587].

This respondent highlights the way that the social context can shape the play of a specific game. Players may ruthlessly seek to push every advantage in a game or they may offer assistance to players and discuss potential moves openly. The style of play is not a product of the game's rules but of the social environment in which it occurs. As Espen Aarseth notes, player understandings of games are often shaped by the social context in which they are first exposed to them:

> The potential player, before becoming an actual player, must receive some instructions, either from the game itself, or from a guide or accompanying material. Thus, the player is created, by these instructions, and by his or her initial learning experience. In many cases, this experience is social, and the player learns from other, more experienced players [2007, p. 130].

Depending upon the social context, a game of *Carcassonne* can border on that of a cooperative game — with rules that explicitly encourage collaboration with the active player — an observation that challenges the notion that the game is competitive. In a competitive sport such as football, this would be the equivalent of making helpful suggestions as to the best player for the opposing team to pass the ball to. As this respondent suggests, the decision of how helpful to be during this phase is largely dependent on the context of the game and the relationship with other players. In this response we begin to see how the goals of the rational player fluctuate depending upon the specific encounter in which play occurs. Notably, the social demands of an encounter may even override the rational pursuit of victory, shifting the emphasis from purely game-related considerations to those of the broader social fabric. As one respondent states, "My first priority is that everyone at the table is having fun" (R728).

In her studies of children's social play, Linda Hughes describes the way in which the structure of the group forms a part of a gaming encounter:

> The concern displayed here for *how* things are done (for "style"), and for modulation of the single-minded pursuit of the stated point of the game ("outs") in light of principles basic to the social life of the group more generally (like "friends"), is a dominant theme among these players, woven throughout all episodes of play [1988, p. 685].

The importance of social cohesion and shared enjoyment is a recurring theme in Hughes' work. In observing girls' play particularly, Hughes notes that the existence of a social matrix overlaying the play of a game meant that "players who played the game according to its rules, competing as individuals, were treated as though they were acting in a totally inappropriate and unacceptable way" (1999, p. 101). While the influence of peer pressure and other social factors might not be so apparent in adult play as what Hughes finds with children, the "social matrix" she describes is clearly present in these survey responses. A number of respondents identified a shared responsibility to maintain the integrity of the social fabric during the game. For these players the unbridled pursuit of victory might be suitable in some situations, while in others an overly competitive approach would be deemed socially inappropriate:

> Although I am usually playing to win the game, what is more important to me is that people want to continue playing the game with me. If I am being an overzealous jerk, I will soon find myself in a situation where nobody wants to play a game with me.... I don't want people to not desire to play games with me regardless of whether the game is *Chess*, *Apples to Apples*, or *Catan* [R569].

Here it is apparent the degree to which a player must negotiate the norms of the specific social setting in which the game occurs. The decision to pursue game goals without reserve may be tempered by the knowledge that this level of competitiveness is unsuitable within a particular social context. While the majority of players attest to pursuing goals generally, when questioned as to when they might not do so, a wide variety of exceptional circumstances emerge.

## Self-Handicapping in Social Play

Given that the social context of a particular gaming encounter has the potential to influence a player's goal-orientedness, players were then asked to identify situations under which they would *not* actively pursue victory. The answers to this question are perhaps the most surprising of any gleaned from this survey — only 15 percent of players would pursue victory regardless of the context of play. Given the degree to which the rational player model of goal-orientedness dominates understandings of player behavior in games, such a level of deviance from this presumed norm is, in itself, remarkable. 85 percent of respondents acknowledge that there are situations in which they would be playing a game without actively seeking to achieve the winning conditions of the game.

By far the most common situations in which goals are abandoned are those in which hobbyists are teaching other players who are inexperienced with a particular game (39 percent). In some cases players displayed the "willingness to help others" that Heide Smith observes in video game players (2006, p. 242). That is, where there is a perceived disparity in understandings of the game mechanics, players will seek to redress this imbalance in order to facilitate a level playing field:

When there are less experienced players, I will coach them on taking a better move or strategy, and explain why I'm doing what I am when I move. It makes it more fun when games are balanced [R590].

If I'm showing some one how to play, or the person isn't that experienced with the game. I always give pointers, and try and make sure the other person playing knows what their doing. Beating some one because they have little or no understanding of what to do, isn't fun at all [R470].

If I were playing with a less experienced player, I would feel it unfair to not assist them in understanding the game's mechanics. A victory would be less rewarding in that situation for me [R503].

While assisting players with understanding how to play the game may appear altruistic, there is clearly a degree of self-interest also evident in these statements. Play with opponents whose skills are not evenly matched often results in an unsatisfactory game not just for the less experienced player, but also for the more experienced participant (Zagal *et al.*, 2006). Although the responses above indicate a degree of latitude in the single-minded pursuit of victory, the proffering of assistance in understanding the mechanics of a game falls short of actually abandoning game goals. More interesting are those respondents who attested to actively self-handicapping through non-optimal play when opponents are mismatched. Such occasions often coincided with teaching new players, but, unlike earlier examples directed at assisting in understanding the game, players here describe actively self-handicapping in order to improve the experience for their opponents:

If I'm in a situation where I can trounce the other players, I change my approach.... The most frequent situation where I ease off is when I'm teaching a new game. Nothing is less fun than having somebody teach you a game, and then wallop you with their experience in the first match. In such situations I'll adjust my technique by secretly adopting a handicap or choose a convoluted approach to winning [R288].

If I was teaching a game that I like to someone who is not inclined to like it, I'll often check myself, and play down to their level, or even let them win so they will have a positive first time experience [R382].

In a one-on-one session when teaching another player to play a game I would deliberately take neutral actions which would prolong the game and provide a more beneficial learning experience to another player. As part of this I would allow the other player to win if they were able to master the basics of the game. This helps in encouraging the player to play again and builds self-confidence in the individual — this could be particularly important if the individual was a younger member of the family or a friend who had no experience of boardgaming. After all, who wants to play a game where they get beat every time and the experience of the game was so poor that they were not learning the game, and, what's more, they felt belittled? [R494].

In contrast to Heide Smith's observations of co-located video game play, these respondents display a willingness to abandon game goals and adopt sub-optimal strategies in order to facilitate a level playing field and to ensure a positive experience for other players. In these cases, concerns about fairness clearly *do* extend into the game space. When faced with players who have less experience of a game, or games generally, players express a tendency to pull back from optimal play in order to artificially maintain a sense of equality. Significantly, these responses also indicate that the overall experience of other players, including whether or not they are children, is a factor in this decision.

The recognition of other players' experience is also evident in the small number of responses where players attest to the de-prioritization of game goals following a series of wins (about 1 percent). Here respondents demonstrate awareness that successive victories can have a similar effect to game-specific imbalance:

> After I have won a few games in a row (of any combination of games that we play), I will begin playing a game by making non-optimal choices to start before pursuing victory (to give other players a chance) [R623].

> If I have been on a particularly hot streak of wins, say I've beat somebody 30 times in a row, I will throw a game to encourage them so I still have people that want to play with me [R706].

Taken together, over 60 percent of players acknowledge voluntary self-handicapping in the face of unevenly matched contests. In the context of play studies, such a phenomenon should not be unexpected. In the act of play-fighting, self-handicapping is a "pervasive feature" which becomes more amplified with increasing asymmetries between antagonists. In the vast majority of such cases, this behavior typically occurs where one participant is "dominant, older or larger," and where the act of self-handicapping confers a competitive advantage to an opponent (Pellis and Pellis, 1998, p. 128). Self-handicapping has been identified in the competitive social play of a number of animal groups, including apes (Lewis, 2005), canines (Bekoff and Allen, 1998; Bauer and Smuts, 2002; Ward *et al.*, 2008), marsupials (Watson and Croft, 1996), and rodents (Pellis, 2002). More significantly, it is also a common feature of children's competitive play (Aldis, 1975; Smith, 1997; Brown, 1998). The qualitative responses from this survey certainly confirm the presence of self-handicapping in the board game play of adult hobbyists.

So far the motivations discussed for de-prioritization of game goals have hinged on the understanding that a level playing field presents a more enjoyable — and fairer — experience for all players. However, within the remarks made by players, we can begin to see how the broader social context of play is a contributing factor to this proclivity. Comments that reference the demoralizing effect of losing a game (or successive games) point to the importance of this social context as influential in a player's decision to self-handicap. In some cases respondents indicated that the social fabric of the gaming encounter was of more importance than the game goals, regardless of any imbalance in player understanding:

> For the enjoyment of the rest of the group, if my winning or aggressive style of play makes the game less enjoyable for others, I'll tame it back [R371].

> I would not actively pursue victory only if doing so would create a lasting grudge between myself and my friends [R458].

> If it was obvious that it would mean I would have to screw up someone else's plans or position in the game to get ahead and they are obviously emotionally done with my previous successes at doing the same thing to them [R212].

> If I see a player ... having a run of bad luck, I will play down to their level to keep them interested, involved, and happy. I will make moves that I know will hurt me and help them [R536].

It is evident in these responses that some, if not all, players prioritize the enjoyment of the game by all participants over the victory condition. Given the importance of social interaction in their enjoyment of games, it is not surprising to find that maintenance of the social fabric is a consideration for some players in their decision to pursue victory. Further evidence of influences from outside of the game is apparent in players who identify longer-term goals in their decision to self-handicap:

> Allowing new learners to win have [sic] a psychological effect on players, increasing their chance on thinking that a game is fun, and that they may replay it again. When new players lose, or lose badly, it is natural that they will have thoughts that this game doesn't really suit them or to their interest [R418].

> When playing with novices, to show them how the game works, no need to win, making a new adept is fun enough [R426].

Clearly present in these statements is the evangelistic tendency of board gaming hobbyists that was identified earlier. Here the desire to introduce new players into the hobby is considered more important than the unbridled pursuit of victory. Whether due to a perceived imbalance between opponents, the press to maintain the social fabric or the desire to introduce new players to the hobby, all of the motivations discussed here for abandoning the stated goals of a game are, to some degree, linked with the context of the game encounter. This alone is enough to indicate that the general goal-orientedness of players cannot be assumed. Yet there is still further evidence in these survey responses of players who engage in sub-optimal play for reasons that are not connected with the social context.

A significant number of players indicate that they may abandon the goals of the game when they perceive themselves as being in a position from which they cannot win the game (16 percent). Still others describe situations where a strategy of risk-aversion is more beneficial than a direct play for victory (about 0.5 percent). For some the desire for personal retribution within the context of a specific game is enough for some players to set aside the goals (3 percent). Some respondents attest to a tendency not to be overly concerned with the prescribed goals of the game when they themselves are learning (8 percent), while others may use the play of a particular game as an opportunity to experiment with new strategies (6 percent). Here the play of the game is not situated as an isolated event, but as part of the ongoing practice of the hobby. Finally, a number of players suggest that their interest in the goals of the game is reduced in games they do not enjoy (3 percent) or in the play of lighter games (6 percent) where the emphasis is explicitly on experience over competition.[6]

As can be seen, players present a wide variety of reasons why they might not actively seek victory in a game. However, the fact that players indicate that there exist situations in which goal-orientation would not be their primary concern does not imply that such behavior is common — for the most part, players tend to play a game to win as prescribed by the rules. Indeed, in all of the situations described here the question arises as to whether players are actually "playing" the game if they are not actively pursuing the victory conditions that are explicitly stated in the rules.

It is tempting here to call on the notion of the "active player" that Heide Smith and Aarseth suggest is of such fascination to game scholars (Heide Smith, 2006, p. 30; Aarseth, 2007). However, in my readings of how the active player is perceived as being engaged in "wondrous acts of transgression" (Aarseth, 2007, p. 133), engaging with the game "in ways not prescribed by the designer" (Heide Smith, 2006, p. 24), I find little in common with the rationale and behaviors that are described by respondents here. None of the activities or motivations described above could be described as "transgressive" in terms of any deliberate attempt to undermine the game design. Arguably, then, these players do not conform to the model of the rational player *or* the active player. This is, perhaps, due to the fact that both of these models are largely concerned with the relationship between the player and the game system. In eurogames the relationship between the social context and the game is significant in shaping the motivations of players. The intersection of the abstract ruleset with the social structures that surround the game constitutes the act of gaming.

Although the term gaming has come to describe the act of game-playing generally,[7] in critical terms the word has a very specific meaning. Hughes describes the activity of gaming as "the processes by which players mold and modulate the raw materials of their games into actual play" (1999, p. 94). The practices Hughes describes arise from the interpersonal interactions that occur during the play of a given game:

> Rules can be interpreted and reinterpreted toward preferred meanings and purposes, selectively invoked or ignored, challenged or defended, changed or enforced to suit the collective goals of different groups of players. In short, players can take the same game and collectively make of it strikingly different experiences [p. 94].[8]

Understanding the gaming encounter as a socially constituted series of exchanges with other players as opposed to a rational series of prescribed inter-actions situates player experience as paramount to understanding the game form. Yet it does not necessarily imply anything transgressive or deviant in the attitudes of players. Embedding play in the context of the social fabric which surrounds it, the teaching, learning and implied social contract of the game become a part of the play activity as much as games between idealized optimizers. The contrived maintenance of the level playing field seems an appropriately fluid response to the differing levels of expertise and social expec-tations present in the encounter. Where voluntary handicapping is present it not only restores the competitive equilibrium that players have come to expect from pseudo-agônistic play but also reinforces the social cohesion that is of such importance to players in the game encounter. This emphasis on the social fabric of the game encounter is further challenged when players are given the opportunity to adversely affect the position of opponents.

## Rationalizing Antagonism

> There is a fine line between trying to win and spoiling others' enjoyment.—R224

The notion that "winning at all costs" might be inappropriate in a par-ticular social setting reflects the way in which the expectations of social behav-ior influence the formal structure of the game. While the expectations of this cooperative element brought to the table by each player may differ, it is evident that players are generally informed by what, in the context of children's play, Borman and Lippincott term the "press to maintain the game" (1982, p. 139). That is, the maintenance of the play environment in a way that benefits all players may constitute a higher priority than the pursuit of the prescribed game goals. Awareness of this issue is evident in responses that claim the social connectedness between players is more important than the game-specified goals:

> I would not pursue victory if I believe I will hurt someone's feelings by doing so. I would not try and ruin another player's chances at winning because I have nothing more constructive to do [R206].

> Most of the enjoyment in the games comes from seeing the game unfold, and if all that is desired is victory, then it opens up to "three turn win or else" strategies which are no fun.... Sure we trash talk and promises can be broken, but there are levels of promise, and while it is ok to backstab now and again, it's not about winning at all costs [R579].

The idea that players are under an implicit obligation to fulfill social responsibilities within the game is one that serves to shape the gaming encounter in a number of ways. As I have indicated, some players are aware that to pursue victory goals too zealously can threaten the stability of the social setting. The question arises, then, of how players evaluate certain actions as being inappropriate, where other actions are perfectly acceptable. While in theory a player can be "rational," in reality an awareness of the social context is essential to the continuation of the game.

The option to deliberately hinder the play of others through direct or indirect action is one area where the awareness of the social fabric is particularly important. In traditional two-player abstract games, the zero-sum nature of the contest demands that players seek to maximize their own position while subverting their opponent — every move effectively hinders the other player. Within multiplayer games, however, the decision to target another player may be an entirely strategic one, but it is also one that runs the risk of being perceived as motivated by factors other than the general goal-orientedness of play. In this case, the choice to target another player is a critical one. The interpretation of a player's intent may disrupt the social fabric in ways not intended by the antagonist.

While 64 percent of respondents perceive no problem with deliberately hindering other players, a noteworthy number qualified their replies by describing specific situations in which they felt such actions were a legitimate tactic. In a number of responses to this question, this decision was framed in particularly rational terms:

> If there were four moves available, this is the order I would take them. Benefits me and hinders an opponent. Benefits me. Hinders opponent. Helps/hinders no one [R753].

Clearly this respondent has a highly organized and reasonable series of priorities that inform the decision to hinder other players. This rationality is also apparent in the comments of those who respond that they would only target the game leader. This approach, colloquially referred to as "bashing the leader," prolongs the game for the other players, affording them opportunities to win the game. Of those players who qualified the appropriateness of hindering other players, 10 percent subscribe to this perspective:

> I will attack a clear leader, but not always attack anyone else unless I have no other option that might reasonably be considered an optimum move [R543].

> If the endgame is near and there is one clear leader and I have no chance at winning, I will hinder the leader to the detriment of my own position [R569].

In contrast, many players adopt a more nuanced approach that is dependent upon the particular social situation and the perceived expectations of others, rather than the game itself:

> I am very conscious of whom I am seated with, and while I want to win, more important to me is whether everyone had a good time. So I will evaluate the players and decide whom I can hinder and have them still enjoy the game, as well as who such tactics will rub wrong [R262].

> I have to be sure that the other person can take the setback. I'd rather lose a game than lose a friend [R316].

> I try to "balance the meanness" around the table. I'll endeavour to hinder different players at different times so as to avoid people feeling victimised and their enjoyment being affected because of it [R704].

> If you are a guest at someone's house for a game night you don't block their route in *Ticket to Ride* [R591].

A number of respondents suggested that their decision to hinder another player is dependent on the game being played, with a sizeable proportion of these making some reference to the rules of the game and whether they explicitly allow and/or encourage this type of play (43 percent). This attitude is also reflected in those respondents who made reference to "the spirit of the game" or the understanding that such plays are acceptable only if they can be construed as "sportsmanlike."

Emerging from these responses is a clear picture of how the goal-orientedness assumed by the rational player model is frequently undermined in practice by the individual perspectives of players, understandings of appropriate forms of play and the need to balance the social world of the gaming encounter with the competitive structure of the game. All of these elements contradict the general assumption that players are rationally motivated agents who always act in pursuit of the game goals. More importantly, perhaps, they also throw into question the notion that enjoyment is derived from the attainment of these goals.

## The Tenuous Relationship Between "Better" Outcomes and Enjoyment

*It is quite simple: When you play a game, you want to win. Winning makes you happy, losing makes you unhappy.* — Juul, 2009

*Heartbreaking losses and lucky last-minute wins are an important and valued part of my gaming experience not because of the win or loss, but because of the reactions of the participants. The playful belly-aching and playful gloating following a game session often leads to laughter and hilarity afterwards. Pursuing victory is a means to this end, not an end in itself.* — R643

The idea that players pursue goals and victorious outcomes as a principal motivation for engagement with the game is a compelling and pervasive one, particularly in writings on game design. For Juul, the enjoyment that can be derived from a "better" outcome (i.e. victory) is one that underpins the psychological state of playing a competitive game to the degree that he uses this condition as a defining element of games (2005, p. 40). It is interesting to note, however, that although Juul's model is ostensibly a distillation of the works of previous scholars, the suggestion that players are attached to one outcome over another is not one that appears in any of the definitions from which he draws his raw material. While the presence of a disequilibrial outcome is included in the definition proposed by Avedon and Sutton Smith (1971b, p. 405) and the quantifiable nature of that outcome is present in that of Salen and Zimmerman (2004, p. 80), the idea that a player is attached in some way to this outcome is a highly speculative one.

In terms of board game hobbyists, a favorite quotation on this subject comes from designer Reiner Knizia: "When playing a game, the goal is to win, but it is the goal that is important, not the winning." Although this statement displays a certain idealism about the nature of competitive gameplay, it reinforces the notion that many players are actively conscious of the separate nature of game goals and the ensuing valorization of outcomes. This emphasis upon process over outcome is explicitly mentioned by a number of survey respondents:

> Playing to win is critical.... Winning itself is wholly inconsequential. I'd much prefer to come in last than to win unchallenged. Did everyone have fun? Good, nothing else matters [R162].

> Trying to win is important, having fun is important, actual winning is not that important [R142].

> It's important that there be a goal. It's not important whether I win as long as I get to try to win [R174].

It [winning] is secondary to the enjoyment of the game and the enjoyment of being and playing with the people there [R206].

This last response brings our attention back to one of the defining elements of games — enjoyment. Although enjoyment is an extremely slippery term to define, psychologist Fabio Paglieri has suggested that it can be seen as a characteristic goal in all play activities (2003a; 2003b). Given the wide variety of reasons identified for why players may abandon the goals that lead to a valorized outcome, a significant question is that of how much importance players place upon the outcome of a game. If Juul is correct and emotional attachment to a "better" outcome is a feature of games, we would expect that winning would contribute to player enjoyment of a game. Thus, as a part of my survey players were asked to what degree a successful outcome contributes to their enjoyment.

The first and most significant observation that arises from responses to this question is that over half of players (53 percent) are not attached to the outcome of the game as a basis for their enjoyment. While 28 percent acknowledge that winning contributes positively to the experience of a game, only 19 percent indicated that this was an important element in their enjoyment of the game encounter. These results stand in stark contrast to Juul's assertion that "the spoilsport is one who refuses to seek enjoyment in winning, or refuses to become unhappy by losing" (2005, p. 40). Of the players who gave more detailed qualitative responses to this question, 36 percent suggested that their own enjoyment of the game was *of more importance* than a victorious outcome, while 15 percent indicated that the enjoyment of all players held more weight in determining whether the game was a success. Clearly players have differing understandings of the relative importance of game outcomes. This observation raises further questions regarding the relationship between enjoyment and player goals within the gaming encounter.

## Enjoyment as a Goal

Paglieri builds upon the work of cognitive psychologists Rosario Conte and Cristiano Castelfranchi, who propose a model of cognition that focuses on mental states based upon *beliefs* and *goals* (1995). Taking as a fundamental characteristic of play the fact that players seek to enjoy the activity, Paglieri uses this model to describe the way that different goal-types shape the experience of, and attitude towards, play (2003a). Although he discusses a number of these goal-types and the way they shape play activities, I will limit the discussion here to the two forms that are most relevant to this survey — those Paglieri describes as the "true player" and the "hedonistic player."[9]

The true player is described by Paglieri as one for whom enjoyment is the *motivation* for play: "The player is playing to have fun and any other goal is a sub-goal for enjoyment, so she presents a strong goal-oriented attitude." There is a clear causal relationship here — the player is engaged in play specifically because they find such play enjoyable; and since they have identified the game experience as one that provides this enjoyment, they are understood to be largely goal-oriented inasmuch as playing by the prescribed rules and goals is perceived as the source of pleasure. Thus, the player demonstrates an attachment to the goals and outcome of the game, since their enjoyment is based upon the goals as defined by the rules. As a consequence, this "also means they can end without a single bit of enjoyment, if they miss their goals" (2003b). There is a clear correlation here between Paglieri's true player and the rational player model, since both are strongly goal-oriented in their play of a game.

A second category of goal-type presented by Paglieri is that of the *meta-goal*. The player for whom enjoyment is a meta-goal is described as the hedonistic player:

> Such players are always fun-driven, but they can be poorly goal-oriented: they have no problem in forsaking goals defined by play rules, whenever doing so could assure them to have more fun. I suggest to characterize them as hedonistic, since they always choose the path of greater enjoyment [2003a].

The presence of the hedonistic player is also suggested by this research. Player responses which focus upon overall pleasure as being a higher priority than the goals defined by the rules clearly indicate a predisposition towards this style of play. In terms of exhibited play styles, objectively determining the differences between the hedonistic player and the true player might prove difficult since one need not expect their behaviors to deviate too strongly. The difference between the two is largely one of attitude and disposition during play that sees the hedonistic player willing to abandon the prescribed goals if they conflict with the pursuit of enjoyment. Responses that suggest this approach were certainly present in this survey, albeit nowhere nearly as common as those that suggested the true player.

As a consequence of the unbridled pursuit of enjoyment, the hedonistic player will presumably have no difficulty with the idea of self-handicapping if it results in a game that is more enjoyable. Certainly this would appear to be the case when players self-handicap in order to achieve an equilibrium that furthers their own enjoyment. Similarly, although based upon longer-term expectations, the decision to self-handicap in order to draw inexperienced players into the game suggests a hedonistic approach that hinges on the idea of exchange as an impetus for social action (Homans, 1958). That is, if the experienced player self-handicaps in this particular play, the potential for drawing the inexperienced player back to the game provides rewards that out-weigh the shorter-term prioritization of game goals.

The use of Paglieri's model is productive here firstly in the way it describes *why* players focus on game goals. When the primary motivation for play is the enjoyment derived from the activity, any deviance from the prescribed form of the play activity will result in a lesser experience — the rules and goals of the game are central to a player's enjoyment. Secondly, this model also explains why some players willingly abandon the game goals in particular situations. Players for whom enjoyment is a meta-goal of the play activity will behave in ways that are not prescribed by the rules in order to further their enjoyment of the play experience. Both of these characteristic approaches to play are evident in the survey responses discussed in this chapter.

## The Social Player

As I have identified, the apparent tensions between the competitive and collaborative demands of social play are managed through both communicative and behavioral acts in the form of proffered assistance and self-handicapping. The pursuit of the over-arching goal, while ostensibly a primary motivation within the play encounter, is understood by many players to be a facilitative rather than prescriptive element of the game. The general goal-orientedness of players can be subverted by the desire to maintain social cohesion for the group and pleasure for the individual. Thus it is clear that players, for the most part, are aware of the distinction between the game goal as described by the formal structure of the game and the valorization of outcome that is derived from the social context. To return to Eggert's opening quote, the game goals of eurogames are of more importance as a device for motivating play than as a valorizing end condition.

The knowledge that player motivations are, in part, shaped by social context highlights an important element in this analysis of play — that is, that the shape and experience of a specific game encounter are highly dependent upon the particular social structure of the game encounter, and the attitudes and expectations of players. In understanding that these elements can have such an impact on issues such as goal-orientedness, there is a clear indication that, as Goffman suggests, the boundary between the game world and the real world can be more accurately imagined as a "membrane" that permits the incursion of one into the other (1961, p. 65). All of the behaviors described here as deviating from the model of the rational player are evidence of this osmotic intrusion. To suggest that a social game can be played without any influence from the social context is to deny the fact that these games are social experiences. The implicit rules engendered by the social gathering that surrounds the play of the game serve to shape the game encounter as much as do the explicit rules to be found within the game itself. In the next chapter I turn my attention to how this process can not only influence the play of the game, but also render the game experience largely dependent upon the norms of the gaming encounter.

# 9

# An Act Apart?

*Obviously, we are never merely playing a game. Or, to say it another way, we are never playing only one game. We are always conscious of the game's relation to the world in which we live, the world in which that game is one small part.* — Sniderman, 1999

So far I have described the way that players negotiate two different imperatives: first, the competitiveness of play that is called upon by the structure of a game, and, second, the sociability that provides the principal source of enjoyment in game play. I concluded that the majority of players do not consider winning — the ostensibly "better" outcome — a significant element in their enjoyment. It seems players are, for the most part, willing to abandon the prescribed goals of the game in order to maintain the social cohesion of the game encounter, particularly by reclaiming a sense of "fair play."

To further explore the influence of the social context of the gaming encounter on the play of board games the player survey included a number of questions related to in-game activities, such as cheating, kibitzing, deception and kingmaking. Responses to these questions reveal the importance that players place on maintaining the separation of the game world from the "real world." Interestingly, differing player expectations and understandings of appropriate forms of play suggest that the explicit rules of a game act primarily as a framework around which the actual play of a game is constructed.

## Cheating

*If you cheat, we are done playing.* — R179

Cheating in the context of multiplayer games is the act of purposefully deceiving other players in acting outside of the explicit rules of game play in order to gain advantage in a game. In the play of board games, the implicit requirement to play by the rules demands a sense of mutual trust between players, even as the sense of competition embedded in the game structure compels them to pursue the game goals. Unlike digital games, where the procedural rules are embedded in the algorithms of the game itself, or organized sports, where the presence of an impartial umpire ensures compliance, board games require that players voluntarily agree to be bound by the arbitrary constraints of the game system in order for the game to function. Reflecting this requirement, 94 percent of respondents expressed a deep displeasure at the thought of engaging in such an activity, or playing games with those who did.

A common reaction to cheating was an insistence that such players would be ejected from game play and would not be entertained as participants in the future (25 percent). Respondents also placed particular emphasis on the notion of mutual trust and the understanding that cheating not only undermines the game structure but also detracts from the enjoyment of other players. Some respondents felt that cheating within the context of a social gaming environment constituted a "pathological act" (R95) suggesting "a severe social disorder" (R56). Some of the more emotive responses to this question included:

> Not only will you never be invited over again, but the person who first invited you along gets thrown in the pool [R239].

> People who cheat who are over 12 should be shot [R215].

> Burn them at the stake [R184].

> Cheaters? Stone 'em [R85].

> Testicular removal is too mild a punishment for cheating [R117].

> Do you mean: Do I send flowers and cards to the surviving members of the cheater's family? And I would say no. I would also not attend the funeral service [R444].

These responses typify the prevalent attitude among hobbyists towards cheating in board games. Interestingly, Mia Consalvo has explored the act of cheating in video games, suggesting that while video game players may have varying ideas as to what constitutes cheating in a game environment, to many, "shortcuts or code alterations are acceptable in the space of the game" because "games offer us a space where we can experience that freedom, without significant consequences" (2005b). In the light of her research, Consalvo suggests that cheating is "a way for individuals to keep playing through boredom, through difficulty, through limited scenarios, and through rough patches or just bad games" (2005a).

However, as Kafai and Fields note, the majority of research on cheating behaviors in games is principally concerned with the consequences for the *game* rather than for rival players (2007). Importantly, the act of cheating in board and table games is differentiated from that in single player video games due to the way that the required duplicity can impact on other players. Because cheating in a multiplayer games involves the act of intentional deception — "the conscious, planned intrusion of an illusion seeking to alter a target's perception of reality, replacing objective reality with perceived reality" (Bell, 2003, p. 244) — it threatens to disrupt the social cohesion of the gaming encounter as well as the integrity of the game. The repeated assertion that players caught cheating will experience a social penalty appears to leave little room for exploring the creative potential of rule-breaking within the play of board games. In order for the social formation of the game encounter to remain intact, the implicit understanding that such deception is prohibited within the confines of the game holds significant weight.

Another observation made by players is that cheating in board games is evidence of the privileging of outcome over process:

> Cheating is for people who would be happy to simply record victories with no regard for the actual game progress [R723].

> The important part of the game is the PROCESS of playing the game, not the outcome. Intentionally violating rules is counterproductive [R582].

> This tends to arise with people who are too wrapped up in winning and not in the experience of play [R161].

> Cheaters don't like gaming [they] just like winning [R203].

As discussed in the previous chapter, most players view an overly strong attachment to the outcome of the game to be inappropriate. Whereas goals are perceived as facilitative of the gaming process, attachment to outcome is derived from factors extrinsic to the game itself. That is to say, that while pursuit of the game goals is a requirement of play, the extent of the attachment to the game outcome is a trait of the player. In its most extreme manifestation this attachment can lead to cheating. If the desire for valorization through winning is prioritized over the play of the game itself, then real-world attachments disrupt the play of the game. This concern is reflected in a number of other issues that, while not as disruptive as cheating, can impact in different ways on the play experience.

## An Act Apart

As a part of the survey, players were asked to identify behaviors that were considered unacceptable within the context of play. Setting aside the significant number of respondents who again expressed their disapproval of cheating, the most common concerns were those that reflected the inability of some players to separate the "real world' from the artifice of the game. Examples of this kind of issue include the taking of loss and aggressive acts personally, complaining about the game situation, personal attacks, collusion, gloating and emotional manipulation.[1] The most common concern among respondents was over behaviors that suggest a player is genuinely unhappy about in-game activities. Becoming upset over a loss or an aggressive move on behalf of another player is viewed as manipulative, as well as disruptive. Once again, the suggestion here is that such behaviors indicate an overly strong attachment to outcome and an inability to separate the artificiality of the game play from the perceived valorization that is derived from winning:

> Getting genuinely angry is just stupid. I don't mind even the shadiest of tactics, but I do get annoyed at people that take things too seriously and gripe when things aren't going their way or blame bad luck for everything. It's just a game, if you can't lose and still have fun, don't play [R221].

> I do not like players who take losses so personally that they would openly intimidate and threaten another player into a course of action which was counter-productive [R494].

> Somebody saying "Oh no!" playfully is alright, but somebody sulking when you interrupted their plan, played in their carefully calculated spot, leading to a sour game experience for everybody else is not cool. It might be because I'm not deadset on winning, but I find sore losing as well as sulking in game to be unacceptable behaviour, and often sours a particular game for me [R288].

Not surprisingly, a number of respondents also considered personal attacks, gloating and taunting as evidence that players are inappropriately allowing real-world emotions to affect in-game behavior. This lack of separation between the game and the wider environment is considered particularly inappropriate in instances where grievances or allegiances from the real world spill into the play context:

> There are ... situations where a metagame effect is present — i.e. one player is deliberately making another player's life miserable, not to advance their own situation but because they have a personal grudge against them. These games are usually uncomfortable to be involved in and often devolve into arguments. It's best not to get involved in such games [R196].

> Apart from ... cheating and kingmaking, the only other thing I would find really unacceptable is in the meta-game merging of internal and external (with respect to the game being played) activities — e.g. using real-world threats, promises or personal relationships to leverage in-game decisions [R477].

> Not acceptable to ally with your girlfriend/boyfriend just cause they're your GF/BF, or to not attack someone 'cause they gave you chocolate [R364].

Hobbyists often refer to this inappropriate intrusion of real-world attachments into the game as metagaming, even though, as I shall discuss a little later, metagame play can take a number of less detrimental forms. Regardless, whether in the form of collusion or in the decision to target another player based upon considerations external to the game, this type of play is typically considered unacceptable.

These responses reflect the understanding that play of a game should ideally be, as Huizinga suggests, "an act apart" from the real world (1950, p. 10). Discussing the conditions surrounding play, Fabio Paglieri proposes that within games, a normative meta-rule exists:

> Within temporal and spatial boundaries of play context, a (meta)rule holds: there must be no practical consequences to the actions performed here, after the play is over. But this rule has a relevant corollary: if a play action has no practical consequences outside play context, then it is permitted while play-ing — no matter what are its nature and moral value elsewhere [2003a].

Here Paglieri affirms the deontic nature of play in that players are assumed to voluntarily uphold this shared meta-rule as one that constrains them during play. The spatial and temporal boundaries commonly assigned to the play of games circumscribe the activity while also creating a context in which players share a set of normative constraints. The context brought about by this nor-mative boundary can be termed "play" so long as there are no consequences external to it. More importantly perhaps, it is understood that in-game actions should have no consequence outside of the game. Players who fail to recognize this meta-rule can disrupt the play experience. As one player describes:

> Going into a game, I suspend the traditional ethical rules and make it clear to others that I do not regard the in-game situations as truly moral in nature [R548].

The observation here that the game world ideally needs to be understood as separate from the real is complicated by the findings of the previous chapter. As I have argued, the act of self-handicapping is commonly motivated by fac-tors external to the game itself. When players respond to these factors in mak-ing a decision not to play aggressively or target another player, real world considerations function to maintain the social fabric. This is clearly a delicate balance, since players whose behavior actively demonstrates real-world attach-ment to the outcome can be considered problematic by other players.

The fact that board games are played within a social context makes it extremely difficult to separate the ideal experience of the "act apart" from the communicative exchanges between players. As one player observes, "Some whining is strategic. Excessive whining ruins the experience" (R413). Although this player perceives genuine complaint as irksome, there is an indication that, in some cases, communicative acts aside from the in-game mechanics can play a part in shaping the flow of play. Indeed, while for some players complaining about an in-game situation is problematic, for others it constitutes an expected part of the gaming encounter:

> We also consider it fair, almost expected, to belly-ache about how poorly you're doing. Even if you're doing quite well. And whining about how poorly you're doing to get out of having someone do something bad to you is also perfectly acceptable — as long as you accept it with grace and/or humor if you get the bad stuff anyway [R232].

For this player, it is clear that the subtle manipulation of other players through communicative acts is not merely a side-effect of play, but another layer of interaction that forms a fundamental aspect of social game play. This type of play, also referred to as metagaming, is interpreted and experienced by players in different ways.

## Playing the Metagame

> *As much as people make noises about being smart and stuff, the best gamers I've ever played against are usually the ones that can control the game above the game: the metagame.* — Solko, 2005

> *If you don't like the metagame, play games against a computer.* — Pollard, 2008

Within the context of games as a leisure pursuit, the term metagame has been used in a variety of ways, most of which are summarized in Richard Garfield's description of the phenomena. Garfield refers to the metagame as "how a game interfaces outside of itself," suggesting four ways that the metagame impacts play of a given game: what players bring to a game, what players take from a game, what players do between games, and what players do during games (2000, p. 16). In terms of the board gaming hobby, all of these elements can be seen to have some degree of impact on the play of a given board game.

Players may bring previous experience of a game or similar games to the encounter. The description offered by Garfield is so broad that one could suggest that any prior play experience can be considered a part of the metagame. As discussed earlier, in cases where particular social relations are manifest on the gaming table in the form of grudges and/or collusion, this type of influence is viewed in a very negative light by most gamers. Similarly, outside of the framework of tournaments that have metagame value in terms of how they affect overall position, it is expected that play occurs in isolation and that previous victories will not be factored into the play of a particular game. Ideally, players do not bring social relations to the table, nor do they allow those real-world relationships to be affected by play of a game. In terms of what occurs between plays, the earlier discussion of hobby gaming culture is replete with evidence of the way that players engage in metagame activities. Indeed, Garfield suggests that what separates hobby games from other forms of game is the compelling form of metagame that is offered by involvement with the hobby (2000, p. 16).

I want to focus here on the last of the forms that Garfield describes, the metagaming that occurs during the play of the game. In doing so, I specifically want to address the social interactions that occur within the game that are perceived by some players as significant in their enjoyment of social play and by others as problematic. This type of metagame activity is clearly described by Csilla Weninger in her analysis of social events in the collectible card game *Magic: The Gathering*:

> The metagame is characterized by language use that topically centers around game analysis: the out-loud deliberation about the co-participant's or one's own moves. It also includes talk about hypothetical courses of action, primarily in the form of players reflecting about what the outcomes of an alternative move might have been [2006, p. 64].

As Weninger implies, it is a natural consequence of social gaming encounters that players engage in conversations that pertain to the play of the game. This interaction is where much of the meaning of the game encounter is produced. Indeed, drawing on the work of Brian Sutton Smith, Boria *et al.* note that the meaning of the video game *Counter Strike* is not only found in the graphical and mechanical elements which reside in the game itself but "in the social mediations that go on between players through their talk with each other" (2002). In face-to-face games this social interaction is often referred to as "table-talk," a name inherited from partner discussions in card games. Although frowned upon in more competitive environments, and specifically forbidden in select games, table-talk in a typical social gaming situation is common. The presence of table-talk is complicated, however, when the conversations that take place over and above the gaming table are specifically employed in ways that are intended to shape the outcome of the game. The term commonly used to describe this activity is kibitzing.

## Kibitzing and Deception

Although the kibitzer is traditionally thought of as a non-player of the game who contributes (usually unwanted) advice, the term has come to refer to any player who offers commentary on a player's move or the game situation generally. Wei-Hwa Huang suggests four motivations for the kibitzer — those of instruction, selfishness, altruism and socializing (Vasel *et al.*, 2006). As Huang notes, it is extremely difficult to discern the motivations of a particular comment, an observation that frequently leads to the interpretation of kibitzing as a manipulative element in the metagame. For some players, table-talk and kibitzing can be problematic:

> Table-talk gets me mad sometimes. If someone sees something that another player may not and suggests it as an option.... I'd be fine when maybe teaching the game and giving hints to new players, but I do get a bit mad when experienced players give other experienced players "suggestions"— especially when they affect my chances of winning [R585].

> (Unacceptable behaviors) ... strategizing openly with another player against a third party ("table-talk"). I specifically don't like this if the move by a third player helps the one giving advice, to my detriment. Often if a new player is making a gross mistake someone may ask the table, "May I give some advice?" Then the group can either agree or not. Without permission to give strategy tips, especially from the one who will be harmed, it is unacceptable to give advice [R308].

For these players, kibitzing disrupts the expectations of autonomy of in-game decision-making. Yet for others this communicative element is fundamental to the play of the game:

> My group meta-games like crazy. As long as people aren't annoying when they do it. We have a good time giving each other "advice" during our games [R463].

> Kibitzing is an integral part of the experience of boardgaming, and is one of the big reasons I find playing games on the computer unrewarding compared to face to face play. Bridge is one of the few gaming experiences that specifically excludes kibitzing; all others nearly require it or the game suffers [Young in Vasel *et al.*, 2006].

As these comments indicate, players have different expectations regarding the permissibility of table-talk and kibitzing at the gaming table. Proffering advice that is intended to benefit the advice-giver rather than the receiver can have a significant effect on the state of the game. It also represents a disruption of the autonomy that some players expect from the game experience in the way that the game shifts from one of independent decision-making to one where decisions are subject to the influence of in-game communication. Clearly the social context impinges on the purity of the game world.

In contrast to this position, consider the following player statement:

> I might make suggestions as to what my possible strategies could be during a game, remaining silent about the one I'm REALLY trying to pursue, as to mis-

lead others. I think this is perfectly acceptable (especially in multiplayer conflict games), and part of the game is not letting yourself getting manipulated by others and seeing through their misleading would-be intentions. All in good laughs and humour though, people should separate game and real life [R351].

This player makes a clear distinction between the game world and the real world, yet clearly included in the understanding of the game world is a form of social manipulation that for other players is problematic. Evidently, some players include in their understandings of game play the banter and kibitzing that often occurs around the table, while for others the game is purely an opportunity to match wits, ideally devoid of any manipulative or persuasive kibitzing. This variability is further highlighted in survey responses to the question of whether misleading opponents is a legitimate strategy in games.

In the context of game-related conversation, 57 percent of players surveyed consider deception an inherent part of effective game play, particularly with regards to player intent. A number of players indicated that this was a necessary part of game play:

Statements regarding intent should never be taken at face value, as telegraphing your moves transparently is obviously not a winning strategy. In many abstract games, intent is the only aspect of play that is hidden, and this requires either complete silence regarding the game or misdirection to achieve your goals [R161].

Respondents who indicated that this type of play was acceptable typically referred to bluffing, feinting, distraction and misdirection as tactics that reflect a degree of gamesmanship. Although perhaps not explicitly encompassed by the ruleset, it seems they are implicitly a part of the broader gaming encounter and are often seen as valuable skills:

As long as you don't lie about the rules or how the game should be played, it is fine. I respect people that can fool others about their intentions really well [R140].

Manipulation is a valued asset of life's tools [R343].

Deception is an important part of gaming. If players take your word so much that they fail to see that you are working contrary to it, then so be it. They had their chance. In-game deceptions such as these are different than cheating, in my opinion [R179].

In contrast to this attitude were the 3 percent of respondents who felt that misleading other players was entirely inappropriate:

I think it is a way for someone to try to compensate for bad play by subterfuge [R529].

It's not "cheating," but I hate people who do that. I tend to just not listen to what people say, and say nothing myself [R538].

Because I see gaming as a social event, I strongly disprove of lying about your intentions during a game. The point of gaming is to strengthen friendships, relationships, etc. [R245].

Of the 38 percent of players who qualified their responses to this question, 88 percent indicated that the decision to mislead other players was dependent upon the game being played. Most of these players indicated that such misdirection must be explicitly encouraged within the rules of the game, typically where they involve mechanics of diplomacy or negotiation:

This depends totally on the kind of game and whether it could be considered within the bounds of the rules. In most games the rules are quite clear about whether bluff is allowed or not. For the vast majority of games involving multiple players it is quite clear to me that misleading others about your intentions is a viable strategy [R340].

In games where trading, negotiating and other verbal skills are clearly part of the game strategy, then I have no issue with it at all. For other games — *Puerto Rico*, for example — where bargaining between players would ruin the game balance in short order, then you shouldn't be talking about your in-game intentions at all, let alone lying about them [R456].

Notably, 10 percent of those who offered conditional responses indicated that the decision to employ such tactics would be dependent upon the other players in the group. Understandably, reference was occasionally made to the inappropriateness of misdirection when teaching or when playing with younger players. Many respondents made reference to the degree of familiarity with the other players, citing explicit discussions or implicit understandings that dictate the degree to which such metagaming is allowed and/or appropriate:

A lot of this relates to the fact that I play with a regular group, and we've learned about each other's general psychological approaches, and can therefore make sensible decisions about claims that other players may make [R587].

If I wanted to play that way, I would discuss it with my group first and make sure everyone's on the same page. There are lots of different styles of gaming interaction that can all work, as long as all the parties involved agree on that style of play [R355].

The context dependence and the variability of player attitudes towards this type of play style suggests that players are often involved in gaming encounters where differing implicit rulesets might be experienced by each player. Clearly, then, groups who play together over a period of time form shared understandings concerning the level of metagame play, suggesting that although two groups might share a set of explicit rules in the form of the game itself, the social metagame in each situation, and hence the game being played, may differ considerably.

One way to highlight the differing understandings of the metagame in relation to the overall experience of play is to analyze situations where players are forced into making decisions that might be influenced by the particular context of play. One such situation is referred to within the hobby as "kingmaking."

## Kingmaking

*If you're not in a position to win outright, than you deserve to fall prey to the metagame.*— R665

Kingmaking in the context of gaming refers to an endgame situation in multiplayer games where one player, who is not in a position to win, has the opportunity to decide through their actions who will. The act of kingmaking is one that is discussed frequently on *boardgamegeek*, largely due to the way that different players perceive the "right thing to do" in such a situation. Knowing the contentious nature of this issue, I included in my survey a question as to how players feel about kingmaking situations. The responses, by and large, reflect very different understandings of how games should be played and the role of the metagame.

The open-ended format of this question led to a variety of reactions. The most common theme running throughout these responses was the inevitability of kingmaking situations in multiplayer games. A number of respondents (7.5 percent) were of the opinion that the potential for kingmaking in a game is evidence of flawed design. However, the most striking observation is the degree to which players differ in their attitudes towards this type of play. 30 percent of respondents felt that kingmaking has a negative impact on games and is often problematic when it occurs. Typically, these responses focused on the arbitrary nature of one player having control over the overall outcome of the game:

> That sort of situation is no fun for anyone. Being handed the win, rather than earning it, is a pointless and anticlimactic end to a game [R688].

> I find it downright rude to those that had good strategies and were vying for the win. I find it ruins a perfectly good gaming session by trivializing the endgame [R710].

> It has a serious negative effect on enjoyment of the game. Usually it's a fault in the game or a player who has ceased to care making a poor play [R580].

A cheap, poorly designed way to make the losers feel like they have more to give the game [R552].

In contrast to these responses were the almost identically sized group of players who felt that kingmaking is an inherent part of any multiplayer game and should be factored into play:

Kingmaking is an essential part of gameplay. The psychology and how you manipulate your opponents is just as important as moving pieces around the board. I always try to make sure it works in my favour if the last player can have an influence on who wins [R195].

It is a necessary mechanic that forces players to make political decisions throughout the game. Without kingmaking a player's actions have no metagame consequences. In other words, good and necessary [R344].

The metagame is always part of the game. If the kingmaker hands your opponent the win, then you obviously did not play the metagame as well as they did [R133].

If your opponents have allowed you to get into a position late in the game where you have the opportunity to decide the winner, more power to you! Let the metagame begin! [R95].

These respondents view kingmaking as a part of the psychological skillset required to play the game. To them, the ability to read a player and tune play around that reading is an inherent part of the game. Importantly, many of the responses were accompanied by a qualification that the decision to elevate the position of another player should not be motivated by factors external to the game:

As long as the player deciding does so based on what has happened in the course of the game, I have no problem with it. If, however, the deciding player has motives outside the game (such as making their significant other win), I do have a problem with that and will let them know before any such decision could be made [R443].

Kingmaking is fine if done within the context of the game (e.g., where it improves your own final result or where it benefits the player who didn't attack you), as these are things which are part of the game (or metagame) which can be controlled. However, I dislike it where it is done through factors outside the game (e.g., holding grudges or favouring relationships), as it takes away the level playing field [R468].

Here again it is clear that players enforce the separation of the game world from the broader social context. The performance of the "act apart" is seen as vital to the integrity of the game. Yet players have differing understandings of the way that actions performed within a game should be understood. For some, it is appropriate for in-game actions to have consequences that remain in the game. For others, in-game actions should not be treated in the same way as those in the real world. For these players, taking into account prior actions in the game constitutes inappropriate play. This is seen most obviously in responses that emphasized a detached rationality should kingmaking situations arise:

> I think they should do the move that is most beneficial to their own position, and whomever that benefits profits from their planning for that scenario [R395].

> I will make the move which increases my relative position the most. If there is no such move, then I will "pass" if possible, or make an irrelevant move [R365].

> If you're at the bottom of the pack you should generally just stick with moves that seem "reasonable" for your position and hit the folks at the top roughly equally [R281].

> The most important thing for me is to make the decision as impersonal as possible [R445].

These players choose not to allow prior actions to affect their decision-making. Instead they are viewing themselves in isolation from other players. One can discern two general approaches to play here. On the one hand there are those players who view the interpersonal psychology of competitive play as being a central element in their understanding of games. For these players the potential ramifications of targeting other players are a consideration in their overall approach to play. On the other hand, there is that group of players who see games from a more abstract and rational perspective. For these players the emphasis on skilful manipulation of the game system, rather than the psychological interplay, is the principal concern. Is it the case, then, that some players choose to play the metagame, while others do not?

## Never Not Playing

> *A game without a metagame is like an idealized object in physics. It may be a useful construct but it doesn't really exist.* — Garfield, 2000

When a group of players sit down around a table to play a game, the social metagame begins. The very act of sitting together to engage in competitive play establishes a framework for social interaction that can never be entirely separated from the play of the game itself. If we sit with children or inexperienced players, this metagame may manifest in self-handicapping.

With more experienced players we may manipulate, kibitz and plead in ways that bring the game to life. Alternatively, we may sit in silence and imagine that this game-above-the-game is not occurring. Nevertheless, as *boardgamegeek* member Mscrivner describes, this does nothing to alter the situation:

> Denying the metagame, or refusing to engage in metagaming is in and of itself a metagame move. One's emotional or attitudinal preferences may be to ignore the metagame in favor of the less complex and chaotic (or, if you prefer, the more mathematically harmonious) patterns of the board game, but that does not mean the metagame ceases to be [2008].

Games such as the ones I have described here take place within a social microcosm that cannot help but influence the flow of a particular game. Some players are content to merely observe this metagame. Others seek to harness it and attempt to shape it through the manipulation of others. As Pulsipher describes:

> [Players] play to enjoy the interaction of the system and the players, to learn how people think and how they can be persuaded to think in certain ways [2009b].

The appreciation of how people think and the development of skills to shape that thinking are at the heart of social board game play. It is this element of play that players describe when they refer to reading other players, predicting behavior, and manipulating players through kibitzing, deception, and even "tactical whining." It is a game that players of board games are never not playing.

Where difficulties arise is when players have conflicting ideas as to what constitutes psychological play and what constitutes unfair leverage of the social metagame. This is because game rules do not typically describe the psychological skills required to play. A good example of this is the card game *Poker*. Despite the centrality of the bluff to the effective play of the game, there is no reference to bluffing in the official rules of *Poker* (Ciaffone, 2004). While this may seem a trivial observation, it might serve to imagine a group of players who have no experience of the game. To these players, the potential for bluffing is not immediately obvious. The game proceeds with players attempting to estimate the worth of their cards based upon probabilities. Yet *Poker* is a game predicated on the possibility of bluffing. Should this type of play emerge, it would be subject to the social norms established by the group. In fact, it is entirely possible that the act of bluffing may be dismissed as "against the spirit of the game."

Though the patterns of board games may appear complex, they are crude and predictable when compared with the patterns of behaviors exhibited by players. For some players it may be the mastery of game patterns that holds their attention, where for others it may be the mastery of other players through observation and psychological play. This research has identified that both social interaction *and* intellectual stimulation are the most significant contributors to player enjoyment of eurogames. Significantly, the framework for intellectual stimulation is explicitly described by the rules of the game. The framework for psychological play is not.

The fact that the implicit rules governing psychological play are never codified means that players bring their own expectations to the game. In order for the game to progress smoothly, these expectations must be managed within the broader framework of the gaming encounter. It is the structure that emerges from this process of negotiation that forms the game, as the nature of each game is largely dependent on the social context in which it occurs. As Garfield observes, "a particular game, played with the exact same rules will mean different things to different people" (2000, p. 16).

## *The Social Construction of the Game*

> Any game requires a gaming society, and any society has norms and hierarchies that interpenetrate the game. Talking about the game independently of the life of the group playing it is an abstraction. — Sutton-Smith, 1997, p. 106

> A board game is not a vacuum; it happens in real life with real people. — R259

Players have their own understandings of the normative constraints that are in play during a game. For the most part they work together to create the game world and enforce its separation from the social context. Importantly, the continued observation and maintenance of the "real' social context is necessarily a requirement of play. Any behavior that has the potential to spill over outside of the play context can threaten the fragility of the play environment. For this reason a significant degree of social awareness and self-regulation is typically required to maintain the play of a game. As Matthew Speier observes in the play of children, social play demands a high degree of competence in terms of situated interaction and the ability to function within an intimate social grouping (1976).

Stephen Sniderman has written on the implicit rules which surround gameplay and which facilitate the perpetuation of the game instance, yet which are not formally codified (1999). The suggestion that an unspoken obligation binds the player to a normative performance within a game is not a new one and is reflected in many discussions of the nature of play. In his observations of children, Lev Vygotsky notes that at a certain period in their development children acquire the understanding that subjugation to internal impulses during social play often results in the maximization of pleasure (1976, p. 549), a theme that also runs through the work of Bernard Suits (1978). Although some writers see this kind of self-regulation in all forms of play, Fabio Paglieri identifies the "crucial element" in the identification of rules as being a sense of social obligation that is established through peer-to-peer negotiation (2005).

As I have identified here, players have many diverse expectations as to the appropriate "way" to play particular games, in particular with regard to the way that the social interaction forms a part of the game itself. While the majority of players agree that social interaction is one of the main reasons for playing, they have a variety of understandings as to what form this interaction should take. From this observation it becomes clear why so many players tend to form into regular groups that meet specifically with the intention of playing games. As players become more familiar with the patterns of communication that exist in established gaming groups, the potential for consequences to spill outside of the game context diminishes. At the same time, the opportunity to play with these social structures as a part of the game increases. When an outsider joins a group, the existing social structure must again be recalibrated to allow for the expectations of the new player.

Clearly the act of gaming is far more complex in terms of situated action and social negotiation than can be accounted for by formalist explanations. The play of the social game brings into being a complex web of interpersonal and metacommunicative actions and behaviors that demand the constant attention of the players, even as they strive to maintain the semblance of ordered rationality that a strategic competition suggests. The bringing together of these elements, the formal game system, the expectations of individual players and the social context of the encounter bring the game to life in the form of play. Despite the temptation to look to the game box and perceive a game within it, this is only half of the picture. It is the players, acting within the context of the gaming encounter, who create the game. To repeat the words of Erving Goffman, "While the game defines the situation it does not bring the situation into lively existence" (1961, p. 41).

This is both the work and the pleasure of the player.

# Conclusion

*In society ... play phenomena are rarely met in prototypical occurrences: they are usually mixed up with different behavioural patterns, involved in many processes at once, and embedded in larger social dynamics. As a result, social definition of play activities requires a certain degree of variation, in which different kinds of play activity, with different social meaning, are taken into account.* — Paglieri, 2003a

In this book I have analyzed a particular form of game and the way that the play of such games is performed, experienced and understood by a very specific group of people. In adopting this approach to the study of social play, I have been guided by a simple assumption — that social play cannot be understood without taking into account the broader cultural and sociological context in which it occurs. For this reason I have drawn on an eclectic range of disciplines. History, ludology, cultural and subcultural studies, leisure studies and play theory have all contributed to the picture I have painted of social play. While this book does not allow an in-depth exploration of any of these areas, I believe that such a multidisciplinary approach is fundamental in the study of social play and games. There can be no understanding of adult social play without this broader context.

Consequently, from a ludo-historical perspective, I have examined the way that hobby games emerged from the serious practice of war simulation to become a form of recreation for a small, highly educated, predominantly male group in society. From the communities that formed around the hobby, the tendency to experiment with rules led directly to the birth of role-playing games, a revolutionary manifestation of social play whose impact is still felt in the tropes of video games today. As hobby gaming grew, so too did the strong sense of community that inevitably accompanies a shared interest among a minority group. Although the emergence of computer games had a significant impact on hobby gaming, the popularity of collectible card games in the 1990s re-affirmed the attraction of engaging in intellectually challenging social play that was arguably lacking in the video games of that era. Hobby gaming survived.

Throughout this period the growth of the hobby industry provided opportunities to experiment with the form of board and table game in ways that ran counter to the prevalent "one size fits all" approach of mainstream games manufacturers. The niche occupied by hobby gaming allowed for the development of innovative approaches to game design that in turn led to new mechanics and conceptions of what a board game could be. Meanwhile, in Germany, designers subject to particular cultural and commercial influences began to evolve a design aesthetic that reflected the increasing sophistication of hobby game designs yet was conceived specifically to facilitate social play among families. As this aesthetic evolved, designers in Germany were forced to reconsider some of the central tenets of game design in order to create games that eschewed direct conflict in favor of family-oriented themes and mechanics.

The design style that materialized from this prolific period of creativity manifested in a genre of game that has come to be known as the eurogame. These games are characterized by accessible themes, simple rules, constrained playing times and a strong emphasis on comparative performance through non-confrontational interaction. In terms of mechanics, this is achieved through a focus on personal achievement over direct conflict that tends to lead to asymmetric goal formation through the process of play. At the same time, the thematic goals that are assigned to players in eurogames are also typically infused with personal achievement rather than domination or sub-jugation. In addition, the loose connection between player roles and the actual mechanics of the game diminishes the need for aggressive role-playing and the possibilities for in-game actions to spill out into the "real world." Taken together, these traits of eurogames lend themselves to a form of convivial social play, with the game acting primarily as a framework for intellectual challenge and social interaction rather than an opportunity for valorization.

With such a strong emphasis on simple rulesets and innovative mechanics, hobby gamers eagerly embraced the games that were emerging from Germany at this time. That the themes and constrained playing times made them more accessible, particularly to older gamers and their peers, only served to enhance the appeal. Small groups of enthusiasts, firstly in the U.K. and later in the U.S., increasingly sought out these games as an alternative to the complex simulation-driven designs that were typical of Anglo-American hobby board games. The explosive growth of the Internet during the late 1990s further accelerated the word-of-mouth interest that eurogames inspired. Before long, hobbyist publishers in the U.S. emerged to meet the growing demand for the genre, and designers worldwide were increasingly influenced by the eurogame aesthetic. By the early 2000s the eurogame had become a staple of hobby gaming.

The emphasis on games as a social and intellectual activity, rather than an opportunity for valorization, made eurogames the perfect match for hobby gamers precisely because hobby game play has always been centrally concerned with *process*, rather than outcome. Wargames have always been primarily an opportunity to play with history, to see how particular decisions shape the outcome of events, to experience that process. This emphasis on process over outcome is reflected in Matthew Kirschenbaum's observations of the wargaming hobby:

> I see a contemporary player and design community (both hobbyist and professional) that values attention to process in the procedural or quantitative representation of complex, often literally contested phenomena.... I see a focus on the in-game experience, and the after the fact analysis and discussion of what happened and why Kirshenbaum, 2011].

In role-playing games, which typically eschew the notion of winners and losers entirely, the emphasis on collaboration leads Fine to suggest that "enjoying the fantasy ... overrides other considerations" (1983, p. 233). Finally, although collectible card games are built around a directly competitive model, they arguably proved popular due to the engaging metagame of deck-building, which gave hobbyists the opportunity to experiment with the process of game design on a small scale.[1] Even when competition does drive player motivation, as Lenarcic and Scollay observe, "social aspects of play itself transcend the mechanics of any particular game" (2005, p. 71).

The play of tabletop games is a complex social activity. Unlike videogames, where "virtual gamers are hidden away in their warrens, logging-on to their server of choice" (Lenarcic and Mackay-Scolley, 2005, p. 71), management of the immediate social setting in tabletop games adds a meta-level of understanding that cannot help but inform the process of play. The social context of the game can indeed shape play in a variety of ways, since players are always mindful of the social environment in which a game encounter takes place. Goal-orientedness, the perception of fairness, the potential for in-game emotions to spill outside of the game, the norms of appropriate play and the leverage of the metagame — all of these factors impact on the process and experience of play. More significantly, the negotiation of these elements is not merely a by-product of play but an essential aspect of the process. That eurogames are strategy games belies the observation that what they are largely *about* is the social structures they create.

The connection I make here between the play of strategy games and wider understandings of social behavior is not a new one. Most famously, in 1959 anthropologists Roberts, Arth and Bush identified an "association between games of strategy and complexity of social organization" in reviewing the role of games in culture (1959b, p. 610). Huizinga explicitly privileged group forms of play as those most closely linked to the formation of culture, describing play, and specifically contests, as "civilising functions" operating in the realm of ritual (1950, p. 47). As Goffman argues, it is through these forms of ritual that individuals become social beings:

> One must look ... to the fact that societies everywhere, if they are to be societies, must mobilize their members as self-regulating participants in social encounters. One way of mobilizing the individual for this purpose is through ritual.... The general capacity to be bound by moral rules may well belong to the individual, but the particular set of rules which transforms him into a human being derives from the requirements established in the ritual organization of social encounters [1967, pp. 44–45].

The ritual of structured interaction found in games acts to bring about a collective social identity. Consequently, the push to maintain the integrity of the social fabric in a gaming encounter frequently supersedes the goals that are defined by the formal ruleset. This observation suggests a correlation between the social structure of games and the functioning of society inasmuch as both are presumed to operate under a form of social contract where "in place of the individual personality of each contracting party, this act of association creates a moral and collective body" (Rousseau, 1762, p. 24). While this is an association frequently cited by games scholars, it is one that has rarely been explored in any depth. For the group of players discussed in this research, the presence of an implicit social contract in the performance of game play is clearly evident.

The idea that hobbyists value the social process of game play over the game outcome is readily apparent in this book. For the majority of hobbyist players, game goals — typically associated with winning and losing — are not of prime importance in terms of the valorization they are imagined to offer. This is because gamers are, almost by definition, people who are interested in the form of games and the process of play. They are players for whom goals are facilitative of the experience they seek rather than the principal source of enjoyment. Hobbyists play to win because playing to win, rather than winning, is enjoyable.

I am by no means the first to argue for the primacy of process in understandings of games. As noted earlier, Suits' definition of games hinges on the notion that the goals and constraints of games are "accepted for the sake of the activity they make possible" (1967, p. 154). Philosopher Hans Gadamer argues that "the purpose of the game is not really the solution of the task, but the ordering and shaping of the movement of the game itself" (1960, p. 107). This is something that gamers intuitively understand. As games writer Tom Rosen observes:

The people who truly fall head over heels for the hobby are the people who forget about the results of a game as soon as it's over. They might ponder what they could have done differently to improve their score, not because they're bitter or upset, but rather because they want to continue exploring the breadth and depth of the rules framework [2009].

This understanding of the nature of game play directly contradicts that proposed by Juul in his classic game model. Clearly, emotional attachment to the outcome of a game cannot be described as a "psychological feature of the game activity" (2005, p. 40), much less a defining one. Yet there can be no doubt that such attachment is commonly attributed to the experience of competitive play. I propose that it is far more constructive to consider the emotional relationship to the outcome of a given game as being derived from factors that lie partially outside of the game itself. In short, emotional attachment to the outcome is a product of the metagame.

In their purest form, the goals of all games are arbitrary outside of the play they facilitate. Yet when metagames infringe upon the play of any particular game, there is a tendency for players and spectators to become emotionally attached to specific outcomes. This is most obvious in professional sports, where the meaning of an individual game is amplified through tournaments, geographical allegiance and an industry that supports the activity. Similarly, wagering on the outcome of a given instance of a game typically intensifies the emotional attachment to outcome. Clearly, here the metagame overlaying the play can change the experience of the game.

In less formal examples, the specific situational and social context surrounding the play of a game can give rise to nuanced metagames that can similarly affect a player's emotional relationship with preferred outcomes. For example, long-standing competitive relationships with other players, a succession of winning outcomes or the understanding that particular players have an adverse reaction to losing may act to shape this emotional attachment. These are all examples of the way that informal — often unspoken — metagames can bring about changes in the way that players relate to the outcome of a game.

Earlier in this book I suggested that Richard Garfield's description of the metagame as "how a game interfaces with real life" (2000, p. 16) could be interpreted so broadly as to suggest that all previous experience of play in a player's life could be considered as contributing to the metagame. Taking this idea literally, it is apparent that all players must come to a given game with a particular framework for understanding the nature of play activities. These predispositions and beliefs then shape their approach to games and to the importance of valorization through outcomes. For some, this is a significant factor in their decision to play; for others it is not. In some cases it may be that the possibility of losing is of such emotional weight that an individual may choose not to play. These attitudes stem largely from personal experience of play and games, but they are also shaped by the schizophrenic attitude with which contemporary western culture frames competitive play.

On the one hand, most children are raised with the understanding that competitive games are principally concerned with facilitating play — that while the pursuit of goals is incumbent upon the player, emotional attachment to these goals is entirely inappropriate. As parents we teach children that winning and losing are not important, it is "how you play the game" that matters. Despite this understanding, our culture typically frames competitive play in the same light as any other goal-driven endeavor. The importance that is placed upon achievement, winning and valorization through the discourses of sport, business and all manner of other competitive fields, has increasingly bled through into understandings of play. It is, perhaps, the prevalence of this attitude that deters many people from the play of competitive social games. If winning matters and losers are *expected* to be unhappy, why take the chance?

Games are one of the few examples of a cultural activity in which goals are entirely arbitrary. Indeed, it is precisely this autotelic aspect of play that leads many to dismiss games as a trivial and ultimately worthless activity. In contrast, our daily lives are filled with the pursuit of goals that have tangible consequences in the real world. Understandably, we are attached to the results of these activities and experience pleasure when we achieve them. In games, however, while emotional attachment to preferred outcomes may enhance enjoyment, it can also serve to diminish the uniqueness of the play activity as a ritual performed purely for its own purpose. The playful element of game play can be jeopardized by the emotional concerns of the players.

Hobby gamers love games. They purchase, collect, compare, discuss and analyze games with a passion that goes far beyond casual interest. Yet the source of their enthusiasm can only truly be realized when they sit down with others to play. The social situation that arises from game play is a culmination of all the peripheral activities that make up the hobby. If these players have an attachment to anything, it is to the quality of the social encounter that circumscribes this moment. As a group who value the process of play above any implied valorization, maintenance of this process is paramount. So while on the one hand they are actively bound to prescribed goals by the social contract of the game, on the other, they tend to avoid overly strong attachment to outcomes in ways that might disrupt the social fabric of the encounter. It is only when this balance is achieved that gamers can immerse themselves in the genuine source of their enjoyment — a convivial environment within which to explore the intellectual engagement that arises from the pursuit of arbitrary goals.

# Chapter Notes

## Preface

1. Advanced, of course (Gygax, 1977).
2. *Against the Giants* (G1-3), *Descent into the Depths of the Earth* (D1-2) and *Queen of the Demonweb Pits* (Q1).
3. Harris, 1983.
4. Eberle, Kittredge & Olotka, 1977.
5. Lamorisse, 1959.
6. Vaccarino, 2008.

## Introduction

1. See also Eskelinen, 2001.
2. Zagal, Rick and Hsi (2006) have analyzed play of the board game *Lord of the Rings* (Knizia, 2000a) to understand how collaborative games might be better implemented on computers. Others have attempted to leverage the inherently social nature of board games in the implementation of electronic games (Björk et al., 2001; de Boer and Lamers, 2004; Peitz et al., 2005). Patrick Crogan interprets the lengthy history of wargames as a "forerunner of contemporary modelling and simulation practices" (2003). This analysis of board games with a view to how they might relate to the design of video games is an approach I have also adopted in the past (Woods, 2009).
3. See, for example, Schwarz and Faber, 1997; Anspach, 2000; Orbanes, 2003; and Orbanes, 2007.
4. For a detailed history of early wargaming, also see Owen, 1990; and Perla, 1990.
5. See, for example, Borgstrom, 2007; Czege, 2007; Mona, 2007; and Cook, 2009.
6. For an example of this activity, see Montola and Stenros, 2004. For examples of other writing on the role-playing genre see Edwards, 2001; Waskul and Lust, 2004; Copier, 2005; Dormans, 2006; Beattie, 2007; and Tychsen *et al.*, 2007.
7. See, for example, Weninger, 2006; and Williams, 2006.
8. Of particular interest are Kevin Jacklin's design analysis of Reiner Knizia's work, John

Kaulfield's discussion of randomness, and Ira Fay's description of overseeing expansion development for Uwe Rosenburg's *Agricola* (2007).
9. Martin Krause (2007) adopts a more business-oriented approach to the success of board games in Germany in his masters thesis.
10. As an example, an issue such as self-handicapping proves particularly difficult to gauge without a clear understanding of both intent and internal attitudes.
11. See, for example, Redhead, 1993; Giulanotti, 1995; and Wheaton, 2002.
12. See, for example, Doyle and Sorenson, 1993.
13. For further information, see http://waboardgamers.org.au.
14. For further information, see http://www.boardgamesaustralia.org.au.

## Chapter 1

1. It is noteworthy that Parlett includes a number of commercially produced abstract games, such as Alex Randolph's *Twixt* (1961) and Piet Hein's *Hex* (1942). For the purposes of this classification, such games are not considered classical but serve as examples of the mechanics Parlett is describing.
2. A number of texts discuss the emergence of commercial board game production during the late 19th and early 20th century, notably Bruce Whitehill's *American Boxed Games and their Makers: 1822–1992* (1992) and *Americanopoly: America as Seen Through Its Games* (2004), Kenneth Brown's *The British Toy Business: A History Since 1700* (1996), Margaret Hofer's *The Games We Played* (2003) and R. C. Bell's *Games to Play* (1988). More company-specific titles include *The Game Makers: The Story of Parker Brothers, from Tiddledy Winks to Trivial Pursuit* (Orbanes, 2003), *Milton Bradley* (Miller, 2004) and *Games We Play: History of J. W. Spear & Sons* (Schwarz & Faber, 1997).

3. Arguably, it is unfair to dismiss Hasbro in this way given the constraints of the U.S. mass-market, particularly in terms of game complexity and the need to sell significant numbers of games in order to justify mass production.

4. For example, the "Hearts family," "Whist/Bridge family" and "Rummy games." Arnold Marks uses a similar categorization method in his book on the topic of card games (Marks, 1995).

5. Interestingly, Stam makes a similar point with regard to film when he says, "Subject matter is the weakest criterion for generic grouping because it fails to take into account how the subject is treated" (2000, p. 14).

6. For example, while Wolf describes "Shoot 'Em Up" and "Dodging" games by the principal player interaction, other examples include "Sports" (theme), "Escape" (goal) and "Card Games" (medium of origin) (2002, p. 117).

7. For example, *Warhammer 40,000 Collectible Card Game* (Peterschmidt and Miller, 2001), *Warlord: Saga of the Storm* (Williams, 2001).

8. The beginnings of this activity can be traced to 1780 and the development of a war game by Helwig, Master of the Pages for the Duke of Brunswick. The game, which was played out on a table of 1666 squares, featured differing abilities for units, terrain effects and early rules for fortresses and entrenchment (Sutton-Smith and Avedon, 1971b, p. 273; Freeman, 1980). At the same time, there is evidence that civilians had taken to modifying the rules of existing games, such as *Chess* and *Draughts*, to better simulate contemporary warfare (Dunnigan, 1997). The first modern military usage of games is usually attributed to the Prussian army in the early 19th century (Freeman, 1980; Dunnigan, 1997; Jones, 1998). Dissatisfied with current forms of training, the Prussians (and, later, the re-unified Germans) utilized games as models for strategic thinking. These early games implemented terrain effects and even more realistic military maps, and were notable for the inclusion of the effects of military intelligence. In some games the presence of an umpire meant that players were not necessarily able to know the position or exact aims of their adversary. The neutral umpire held such information and revealed only what was logically "knowable" to the commander of the force. This group of games, known as *Kriegspiel*, were divided by the emergence of "free" *Kriegspiel*, in which an umpire suitably versed in the art of warfare made critical judgments over success and failure — as opposed to the "rigid" *Kriegspiel* in which all judgments were rigorously decided by a complex set of tables.

9. In 1913, science fiction writer H. G. Wells published *Little Wars* (1913). The book, which detailed a ruleset for playing wargames with lead miniatures, can be considered the precursor to modern miniatures wargaming. For just over forty years, Wells' rules, along with those of Naval historian Fletcher Pratt (1943), constituted the only form of recreational wargaming (Freeman, 1980, p. 14).

10. This was largely due to the efforts of Jack Scruby in the U.S. who developed a method for producing figures from rubber moulds, and Don Featherstone in the U.K. The pair worked together on the early newsletter *War Game Digest* (Beattie, n.d.; Gray, 2008).

11. For example, *Gettysburg* (Roberts, 1958a), *Waterloo* (Shaw and Schutz, 1962), *D-Day* (Roberts, 1961).

12. Originally an amateur fanzine produced by U.S. serviceman Chris Wagner, *Strategy & Tactics* helped to cement the community that was gathering around the hobby by soliciting the opinions of players regarding the types of games they wished to see produced, and by active discussion of products other than those offered by SPI (Costikyan, 1996).

13. Although Costikyan's claim is somewhat outdated, it is unlikely, especially given the decline of the wargaming hobby, that any title has surpassed the sales of *Squad Leader*.

14. Avalon Hill also grew their product line through the acquisition of companies such as Sports Illustrated Games, 3M Games and Battleline, whose successful titles *Wooden Ships and Iron Men* (Taylor, 1975) and the *Diplomacy*-inspired *Machiavelli* (Taylor and Wood, 1977) were brought into the company's product line. Importantly, the company also purchased the rights to *Diplomacy* and gave the game widespread distribution.

15. For example, *Terrible Swift Sword* (Berg, 1976) and *Sniper!* (Dunnigan, 1973).

16. *Broadsides and Boarding Parties* was an elaborately produced version of Harris' game, originally released as a paper and chit wargame by Citadel Game Systems in 1981.

17. Known as the Gamemaster series, the line was made up of *Axis and Allies* (Harris, 1981), *Broadsides and Boarding Parties*, *Conquest of the Empire* (Harris, 1984), *Fortress America* (Gray, 1986a) and *Shogun* (Gray, 1986b), later renamed *Samurai Swords*.

18. For example, TSR's *Onslaught* (Niles, 1987) and the book/film-related *The Hunt for Red October* (Niles, 1988), GDW's *Battle for Moscow* (Chadwick, 1986), and Avalon Hill's *Platoon* (Taylor, 1986) and *Gettysburg* (Taylor, 1988).

19. The story of the series of events that led up to the "invention" of *Dungeons & Dragons* is a complex one involving many players, each with their own interpretation and recollection of events. More detailed descriptions of the origins of the game can be found in Fine, 1983; Mason, 2004; and Mona, 2007.

20. The game was turned down by a number

of game companies, and the first 1000 copies produced by Gygax's own company, Tactical Studies Rules (TSR), would take 11 months to sell (Fine, 1983, p. 15).

21. Among the first of these were *Tunnels and Trolls* (Andre, 1975), a simpler game notable for the inclusion of solo rules; Chaosium's *Runequest* (Perrin *et al.*, 1978), another fantasy offering that described an elaborate pseudo–bronze age world and was the first to incorporate a system of character skills (Jaquays, 2007); and Marc Miller's *Traveller* (Miller, 1977), a science fictional take on the genre that famously described an elaborate fictional universe, the Third Imperium, with a history stretching over hundreds of thousand of years (Pondsmith, 2007).

22. TSR expanded their range to include post-apocalyptic (Jaquet and Ward, 1978), western (Gygax and Blume, 1975) and spy thriller settings (Rasmussen, 1980), with other companies soon following suit in the search for new material. Superheroes received the role-playing treatment in the 1980s with both Hero Games' *Champions* (MacDonald *et al.*, 1981) and TSR's own *Marvel Super Heroes* (Grubb, 1984). *Champions* was among the first role-playing games to use a balanced points system to establish character traits (earlier games had relied on random die rolls) (Bridges, 2007), while *Marvel Super Heroes* took the opposite approach in supplying characters with wildly imbalanced attributes that were intended to mirror the fictional realities of the Marvel comic universe (Kenson, 2007). Horror-themed games quickly appeared, the most successful of which was Chaosium's *Call of Cthulhu* (Peterson, 1981). Based upon the mythos of H. P. Lovecraft, *Call of Cthulhu* saw the familiar notion of gradual character development replaced by a slow descent into insanity.

23. The flexibility of role-playing was amply demonstrated by games such as *Paranoia* (Costikyan *et al.*, 1984), a darkly humorous take on a dystopian computer-controlled society that often pitted players against each other through hidden agendas, and *Toon* (Costikyan and Spector, 1984), simultaneously a comedic attempt to mirror the lunacy of cartoons and a subtle jibe at the seriousness of the role-playing genre.

24. Lion Rampant's *Ars Magica* (Tweet and Rein-Hagen, 1987) is indicative of this evolution, as players take turns in the role of game master (story guide) and switch between characters (each player initially creates three characters) as the story progresses. Erick Wujcik pushed this emphasis still further in the introduction of *Amber Diceless* (1991), a game set in the universe of Roger Zelazny's series of science fiction books, *The Chronicles of Amber*, which, as the title suggests, dispensed with the use of dice completely.

25. *Werewolf: The Apocalypse* (Rein-Hagen,

1992), *Mage: The Ascension* (Wieck *et al.*, 1993), *Wraith: The Oblivion* (Rein-Hagen *et al.*, 1994), *Changeling: The Dreaming* (Rein-Hagen *et al.*, 1995), *Hunter: The Reckoning* (Rein-Hagen *et al.*, 1999), *Mummy: The Resurrection* (Achilli *et al.*, 2001) and *Demon: The Fallen* (Stolze and Tinworth, 2002).

26. Live action role-playing games (LARPs) are a form of role-playing that, as the name suggests, take play away from the tabletop environment to a larger theatrical scale.

27. "Gamism is expressed by competition among participants (the real people); it includes victory and loss conditions for characters, both short-term and long-term, that reflect on the people's actual play strategies. The listed elements provide an arena for the competition" (Edwards, 2001).

28. Among those games that continue to demonstrate innovation in the independent role-playing genre are *Dust Devils* (Snyder, 2002), a spaghetti-western RPG which incorporates an innovative poker mechanic for event resolution; *My Life with Master* (Czege, 2003), a comedic take on the gothic horror genre which sees players taking the role of servants to an evil master; and *Donjon* (Nixon, 2002), an interesting attempt to revisit early fantasy role-playing games while further empowering players to create the game in conjunction with the game master.

29. The game was published by Wizards of the Coast in 1994 (Garfield, 1994).

30. Renamed *Vampire: The Eternal Struggle* in 1995.

31. Derived from the gameworld of the RPG game *Feng Shui* (Laws, 1996).

32. For example, *Netrunner* (Garfield, 1996), *Deadlands: Doomtown* (Williams, 1998), adapted from the *Deadlands* RPG (Hensley, 1996), and *Legend of the Burning Sands* (Williams and Lau, 1998), set in the same fictional universe as *Legend of the Five Rings*.

33. For example, *Highlander TCG* (Sager, 1996), *James Bond 007 GoldenEye* (Winter, 1995), *X-Files* (Macdonell and Kent, 1996) and *Xena: Warrior Princess CCG* (1998).

## Chapter 2

1. Interestingly, this was not the first time that a bookshelf design had been utilized for games. McLoughlin Brothers had adopted a similar design style for a range of games as early as 1875 (Whitehill, 1992, p. 165).

2. The full list of 3M's Bookshelf series comprises the independently designed *Acquire* (Sackson, 1962), *Bazaar* (Sackson, 1967), *Breakthru* (Randolph, 1965), *Challenge Football* (Herschler, 1972a), *Challenge Golf at Pebble Beach*

(Herschler, 1972b), *Contigo* (Thibault, 1974), *Events* (1974), *Executive Decision* (Sackson, 1971), *Facts in Five* (Onanien, 1967), *Feudal* (Buestchler, 1967), *Foil* (Herschler, 1968), *High Bid* (Winters and Winters, 1962), *Image* (Szwarce, 1973), *Jumpin* (1964), *Mr. President* (Carmichael, 1967), *Oh-Wah-Ree* (a mancala variant) (Randolph, 1962), *Phlounder* (Bernett, 1962), *Ploy* (Thibault, 1970), *Point of Law* (Lipman, 1972), *Quinto* (1964), *Stocks and Bonds* (1964) and *Twixt* (Randolph, 1961), along with versions of *Backgammon, Challenge Bridge* (a *Bridge* variant), *Chess* and *Go*, and the unreleased *Jati* (Havens, 1965) and *Mad Mate* (Randolph, 1972).

3. After living in Japan for a short period, Randolph moved to Venice, where, along with designers Leo Colovini and Dario de Toffoli, he established the publisher Venice Connections in 1995. Over the course of his life Randolph would design a number of *Spiel des Jahres* contenders before his death in 2004. An active member of the game design community, Sackson too had a significant number of games short listed for the *Spiel des Jahres* and is also reputed to have accumulated the largest private collection of games in the world before his death in 2002. Along with his design work, Sackson wrote a short column for *Strategy & Tactics* magazine, discussing non-wargames in the 1970s, and authored *A Gamut of Games* (1969), a compendium of rules for abstract games, some of which were later published as boxed games.

4. Klaus Teuber and Wolfgang Kramer, among others, list Sackson as being influential in their work ("Interview with Klaus Teuber," 2005; Vasel, 2005a).

5. The majority of the information contained in this section discussing the early years of the gaming hobby in the U.K. was provided in a series of interviews with gaming writer Stuart Dagger, to whom I am exceedingly grateful.

6. Later republished by Parker Brothers in Germany as *Ultra*.

7. Published by Milton Bradley, among others, as *Conspiracy*.

8. Ariel began life as a small division of Philmar Ltd., a card game manufacturer who expanded into board games during the 1960s (Bloomfield, 2005).

9. Strangely enough, the success of this arguably mediocre game is attributed to its inclusion in the first versions of Gygax and Arneson's *Dungeons and Dragons*. In the booklet describing wilderness encounters, the authors assume that players have access to Dunnigan's game (Gygax and Arneson, 1974b).

10. Part of a trilogy that also included *Outreach* (Hardy, 1976) and *Starsoldier* (Walczyk, 1977).

11. Other SPI Science Fiction–themed games during this period include *Battle Fleet Mars* (Simonsen, 1977), *Titan Strike* (Kosnett, 1979), *John*

*Carter Warlord of Mars* (Herman and Goldberg, 1979), *Wreck of the B.S.M. Pandora* (Dunnigan, 1980b), *The Sword and the Stars* (Smith, 1981), *The Return of the Stainless Steel Rat* (Costikyan and Simonsen, 1981), and *Star Trader* (Simonsen, 1982). Many more games were published in SPI's dedicated science fiction and fantasy gaming magazine *Ares*.

12. *War of the Ring* (Berg and Barasch, 1977), *Gondor* (Berg, 1977) and *Sauron* (Mosca, 1977)

13. The complete line of Metagaming's Microgame line comprised *Ogre* (Jackson, 1977b), *Chitin I* (Thompson, 1977a), *Melee* (Jackson, 1977a), *Warp War* (Thompson, 1977b), *Rivets* (Taylor, 1977), *Wizard* (Jackson, 1978b), *Olympica* (Willis, 1978), *G.E.V.* (Jackson, 1978a), *Ice War* (Gross, 1978), *Black Hole* (Taylor, 1978), *Sticks and Stones* (Ray, 1978), *Invasion of the Air-Eaters* (Gross, 1979), *Holy War* (Willis, 1979), *Annihilator and One World* (Armintrout, 1980), *Hot Spot* (Armintrout, 1979), *Artifact* (Williams, 1980), *Dimension Demons* (Askew, 1981), *The Lords of Underearth* (Gross, 1981), *Helltank* (Kosnett, 1981), *Trailblazer* (Costikyan, 1981), *Starleader: Assault!* (Thompson, 1982), and *Helltank Destroyer* (Kosnett, 1982).

14. Jackson's *Car Wars* (Jackson and Irby, 1981), which takes its thematic cue from movies such as *Deathrace 2000* and *Mad Max*, is a notable microgame that spawned a number of successful expansions and being eventually re-released as a boxed game.

15. Interestingly, *Cosmic Encounter* was originally licensed by Parker Brothers, but after negotiations fell through, the Eon team self-published the game (Vasel, 2005b).

16. For example, Bruno Faidutti: "*Cosmic Encounter* would later impact my own game designs the most profoundly" (2007); Richard Garfield: "Though there are about a dozen games that have directly influenced *Magic* in one way or another, the game's most influential ancestor is a game for which I have no end of respect: *Cosmic Encounter*" (as cited in Mulligan, 2002); and Steve Jackson, on the design of *Illuminati* (1983): "I'm a great admirer of Eon's *Cosmic Encounter*. I decided to go for the same free-wheeling, backstabbing play style. Another similarity to CE was the idea that each player would have his own special power" (Jackson, n.d.).

17. West End Games in 1986, Mayfair Games in 1991, and Avalon Hill in 2000. Fantasy Flight Games re-issued the game in late 2008.

18. Strangely enough, Sid Meier, developer of the original *Civilization* computer game (1991), has claimed that he had not played Tresham's design, yet Bruce Shelley, Meier's co-designer at Microprose, was an ex–Avalon Hill employee who had worked on the localization of Tresham's *1829* for the company and played *Civilization* fre-

quently (Edwards, 2007). Following a string of successful sequels to the computer game, in 2002 Eagle Games published *Sid Maier's Civilization: The Board Game* (Drover, 2002), an adaptation of *Civilization III* (Briggs and Johnson, 2001). In 2010, Fantasy Flight Games published an entirely different game by the same name (Wilson, 2010), adapted from *Civilization V* (Schafer, 2010).

19. The game upon which *Dover Patrol* was based was *L'Attaque*, designed by Frenchwoman Hermance Edan (1909).

20. Among the games that have re-implemented Pulsipher's design in different historical contexts are *Maharaja* (Sandercock and Martin, 1994), Charles Vasey's *Chariot Lords* (1999) and the more recent *The Dragon and the Pearl* (Richardson, 2004).

21. *Dungeon!* was later published by Parker Brothers, among others, and was revised to facilitate more cooperative play in 1989 and 1992 as *The New Dungeon!* and *The Classic Dungeon!* respectively.

22. Notably, the 2007 re-implementation adds several additional mechanisms and shortens the game significantly. Changes were contributed by European designers Bruno Faidutti and Pierre Clequin, and Fantasy Flight's Corey Konieczka (Carver, 2006; Dagger, 2006a).

23. Or *Blood Royal*—Carver insists the extra "e" is incorrect! (Carver, 2008)

24. *Talisman Expansion Set* (Harris, 1986), *Talisman: The Adventure* (Merrett *et al.*, 1986), *Talisman Dungeon* (Harris, 1987), *Talisman Timescape* (Bourque, 1988), *Talisman City* (Morrow and Friedman, 1989) and *Talisman Dragons* (Morrow and Friedman, 1993).

25. For example, *British Rails* (Henninger *et al.*, 1984), *Mexican Rails* (1989), *North American Rails* (1992), *Eurorails* (Bromley, 1990), *Nippon Rails* (1992), *Australian Rails* (Roznai, 1994), *India Rails* (Fawcett, 1999), *Iron Dragon* (Bromley and Wham, 1996), *Lunar Rails* (Stribula, 2003), *Russian Rails* (Soares, 2004), and *China Rails* (Dreiling, 2007).

26. Reworked for the U.S. market as *1830: The Game of Railroads and Robber Barons* (Tresham, 1986).

27. Originally published by the Swiss company Fata Morgana.

28. Avalon Hill acquired the rights to Battleline's *Circus Maximus* upon taking over the company. The game was subsequently reworked and split into two games—*Gladiator* (Matheny, 1981), which focused upon arena combat, and *Circus Maximus*, a race game.

29. Famously, the rules include a section on sanctioned rule-breaking.

30. Designer John Wick has compared this element of the game to *Magic: The Gathering* (2007).

31. "Beer and pretzel" is a term commonly used to describe games that feature a large amount of randomness and a light theme.

32. *Arkham Horror* was redesigned and released by Fantasy Flight Games in 2005 (Wilson, 2005).

## Chapter 3

1. *Memory* has subsequently sold approximately 50 million copies (Hanson, 2006, p. 45).

2. In 2010 Spielbox began simultaneous publication in English.

3. Tepper estimates that a *Spiel des Jahres*–winning game can expect to sell between 300,000 to 500,000 copies (2007), though some have easily surpassed this figure (e.g., *Carcassonne*, *Die Siedler von Catan*).

4. Strangely, in a more recent interview, Werneck has suggested that this "pressure on the game industry" was largely incidental: "The originators of Spiel des Jahres were—and still are—game critics. We are responsible to our 'customers' which are the readers of our columns. There is no responsibility to either trade or industry. So our aim was to focus on good games. The fact that trade or industry would benefit from our decision was willingly tolerated, since we know that companies can only invest in better products if they had earned money before" (Yu, 2011a).

5. This was awarded in 2001 to Reiner Knizia's *Der Herr der Ringe* (2000a), a cooperative game based upon Tolkien's *Lord of the Rings*.

6. The International Gamers Awards were established in the U.S. in 2000 "to recognize outstanding games and designers, as well as the companies that publish them" (Schloesser, 2008b).

7. Originally established in 1974 as the Charles S. Roberts Awards, the U.S.–based Origins Awards are voted upon by members of the Academy of Adventure Gaming, Arts and Design, and announced at the annual Origins Game Fair. In 1987 the awards were separated, with the Charles S. Roberts award now independently awarded at the World Boardgaming Championships (formerly Avaloncon) ("Academy of Adventure Gaming," 2008).

8. The Spiel des Jahres jury has acknowledged more complex games with the *Sonderpreis Komplexes Spiel* and, more recently, with the *Kennerspiel des Jahres*.

9. As well as an overall prize, the *Spiel der Spiele* recommends games for families, games for friends, games for children, games for everyone, games for two and games for experts ("Spielen in Österreich," 2008).

10. Although, as previously noted, this practice had also been common in wargames.

11. So called because the initial proclamation

was signed on the back of a beer coaster. Initiated by Reinhold Wittig, the thirteen signatories were Wittig, Helge Andersen, Hajo Bücken, Erwin Glonegger, Dirk Hanneforth, Max Kobbert, Wolfgang Kramer, Joe Nikisch, Gilbert Obermeier, Alex Randolph, John Rüttinger, Roland Siegers and an as yet unidentified designer ("Game Designers — A Plea," 2010).

12. It is a testimony to Wittig's combination of these two pursuits that he has won no less than five *Sonderpreis "Schönes Spiel"* for, chronologically, *Das Spiel* (1980), a game comprising 281 dice in a pyramid formation, *Wir füttern die kleinen Nilpferde* (1983), a children's game, *Müller & Sohn* (1986), a two player roll and move game themed around mill construction, *Kula Kula* (1993), a nautical set collection game that utilizes sea shells and wooden boats, and the beautiful abstract *Doctor Faust* (1994).

13. Interestingly, "Game Designer's Association" is the translation offered up for international members.

14. Originally entitled *Rafting*.

15. Originally entitled *Das Spiel der Weinberge*.

16. *Münchner Spielwies'n* (2008).

17. *Spielefest* (2008).

18. Wargames.

19. It is interesting to note that this aversion to violence also applies to video games, where Germany is described as having "the most stringent anti-violence laws" in Europe (Thayer and Kolko, 2004, p. 486).

20. Thornquist is here referring to the Essen Games Fair, discussed later in this chapter.

21. Game Manufacturer's Association.

22. In 2010 the collection of the *Deutches Spiele-Archiv* was purchased by the city of Nuremberg (Helldörfer, 2010).

## Chapter 4

1. For example, Kosmos (previously Franckh Spiele-Galerie), an imprint of Franckh-Kosmos Verlags-GmbH & Co.; and Goldsieber, an imprint of Simba Toys, formed in 1995.

2. For example, Amigo Spiel (1980), Queen Games (1992), Drei Magier Spiele (1994), and Adlung-Spiuele (1990).

3. Originally commissioned by a German road haulage company (Walker, 1989).

4. Between these two *Spiel des Jahres*–winning games, Kramer and his wife Ursula also designed the highly regarded *Wildlife Adventure* (1985), a reworking of which, *Expedition* (Kramer, 1996b), would be nominated for the award in 1996.

5. *The General* was Avalon Hill's in-house magazine.

6. In 2004 Walker temporarily revived

*Games International* in both a print and online format, but publication ceased again in 2006.

7. Moon published three games in Germany in 1990: *Wer Hat Mehr?* (1990c), later reprinted as *Where's Bob's Hat?*; *Gespenster* (1990b), a re-release of the game *Black Spy* (1981), which Moon had designed while at Avalon Hill; and *Airlines* (1990a), a reimplementation of which, *Union Pacific* (1999), would be nominated for the *Spiel des Jahres* in 1999.

8. Re-issued by Milton Bradley as *Daytona 500*, *Quandary*, *Bandu* and *Dragon Tales Matching Game*, respectively.

9. Reprinted by Avalon Hill in the U.S. as *Adel Verpflichtet* (subtitled "The Great Bluffing Game from Germany") and, later, as *By Hook or Crook* (1990b); in the U.K. by Gibsons Games as *Fair Means or Foul* (1990c); and by Überplay worldwide in 2004 as *Hoity Toity*.

10. Interestingly, *6-Tage Rennen* was not produced by a dedicated games company but by a group promoting cycling, Holtmann VIP.

11. Vasey was co-author of the popular war game review magazine *Perfidious Albion*. Farquhar would later become a playtester for Reiner Knizia and contribute substantially to *Der Herr der Ringe* and *Blue Moon*, Knizia's expandable card game (2004c), among other titles.

12. Breese is the designer and publisher of *Reef Encounter* (2004) and the successful "Key" series of games in the European mold, *Keywood* (1995), *Keydom* (1998), *Keytown* (2000), *Keythedral* (2002) and *Keyharvest* (2007).

13. Bob Scherer-Hoock (Scherer-Hoock, 2003) notes that among the games played at the event were: *Ausbrecher* (Bücken, 1988), *Cash* (Kramer and Grunau, 1990), *Civilization*, *Die Macher*, *Drachenlachen* (Wittig, 1984), *Favoriten* (Müller, 1989), *Hare & Tortoise*, *Haithabu* (Ross, 1975), *Homas Tour* (Bontenbal, 1979), *Jump the Queue* (1989), *Karawane* (Bartl et al., 1990), *Karriere Poker* (1988), *McMulti*, *Niki Lauda's Formel 1*, *Ogallala* (Hoffmann, 1975), *Railway Rivals*, *Sahara* (Bücken, 1990), *Traber Derby* (Urack, 1989), *Up the River* (Ludwig, 1988), *Wildlife Adventure* and *Adel Verpflichtet*.

14. A problematic issue with the submission of game designs is that companies will often refuse to view unpublished prototypes lest they make themselves vulnerable to later claims of copyright infringement.

15. *Junior Labyrinth* (Kobbert, 1995), *Labyrinth der Ringe* (Kobbert, 1998), *Labyrinth: Das Kartenspiel* (Kobbert, 2000), *3D Labyrinth* (Kobbert, 2002), *Lord of the Rings Labyrinth* (Kobbert, 2003), *Labyrinth — Die Schatzjagd* (Baars, 2005) and *Master Labyrinth* (Kobbert, 2007).

16. A re-release of the earlier *Homas Tour* (Bontenbal, 1979).

17. A degree of confusion surrounds the origins of Borg's game. Originally titled *Liars Dice* and published by Milton Bradley in 1987, the game is similar to the public domain game known as *Dudo* or *Perudo*.

18. Originally published by the German company Moskito.

19. Falco, 1991.

20. Eventually Mike Siggins would contribute to the site in a deal which allowed Tidwell to transcribe the majority of *Sumo*'s back issues onto *The Game Cabinet* (Tidwell, 2008).

21. The English translation of *Die Siedler von Catan* is *The Settlers of Catan*.

22. Dott was the president of Avalon Hill at the time.

23. *1835* was a German take on Tresham's railroad designs.

24. Reprinted as *Detroit-Cleveland Grand Prix*.

25. Reprinted as *Streetcar*.

26. Interestingly, *Entdecker* was a part of a larger game that Teuber had presented to Kosmos. The publisher was reluctant to produce such an expansive design, encouraging Teuber to break up the game into its constituent parts. *Entdecker* was the result of the first explorative portion of the game, while *Die Siedler von Catan* came from the development-focused endgame ("Interview with Klaus Teuber," 2005).

27. Re-issued (updated) in 2007 as *El Capitan* (Rösner and Kramer, 2007).

28. Clifford, 2000.

29. Tummelson discusses this decision in an interview with Stephen Glenn:

The Bromley family decided to leave Mayfair and tried to sell it. I really thought that there was a market — or should be — for the German style games in the U.S. so I decided to create my own company to do it. The first step was to try to buy Mayfair, but the family wanted too much for the company — so I just started my own company and forged ahead. Using what I had learned at Mayfair: primarily the mistake of reprinting and not cooperating with the Germans (Tummelson in Glenn, 1999b).

30. *Fossil, Mississippi Queen, Mississippi Queen: The Black Rose* (Hodel, 1998b), *Edison & Co.* (Burkhardt, 1998), *Löwenherz* (Teuber, 1998) and *Ido* (Weber, 1998).

31. *Mamma Mia* (Rosenberg, 1999).

32. *Tikal* (Kramer and Kiesling, 1999).

33. *Torres* (Kramer and Kiesling, 2000a).

34. Branham, an active game designer and writer, was also responsible for *The Gaming Dumpster*, an online rules resource.

35. Action Points — a mechanic whereby several actions are available to a player in their turn but limited by the expenditure of action points.

36. *Carcassonne—Wirtshäuser und Kathedralen* (Wrede, 2002), *Carcassonne—Händler & Baumeister* (Wrede, 2003a), *Carcassonne—Burgfräulein und Drache* (Wrede, 2005), *Carcassonne—Der Turm* (Wrede, 2006), *Carcassonne—Abtei und Bürgermeister* (Wrede, 2007b), *Carcassonne—Graf, König und Konsorten* (Wrede, 2008).

37. *Carcassonne: Neues Land* (Wrede and Colovini, 2005), *Carcassonne: Die Burg* (Wrede and Knizia, 2003).

38. For example, designers such as Martin Wallace and Richard Breese (U.K.), Bruno Faidutti (France), Leo Colovini (Italy) and Philippe Keyaerts (Belgium).

39. South Korea has a particularly active board game community.

40. *Ticket to Ride: Europe* (Moon, 2005), *Ticket to Ride: Märklin Edition* (Moon, 2006), *Ticket to Ride: Nordic Countries* (Moon, 2007a) *Ticket to Ride: The Card Game* (Moon, 2008a) and *Ticket to Ride: The Dice Game* (Moon, 2008c).

41. *Ticket to Ride: Mystery Train Expansion* (Moon, 2004b), *Ticket to Ride: Switzerland* (Moon, 2007b) and *Ticket to Ride: The Dice Expansion* (Moon, 2008b).

42. A re-working of Michael Schacht's *Kardinal & König* (2000).

43. A subsidiary of Überplay, Inspiration Games, published religious-themed variations on popular games, such as *The Settlers of Zarahemla* (Teuber, 2003) and *The Ark of the Covenant* (Wrede, 2003b), re-workings of *Die Siedler von Catan* and *Carcassonne*, respectively.

44. For example, *Primordial Soup* (originally published as *Ursuppe* (Matthäus and Nestel, 1997), *Santiago* (Hely & Pelek, 2003) and *Il Principe* (Ornella, 2005).

45. For example, *Parthenon: Rise of the Aegean* (Parks and Hawkins, 2005), *Pandemic* (Leacock, 2008) and *Wasabi* (Gertzbein and Cappel, 2008).

46. For example, *Twilight Imperium 3rd Edition* (Petersen, 2005), *Battlelore* (Borg, 2006), *Bootleggers* (Beyer *et al.*, 2004), and *Nexus Ops* (Catino, 2005).

47. *Voltage* (Yu, 2006a) and *Desert Bazaar* (Yu, 2006b).

48. *Risk (Revised Edition)* (Daviau, 2008). Designer Rob Daviau has acknowledged the influence of eurogames in the development of more recent Hasbro titles (Vasel, 2005d).

49. The designer, Donald Vaccarino, had been involved in the development of cards for *Magic: The Gathering*.

## Chapter 5

1. A number of titles included in this sample would likely not be considered eurogames by hobbyists or publishers (e.g., *Die Werwölfe von Düsterwald* (Davidoff *et al.*, 2001) and Kris Burm's *Gipf* series of games: *Dvonn* (2001), *Gipf*

(1997). To exclude these from this sample would be to impose a definition of the eurogame before embarking on the analysis — a somewhat specious approach.

2. With apologies to Damon Knight!

3. Examples of this are card games such as *Bohnanza* (Rosenberg, 1997), *Bang!* (Sciarra, 2002) and *Race for the Galaxy* (Lehmann, 2007).

4. For example, *Ra* (Knizia, 1999a) and the central board of *Agricola* (Rosenberg, 2007).

5. For example, card placement in *Lost Cities* (Knizia, 1997b) and *Blue Moon* (Knizia, 2004c).

6. For example, *El Grande* (Kramer and Ulrich, 1995) and *Rheinländer* (Knizia, 1999b).

7. For example, *Goldbräu* (Delonge, 2004) and *Mall World* (Meyer, 2004).

8. For example, *Carcassonne* and *Gheos* (Wiersma, 2006).

9. For example, *Goa* (Dorn, 2004) and *Wasabi* (Cappel, 2008).

10. For example, Franz Vohwinkel, Doris Matthaus and Michael Menzel.

11. Perhaps the most humorous example of this attention to detail is found in Richard Berg's *The Campaign for North Africa* (1978), in which the Italian troops require additional water in order that they may enjoy pasta.

12. Those familiar with eurogames will recognize that I have chosen a title where the emphasis on restricted choice is most transparent. Still, as I have identified, this type of choice-driven play is extremely prevalent throughout the genre. *Tikal* is used here precisely because the mechanic is so explicitly realized.

13. The bidding mechanic is only utilized in the advanced "auction version" of the game.

14. Marcel-André Casasola Merkle's *Verräter* (Casasola Merkle, 1998) and Phillipe Keyaert's *Vinci* (Keyaerts, 1999).

15. Richard Morgan's *Chess* and *Checkers*-derived abstract strategy game *La-Trel* (Morgan, 1994).

16. See, for example, *Euphrat & Tigris* (Knizia, 1997a).

17. For example, hobbyists refer to Reiner Knizia's *Euphrat & Tigris* (1997a), *Samurai* (1998b) and *Durch die Wüste* (1998a) as a tile-placement trilogy, though the latter does not involve the placement of tiles during the game but three-dimensional camel-shaped tokens.

18. A similar limitation is seen in Richard Breese's *Key Harvest* (2007).

19. This is a common mechanic in connection games, such as *Linie Eins* (Dorra, 1995), *Tsuro* (McMurchie, 2005) and any number of transport-themed games.

20. For example, *Zooloretto* (Schacht, 2007) and *Agricola* (Rosenberg, 2007).

21. For example, *Alhambra* (Henn, 2003).

22. While gaming writer Shannon Appelcline has argued that most game mechanics can be abstracted to a form of auction (2005), I shall limit here the description of auctions to the more transparent implementation of bidding mechanics.

23. For example, *Modern Art* (Knizia, 1992a), *High Society* (Knizia, 1995a) and *For Sale* (Dorra, 1997).

24. For example, *Age of Steam* (Wallace, 2002) and *Power Grid* (Friese, 2004).

25. For example, *Ra* (Knizia, 1999a) and *Die Fürsten von Florenz* (Kramer and Ulrich, 2000).

26. For example, *Wildlife* (Kramer, 2002) and *Modern Art* (Knizia, 1992a).

27. For example, *Age of Steam* (Wallace, 2002) and *Löwenherz* (Teuber, 1998).

28. For example, *Die Macher* (Schmeil, 1986), *Serenissima* (Ehrhard and Vitale, 1996) and *Indonesia* (Doumen and Wiersinga, 2005).

29. For example, *New England* (Weissblum and Moon, 2003) and *El Grande* (Kramer and Ulrich, 1995).

30. For example, *Vom Kap bis Cairo* (Burkhardt, 2001) and *New England*.

31. For example, *High Society* (Knizia, 1995a) and *Geschenkt* (Gimmler, 2004).

32. Designer Shannon Appelcline refers to this variation on the English auction as "Turn-Based Continuous Bidding" (2004).

33. For example, *Medici* (Knizia, 1995b) and *Industria* (Schacht, 2003b).

34. A somewhat uncharacteristic reliance on technology for a eurogame.

35. Referred to by hobbyists as "downtime."

36. *Die Siedler von Catan* is a good example of this, with runaway leaders typically encountering difficulty in performing trades that would benefit them.

37. For example, *Die Siedler von Catan* and *Antike* (Gerdts, 2005).

38. For example, *Roads and Boats* and *Caylus*.

39. For example, *Union Pacific* (Moon, 1999) and *Stephenson's Rocket* (Knizia, 1999c).

40. For example, *Imperial* (Gerdts, 2006) and *Goldbräu* (Delonge, 2004).

41. For example, Andreas Seyfarth's *Manhattan* (1994) incorporates an area control element.

42. Although simultaneous action selection is also a common mechanic in eurogames. See, for example, *Raja: Palastbau in Indien* (Kiesling and Kramer, 2004), *6-Nimmt!* (Kramer, 1994), *Diamant* (Moon and Faidutti, 2005) and *Piratenbucht* (Randles and Stahl, 2002).

43. Wargames commonly cast players in asymmetrical roles from the outset of the game, while role-playing is founded upon the notion of players occupying separate and distinct character roles.

44. Interestingly, as noted earlier, this was also one of the few early eurogames to involve direct conflict.

45. Kramer and Ulrich's earlier *El Grande* employs a very similar mechanic, although the action cards are not tied to specific phases of the turn.

46. Acknowledging the derivation, Faidutti writes on his website: "I am indebted to that old teenager, Marcel-André Casasola Merkle, for taking from *Verrater* the character system of my game *Citadels*. I had most of the building system, the scoring system, some character effects, but I did not know how to distribute the characters among the players in a tactical way while allowing some bluffing with it. Then I read the rules of *Verrater* [sic] — even before playing the game — and I directly moved the character choosing system from his game to mine" (n.d.).

47. In *Puerto Rico* players select a role on their turn that is then used by all players, but with the selector receiving an additional privilege. The role is then unavailable for the remainder of the round.

48. Splotter Spellen's *Bus* (Doumen and Wiersinga, 1999a) and Martin Wallace's *Way Out West* (2000) can also be considered early examples of this mechanic.

49. Breese employed the worker placement mechanic in a purer form in his later game *Keythedral* (2002).

50. Games scholar Jesper Juul explicitly foregrounds the player relationship to the over-arching goal by arguing that player movement towards the goal is reinforced by an emotional attachment to the game outcome, an assertion I shall discuss in greater detail in a later chapter.

51. Translated as "the Kramer track," it was first implemented by Wolfgang Kramer in *Das Große Unternehmen Erdgas* (1982).

52. In both of these cases, auctions.

53. Or, more accurately, narrativist (Frasca, 2003).

54. See Cameron, 1995; Murray, 1997; Frasca, 1999; Finn, 2000; Eskelinen, 2001; Frasca, 2001a; Juul, 2001a; Juul, 2001b; Carlquist, 2002; Jenkins, 2002a; Atkins, 2003; Frasca, 2003; Eskelinen, 2004; Murray, 2005; Pearce, 2005; Brown, 2007; Stern and Mateas, 2007, among many others, for the details of this debate.

55. I am aware that Eskelinen has critiqued scholars for taking these words out of context in the past (Eskelinen, 2005). To the extent that he clarifies his position, I agree with Eskelinen that the study of theme or narrative has little to offer in terms of understanding the nature of games as a "different transmedial mode and cultural genre of expression and communication than stories." However, as thematic elements in eurogames *are* marketing tools, they are more than worthy of exploration here.

56. As a concrete example, role-playing games are, without exception, built upon the notion of narrative and thematic immersion. It is the theme and story of these games, the "collective creation of fantasy" (Fine, 1983, p. 230), that provides one of the keys to their attraction. Although many examples could be reduced to the level of abstract die rolling, this compelling element would be lost in the process.

57. Although, as mentioned earlier, the quality of graphic design within eurogames is notably high, designer Mike Doyle has criticized the genre for its somewhat formulaic approach to box design: "There has been, for many generations, a general formula for creating box covers that basically has not changed. With the themed Euro-style games, for example, you will find a big, illustrated image, usually depicting an event related to the theme, the big game name on top and the publisher's logo on bottom — usually on the right hand corner. Illustration styles can vary and often will depict a period look.... So why do I think this formula needs rethinking? With the new generation of gaming at hand, the visual language remains identical to its predecessors — it does not communicate that something new is happening here" (Doyle in Bretsch, 2005).

58. The graphic design of the game is by Franz Vohwinkel.

59. Aleknevicus is speaking here with a degree of levity, but the criticism is nevertheless valid.

60. Despite this observation, Knizia has claimed repeatedly that theme is an important element in his designs: "The theme, mechanics and the materials in the game must work as one unit and if they don't gel together I think the game is not complete. Sometimes people say that my games are a bit abstract. I'm a more scientific man. My approach is that the game should have very simple rules and depth of play comes out of these simple and unified rules. There may be a lot of details, but usually I have a good thematic reason for these additions" (Knizia in Batty, 2006a). See also Glenn, 2002; and Knizia, 2004b.

61. While some of these changes are relatively minimal (see, for example, *Ave Caesar* [Riedesser, 1999], a chariot racing game rethemed as spaceship racing in *Q-Jet 21ZXX* [Riedesser, 2005] for the Japanese market), others are a complete reworking of the theme (for example, Queen's retheming of Dirk Henn's game of theater management, *Show Manager* [1996], to one of ocean cruises in *Atlantic Star* [2001]).

62. For the purposes of this analysis, historical periods have been broken down into prehistoric, ancient, middle ages, early modern and modern. Importantly in the case of games identified as being themed within the Middle Ages, this does not refer to a specific location (i.e. Europe) that is typically associated with the term, merely to a time period (Approximately 400 A.D. to 1500 A.D.). Thus a game such as *Raja* (Kiesling and Kramer, 2004), although taking place

in India, is categorized according to the time period in which the game is set.

63. Although this is typically not the classic Tolkien-inspired fantasy that dominates Anglo-American designs, but rather a generic medieval setting with fantastic elements — for example, *Ohne Furcht und Adel*, *Das Amulett* (Weissblum and Moon, 2001) or, in the case *of Die Siedler von Catan*, a fictional historical setting.

64. German writer Morritz Eggert attributes the rarity of science fiction as a game theme in Germany to cultural memories of the way the Nazi regime "defined itself in a kind of futuristic aesthetic" (Eggert, 2005).

65. In the case of *6 Nimmt!* and *Hol's der Geier*, these games use plays on German colloquialisms to locate the theme. The presence of oxen in *6 Nimmt!* is a play on the common pejorative term hornochsen. The expression Hol's der Geier is an exclamation in German, with the word geier also referring to the vultures featured on the game's cards. In *Coloretto* the employment of chameleons is a reference to the goal of the game — collecting different colored cards.

66. Two games, *Kahuna* (Cornett, 1998) and *Alles im Eimer* (Dorra, 2002), simultaneously encourage the player to build and destroy the accomplishments of other players. *Kahuna* adopts a fantasy theme, with players competing through the use of magic, while the theme of *Alles im Einer* casts players as children in a friendly competition set in a farmyard. In both cases it is buildings, rather than people or animals, which are the targets of the destruction. Both *Verräter* and *David & Goliath* (Staupe, 1998) explicitly task players with fighting, though the relationship between the thematic and functional goals in the latter is extremely tenuous, *David & Goliath* being a variation on a traditional trick-taking card game. Only one game, notably a French design, has the thematic goal of conquering — *Condottiere* (Ehrhard and Vitale, 1995). Finally, *Die Werwölfe von Düsterwald* (Davidoff *et al.*, 2001), which falls under the umbrella of this analysis due to its appearance on the Spiel des Jahres shortlist, is a commercial version of Dimma Davidoff's party game *Mafia* that includes player elimination.

67. A number of eurogames do employ simultaneous actions, however; for example, *Adel Verpflichtet* and *Wallenstein* (Henn, 2002).

68. Referred to in game theory as payoffs.

69. Following the initial set-up of the board, *Caylus* can be considered a game of perfect information, as can *Packeis am Pol* (Jakeliunas and Cornett, 2003) and *Age of Steam* (Wallace, 2002).

70. For example, *Attika* (Casasola Merkle, 2003), *Elfenland* and *Notre Dame* (Feld, 2007b).

71. For example, *Goa*, *Amon Ra* (Knizia, 2003) and *Sankt Petersburg* (Brunnhofer and Tummelhofer, 2004).

72. For example, *Ra*, *Lost Valley* and *Euphrat & Tigris*.

73. For example, *Die Siedler von Catan* and *Piratenbucht* (Randles and Stahl, 2002).

74. For example, *Ticket to Ride* and *Elfenland*.

75. For example, *Snakes and Ladders* and *Candyland*.

76. Beginning in approximately 2005, dice began to appear far more commonly in eurogames — for example in *Um Krone und Kragen* (Lehmann, 2006), *Yspahan* (Pauchon, 2006), *Königsburg* (Chiarvesio and Iennaco, 2007) and *Giganten der Lüfte* (Seyfarth, 2007). More recently, publishers have begun releasing dice-based games that leverage the familiarity of already popular franchises — for example, *Alhambra — Das Würfelspiel* (Henn, 2006), *Die Siedler von Catan: Das Würfelspiel* (Teuber, 2007b) and *Ra: The Dice Game* (Knizia, 2009b).

77. Naturally there are many counter-examples in early hobby games, but the generalization stands.

78. Even if this is a position that some hobby gamers might argue.

79. For example, *Euphrat & Tigris, Sankt Petersburg* and *Funkenschlag (Second Edition)* (Friese, 2004).

80. For example, *Piratenbucht* (Randles and Stahl, 2002), *Die Siedler von Catan* and *Ticket to Ride*.

81. For example, *Zooloretto* and *Agricola*.

82. Variations on this system can be seen in a wide variety of games, including *Hase und Ingel*, *Adel Verpflichtet*, *Ursuppe* (Matthäus and Nestel, 1997), *Torres* and *Das Zepter von Zavandor* (Drögemüller, 2004), among others.

83. Stepak vs. Mashian, Israel Championship Semifinals, 1980. See Krabbé, 2009.

84. In both cases, twelve rounds.

85. Other examples that use this technique include *El Grande*, *Piratenbucht* (Randles and Stahl, 2002), *Notre Dame* (Feld, 2007b), *Agricola* and *Yspahan* (Pauchon, 2006).

86. For example, *Tikal*, *Euphrat & Tigris*, *Ticket to Ride* and *Puerto Rico*.

87. See Faidutti, 2006, for examples.

## Chapter 6

1. In the USA and U.K., the top 4,000.

2. The data regarding marital status was drawn from an informal poll conducted by user LankyEngineer in 2008. This data is based on 2256 respondents as of January 2010 (LankyEngineer, 2008b).

3. Based on 2957 responses as of February 20, 2009.

4. For example, although data on gaming in

the general population is closely guarded by the industry, a 2000 report by Wizards of the Coast indicates that approximately 3 percent of the population play role-playing games at least once a month, compared with 16 percent in this survey (Dancey, 2000).

5. National gaming conventions such as Origins and Gencon offer players the possibility of participating in tournament play and/or set aside areas for open gaming, as do smaller local conventions. Usually attended by industry professionals and the general public, the larger conventions serve as a way for companies to reach their target audience, demonstrate upcoming releases and organize tournaments to bolster awareness of particular games. Typically, larger conventions cover all aspects of the broader gaming culture, while smaller local conventions are generally genre specific. Of the two U.S. national conventions, Origins is anecdotally considered a more gamer-focused event due to the greater opportunities for casual/open gaming, while Gencon is perceived as a larger, more industry-focused event at which many companies debut new titles. Both feature organized tournament play. Local conventions are numerous in the U.S., with most organized by regional gaming clubs.

Tournaments on a large scale occur at the World Boardgaming Championships in Lancaster, Pennsylvania, an event specifically dedicated to board games ("Boardgame Players Association," 2009). Organized by the non-profit Boardgame Players Association, the WBC replaced Avalon Hill's dedicated convention in 1999 and continues to draw audiences of around 1300 players each year. As with the broader board gaming hobby, the shift towards European-style games has been considerable since the inception of the convention. Further reflecting this shift, since 2001 the Boardgame Players Association, along with the Games Club of Maryland, has been organizing Euroquest, a convention specifically dedicated to European-style games that includes tournament events linked to the WBC.

6. Fine cites two 1978 surveys, one from the *Judges Guild Journal* which found that 2.3 percent of players of RPGs were female, and another in Metagaming's *The Space Gamer* in which only 0.4 percent of respondents were female.

7. Eighty-three percent of respondents were under 35, and only 40 percent had been married.

8. The survey covers players of role-playing games, wargames and collectible card games.

9. In 2004, Deppey reports that the average age of a comic book reader is 34 years.

10. Fine notes that, of gamers over 21, 51 per-

cent had achieved more than undergraduate education.

11. Although Bordenet's survey indicates that only 11 percent of participants have completed an undergraduate degree, the age group surveyed is significantly lower. When taking into account those respondents who have completed "some college," the figure rises to 51 percent. Given the age range identified in his survey (38 percent are under 25), it is safe to assume that a sizeable proportion of these respondents were engaged in study at the time of the survey.

12. The reference here to "slans" is a notable one. Within Science Fiction fandom, the notion of slans is used to identify a particular type of fan, or at least the attitude of a specific subset, who have subverted the perceived marginalization of their interests to the point where they see themselves as belonging to a community that "possess[es] a truth which is denied to outsiders" (James, 1994, p. 135). The idea that gamers are also in possession of a truth that might benefit the broader culture is a topic I explore later in this chapter.

13. It is also likely that the communities overlap. Certainly my local gaming group, the West Australian Boardgaming Association, shows significant overlap with West Australian science fiction fandom.

14. Again, the comparison with fans, who Bruner and Thorne describe as "focus[ing] their time energy and resources intently on a specific area of interest," is unavoidable (2006, p. 53).

15. As of August 2011, only one of the top 100 games on *boardgamegeek* is produced by a mainstream manufacturer—this being Hasbro's reprint of Sid Sackson's *Acquire*. There have been several exceptions to this general dismissal of mainstream games. Interestingly, the two most notable have come from the area of dexterity games. *Loopin Louie* (Wiselely, 1992) is a children's dexterity game manufactured by Milton Bradley that was awarded the Kinderspiele des Jahres in 1994. The game experienced a boost in popularity among gamers after being played heavily at Alan Moon's Gathering of Friends events in the late 1990s. In 2008 the mass-market *Sorry Sliders!* (Van Ness, 2008) received similar attention as a substitute for the well-regarded but expensive public domain game *Crokinole*.

16. See, in particular, Bordieu, 1979.

17. Based on 137 responses as of January 10, 2010.

18. The use of this way of measuring the value of games has been taken up by other members of the hobby in the form of "five and dime lists." In the transition, however, the original purpose has been largely forgotten, and such lists are now seen as an indicator of the popularity of specific games over time. See Jackson, 2006.

19. For examples, see threads *Estimating CCP (Cost Per Play) of my collection* (Kobral, 2005), *How many plays should we expect out of a game?* (Jome, 2008) and *Boardgames: Higher Entertainment Value Than You Thought!* (flabber23, 2007).

20. Based on 2834 respondents as of January 9, 2009.

21. Based on 421 responses as of January 10, 2010. The phenomenon of the "unplayed game" has led Australian user John Farrell to establish a supplementary site where player statistics from BGG are analyzed to determine, among other things, a "Friendless metric" which indicates how much of a collection is played with any regularity (2009).

22. For example, Alea produces three series of numbered games: big, medium and small box, most of which have been reprinted in English by Rio Grande Games. However, since English language versions of *Chinatown* and *Adel Verpflichtet* were not produced, original German versions of these titles are sought after by collectors. The recent "Bookshelf Series" of titles released by Gryphon Games also employs numbering.

23. Although this is probably due in most cases to economic convenience, publishers arguably leverage this similarity in creating "lines," such as the Kosmos 2-Player line. Clearly, the use of similar presentation establishes coherency in a company's product range, with the perception of groups as a "set" a fortunate side-effect.

24. Reflecting the gendered nature of the hobby, such spaces have been referred to as "man-caves."

25. "PrOn" being Internet slang for pornography, a term originally used on usenet groups as a way to bypass language filters.

26. Fiske is here writing before the advent of the World Wide Web. While his comments remain true in principle, the potential for fan-created texts to reach an audience outside of the community is greatly increased.

27. As an example, the English version of the fantasy-themed adventure game *Die Rückkehr der Helden* (Stepponat, 2003) suffers from a ruleset that is written as an ongoing discussion between the player characters in the game. Despite being extremely humorous, it is generally considered a failure in terms of rule clarity. User Christopher Young has rewritten the entire ruleset in a way that makes the game far more accessible (Young, 2007). In an example of the value of this feedback loop, designer Lutz Stepponat has since suggested that discussions on the website have informed his decision to rewrite the rules in an upcoming edition (Stepponat, 2008).

28. See, for example *Carcassonne: The Well and the Donkey* (Exit191, 2006b), *Carcassonne: Dragon Riders and Slayers* (Exit191, 2006a), *Carcassonne:*

*Fruit Trader* (Wu, 2005), and *Carcassonne: Treasure Hunt* (Wu, 2008).

29. The original version of the game positions the players as the heads of feuding Scottish clans.

30. Exemplar of this level of commitment is Karim Chakroun's redesign of Richard Hamblen's fantasy game *Magic Realm* (1978), a project that required over 300 hours of work (Chakroun, 2009).

31. Designers Andrea Angiolino, Bruno Faidutti, Friedemann Friese, Richard Breese, William Attia, Jeroen Doumen, Martin Wallace, Marcel-André Casasola Merkle, Kevin Wilson, Bruno Cathala and Lewis Pulsipher, among many others, are contributors to the site.

32. For example, in 2009 designer Rüdiger Dorn actively enrolled site members in discussing changes prior to the re-release of his game *Goa* (Dorn, 2009). Similarly, one of the designers of Avalon Hill's *Betrayal at House on the Hill* (McQuillan *et al.*, 2004), Bruce Glassco, solicited input and ideas from hobbyists for inclusion in the second edition of the game (Glassco, 2009).

33. For example, the German-to-English translation of Uwe Rosenberg's *Agricola* was initially undertaken by Australian *boardgamegeek* member Melissa Rogerson due to hobbyist interest in the German version. The English version of the game produced by Z-Man utilized Rogerson's translation. Rogerson subsequently worked on the translation of Rosenberg's next game, *Le Havre* (Rosenberg, 2008).

34. Pope, 2006.

35. Designed by Yehuda Berlinger, another example of a hobbyist turned designer (Berlinger, 2007).

36. Pope and Cheatham, 2008.

37. A geeklist is a function of the site that allows users to list a series of games with commentary after each. Although initially conceived as a way to group games with something in common, the feature has subsequently been utilized by users in a myriad of creative ways. Geeklists have become a central feature of the site, operating as a facility for community building and the development of cultural capital.

38. In another intertextual reference, the currency employed in the game is Florins, a particularly ubiquitous currency in eurogames.

39. "These Games of Ours"—a now rarely used acronym dating from an early discussion on *rec.games.board* of an alternate name for German-style games.

## Chapter 7

1. For example, evolutionist and political theorist Herbert Spencer saw play as a method

of using up excess energy and directing that energy towards activities that were of particular interest to the individual (Spencer, 1855). Another proponent of this idea, German poet Friedrich Schiller, saw the function of play as lying in the balance drawn between the rational and spiritual instincts, claiming that "the double action of the two ... instincts, will content the mind at once morally and physically" (1954). In contrast, the "relaxation" or "recreation" theory proposed by Moritz Lazarus and George Patrick suggests that the function of play is primarily a restorative one (Lazarus, 1883; Patrick, 1916).

2. For example, Karl Groos' instrumentalist theory proposes that play constitutes a child's way of preparing for adult life (1898; 1901). Indeed, a number of early psychological theorists view child's play as a recapitulation of cultural development that allows the child to "play out" the steps in the evolution of mores (Wundt, 1902; Hall, 1906). More recently, social psychologist Kurt Lewin interprets play as being reflective of the unstructured state of the infant mind, flitting between the real and unreal (Sutton-Smith and Herron, 1971). Similarly, Frederick Buytendijk suggests that due to this incoherent cognitive and emotional state, play is the only activity of which a child is capable (Helms and Turner, 1981). Psychoanalytic theory tends to focus on the fantasy element of play in the growth of the human psyche. Anna and Sigmund Freud propose that play allows the child to express negative emotions over problems which she is unable to exert control in real life (Freud, 1959; Freud, 1968).

3. Most famously, Jean Piaget's theory of cognitive development identifies a series of developmental stages through which children pass sequentially, progressing through play which emphasizes sensorimotor, preoperational, concrete operational and formal operational thought processes. In each of these stages the child is said to develop new knowledge through a state of cognitive disequilibrium that must be brought into balance through accommodation (attempting to imitate and physically interact with the environment) and assimilation (attempting to integrate external precepts or actions) (Gruber and Voneche, 1977).

4. For example, Lev Vygotsky places a strong emphasis on the interpersonal nature of learning and the way in which understandings are developed through the use of symbolic tools such as language (Crawford, 1996). For Vygotsky, forms of play are not primarily determined by any innate factor but are reflective of the individuals, social institutions and culture in whose proximity the child develops (Vygotsky, 1962; Goldfarb, 2001). Of particular interest are Vygotsky's observations on the way in which children self regulate in play activities. As an example, a child involved in a running race resists the urge to begin before the agreed moment in order to experience the pleasure of social play. In this way, the rules of play become the strongest impulse; "to carry out the rule is a source of pleasure" (Vygotsky, 1976, p. 549).

5. Reflecting the complexity of this question, researchers have also identified control (Barnett *et al.*, 1997; Grodal, 2000; Vorderer, 2000; Newman, 2002), competition (Vorderer *et al.*, 2003), escapism (Barnett *et al.*, 1997), sociality (Jansz and Martens, 2005), self-efficacy (Klimmt and Hartmann, 2006), identification with a player character (Hefner *et al.*, 2007) and suspense (Klimmt *et al.*, 2009) as other potential sources of pleasure for players in different forms of games.

6. Although the issue of time commitment that Juul describes is not so constraining as it is in video games — which can take days of a player's life to complete — I have already identified how game length effects general gaming preferences among hobbyists.

7. The categories originally included in the survey were "Do Not Enjoy," "Rarely Enjoy," "Usually Enjoy" and "Always Enjoy."

8. Variable phase order is a term that refers to games where each turn may have a different order. Although not, strictly speaking, a "mechanic," it typically stems from the use of mechanics, such as role selection and worker placement.

9. Hand management is a commonly used mechanic in eurogames; however, it is also present in many American hobby games and, of course, collectible card games.

10. Ninety-six percent of respondents indicate that replayability is either very important (67 percent) or quite important (29 percent).

11. Exceptions exist in the case of "speedruns" (Lowood, 2005) and games that offer multiple endings, but the generalization holds.

12. Although some board games do have elements of progression in them (e.g., *Tales of the Arabian Nights* [Goldberg, 1985]), most are largely emergent. Juul suggests that multiplayer board games are the purest examples of this game form (2005, p. 71).

13. Although some of the ideas discussed in this section were originally presented in my article "Playing with an Other: Ethics in the Magic Circle" (2007), these thoughts were subsequently crystallized through reading designer Lewis Pulsipher's blog post "The system and the psychological in games" (2009b).

14. Eighty-six percent of respondents cite direct interaction as either quite important (48 percent) or very important (37 percent) in their enjoyment. Eighty percent consider indirect in-

teraction either quite important (62 percent) or very important (18 percent).

15. Only 45 percent of respondents indicated that the presence of direct conflict was either very important (9 percent) or quite important (36 percent) to their enjoyment of a game.

16. While early eurogames were highly interactive, as Michael Barnes notes, games such as *Puerto Rico*, *Die Fürsten von Florenz* and *Goa* ushered in the style of games that are commonly perceived as having very little interaction (2008a). Notably, these titles are at the more complex end of the spectrum of eurogame titles.

17. Aleknevicus cites the American game *Set* (Falco, 1991), Alex Randolph's *Rasende Roboter* (1999), Bruno Faidutti's *Bongo* (2000a) and the English-designed *Take It Easy* (Burley, 1983) as examples of true multi-player solitaire. To these titles can be added similar games such as Splotter Spellen's *Oraklos* (Wiersinga and Jannink, 2002), Friedemann Friese's *Turbo Taxi* (2000) and the more recent Reiner Knizia game *Fits* (2009a). All of these titles can be more accurately described as puzzles that are simultaneously completed by several people. Moreover, many require pattern recognition on the part of players, a mechanic that was not well regarded by survey respondents.

18. See, for example, Haddon, 1981; Crawford, 1982; Zagal, 2000; Costikyan, 2002; and Björk and Holopainen, 2003.

19. Indeed, although Gingold's thesis deals almost entirely with video games, he explicitly cites the board game *Go* as an example of a "miniature garden" (Gingold, 2003, p. 7).

20. In a mathematical sense the term chaos describes "stochastic behavior occurring in a deterministic system," where stochastic refers to a probabilistic distribution that can be analyzed but not predicted precisely. In effect, the behavior is random (Stewart, 1989, p. 17). Setting aside the apparent contradiction of random events occurring in deterministic systems, the way the term chaos is used by hobbyists aligns very closely with this definition.

21. Responses to this question were analyzed in a method akin to that used in a grounded theoretical approach (Glaser and Strauss, 1967; Martin and Turner, 1986) — that is, key themes and concepts that were mentioned in player responses were assigned codes that revealed elements that players considered important.

22. In discussing games that are not played face-to-face, Goffman refers to examples such as *Hide-and-Seek*, "war exercises" and games such as *Chess* that can be played via mail (Goffman, 1961, p. 36).

23. Pleasure derived from the misfortune of others.

## Chapter 8

1. The rules governing the winning condition have been variously termed the "ludus" rules (Frasca, 2001b, p. 9), the "evaluation" rules (Egenfeldt-Nelson *et al.*, 2008) and the "outcome valorization" rules by video game scholars.

2. Heide Smith identifies the "susceptible player," most commonly assumed in effects-based research, and the "selective player," which has been used to predict media choices (p. 257).

3. For example, Crawford, 1982; Costikyan, 1994; and Koster, 2005.

4. *FIFA Soccer 2004* (2003), *Champions of Norrath* (2004), *Mashed: Drive to Survive* (2004).

5. Examples of studies drawing on this model include those focusing on player activities within MUDs and MMORPGs (Bartle, 1996; Mortensen, 2003; Steinkuehler, 2005; Pearce, 2006; Taylor, 2006), other online multiplayer games (Manninen, 2001; Boria *et al.*, 2002), and those that examine disruptive practices (Foo and Koivisto, 2004; Kücklich, 2004; Consalvo, 2005a).

6. Party games were the most commonly cited examples here.

7. More specifically, the term is commonly used to describe gambling or video game play.

8. Hughes' study of the children's game *Four Square* is a detailed examination of this process (1983; 1988; 1989).

9. These being enjoyment as motivation, enjoyment as expected effect, enjoyment as terminal goal, enjoyment as sub-goal and enjoyment as function (Paglieri, 2003a).

## Chapter 9

1. A secondary theme that emerges is that of inattentiveness that can distract from focus upon the game or interrupt the proper flow (e.g., premature resignation, a lack of attention, slow play and inappropriate breaks). Since this topic offers a similar distraction from the focus of this chapter, I set it aside as only tangentially related to the act of play.

## Chapter 10

1. While the valorization of formal tournaments often provides an impetus for this activity, the nature of such tournaments is that they provide the "collective affirmation of a room full of people engaged in playful unison" (Lenarcic and Scolley, 2005, p. 71) in a very similar way to the eurogames described here.

# Bibliography

Aarseth, E. *Playing Research: Methodological Approaches to Game Analysis*. Paper presented at the Digital Arts & Culture Conference, Melbourne, 2003.

_____. Genre Trouble: Narrativism and the Art of Simulation. In *First Person: New Media as Story, Performance and Game*, edited by N. Wardrip-Fruin and P. Harrigan, 45–49). Massachusetts: MIT Press, 2004.

_____. *I Fought the Law: Transgressive Play and The Implied Player*. In Proceedings of the DiGRA 2007 Conference — Situated Play, 130–133. Tokyo, 2007.

Abbott, E. Candyland [Board Game]. Milton Bradley, 1949.

Abbott, R. Epaminondas [Board Game]. Ariel/Philmar, 1975.

Academy of Adventure Gaming, Arts and Design, 2008. Retrieved January 4, 2008, from http://www.originsgamefair.com/aagad/.

Achilli, J., T. Avers, A. Bates, K. Blackwelder, P. Boulle, C. Bowen, et al. Mummy: The Resurrection [Role-Playing Game]. White Wolf, 2001.

Alden, S. The Aldie Show #008: Interview with Friedemann Friese [Podcast], Boardgamegeek.com, 2008.

Alden, S., and D. Solko. Boardgamespeak — Interview with Rick Thornquist and Greg Schloesser [Podcast], Boardgamegeek.com, 2004a.

_____. Boardgamespeak — Aldie and Derk Interview [Podcast], Boardgamegeek.com, 2004b.

_____. Boardgamespeak — Interview with Jay Tummelson [Podcast], Boardgamegeek.com, 2005.

_____. Geekspeak 2.0: Interview with Reiner Knizia Part One [Podcast], Boardgamegeek.com, 2009a.

_____. Geekspeak 2.0: Interview with Gordon Calleja Part One [Podcast], Boardgamegeek.com, 2009b.

Aldis, O. *Play Fighting*. New York: Academic Press, 1975.

Aleknevicus, G. Hippodice Game Competition. *The Games Journal* 2007, from http://www.the gamesjournal.com/articles/Hippodice.shtml, 2001a.

_____. "Specialize! Diversify! *Counter* 15 (2001b): 20–24.

_____. "Player Interaction in Games." *Counter* 16 (2002): 16–22.

_____. "German Games Are Fraudulent." Retrieved August 14, 2008, from http://www.the gamesjournal.com/articles/Fraudulent.shtml, 2004.

_____. Email Interview, 2008.

Alexander, W., and R. Tait. Cranium [Board Game]. Cranium Inc., 1998.

Alvaro, G. "Re: My Confession: Some Bothersome Things I've Realized About My Approach to the Gaming Hobby." Retrieved February 15, 2009, from http://www.boardga megeek.com/article/2198693#2198693, 2008.

Aminzadah, S. M. "Some Reasons Behind the Success of 'The Settlers of Catan': What Makes This Contemporary Board Game so Attractive to Players?" Paper presented at the Board Game Studies Colloquia VII, Philadelphia, 2004.

Anderson, B. *Imagined Communities: Reflections on The Origin and Spread of Nationalism*. London: Verso, 1983.

Andre, K. S. Tunnels and Trolls [Role-playing Game]. Flying Buffalo, 1975.

Angel, R. Pictionary [Board Game]. Parker Brothers, 1985.

Anspach, R. *The Billion Dollar Monopoly Swindle*. Philadelphia: Xlibris, 2000.

Appelcline, S. "Trials, Triumphs & Trivialities #112: Designing Strategy: Hidden Information." Retrieved October 11, 2009, from http://www.skotos.net/articles/TTnT_112.shtml, 2003.

_____. "Trials, Triumphs & Trivialities #144:

Strategic Insights: Auction Games." Retrieved May 9, 2009, from http://www.skotos.net/articles/TTnT_144.phtml, 2004.

_____. "Trials, Triumphs & Trivialities #161: Designing Strategy: The Auction Grand Unification Theory." Retrieved March 23, 2008, from http://www.skotos.net/articles/TTnT_161.phtml, 2005a.

_____. "Trials, Triumphs & Trivialities #162: Strategic Insights: Majority Control." Retrieved April 15th, 2008, from http://www.skotos.net/articles/TTnT_/TTnT_162.phtml, 2005b.

_____. "Professor of Chaos." *Knucklebones* (November 2006): 16–19.

_____. "A Brief History of Game #1: Wizards of the Coast." Retrieved June 1, 2007, from http://www.rpg.net/columns/briefhistory/briefhistory1.phtml, 2006b.

_____. "A Brief History of Game #11: White Wolf, Part One, 1986–1995." Retrieved April 2, 2008, from http://www.rpg.net/columns/briefhistory/briefhistory11.phtml, 2007.

Armintrout, W. G. Hot Spot [Board Game]. Metagaming, 1979.

_____. Annihilator & One World [Board Game]. Metagaming, 1980.

Armstrong, A., and J. Hagel. "The Real Value of On-Line Communities." *Harvard Business Review* (May–June 1996): 131–141.

Arneson, E. "Bruno Faidutti: Jeux sans Strategie." Retrieved March 14, 2009, from http://boardgames.about.com/library/weekly/aa080100a.htm, 2000.

Askew, F. Dimension Demons [Board Game]. Metagaming, 1981.

Atkins, B. *More Than a Game: The Computer Game as a Fictional Form.* Manchester: Manchester University Press, 2003.

Attia, W. Caylus [Board Game]. Ystari, 2005.

*The Avalon Hill General Index and Company History 1952–1980, Volume 1–Volume 16.* Baltimore: Avalon Hill, 1980.

Baars, R. G. Labyrinth — Die Schatzjagd [Board Game]. Ravensburger, 2005.

Babinsack, J. "By the Book." *Knucklebones* (May 2007): pp. 22–26.

Barnes, M. "Re: A Tribute to Ameritrash." Retrieved February 19, 2009, from http://www.boardgamegeek.com/geeklist/16485?commentid=142850#comment142850, 2006.

_____. "Do Eurogames Hate Us for Our Freedom?" Retrieved December 4, 2009, from http://www.gameshark.com/entertainment/features/525/Cracked-LCD-73-Always-Trust-the-French.htm, 2008a.

_____. Email Interview, 2008b.

Barnett, M. A., G. D. Vitaglione, K. K. G. Harper, S. W. Quackenbush, L. A. Steadman, and B. S. Valdez. "Late Adolescents' Experiences with and Attitudes Toward Videogames." *Journal of Applied Social Psychology* 27, no. 15 (1997): 1316–1334.

Bartl, A., A. Bernabe, and N. Grill. Karawane [Board Game]. Ravensburger, 1990.

Bartle, R. "Hearts, Clubs, Diamonds, Spades — Players Who Suit MUDs." Retrieved January 3, 2007, from http://www.mud.co.uk/richard/hcds.htm, 1996.

Batty, W. Reiner Knizia by the Numbers. *The Game Table* Retrieved March 17th, 2008, from http://gametable.blogspot.com/2006/04/reiner-knizia-by-numbers.html, 2006a.

_____. "The Life and Times of Alan R. Moon." Retrieved June 15, 2008, from http://www.boardgamenews.com/index.php/boardgamenews/comments/the_life_times_of_alan_r_moon/, 2006.

Baudrillard, J. "The System of Collecting." In *The Cultures of Collecting*, edited by J. Elsner and R. Cardinal, 7–24. Cambridge: Harvard University Press, 1994.

Bauer, E. B., and B. B. Smuts. "Role Reversal and Self-Handicapping During Playfighting in Domestic Dogs, Canis Familiaris." Paper presented at the Meetings of the Animal Behavior Society, Indiana University, Indiana, 2002.

Beattie, R. "The Courier Presents a Timeline of the Historical Miniatures Wargaming Hobby." Retrieved May 2, 2009, from http://www-personal.umich.edu/~beattie/timeline2.html, n.d.

Beattie, S. "Voicing the Shadow: Rule-Playing and Roleplaying in Wraith: The Oblivion. *Law, Culture and the Humanities* 3, no. 3 (2007): 477–492.

Beierer, C. Tal Der Könige [Board Game]. Kosmos, 1992.

Bekoff, M., and C. Allen. "Intentional Communication and Social Play: How and Why Animals Negotiate and Agree to Play." In *Animal Play: Evolutionary, Comparative, and Ecological Perspectives*, edited by M. Bekoff and J. A. Byers, 97–114. Cambridge University Press: Cambridge, 1998.

Belk, R. W. *Collecting in a Consumer Society.* London: Routledge, 1995.

Belk, R. W., and M. Wallendorf. "Of Mice and Men: Gender Identity and Collecting." In *Interpreting Objects and Collections*, edited by S. M. Pearce, 240–253. London: Routledge, 1994.

Belk, R. W., M. Wallendorf, J. Sherry, M. Holbrook, and S. Roberts. "Collectors and Collecting." In *Advances in Consumer Research Volume 15*, edited by M. J. Houston, 548–553. Provo, UT: Association for Consumer Research, 1988.

Bell, J. B. "Toward a Theory of Deception." *In-*

*ternational Journal of Intelligence and Counterintelligence* 16, no. 2 (2003): 244–279.

Bell, R. C. *Board and Table Games from Many Civilizations.* New York: Dover, 1979.

_____. *Games to Play: Board and Table Games for All the Family.* London: Dunestyle, 1988.

Berg, R. H. Terrible Swift Sword [Board Game]. Simulations Publications Inc., 1976.

_____. Gondor [Board Game]. Simulations Publications Inc., 1977.

_____. The Campaign For North Africa [Board Game]. Simulations Publications Inc., 1978.

Berg, R. H., and H. Barasch, H. War of the Ring [Board Game]. Simulations Publications Inc., 1977.

Berger, T. U. *Cultures of Antimilitarism: National Security in Germany and Japan.* Baltimore, MA: John Hopkins University, 1998.

Bergman, M. Census Bureau Data Underscore Value of College Degree. Retrieved January 12, 2009, from http://www.census.gov/Press-Release/www/releases/archives/education/007660.html, 2006.

Berlinger, Y. It's Alive! [Board Game]. Reiver Games, 2007.

_____. "Games Are Art: 'Eurogames' Is an Art Period." Retrieved April 30, 2009, from http://jergames.blogspot.com/2009/04/games-are-art-eurogames-is-art-period.html, 2009a.

_____. "The Modern Eurogame Revolution." Paper presented at the Board Game Studies Colloquia XII, Jerusalem, 2009b.

Bermuda Triangle [Board Game]. Milton Bradley, 1976.

Bernett, H. Phlounder [Board Game]. 3M, 1962.

Beyer, D. "Re: Is There a Boardgaming Demographic?" Retrieved February 17, 2009, from http://www.boardgamegeek.com/article/546745#546745, 2005.

Beyer, D., R. Eifler, and S. Gross, S. Bootleggers [Board Game]. Eagle Games, 2004.

"Big Game Hunter: The Search for the Next Monopoly." Retrieved January 9, 2010, from http://www.independent.co.uk/life-style/big-game-hunter-the-search-for-the-next-monopoly-1813587.html, 2009.

Bistro, M. "Art vs. Craft and the Rise of the Mongrel Aesthetic." Retrieved February 21, 2009, from http://fortressat.com/index.php?option=com_content&task=view&id=882&Itemid=551, 2009.

Bisz, J. "The Birth of a Community, the Death of the Win: Player Production of the Middle-Earth Collectible Card Game. *Transformative Works and Cultures,* 2. Retrieved May 4, 2008, from http://journal.transformativeworks.org/index.php/twc/article/view/90/99, 2009.

Björk, S., and J. Holopainen, J. *Describing Games: An Interaction-Centric Structural Framework.* In Proceedings of the DiGRA 2003 Conference — Level Up, Utrecht, 2003.

_____. *Patterns in Game Design.* Charles River Media, 2005.

Björk, S., J. Falk, R. Hansson, and P. Ljungstrand, P. "Pirates! Using the Physical World as a Game Board." Paper presented at the Human-Computer Interaction Conference — Interact 01, Tokyo, 2001.

Bloomfield, E. "Confrontation: The Ultimate Endgame." *Counter* 30 (2005): 62–63.

Board Game Designers Forum. Retrieved February 20, 2009, from http://www.bgdf.com/, 2009.

Boardgame Players Association. Retrieved February 20, 2009, from http://www.boardgamers.org/, 2009.

Boardgamegeek.com. Retrieved January 4, 2010, from http://www.alexa.com/siteinfo/www.boardgamegeek.com?p=tgraph&r=home_home, 2010.

Boellstorff, T. "A Ludicrous Discipline? Ethnography and Game Studies." *Games and Culture* 1, no. 1 (2006): 29–35.

Bonds, J., and D. Glimne, D. Drakborgen [Board Game]. Alga, 1985.

Bontenbal, R. Homas Tour [Board Game]. Homas Spielen, 1979.

_____. Um Reifenbreite [Board Game]. Jumbo, 1991.

Bordenet, M. *An Introduction into the World of Gaming and How One Achieves the Identity of a Gamer.* Unpublished Master's Thesis, West Virginia University, 2000.

Bordieu, P. *Distinction: A Social Critique of the Judgment of Pure Taste.* Cambridge: Harvard University Press, 1979.

Borg, R. Liar's Dice [Board Game]. Milton Bradley, 1987.

_____. Bluff [Board Game]. F.X. Schmidt, 1993.

_____. Battlelore [Board Game]. Days of Wonder, 2006.

Borgstrom, R. "Structure and Meaning in Role-Playing Game Design." In *Second Person: Role-Playing and Story in Games and Playable Media.*, edited by P. Harrigan and N. Wardrip-Fruin. Cambridge: MIT Press, 2007.

Boria, E., T. Wright, and P. Breidenbach,. "Creative Player Actions in FPS Online Video Games: Playing Counter-Strike." *Game Studies: The International Journal of Computer Game Research* 2, no. 2 (2002).

Borman, K. M., and N. T. Lippincott. "Cognition and Culture: Two Perspectives on 'Free Play.'" In *The Social Life of Children in a Changing Society,* edited by K. M. Borman, 123–142. Norwood: Ablex, 1982.

Boulton, M., and P. K. Smith. "The Social Nature of Play Fighting and Play Chasing: Mechanisms and Strategies Underlying Cooperation and Compromise." In *The Adapted Mind: Evolutionary Psychology and the Generation of Culture*, edited by J. H. Barkow, L. Cosmides, and J. Tooby, 429–444. New York: Oxford University Press, 1992.

Bourque, F. Talisman Timescape [Board Game Expansion]. Games Workshop, 1988.

Bowman, S. *The Function of Role-Playing Games: How Participants Create Community, Solve Problems and Explore Identity.* Jefferson NC: McFarland, 2010.

Braunlich, T., R. Tesh, E. Lorentz, and B. Martinson. Star Trek: The Next Generation Customizable Card Game [Card Game]. Decipher, 1994.

Breese, R. Keywood [Board Game]. R&D Games, 1995.

_____. Keydom [Board Game]. R&D Games, 1998.

_____. Keytown [Board Game]. R&D Games, 2000.

_____. Keythedral [Board Game]. R&D Games, 2002.

_____. Reef Encounter [Board Game]. R&D Games, 2004.

_____. Key Harvest [Board Game]. R&D Games, 2007.

Bretsch, R. Mike Doyle Interview. Retrieved August 9, 2008, from http://www.thegamesjournal.com/articles/MikeDoyle.shtml, 2005.

Bridges, B. "Champions." In *Hobby Games: The 100 Best*, edited by J. Lowder, 52–54. Renton: Green Ronin, 2007.

Briggs, J., and S. Johnson. Civilization III [Video Game]. Firaxis Games, 2001.

Bromley, D. Eurorails [Board Game]. Mayfair Games, 1990.

Bromley, D., and B. Fawcett. Empire Builder [Board Game]. Mayfair Games, 1980.

Bromley, D., and T. Wham. Iron Dragon [Board Game]. Mayfair Games, 1996.

Brown, D. "Gaming DNA — on Narrative and Gameplay Gestalts." In Proceedings of the DiGRA 2007 Conference — Situated Play, 58–65. Tokyo, 2007.

Brown, D. "Even in Recession, Board Games Roll Up a Win." Retrieved January 4, 2010, from http://www.denverpost.com/lifestyles/ci_14059493, 2009.

Brown, E. "Pastimes and Paradigms: Games We Play." Retrieved May 1, 2008, from http://rmc.library.cornell.edu/games/plethora/index.html, 2004.

Brown, K. *The British Toy Business: A History Since 1700.* London: Hambledon Continuum, 1996.

Brown, S. (1998). "Play as an Organizing Principle: Clinical Evidence and Personal Observations." In *Animal Play: Evolutionary, Comparative, and Ecological Perspectives*, edited by M. Bekoff and J. A. Byers, 243–259. 1998.

Bruner, G., and S. Thorne, S. "An Exploratory Investigation of the Characteristics of Consumer Fanaticism." *Qualitative Market Research: An International Journal* 9, no. 1 (2006): 51–72.

Brunnhofer, B., and M. Tummelhofer, M. Sankt Petersburg [Board Game]. Hans im Glück, 2004.

_____. Stone Age [Board Game]. Hans im Glück, 2008.

Bücken, H. Ausbrecher AG [Board Game]. Ravensburger, 1988.

_____. Sahara [Card Game]. Hexagames, 1990.

Buestchler, F. Feudal [Board Game]. 3M, 1967.

Bull, G. Buccaneer [Board Game]. Waddingtons, 1938.

Burgess, E. "Board Game Babylon Volume 51— Q&A with Steve Jackson at Orccon 2008 (with special co-host Paul Tevis)" [Podcast]: Board Game Babylon, 2008a.

_____. Email Interview, 2008b.

Burggraf, M., W. Schlegel, D. Garrels, F. Ifland, W. Scheerer, and W. Hoermann, W. Scotland Yard [Board Game]. Ravensburger, 1983.

Burkhardt, G. Edison & Co. [Board Game]. Goldsieber, 1998.

_____. Vom Kap bis Cairo [Card Game]. Adlung-Spiele, 2001.

Burley, P. Take It Easy [Board Game]. Spears, 1983.

Burm, K. Gipf [Board Game]. Don & Co, 1997.

_____. Dvonn [Board Game]. Don & Co, 2001.

Burton, A. "Design History and the History of Toys: Defining a Discipline for the Bethnal Green Museum of Childhood." *Journal of Design History* 10, no. 1 (1997): 1–21.

Butsch, R. "Leisure and Hegemony in America." In *For Fun and Profit: The Transformation of Leisure into Consumption*, edited by R. Butsch, 3–27. Philadelphia: Temple University Press, 1990.

Butterfield, J. H., and H. Barasch. Freedom in the Galaxy [Board Game]. Simulations Publications Inc, 1979.

Butts, A. M. Scrabble [Board Game]. Production & Marketing Co, 1948.

Caillois, R. *Man, Play, and Games.* New York: Free Press, 1958.

Calhamer, A. Diplomacy [Board Game]. Game Research, 1959.

Cameron, A. Dissimulations — Illusions of Interactivity. *Millennium Film Journal* 28 (1995): 33–47.

Campaign [Board Game]. Waddingtons, 1971.

Candyland — Dora the Explorer Edition [Board Game]. Hasbro Inc, 2005.

Candyland — Winnie The Pooh Edition [Board Game]. Hasbro Inc., 2008.

Cappel, J. Wasabi! [Board Game]. Z-Man Games, 2008.

Carlquist, J. "Playing the Story — Computer Games as a Narrative Genre." *Human IT* 6, no. 3 (2002): 7–53.

Carmichael, J. Mr. President [Board Game]. 3M, 1967.

Carr, N. "Re: How Do You Explain Your Hobby to Strangers?" Retrieved February 3, 2009, from http://www.boardgamegeek.com/article/632019#632019, 2005.

Carroll, P. "Re: I Don't Get Game Publisher Economics." Retrieved January 12, 2010, from http://www.boardgamegeek.com/article/2887705m, 2008a.

_____. "Re: A Metagame?" Retrieved January 9, 2010, from http://www.boardgamegeek.com/article/2791076#2791076, 2008b.

Carter, E. *How German Is She?: Postwar West German Reconstruction and the Consuming Woman.* Detroit: University of Michigan Press, 1997.

Carver, D. Doctor Who: The Game of Time and Space [Board Game]. Games Workshop, 1980.

_____. Showbiz [Board Game]. Prestige Games, 1985a.

_____. Warrior Knights [Board Game]. Games Workshop, 1985b.

_____. Blood Royale [Board Game]. Games Workshop, 1987.

_____. "Warrior Knights 2: A Reply to Stuart." *Counter* 35 (2006): 71–74.

_____. "Re: Doctor Who: The Game of Time and Space: A Review from Memory." Retrieved May 15, 2008, from http://www.boardgamegeek.com/article/1627578#1627578, 2007.

_____. (2008). Email Interview.

Casasola Merkle, M.-A. Verräter [Card Game]. Adlung-Spiele, 1998.

_____. Attika [Board Game]. Hans im Glück, 2003.

_____. Taluva [Board Game]. Hans im Glück, 2006.

Cathala, B., and B. Faidutti, B. Queen's Necklace [Card Game]. Days of Wonder, 2003.

Cathala, B., and S. Laget, S. Shadows Over Camelot [Board Game]. Days of Wonder, 2005.

Catino, C. Nexus Ops [Board Game]. Avalon Hill, 2005.

Chadwick, F. Battle for Moscow [Board Game]. Game Designers' Workshop, 1986.

Chadwick, F., and P. Banner, P. Drang Nach Osten [Board Game]. Game Designers' Workshop, 1973.

Chakroun, K. Email Interview, 2009.

Champions of Norrath [Video Game]. Sony Online Entertainment, 2004.

Charlton, C. Middle Earth CCG [Card Game]. Iron Crown Enterprises, 1995.

Chiarvesio, A., and L. Iennaco, L. Königsburg [Board Game]. Heidelberger Spieleverlag, 2007.

Ciaffone, R. Robert's Rules Of Poker Version 4. Retrieved May 2, 2010, from http://www.pokercoach.us/RobsPkrRules4.htm, 2004.

Clifford, M. "Essen 2000." *Counter* 11 (2000): 21–22.

The Coaster Proclamation of 1988. Retrieved May 31, 2010, from http://www.spieleautorenzunft.de/coaster-proclamation.html, 2010.

Cornett, G. Kahuna [Board Game]. Kosmos, 1998.

Confrontation [Board Game]. Ariel/Philmar, 1974.

Conrad, C. Vino [Board Game]. Goldsieber, 1999.

Consalvo, M. *Gaining Advantage: How Videogame Players Define and Negotiate Cheating.* In Proceedings of the DiGRA 2005 Conference: Changing Views — Worlds in Play, Vancouver, 2005a.

_____. "Rule Sets, Cheating, and Magic Circles: Studying Games and Ethics." *International Review of Information Ethics* 3 (2005b): 7–12.

Conte, R., and C. Castelfranchi. *Cognitive and Social Action.* London: University College, 1995.

Cook, M. "The Game Master and the Role-Playing Game Campaign." In *Third Person : Authoring and Exploring Vast Narratives*, edited by P. Harrigan and N. Wardrip-Fruin, 97–104. Cambridge, MA: MIT Press, 2009.

Copier, M. "Connecting Worlds: Fantasy Role-Playing Games, Ritual Acts and the Magic Circle." Paper presented at the DiGRA 2005 Conference: Changing Views — Worlds in Play, Vancouver, 2005.

Costikyan, G. Swords and Sorcery [Board Game]. Simulations Publications Inc., 1978.

_____. The Creature That Ate Sheboygan [Board Game]. Simulations Publications Inc., 1979.

_____. Trailblazer [Board Game]. Metagaming, 1981.

_____. "I Have No Words and I Must Design." *Interactive Fantasy* 3. Retrieved May 4, 2007, from http://www.costik.com/nowords.html, 1994.

_____. "A Farewell to Hexes." Retrieved May 5, 2008, from http://www.costik.com/spisins.html, 1996.

_____. "Don't Be a Vidiot: What Computer Game Designers Can Learn from Non-Electronic Games." Retrieved June 11, 2004, from http://www.costik.com/vidiot.html, 1998.

_____. "I Have No Words and I Must Design: Toward a Critical Vocabulary for Games." In *Proceedings of the Computer Games and Digital Cultures Conference*, edited by F. Mäyrä, 9–33. Tampere, Finland: Tampere University Press, 2002.

_____. "German Boardgames as Fraud." Retrieved October 13, 2009, from http://www.costik.com/weblog/2004_08_01_blogchive.html#109217452587191819, 2004.

_____. "The Revolution Began with Paper." Retrieved April 4, 2008, from http://www.escapistmagazine.com/articles/view/issues/issue_42/253-The-Revolution-Began-With-Paper.2, 2006.

_____. "Games, Storytelling and Breaking the String." In *Second Person: Role-Playing and Story in Games and Playable Media*, edited by P. Harrigan and N. Wardrip-Fruin, 5–13. Cambridge: MIT Press, 2007.

_____. "Randomness: Blight or Bane?" Retrieved December 4, 2009, from http://www.gamasutra.com/blogs/GregCostikyan/20091113/3552/Randomness_Blight_or_Bane.php, 2009.

Costikan, G., and D. Davidson, et al. (eds.). *Tabletop: Analog Game Design*. ETC Press, 2011.

Costikyan, G., D. Gelber, and E. Goldberg. Paranoia [Role-playing Game]. West End Games, 1984.

Costikyan, G., and R. A. Simonsen. The Return of the Stainless Steel Rat [Board Game]. Simulations Publications, Inc., 1981.

Costikyan, G. and W. Spector. Toon [Role-playing Game]. Steve Jackson Games, 1984.

Cover, J. *The Creation of Narrative in Tabletop Role-Playing Games.* Jefferson NC: McFarland, 2010.

Cowley, B., D. Charles, M. Black, and R. Hickey. "Toward an Understanding of Flow in Video Games." *ACM Computers in Entertainment* 6, no. 2 (2008).

Cox, R. "Re: Non-Gamers Rate Boardgames (Including Shogun, Modern Art.) — Large Test in Newspaper. Retrieved March 9, 2010, from http://www.boardgamegeek.com/article/2875259#2875259, 2008.

Crapuchettes, D. Wits and Wagers [Board Game]. North Star Games, 2005.

_____. Email Interview, 2008.

Crawford, C. "The Art of Computer Game Design." Washington State University. Retrieved May 7, 2006, from http://www.vancouver.wsu.edu/fac/peabody/gamebook/Coverpage.html, 1982.

Crawford, K. "Vygotskian Approaches in Human Development in the Information Era." *Educational Studies in Mathematics* 31, no. 1/2 (1996): 43–62.

Crogan, P. "Wargaming and Computer Games: Fun with the Future." In Proceedings of the DiGRA 2003 Conference — Level Up, Utrecht, 2003.

Csikszentmihalyi, M. *Flow: The Psychology of Optimal Experience*. New York: Harper and Row, 1990.

Culin, S. "Street Games of Boys in Brooklyn." *Journal of American Folklore 4* (1891): 221–237.

_____. Mancala, the National Game of Africa. *Annual Report of the U.S. National Museum 1894*, 597–606.

_____. *Korean Games, with Notes on the Corresponding Games at China and Japan*. University of Pennsylvania Press, 1895 (reprinted as *Games of the Orient*. Rutand, VT: Charles Tuttle Co., 1958).

_____. Hawaiian Games. *American Anthropologist 1*, no. 2 (1899): 201–247.

_____. Philippine Games. *American Anthropologist 2* (1900): 643–656.

_____. *24th Annual Report of the Bureau of American Ethnology: Games of North American Indians*. Washington, D.C: United States Government Printing Office, 1907.

Curry, A. "Monopoly Killer: Perfect German Board Game Redefines Genre." *Wired* (April 2009): 60–72

Czege, P. My Life with Master [Role-playing Game]. Half Meme Press, 2003.

_____. "My Life with Master: The Architecture of Protagonism." In *Second Person: Role-Playing and Story in Games and Playable Media*, edited by P. Harrigan and N. Wardrip-Fruin, 67–68. Cambridge: MIT Press, 2007.

Dagger, S. "Es War Einmal." *The Games Journal.* Retrieved June 8, 2007, from http://www.thegamesjournal.com/articles/GermanHistory.shtml, 2003.

_____. "Warrior Knights Old and New." *Counter* 34 (2006a): 73–76.

_____. "What Is a Game Worth? The Misguided Game Buyer Looks at Value. *Counter* 33 (2006b): 14–16.

_____. "Of Dice and Men" (editorial). *Counter* 36 (2007): 4–5.

_____. Email Interview, 2008.

Dancey, R. S. "Adventure Game Industry Market Research Summary (RPGs), V1.0." Retrieved January 2, 2009, from http://www.seankreynolds.com/rpgfiles/gaming/WotCMarketResearchSummary.html, 2000.

Dancing with the Stars Board Game [Board Game]. University Games, 2008.

Darcy, J., R. Tesh, and T. Braunlich. Star Wars CCG [Card Game]. Decipher, 1995.

Darrow, C., and E. Magie. Monopoly [Board Game]. Parker Brothers, 1935.

Daviau, R. Risk (Revised Edition) [Board Game]. Parker Brothers, 2008.

Davidoff, D., H. Marly, and P. Des Pallières. Die Werwölfe von Düsterwald [Role-playing Game]. 999 Games, 2001.

De Boer, C. J., and M. H. Lamers, M. H. "Electronic Augmentation of Traditional Board Games." In M. Rauterberg (ed.), ICEC 2004.

LNCS, vol. 3166: 441–444. Springer, Heidelberg, 2004.

Degann, J. "What Is This Board Game About?" Retrieved August 4, 2009, from http://jbd games.blogspot.com/2008/02/what-is-this-game-about.html, 2008.

Delfanti, G., P. Trigaux, and G. Mathieu. Full Métal Planète [Board Game]. Ludodelire, 1988.

Delonge, F.-B. Goldbräu [Board Game]. Zoch Verlag, 2004.

Deppey, D. "X-Men. Retreat!" *The Comics Journal,* Retrieved May 14, 2009, from http://www.tcj.com/index.php?option=com_con tent&task=view&id=324&Itemid=48, 2004.

De Rosa, P. The Fall of Avalon Hill. *The Strategist,* 7–8. Retrieved June 7, 2008, from http://gis.net/~pldr/fah.html, 1998.

Deutscher Spiele Preis. Retrieved February 2, 2008, from http://www.deutscherspielepreis. de/, 2008.

Deutsches Spiele-Archiv. Retrieved January 9, 2008, from http://www.deutsches-spiele-arch iv.de/, 2008.

Deutsches Spielemuseum e.V. Retrieved January 18, 2008, from http://www.deutsches-spielem useum.de/, 2008.

Dexter: The Board Game [Board Game]. GDC-GameDevCo Ltd., 2010.

Dixon, B. 1870 [Board Game]. Mayfair Games, 1994.

Dontanville, M. "Musings on ... Hybrid Games." Retrieved May 4, 2008, from http://www. boardgamenews.com/index.php/boardgame news/comments/musings_on_hybrid_games_ 32/, 2006.

Dormans, J. "On the Role of the Die: A Brief Ludologic Study of Pen-and-Paper Roleplaying Games and Their Rules." *Game Studies: The International Journal of Computer Game Research* 6, no. 1 (2006).

Dorn, R. Die Händler von Genua [Board Game]. Alea, 2001a.

_____. The Traders of Genoa [Board Game]. Rio Grande Games, 2001b.

_____. Goa [Board Game]. Hans im Glück, 2004.

_____. Louis XIV [Board Game]. Alea, 2005.

_____. Goa — New Version. Retrieved January 5, 2009, from http://www.boardgamegeek. com/thread/381155/goa-new-version, 2009.

Dorra, S. Intrige [Board Game]. F.X. Schmidt, 1994.

_____. Linie Eins [Board Game]. Goldsieber, 1995.

_____. For Sale [Card Game]. Ravensburger, 1997.

_____. Alles im Eimer [Card Game]. Kosmos, 2002.

Doumen, J., and J. Wiersinga. Bus [Board Game]. Splotter Spellen, 1999a.

_____. Roads and Boats [Board Game]. Splotter Spellen, 1999b.

_____. Indonesia [Board Game]. Splotter Spellen, 2005.

Dreiling, M. China Rails [Board Game]. Mayfair Games, 2007.

Drew. (2007). "Re: Why I'm a Eurogamer." Retrieved January 1, 2009, from http://www. boardgamegeek.com/article/1376679#137667 9, 2007.

Drögemüller, J. Das Zepter von Zavandor [Board Game]. Lookout Games, 2004.

Drover, G. Sid Meier's Civilization: The Boardgame [Board Game]. Eagle Games, 2002.

Drover, G., and M. Wallace. Railroad Tycoon [Board Game]. Eagle Games, 2005.

Drude, H. "BGG at Göttingen Game Designers' Convention." Retrieved May 6, 2010, from http://www.boardgamegeek.com/thread/522 405/bgg-at-gottingen-game-designers-conve ntion, 2010.

Dubin, D. "Re: My Confession: Some Bothersome Things I've Realized About My Approach to the Gaming Hobby." Retrieved January 12, 2009, from http://www.boardgamegeek.com/ article/2198747#2198747, 2008.

Duke, R. *Gaming: The Future's Language.* New York: Sage, 1974.

Dunnigan, J. F. PanzerBlitz [Board Game]. Avalon Hill, 1970.

_____. Outdoor Survival [Board Game]. Avalon Hill, 1972.

_____. Sniper! [Board Game]. Simulations Publications Inc., 1973.

_____. War in Europe [Board Game]. Simulations Publications Inc., 1976a.

_____. War in the West [Board Game]. Simulations Publications Inc., 1976b.

_____. The Complete Wargames Handbook. New York: William Morrow, 1980a.

_____. Wreck of the B.S.M. Pandora [Board Game]. Simulations Publications Inc., 1980b.

_____. *The Complete Wargames Handbook.* Retrieved August 18, 2007, from http://www. hyw.com/books/wargameshandbook/5-histor. htm, 1997.

_____. Year 2000 Introduction for the Wargames Handbook. In *The Wargames Handbook, Third Edition.* Writers Club Press, 2000.

Eberle, B., J. Kittredge, and P. Olotka. Cosmic Encounter [Board Game]. Eon Games, 1977.

_____. Dune [Board Game]. Avalon Hill, 1979.

_____. Quirks [Board Game]. Eon, 1980.

_____. Borderlands [Board Game]. Eon, 1982.

Edan, H. L'Attaque [Board Game]. Au Jeu Retrouvé, 1909.

Edwards, B. "The History of Civilization." Retrieved December 9, 2007, from http://www. gamasutra.com/view/feature/1523/the_his tory_of_civilization.php?page=1, 2007.

Edwards, R. "GNS and Other Matters of Role-Playing Theory." Retrieved June 4, 2008, from http://www.indie-rpgs.com/articles/1/, 2001.

Edwards, R., S. Goldberg, and Grady. Sherlock Holmes Criminal-Cabinet [Board Game]. Franckh-Kosmos, 1981.

Egenfeldt-Nelson, S., J. H. Smith, and S. Tosca. *Understanding Video Games*. New York: Routledge, 2008.

Eggert, M. "Rick Heli Plays Board Games in the San Francisco Bay Area." Retrieved July 1, 2008, from http://www.spotlightongames.com/interview/heli1.html, 2005.

_____. "What Is a "Pöppel"? Retrieved February 9, 2008, from http://www.westpark-gamers.de/index.html?/transcripts/ggn17, 2006a.

_____. "Why There Are No Wargames in Germany." Retrieved May 14, 2008, from http://www.westpark-gamers.de/transcripts/german wargames.html, 2006b.

Ehrhard, D., and D. Vitale. Condottiere [Board Game]. Descartes Editeur, 1995.

_____. Serenissima [Board Game]. Eurogames, 1996.

Election [Board Game]. Intellect Games, 1972.

Elias, S., J. Tweet, and R. Heinsoo, R. Dungeons and Dragons Miniatures [Collectible Miniatures Game]. Wizards of the Coast, 2003.

Erickson, R. S., and T. Erickson Jr. Rail Baron [Board Game]. Avalon Hill, 1977.

Eskelinen, M. "The Gaming Situation." *Game Studies: The International Journal of Computer Game Research* 1, no. 1 (2001).

_____. "500 Words on 'Game Design as Narrative Architecture' by Henry Jenkins." In *First Person*, edited by N. Wardrip-Fruin and P. Harrigan. Cambridge MA: MIT Press, 2004.

_____. "Explorations in Game Ecology, Part 1." *Jahrbuch für Computerphilologie* 7 (2005): 93–110.

Eskin, B. "Extraordinary Meeples." Retrieved May 25, 2009, from http://www.printmag.com/design_articles/extraordinary_meeples/tabid/365/Default.aspx, 2008.

_____. "Like Monopoly in the Depression, Settlers of Catan Is the Board Game of Our Time." Retrieved August 4, 2011, from http://www.washingtonpost.com/wp-dyn/content/article/2010/11/24/AR2010112404140.html?hpid=opinionsbox1, 2010.

Essen Feather. Retrieved February 4, 2008, from http://www.deutscherspielepreis.de/p070.php p4, 2008.

Events [Board Game]. 3M, 1974.

Exit191. Carcassonne: Dragon Riders and Slayers [Board Game Expansion]. Web Published, 2006a.

_____. Carcassonne: The Well and the Donkey [Board Game Expansion]. Web Published, 2006b.

EYE of NiGHT. "Re: How Do You Explain Your Hobby to Strangers?" Retrieved January 14, 2010, from http://www.boardgamegeek.com/article/632748#632748, 2005.

Faidutti, B. Bongo [Dice Game]. Heidelberger Spieleverlag, 2000a.

_____. Ohne Furcht und Adel [Card Game]. Hans im Glück, 2000b.

_____. "A Theme, What For?" Retrieved August 5, 2008, from http://www.faidutti.com/index.php?Module=divers&id=455, 2005a.

_____. "Theme and Mechanics 1.0." Retrieved March 14, 2007, from http://www.thegamesjournal.com/articles/ThemesMechanics1.shtml, 2005b.

_____. "Theme Changed by Publisher." Retrieved April 4, 2008, from http://boardgamegeek.com/geeklist/16285/page/1, 2006.

_____. "Cosmic Encounter." In *Hobby Games: The 100 Best*, edited by J. Lowder, 66–68. Renton: Green Ronin, 2007.

_____. Email Interview, 2008.

_____. "The Traitor and the Mutineer." Retrieved August 14, 2009, from http://www.faidutti.com/index.php?Module=mesjeux&id=328&fichier=107, n.d.

Faidutti, B., P. Clequin, D. Carver, and C. Konieczka. Warrior Knights [Board Game]. Fantasy Flight Games, 2006.

Faidutti, B., and M. Schacht. Fist of Dragonstones [Card Game]. Days of Wonder, 2002.

Falco, M. Set [Card Game]. Set Enterprises, 1991.

Farrell, C. "Re: Giving Up on Games Too Quickly." Retrieved July 14, 2008, from http://www.boardgamegeek.com/article/453590#453590, 2005.

Farrell, J. "BGG Extended Stats." Retrieved January 24, 2009, from http://friendless.serveg ame.org/stats/, 2009.

Fawcett, B. India Rails [Board Game]. Mayfair Games, 1999.

Fay, I. "Filtering Feedback." In *Tabletop: Analog Game Design*, edited by G. Costikan and D. Davidson, et al., 54–60. ETC Press, 2011.

Featherstone, M. *Consumer Culture and Postmodernism*. New York: Sage, 1991.

Feld, S. Im Jahr des Drachen [Board Game]. Alea, 2007a.

_____. Notre Dame [Board Game]. Alea, 2007b.

Fenchel, G. La Città [Board Game]. Kosmos, 2000.

Fenwick, R. Fortune [Board Game]. Ariel/Philmar, 1979.

FIFA Soccer 2004 [Video Game]. Electronic Arts, 2004.

Fine, G. A. *Shared Fantasy: Role-Playing Games as Social Worlds*. Chicago: University of Chicago Press, 1983.

_____. "Mobilizing Fun: Provisioning Resources

in Leisure Worlds." *Sociology of Sport* 6, no. 4 (1989): 319–334.

Finn, M. Computer Games and Narrative Progression. *M/C: A Journal of Media and Culture* 3, no. 5. Retrieved May 7, 2007, from http://journal.media-culture.org.au/0010/narrative.php, 2000.

Fiske, J. "The Cultural Economy of Fandom." In *The Adoring Audience: Fan Culture and Popular Media*, edited by L. A. Lewis, 30–49. New York: Routledge, 1992.

Flabber23. "Boardgames: Higher Entertainment Value Than You Thought!" Retrieved January 6, 2009, from http://www.boardgamegeek.com/thread/231584, 2007.

Foo, C. Y., and E. M. I. Koivisto. "Defining Grief Play in MMORPGs: Player and Developer Perceptions." Paper presented at the ACM SIGCHI International Conference on Advances in Computer Entertainment Technology, National University of Singapore, 2004.

Frasca, G. "Ludology Meets Narratology: Similitude and Differences Between (Video)Games and Narrative." Retrieved January 8, 2003, from http://www.ludology.org/articles/ludology.htm, 1999.

_____. "Simulation 101: Simulation Versus Representation." Retrieved June 30, 2004, from http://www.ludology.org/articles/sim1/simulation101.html, 2001a.

_____. *Videogames of the Oppressed: Videogames as a Means for Critical Thinking and Debate.* Unpublished Master's Thesis, Georgia Institute of Technology, Atlanta, 2001b.

_____. "Ludologists Love Stories, Too: Notes from a Debate That Never Took Place." In Proceedings of the DiGRA 2003 Conference — Level Up: Utrecht, 2003.

Freeman, J. *The Complete Book of Wargames.* New York: Simon and Schuster, 1980.

Freud, A. *The Psychoanalytic Treatment of Children.* New York: International Universities Press, 1968.

Freud, S. *Beyond the Pleasure Principle* (translated by J. Strachey). New York: Norton, 1959.

Freund, W. "Pretty German Games." Retrieved April 18, 2008, from http://www.magazine-deutschland.de/magazin/US-Spiele_3-05_ENG_E5.php, 2005.

Friedman, M. (ed.). *Consumption and Identity.* Washington, DC: Taylor and Francis.

Friese, F. Turbo Taxi [Board Game]. 2F-Spiele, 2000.

_____. Funkenschlag (Second Edition) [Board Game]. 2F-Spiele, 2004.

Gadamer, H.-G. *Truth and Method, Second Edition* (translated by J. Weinsheimer and D. Marshall). New York: Crossroad, 1960.

Galanti, G. "Tete-a-Tete with JSP." *GiocArea*

OnLine. Retrieved March 14, 2008, from http://www.davincigames.it/giocarea_eng/17/cover.htm, 2005.

The Game Cabinet. Retrieved April 17, 2008, from http://www.gamecabinet.com/, 2000.

Game Designers — A Plea with Historic Overview. Retrieved May 31, 2010, from http://www.spieleautorenzunft.de/a-plea-with-historic-overview.html, 2010.

The Game of Life — Pirates of the Caribbean [Board Game]. Hasbro Inc., 2004.

The Game of Life — Simpsons Edition [Board Game]. Hasbro Inc., 2004.

Garfield, R. Magic: The Gathering [Card Game]. Wizards of the Coast, 1993.

_____. Roborally [Board Game]. Wizards of the Coast, 1994.

_____. Netrunner [Card Game]. Wizards of the Coast, 1996.

_____. "Metagames." In J. Dietz *Horsemen of the Apocalypse: Essays on Roleplaying*, edited by J. Dietz, 16–21. Charleston, IL: Jolly Roger Games, 2000.

Garfield, R., L. S. Johnson, and R. Goudie. Vampire: The Eternal Struggle [Card Game]. Wizards of the Coast, 1994.

"Gary Gygax Interview." Retrieved October 12th, 2007, from http://www.gamebanshee.com/interviews/garygygax1.php, 2000.

Gerdts, M. Antike [Board Game]. Eggertspiele, 2005.

_____. Imperial [Board Game]. Eggertspiele, 2006.

Gertzbein, A., and J. Cappel, J. Wasabi [Board Game]. Z-Man Games, 2008.

Gibson, H. Dover Patrol [Board Game]. Gibsons Games, 1911.

Giles, G. "House of Cards." Retrieved June 8, 2008, from http://www.metroactive.com/papers/sonoma/11.09.95/magic.html, 1995.

Gimmler, T. Geschenkt [Card Game]. Amigo Spiele, 2004.

Gingold, C. *Miniature Gardens and Magic Crayons: Games, Spaces, and Worlds.* Unpublished Master's Thesis, Georgia Institute of Technology, 2003.

Giulanotti, R. "Participant Observation and Research into Football Hooliganism: Reflections on the Problems of Entree and Everyday Risks." *Sociology of Sport* 12, no. 1 (1995): 1–20.

Glaser, B., and A. Strauss, A. *Discovery of Grounded Theory: Strategies for Qualitative Research.* London: Wledenfeld and Nicholson, 1967.

Glassco, B. "Betrayed Once More — 2nd Edition Is Now a Go!" Retrieved January 4, 2010, from http://www.boardgamegeek.com/thread/466307/betrayed-once-more-2nd-edition-is-now-a-go, 2009.

Glee Board Game [Board Game]. Cardinal, 2010.

Glenn, S. "Interview with Reiner Knizia — Fall 1999." Retrieved May 1, 2008, from http://www.funagain.com/control/rc?p=knizia99, 1999a.

_____. "Interview with Jay Tummelson — Winter 1999." Retrieved May 2, 2008, from http://www.funagain.com/control/rc?p=tummelson99, 1999b.

_____. "Interview with Reiner Knizia — Fall 2002." Retrieved May 4, 2008, from http://www.convivium.org.uk/kgfgi.htm, 2002.

_____. Balloon Cup [Card Game]. Kosmos, 2003.

Gobet, F., A. De Voogt, and J. Retschitzki. *Moves in Mind: The Psychology of Board Games.* Hove: Psychology Press, 2004.

Goffman, E. "Fun in Games." In *Encounters: Two Studies in the Sociology of Interaction*, 15–81. Indianapolis: Bobbs-Merrill, 1961.

Goldberg, E. Tales of the Arabian Nights [Board Game]. West End Games, 1985.

Goldfarb, M. E. "The Educational Theory of Lev Semenovich Vygotsky (1896–1934)." Retrieved June 4, 2002, from http://www.newfoundations.com/GALLERY/Vygotsky.html, 2001.

Goslar, R., and T. Goslar, T. Lost Valley [Board Game]. Heidelberger Spieleverlag, 2004.

Gossip Girl Never Have I Ever Game [Board Game]. Imagination Games, 2009.

Gray, M. Fortress America [Board Game]. Milton Bradley, 1986a.

_____. Shogun [Board Game]. Milton Bradley, 1986b.

Gray, M., G. Gygax, L. Kessling, D. Megarry, S. Schwab, and S. Winter, S. Dungeon! [Board Game], TSR, 1975.

Gray, W. "History of Wargaming." Retrieved May 4, 2009, from http://www.hmgs.org/history.htm, 2008.

Greenwood, D. Advanced Squad Leader [Board Game]. Avalon Hill, 1985.

Greenwood, D., and M. Matheny, M. Circus Maximus [Board Game]. Avalon Hill, 1979.

Grodal, T. "Video Games and the Pleasures of Control." In *Media Entertainment*, edited by D. Zillman and P. Vorderer, 197–212. 2002.

Groos, K. *The Play of Animals.* New York: D. Appleton and Co., 1898.

_____. *The Play of Man.* New York: D. Appleton and Co., 1901.

Gross, K. Ice War [Board Game]. Metagaming, 1978.

_____. Invasion of the Air-Eaters [Board Game]. Metagaming, 1979.

_____. The Lords of Underearth [Board Game]. Metagaming, 1981.

Grossberg, L. *We Gotta Get Out of This Place: Popular Conservatism and Postmodern Culture.* London: Routledge, 1992.

Grubb, J. Marvel Super Heroes [Role-Playing Game]. Tactical Studies Rules, 1984.

Grubb, J., D. Megarry, and S. Winter. The New Dungeon! [Board Game], TSR, 1989.

_____. The Classic Dungeon! [Board Game], TSR, 1992.

Grubb, J., J. Tweet, B. Slavicsek, and R. Watkins. Star Wars Miniatures [Collectible Miniatures Game]. Wizards of the Coast, 2004.

Gruber, H. E., and J. J. Voneche (eds.). *The Essential Piaget.* New York: Basic Books, 1977.

Gygax, G. Advanced Dungeons and Dragons [Role-playing Game]. Tactical Studies Rules, 1977.

Gygax, G., and D. Arneson, D. Dungeons and Dragons [Role-playing Game]. Tactical Studies Rules, 1974a.

_____. Dungeons and Dragons Vol. 3: Wilderness and Underworld Adventures [Role-playing Game]. Tactical Studies Rules, 1974b.

Gygax, G., and B. Blume. Boot Hill [Role-playing Game]. Tactical Studies Rules, 1975.

Gygax, G., and J. Perren, J. *Chainmail: Rules for Medieval Miniatures.* Guidon Games, 1971.

Haag, A. "Games International — The Journal of Fun and Games." Retrieved June 4, 2008, from http://www.westpark-gamers.de/index.html?/Artikel/gamesintl.html&http%3A//www.westpark-gamers.de/Artikel/GIinterview.html, 2003.

Haddon, L. "Electronic and Computer Games: The History of an Interactive Medium." *Screen* 29, no. 2 (1981): 52–73.

Hall, G. S. *Youth.* New York: D. Appleton and Co., 1906.

Hamblen, R. Magic Realm [Board Game]. Avalon Hill, 1978.

_____. Gunslinger [Board Game]. Avalon Hill, 1982.

Hamburg, M. "Re: Why FASTER FASTER FASTER??? Why?" Retrieved November 4, 2008, from http://www.boardgamegeek.com/article/586852#586852, 2005.

Hamlin, D. "The Structures of Toy Consumption: Bourgeois Domesticity and Demand for Toys in Nineteenth-Century Germany." *Journal of Social History* 36, no. 4 (2003): 857–869.

Haney, C., and S. Abbot. Trivial Pursuit [Board Game]. Horn Abbot, 1981.

Hanson, A. "Ravensburger Takes Flight." *Knucklebones* (March 2006): 44–46.

Hardin, A. "Is It Really About Theme vs. Mechanic?" *The Games Journal* Retrieved February 12, 2008, from http://www.thegamesjournal.com/articles/ThemeVsMechanics.shtml. 2001.

Hardy, I. B. Outreach [Board Game]. Simulations Publications Inc., 1976.

Harper, B., L. Banerd, J. Eliason, J. Groteboer,

E. Hunter, S. Padgett, et al. Advanced Civilization [Board Game Expansion]. Avalon Hill, 1991.

Harrigan, P., and N. Wardrip-Fruin (eds.). *First Person: New Media as Story Performance and Game.* Cambridge, MA: MIT Press, 2004.

_____. *Second Person: Role-Playing and Story in Games and Playable Media.* Cambridge, MA: MIT Press, 2007.

_____. *Third Person: Authoring and Exploring Vast Narratives.* Cambridge, MA: MIT Press, 2009.

Harris, L. H. Axis and Allies [Board Game]. Milton Bradley, 1981.

_____. Broadsides and Boarding Parties [Board Game]. Milton Bradley, 1982.

_____. Conquest of the Empire [Board Game]. Milton Bradley, 1984.

Harris, R. Talisman [Board Game]. Games Workshop, 1983.

_____. Talisman Expansion Set [Board Game Expansion]. Games Workshop, 1986.

_____. Talisman Dungeon [Board Game Expansion]. Games Workshop, 1987.

_____. Talisman: The Magical Quest Game. Retrieved June 8, 2007, from http://www.harris-authors.com/talisman_history.html, 2007.

Hartwell, David G. *Age of Wonders: Exploring the World of Science Fiction.* New York: Walker and Company, 1984.

Hartwig, K. Chinatown [Board Game]. Alea, 1999.

Hauser, E. "Ravensburger AG." In *International Directory of Company Histories,* 64. 1993.

Havens, E. Jati [Board Game]. 3M, 1965.

Hefner, D., C. Klimmt, and P. Vorderer. "Identification with the Player Character as Determinant of Video Game Enjoyment." Paper presented at the ICEC 2007, 6th International Conference on Entertainment Computing, 2007.

Heide Smith, J. "The Aesthetics of Antagonism." Paper presented at the Aesthetics of Play Conference, Bergen. Retrieved May 7, 2007, from http://www.aestheticsofplay.org/papers/smith2.htm, 2005.

_____. *Plans and Purposes: How Videogame Goals Shape Player Behaviour.* Unpublished Doctoral Dissertation, I.T. University of Copenhagen, Copenhagen, 2006.

Hein, P. Hex [Board Game]. Piet Hein A/S, 1942.

Heli, R. "State of the Board Games World." Retrieved June 5, 2007, from http://www.spotlightongames.com/list/history.html, 2004.

_____. "Moritz Eggert Plays Board Games in Munich, Germany." Retrieved April 5, 2008, from http://www.spotlightongames.com/interview/eggert.html, 2007.

Helldörfer, C. ("Sammlung des Deutschen Spiele-Archivs Kommt Nach Nürnberg." Retrieved April 29, 2010, from http://www.nz-online.de/artikel.asp?art=1210751&kat=317&man=3, 2010.

Helms, D. B., and J. S. Turner. *Exploring Child Behaviour.* Japan: Holt-Saunders, 1981.

Hely, C., and R. Pelek. Santiago [Board Game]. Amigo Spiele., 2003.

Hemberger, S. "Re: Why FASTER FASTER FASTER??? Why?" Retrieved January 9, 2009, from http://www.boardgamegeek.com/article/587231#587231, 2005.

Henn, D. Show Manager [Board Game]. Queen, 1996.

_____. Metro [Board Game]. Queen, 1997.

_____. Atlantic Star [Board Game]. Queen, 2001.

_____. Wallenstein [Board Game]. Queen, 2002.

_____. Alhambra [Board Game]. Queen, 2003.

_____. Alhambra — Das Würfelspiel [Board Game]. Queen, 2006.

Henninger, E., J. Roznai, J. Griffin, and B. Roznai. British Rails [Board Game]. Mayfair Games, 1984.

Hennion, A. "Those Things That Hold Us Together: Taste and Sociology." *Cultural Sociology* 1, no. 1 (2007): 97–114.

Hensley, S. L. Deadlands [Role-playing Game]. Pinnacle Entertainment Group, 1996.

Herman, M., and E. Goldberg. John Carter: Warlord of Mars [Board Game]. Simulations Publications Inc., 1979.

Hermosa, C. "User Profile." Retrieved January 15, 2009, from http://www.boardgamegeek.com/user/MScrivner, 2007.

Hersch, B. Outburst! [Board Game]. Hersch and Company, 1986.

_____. Taboo [Board Game]. Hasbro GMBH, 1989.

Herschler, F. A. Foil [Card Game]. 3M, 1968.

_____. Challenge Football [Card Game]. 3M, 1972a.

_____. Challenge Golf at Pebble Beach [Board Game]. 3M, 1972b.

Hertzano, E. Rummikub [Board Game]. Intelli/Arxon, 1977.

Hill, J. Squad Leader [Board Game]. Avalon Hill, 1977.

"Hippodice Spieleclub e.V." Retrieved June 21, 2008, from http://www.hippodice.de/index.php?option=com_content&view=article&id=8&Itemid=1, 2008.

Hodel, W. Mississippi Queen [Board Game]. Goldsieber, 1998a.

_____. Mississippi Queen: The Black Rose [Board Game Expansion]. Goldsieber, 1998b.

Hofer, M. K. *The Games We Played: The Golden Age of Board and Table Games.* New York: Princeton Architectural Press, 2003.

Hoffmann, R. Ogallala [Card Game]. Pelikan, 1975.

Holt, R., and J. Mitterer. "Examining Video Game Immersion as a Flow State." Paper presented at the 108th Annual Psychological Association Conference, Washington DC, 2000.

Holzgrafe, R. "Re: You Know What I Realized?" Retrieved January 14, 2009, from http://www.boardgamegeek.com/article/1195713#1195713, 2006.

Homans, G. C. "Social Behavior as Exchange." *American Journal of Sociology* 63, no. 6 (1958): 597–606.

Hostettler, U. Kremlin [Board Game]. Avalon Hill, 1988.

Huber, J. Email Interview, 2008.

Hughes, L. A. "Beyond the Rules of the Game: Why are Rooie Rules Nice?" In *The World of Play: Proceedings of the 7th Annual Meeting of the Association of the Anthropological Study of Play*, edited by F. E. Manning, 188–199. New York: Leisure Press, 1988.

_____. "'But That's Not Really Mean': Competing in a Cooperative Mode." *Sex Roles* 9, no. 11/12 (1988): 669–687.

_____. "Foursquare: A Glossary and 'Native' Taxonomy of Game Rules." *Play and Culture* 2, no. 2 (1989): 102–136.

_____. "Children's Games and Gaming." In *Children's Folklore: A Sourcebook*, edited by B. Sutton-Smith, J. Mechling, T. W. Johnson, and F. R. McMahon, 93–119. New York: Garland, 1999.

Huizinga, J. *Homo Ludens: A Study of the Play Element in Culture*. Boston: Beacon Press, 1950.

Hunicke, R., M. LeBlanc, and R. Zubek. "MDA: A Formal Approach to Game Design and Game Research." In Proceedings of the Challenges in Game AI Workshop, 19th National Conference on Artificial Intelligence, San Jose, CA: AAAI Press, 2004.

Hurter, W. Memory [Board Game]. Ravensburger, 1959.

Huzzey, R. A. "Games Mecca?" *The Games Journal*. Retrieved June 8, 2007, from http://www.thegamesjournal.com/articles/GamingMecca.shtml, 2002.

"Internationale Spieltage." Retrieved May 15, 2008, from http://www.merz-verlag.com/spiel/index.php4, 2008.

"Interview with Klaus Teuber." Retrieved May 3, 2008, from http://catanonline.com/news/klausteuberinterview01.htm?, 2005.

Jacklin, K. "Simply Knizia: The Art in Keeping Game Design Simple." In *Tabletop: Analog Game Design*, edited by G. Costikan and D. Davidson, et al., 47–53. ETC Press, 2011.

Jackson, M. "Five & Dime: How It All Started." Retrieved January 14, 2009, from http://akapastorguy.blogspot.com/2006/01/five-dime-how-it-all-started.html, 2006.

Jackson, S. Melee [Board Game]. Metagaming, 1977a.

_____. Ogre [Board Game]. Metagaming, 1977b.

_____. G.E.V. [Board Game]. Metagaming, 1978a.

_____. Wizard [Board Game]. Metagaming, 1978b.

_____. Illuminati [Card Game]. Steve Jackson Games, 1983.

_____. Generic Universal Role Playing System (GURPS) [Role-playing Game]. Steve Jackson Games, 1986.

_____. "Illuminati Designer." Retrieved May 9, 2008, from http://www.sjgames.com/illuminati/designart.html, n.d.

Jackson, S., and C. Irby, C. Car Wars [Board Game]. Steve Jackson Games, 1981.

Jacobi, P. 1876 [Board Game]. Chris Lawson, 1996.

Jakeliunas, A., and G. Cornett, G. Packeis am Pol [Board Game]. Bambus Spieleverlag, 2003.

James, E. *Science Fiction in the Twentieth Century*. Oxford: Oxford University Press, 1994.

Jansz, J., and L. Martens, L. "Gaming at a LAN Event: The Social Context of Playing Videogames." *New Media and Society* 7, no. 3 (2005): 333–355.

Jaquays, P. "Runequest." In *Hobby Games: The 100 Best*, edited by J. Lowder, 261–264. Renton: Green Ronin, 2007.

Jaquet, G., and K. M. Ward. Gamma World [Role-playing Game]. Tactical Studies Rules, 1978.

Järvinen, A. *Games Without Frontiers: Theories and Methods for Game Studies and Design*. Saarbrücken: Verlag Dr. Müller, 2009.

Jenkins, H. *Textual Poachers: Television Fans and Participatory Culture*. New York: Routledge, 1992.

_____. "Game Design as Narrative Architecture." In *First Person: New Media as Story, Performance and Game*, edited by P. Harrington and N. Frup-Waldrop, 118–130. Cambridge: MIT Press, 2002a.

_____. "Interactive Audiences?: The 'Collective Intelligence' of Media Fans." In *The New Media Book*, edited by D. Harries, 157–170. London: British Film Institute, 2002b.

Jenkins, J. "Re: Are we at the Start of a Resurgence of Boardgame Popularity?" Retrieved January 12, 2010, from http://www.boardgamegeek.com/article/2794381#2794381, 2008.

Jensen, J. "Fandom as Pathology: The Consequences of Characterization." In *The Adoring Audience: Fan Culture and Popular Media*, edited by L. A. Lewis, 9–29. London: Routledge, 1992.

Jolly, T. Wiz War [Board Game]. Jolly Games, 1983.

Jome, E. "How Many Plays Should We Expect Out of a Game?" Retrieved January 9, 2009, from http://www.boardgamegeek.com/thread/291911, 2008.

Jones, K. "Playing It for Real." *Simulation and Gaming* 29, no. 3 (1998): 351–354.

Jump the Queue [Board Game]. Spears, 1989.

Jumpin [Board Game]. 3M, 1964.

Juul, J. *A Clash Between Game and Narrative.* Unpublished Master's Thesis, University of Copenhagen, Copenhagen, 2001a.

_____. "Games Telling Stories? — A Brief Note on Games and Narrative." *Game Studies: The International Journal of Computer Game Research* 1, no. 1 (2001b).

_____. "The Open and the Closed: Games of Emergence and Games of Progression." In *Proceedings of the Computer Games and Digital Cultures Conference,* edited by F. Mäyrä, 323–330. Tampere, Finland: Tampere University Press, 2002.

_____. *Half Real: Video Games Between Real Rules and Fictional Worlds.* Cambridge: MIT Press, 2005.

_____. "Fear of Failing? The Many Meanings of Difficulty in Video Games." In *The Video Game Theory Reader 2,* edited by M. J. P. Wolf and B. Perron, 237–252. New York: Routledge, 2009.

_____. *A Casual Revolution.* Cambridge, MA: MIT Press, 2010.

Kafai, Y. B., & Fields, D. A. "Stealing from Grandma or Generating Cultural Knowledge? Contestations and Effects of Cheats in a Tween Virtual World." In Proceedings of the DiGRA 2007 Conference — Situated Play, 1–9. Tokyo, 2007.

Karriere Poker [Card Game]. Hexagames, 1988.

Katriel, T., and B. Danet, B. "No Two Alike: Play and Aesthetics in Collecting." In *Interpreting Objects and Collections,* edited by S. M. Pearce, 220–239. London: Routledge, 1994.

Kaulfield, J. "Randomness, Player Choice and Player Experience." In *Tabletop: Analog Game Design,* edited by G. Costikan and D. Davidson, et al., 24–29. ETC Press, 2011.

Kelley, J. A., and M. Lugo. *The Little Giant Book of Dominoes.* New York: Sterling Publishing, 2003.

"Kennerspiel des Jahres." Retrieved August 3, 2011, from http://www.spiel-des-jahres.com/cms/front_content.php?idcat=180, 2011.

Kenson, S. "Marvel Super Heroes." In *Hobby Games: The 100 Best,* edited by J. Lowder, 196–199. Renton: Green Ronin, 2007.

Key, A. "Letters." *Sumo* 5 (1991).

Keyaerts, P. Vinci [Board Game]. Descartes Editeur, 1999.

Keys, S. "Settlers of Catan: How a German Board Game Went Mainstream." Retrieved August 4, 2011, from http://www.theatlantic.com/entertainment/archive/2011/06/settlers-of-catan-how-a-german-board-game-went-mainstream/239919/, 2011.

Kiesling, M., and W. Kramer. Raja: Palastbau in Indien [Board Game]. Phalanx Games, 2004.

Kilgore, T. "Re: More Thoughts on Gamers vs. Non-Gamers and Such." Retrieved January 2, 2009, from http://www.boardgamegeek.com/article/455516#455516, 2005.

King, B. "Re: Non-Gamers Rate Boardgames (Including Shogun, Modern Art) — Large Test in Newspaper." Retrieved March 14, 2009, from http://www.boardgamegeek.com/article/2874369#2874369, 2008.

Kirschenbaum, M. "War Stories: Board Wargames and (Vast) Procedural Narratives." In *Third Person: Authoring and Exploring Vast Narratives,* edited by P. Harrigan and N. Wardrip-Fruin, 357–372. Cambridge, MA: MIT Press, 2009.

_____. "War, What Is It Good For? Learning from Wargaming." Retrieved August 24, 2011, from http://www.playthepast.org/?p=1819, 2011.

Klamer, R. The Game of Life [Board Game]. Milton Bradley, 1960.

Klimmt, C., and T. Hartmann, T. "Effectance, Self-Efficacy and the Motivation to Play Video Games." In *Playing Video Games: Motives, Responses, and Consequences,* edited by P. Vorderer and J. Bryant, 133–146. Mahwah, NJ: Erlbaum, 2006.

Klimmt, C., A. Rizzo, P. Vorderer, J. Kock, and T. Fischer. "Experimental Evidence for Suspense as Determinant of Video Game Enjoyment." *CyberPsychology and Behaviour* 12, no. 1 (2009): 29–31.

Knizia, R. Goldrausch [Card Game]. Hans im Glück, 1990.

_____. Modern Art [Board Game]. Hans im Glück, 1992a.

_____. Quo Vadis [Board Game]. Amigo Spiele, 1992b.

_____. Auf Heller und Pfennig [Board Game]. Hans im Glück, 1994a.

_____. Flinke Pinke [Card Game]. Amigo Spiele, 1994b.

_____. High Society [Card Game]. Ravensburger, 1995a.

_____. Medici [Board Game]. Amigo Spiele, 1995b.

_____. Euphrat and Tigris [Board Game]. Hans im Glück, 1997a.

_____. Lost Cities [Card Game]. Kosmos, 1997b.

_____. Durch die Wüste [Board Game]. Kosmos, 1998a.

_____. Samurai [Board Game]. Hans im Glück, 1998b.

_____. Ra [Board Game]. Alea, 1999a.

_____. (Rheinländer [Board Game]. Hasbro GMBH, 1999b.

_____. Stephenson's Rocket [Board Game]. Pegasus Spiele, 1999c.

_____. Dice Games Properly Explained. Reading: Elliot Right Way, 1999d.

_____. Schotten Totten [Card Game]. Schmidt Spiele, 1999e.

_____. Der Herr der Ringe [Board Game]. Kosmos, 2000a.

_____. Die Kaufleute von Amsterdam [Board Game]. Jumbo, 2000b.

_____. Battle Line [Card Game]. GMT Games, 2000c.

_____. Tadsch Mahal [Board Game]. Alea, 2000d.

_____. Amon Ra [Board Game]. Hans im Glück, 2003.

_____. Razzia! [Card Game]. Amigo Spiele, 2004a.

_____. "The Design and Testing of the Board Game — Lord of the Rings." In Rules of Play: Game Design Fundamentals, edited by K. Salen and E. Zimmerman, 22–27. Cambridge, MA: MIT Press, 2004b.

_____. Blue Moon [Card Game]. Kosmos, 2004c.

_____. Ra [Board Game]. Uberplay, 2005.

_____. Fits [Board Game]. Ravensberger, 2009a.

_____. Ra: The Dice Game [Board Game]. Abacus, 2009b.

Kobbert, M. J. Das Verrückte Labyrinth [Board Game]. Ravensburger, 1986.

_____. Das Labyrinth der Meister [Board Game]. Ravensburger, 1991.

_____. Junior Labyrinth [Board Game]. Ravensburger, 1995.

_____. Labyrinth der Ringe [Board Game]. Ravensburger, 1998.

_____. Labyrinth: Das Kartenspiel [Card Game]. Ravensburger, 2000.

_____. 3-D Labyrinth [Board Game]. Ravensburger, 2002.

_____. Lord of the Rings Labyrinth [Board Game]. Ravensburger, 2003.

_____. Master Labyrinth [Board Game]. Ravensburger, 2007.

Kobral. "Estimating CCP (Cost Per Play) of My Collection." Retrieved January 9, 2009, from http://www.boardgamegeek.com/thread/892 44, 2005.

Konzack, L. "Geek Culture: The 3rd Counter-Culture." Paper presented at the Fun and Games Conference, Preston, UK. Retrieved June 5, 2008, from http://www.scribd.com/doc/270364/Geek-Culture-The-3rd-CounterCulture, 2006.

Koplow, J. Organized Crime [Board Game]. Koplow Games, 1974.

Kosman, J. "Our Panel Plays, Grades the Board Games of 2009." Retrieved January 4, 2010, from http://www.sfgate.com/cgi-bin/article.cgi?f=/c/a/2009/11/27/PK39IANHRI.DTL&type=entertainment, 2009.

Kosnett, P. S. Titan Strike [Board Game]. Simulations Publications Inc., 1979.

_____. Helltank [Board Game]. Metagaming, 1981.

_____. Helltank Destroyer [Board Game]. Metagaming, 1982.

Koster, R. A Theory of Fun for Game Design. Scottsdale: Paraglyph Press, 2005.

Krabbé, T. "Chess Records." Retrieved October 9, 2009, from http://www.xs4all.nl/~timkr/records/records.htm, 2009.

Kramer, W. Niki Lauda's Formel 1 [Board Game]. Altenburger und Stralsunder Spielkarten-Fabriken, 1980.

_____. Das große Unternehmen Erdgas [Board Game]. Information Erdgas, 1982.

_____. Heimlich and Co. [Board Game]. Ravensburger, 1984.

_____. Auf Achse [Board Game]. F.X. Schmidt, 1987.

_____. 6-Nimmt! [Card Game]. Amigo Spiele, 1994.

_____. Detroit-Cleveland Grand Prix [Board Game]. Mayfair, 1996a.

_____. Expedition [Board Game]. Ravensburger, 1996b.

_____. "The German Game Market." The Games Journal. Retrieved June 8, 2007, from http://www.thegamesjournal.com/articles/GermanGameMarket.shtml, 2000a.

_____. "What Is a Game?" The Games Journal. Retrieved June 8, 2007, from http://www.thegamesjournal.com/articles/WhatIsaGame.shtml, 2000b.

_____. Wildlife [Board Game]. Uberplay, 2002.

Kramer, W., and J. P. Grunau. Cash [Card Game]. Ravensburger, 1990.

Kramer, W., and M. Kiesling. Tikal [Board Game]. Ravensburger, 1999.

_____. Torres [Board Game]. Ravensburger, 2000a.

_____. Java [Board Game]. Ravensburger, 2000b.

Kramer, W., and U. Kramer. Wildlife Adventure [Board Game]. Ravensburger, 1985.

Kramer, W., and H.-R. Rösner. Tycoon [Board Game]. Jumbo, 1998.

Kramer, W., and R. Ulrich, R. El Grande [Board Game]. Hans im Glück, 1995.

_____. Die Fürsten von Florenz [Board Game]. Alea, 2000.

Krause, M. R. Nicht-Digitale Spiele: über das Medium, das Produkt und den Markt für Nicht-Digitale Spiele in Deutschland. Unpublished Master's Thesis, University of Applied Sciences, Hamburg, 2007.

Kücklich, J. "Other Playings: Cheating in Computer Games." Paper presented at the Other Players Conference, University of Copenhagen, 2004.

Lammes, S. "Approaching Game-Studies: Towards a Reflexive Methodology of Games as Situated Cultures." In Proceedings of the DiGRA 2007 Conference — Situated Play, 25–30. Tokyo, 2007.

Lamorisse, A. Risk [Board Game]. Parker Brothers, 1959.

LankyEngineer. "Re: Largest BGG Collections." Retrieved January 9, 2009, from http://www.boardgamegeek.com/article/2590596#25905 96, 2008a.

_____. "Who the Hell Are You? (A Series of Geek Polls)." Retrieved February 17, 2009, from http://www.boardgamegeek.com/article/252 5352#2525352, 2008b.

Lanza, M. T. "Germany's Game Plan." *Knucklebones* (November 2006): 20–23.

Lau, M. 18MY [Board Game]. Marcus Lau, 2006.

Launius, R. Arkham Horror [Board Game]. Chaosium, 1987.

Laws, R. D. Feng Shui [Role-playing Game]. Daedalus Entertainment, 1996.

Laws, R. D., and J. Garcia. Shadowfist [Card Game]. Shadowfist Games, 1995.

Lazarus, M. *Die Reize Des Spiels*. Berlin: Fred dummlers-Verlagsbuch-handlung, 1883.

Lazzaro, N. "Why We Play Games: Four Keys to Emotion Without Story." Paper presented at the Game Developers Conference, San Jose, CA, 2004.

Leacock, M. Pandemic [Board Game]. Z-Man Games, 2008.

LeBlanc, M. "8kindsoffun.com." Retrieved September 27, 2010, from http://www.8kindsof fun.com/, 2005.

Lee, J. Zombies in my Pocket [Card Game]. Cambridge Games Factory, 2009a.

_____. "Re: Are You a Gamer Who Has Published Since Joining the Geek?" Retrieved January 11, 2010, from http://boardgamegeek. com/article/3076387#3076387, 2009b.

Lehmann, T. Race for the Galaxy [Card Game]. Rio Grande Games, 2007.

_____. Um Krone und Kragen [Board Game]. Amigo, 2006.

Lenarcic, J., and J. Mackay-Scollay. "Trading Card Games as a Social Learning Tool." *Australian Journal of Emerging Technologies and Society* 3, no. 2 (2005): 64–76.

Levy, L. "Borderlands." *Counter* 7 (1999): 85–89.

_____. "Special K — Klaus Teuber." *The Games Journal*. Retrieved June 8, 2007, from http://www.thegamesjournal.com/articles/Special K3.shtml, 2001a.

_____. "Special K — Reiner Knizia." *The Games Journal*. Retrieved June 8, 2007, from http://

www.thegamesjournal.com/articles/Special K4.shtml, 2001b.

_____. "Special K — Wolfgang Kramer." *The Games Journal*. Retrieved June 8, 2007, from http://www.thegamesjournal.com/articles/Sp ecialK2.shtml, 2001c.

_____. "Re: Why I'm a Eurogamer." Retrieved May 4, 2008, from http://www.boardgame geek.com/article/1377102#1377102, 2007.

Lewis, K. P. "Social Play in the Great Apes." In *The Nature of Play: Great Apes and Humans*, edited by A. D. Pellegrini and P. K. Smith, 27–53. New York: Guilford Press, 2005.

Liesching, T. Niagara [Board Game]. Zoch Verlag, 2005.

Lipman, M. Point of Law [Board Game]. 3M, 1972.

Lowder, J. (ed.). *Hobby Games: The 100 Best*. Seattle: Green Ronin, 2007a.

Lowder, J. "Interview with James Lowder, Editor of *Hobby Games: The 100 Best*." Retrieved May 4, 2010, from http://www.greenronin. com/hg100_interview.html, 2007b.

Lowood, H. "Real-Time Performance: Machinima and Game Studies." *The International Digital Media and Arts Association Journal* 2, no. 1 (2005): 10–17.

Ludwig, M. Flußaufwärts [Board Game]. Ravensburger, 1988.

MacDonald, G., S. Peterson, B. Harlick, and R. Greer. Champions [Role-playing Game]. Hero Games, 1981.

Macdonell, D., and R. Kent. X-Files [Card Game]. US Playing Card Co., 1996.

Mackay, D. *The Fantasy Role Playing Game: A New Performing Art*. Jefferson, NC: McFarland, 2001.

Mackay, H. (ed.). *Consumption and Everyday Life*. Thousand Oaks, CA: Sage., 1997.

Manninen, T. "Rich Interaction in the Context of Networked Virtual Environments — Experiences Gained from the Multi-Player Games Domain." Paper presented at the HCI 2001 and IHM 2001 Conference, London, 2001.

Marks, A. *Card Games Properly Explained*. Reading: Elliot Right Way, 1995.

Martin, P. Y., and B. A. Turner. "Grounded Theory and Organizational Research." *The Journal of Applied Behavioral Science* 22, no. 2 (1986): 141–157.

Mason, P. "In Search of the Self: A Survey of the First 25 Years of Anglo American Role-Playing Game Theory." Paper presented at the Solmukohta Conference, Helksinki, 2004.

Matheny, M. Gladiator [Board Game]. Avalon Hill, 1981.

Matthäus, D., and F. Nestel. Ursuppe [Board Game]. Doris and Frank, 1997.

McAllister, J. B., and D. A. Trampier. Titan [Board Game]. Avalon Hill, 1980.

McCafferty, J. "Dear Santa: Sprechen Sie Deutsch?" Retrieved April 28, 2008, from http://www.drtoy.com/about_drtoy/sprechen.html, 1999.

McMurchie, T. Tsuro [Board Game]. Kosmos, 2005.

McNeil, A. Kingmaker [Board Game]. Ariel/Philmar, 1974.

_____. "The Making of Avalon Hill's King-maker." *Games and Puzzles* 72 (Spring 1979). Retrieved March 4, 2007, from http://www.diplom.org/~diparch/resources/other_games/kingmaker.htm.

McQuillan, B., B. Glassco, M. Selinker, R. Daviau, and T. Woodruff. Betrayal at House on the Hill [Board Game]. Avalon Hill, 2004.

Meier, S. Sid Meier's Civilization [Video Game]. Microprose, 1991.

Merrett, A., C. Johnson, E. Campbell, and A. Morrison. Talisman: The Adventure [Board Game Expansion]. Games Workshop, 1986.

Merrick, H. "'We Was Cross-Dressing 'Afore You Were Born!' Or, How SF Fans Invented Virtual Community." *Refractory: A Journal of Entertainment Media* 6 (2004): 1–10.

Mexican Rails [Board Game]. Mayfair Games, 1989.

Meyer, A. Mall World [Board Game]. Be-Witched Spiele, 2004.

Miller, M. Traveller [Role-Playing Game]. Game Designers' Workshop, 1977.

_____. "Re: Are We at the Start of a Resurgence of Boardgame Popularity?" Retrieved February 13, 2009, from http://www.boardgamegeek.com/article/2762391#2762391, 2008.

Miller, R. *Milton Bradley.* Farmington, MI: Greenhaven Press, 2004.

Mitchell, R. G. "Sociological Implications of the Flow Experience." In *Optimal Experience: Psychological Studies of the Flow State in Consciousness,* 36–59. Cambridge: Cambridge University Press, 1988.

Mixon, K. "Re: Giving Up on Games Too Quickly." Retrieved March 14, 2008, from http://www.boardgamegeek.com/article/453516#453516, 2008.

Mogendorff, J. J. Stratego [Board Game]. Milton Bradley, 1947.

Mona, E. "From the Basement to the Basic Set: The Early Years of Dungeons and Dragons." In *Second Person: Role-Playing and Story in Games and Playable Media,* edited by P. Harrigan and N. Wardrip-Fruin, 25–30. Cambridge: MIT Press, 2007.

Monopoly — Spiderman 3 Edition [Board Game]. Hasbro Inc., 2007.

Monopoly — SpongeBob Squarepants Edition [Board Game]. Hasbro Inc., 2005.

Monopoly — Transformers Collector's Edition [Board Game]. Hasbro Inc., 2007.

Montola, M., and J. Stenros (eds.). *Beyond Role and Play: Tools, Toys and Theory for Harnessing the Imagination.* Retrieved March 5, 2007, from http://www.ropecon.fi/brap/brap.pdf, 2004.

Moon, A. R. Black Spy [Card Game]. Avalon Hill, 1981.

_____. Airlines [Board Game]. Abacus, 1990a.

_____. Gespenster [Card Game]. Hexagames, 1990b.

_____. Wer Hat Mehr? [Card Game]. Piatnik, 1990c.

_____. Elfenroads [Board Game]. White Wind, 1992.

_____. Elfenland [Board Game]. Amigo Spiele, 1998.

_____. Union Pacific [Board Game]. Amigo, 1999.

_____. Ticket to Ride [Board Game]. Days of Wonder, 2004a.

_____. Ticket to Ride: Mystery Train Expansion [Board Game Expansion]. Days of Wonder, 2004b.

_____. Ticket to Ride: Europe [Board Game]. Days of Wonder, 2005.

_____. Ticket to Ride: Märklin Edition [Board Game]. Days of Wonder, 2006.

_____. Ticket to Ride: Nordic Countries [Board Game]. Days of Wonder, 2007a.

_____. Ticket to Ride: Switzerland [Board Game Expansion]. Days of Wonder, 2007b.

_____. Ticket to Ride: The Card Game [Card Game]. Days of Wonder, 2008a.

_____. Ticket to Ride: The Dice Expansion [Board Game Expansion]. Days of Wonder, 2008b.

_____. Ticket to Ride: The Dice Game [Dice Game]. Days of Wonder, 2008c.

Moon, A. R., and B. Faidutti. Diamant [Board Game]. Schmidt Spiele, 2005.

Morgan, R. La-Trel [Board Game]. ASS (Altenburger und Stralsunder Spielkarten-Fabriken), 1994.

Moromisato, G., A. Shubert, D. Collins, I. Schrieber, C. Davis, C., and M. Holden. Chron X [Video Game]. Darkened Sky Studios, 1997.

Morrow, P., and E. Friedman, E. Talisman City [Board Game Expansion]. Games Workshop, 1989.

_____. Talisman Dragons [Board Game Expansion]. Games Workshop., 1993.

Mortensen, T. E. *Pleasures of the Player: Flow and Control in Online Games.* Unpublished Doctoral Dissertation, University of Bergen, Bergen, 2003.

Mosca, R. Sauron [Board Game]. Simulations Publications Inc., 1977.

Mscrivner. "Re: To Game or Metagame?" Retrieved May 4, 2010, from http://www.board

gamegeek.com/article/2866037#2866037, 2008.

Muller, L. "Is Hasbro's Cash Cow Being Led to the Slaughter?" Retrieved October 4, 2009, from http://www.toydirectory.com/monthly/article.asp?id=3680, 2009.

Müller, W. Favoriten [Board Game]. Walter Müller's Spielewerkstatt, 1989.

Mulligan, J. "Cosmic Encounters from the Old Days." Retrieved May 9, 2008, from http://www.skotos.net/articles/BTH_24.shtml, 2002.

"Münchner Spielwies'n." Retrieved June 14, 2008, from http://www.spielwiesn.de/, 2008.

Murray, H. J. R. *A History of Board-Games Other Than Chess.* Oxford: Oxford University Press, 1952.

Murray, J. H. *Hamlet on the Holodeck—The Future of Narrative in Cyberspace.* Cambridge MA: MIT Press, 1997.

_____. "The More We Talk, the Smarter We Get: The Conversation Between Game Designers and Researchers." Retrieved September 19, 2003, from http://www.igda.org/columns/ivorytower/ivory_Jun03.php, 2003.

_____. "The Last Word on Ludology v Narratology in Game Studies." In Proceedings of the DiGRA 2005 Conference: Changing Views—Worlds in Play, Vancouver, 2005.

Myers, D. "Computer Game Genres." *Play and Culture* 3 (1990): 286–301.

_____. *The Nature of Computer Games: Play as Semiosis.* New York: Peter Lang, 2003.

Nader, L. *Naked Science: Anthropological Inquiry into Boundaries, Power, and Knowledge.* New York: Routledge, 1996.

Nettles, M. T., and C. M. Millett. *Three Magic Letters.* Baltimore: John Hopkins University, 2006.

Newman, J. "In Search of the Video Game Player." *New Media and Society* 4, no. 3 (2002): 405–422.

Niles, D. Onslaught: D-Day to the Rhine [Board Game]. TSR, 1987.

_____. The Hunt for Red October [Board Game]. TSR, 1988.

Nixon, C. R. Donjon [Role-Playing Game]. Anvilwerks, 2002.

North American Rails [Board Game]. Mayfair Games, 1992.

Odenhoven, T. Portobello Market [Board Game]. Schmidt Spiele, 2007.

Ohley, H., and A. Romoth, A. 1895 Namibia [Board Game]. Helumt Ohley and Adam Romoth, 2005.

Oker, E. "Eugene Oker." Retrieved May 1, 2009, from http://www.eugen-oker.de/, 2004.

Olotka, P. "Risk." In *Family Games: The 100 Best,* edited by J. Lowder, 283–285. Seattle: Green Ronin, 2010.

Onanien, R. Facts in Five [Board Game]. 3M, 1967.

Orbanes, P. E. *The Game Makers: The Story of Parker Brothers, from Tiddledy Winks to Trivial Pursuit.* Boston: Harvard Business School Press, 2003.

_____. *Monopoly: The World's Most Famous Game—and How It Got That Way.* New York: Da Capo Press, 2007.

Ornella, E. Il Principe [Board Game]. Amigo Spiele, 2005.

Ortega-Grimaldo, F. *Games as Cultural Practice: Postcolonial Imaginations.* Unpublished Doctoral Dissertation, Texas Tech University, 2008.

Owen, S. "The History of Wargaming 1975–1990." *Strategy and Tactics* (July 1990).

Paglieri, F. "Frame Games: The Role of Context in Defining Play Behavior." Retrieved December 27, 2008, from http://www.media.unisi.it/cirg/fp/frames03.pdf, 2003a.

_____. "Modelling Play: Towards a Cognitive Model for Playful Activities." Retrieved January 4, 2009, from http://www.media.unisi.it/cirg/fp/mopl03.pdf, 2003b.

_____. "Playing by and with the Rules: Norms and Morality in Play Development." *Topio* 24 (2005): 149–167.

Palesch, K. Fossil [Board Game]. Goldsieber, 1998.

Palmer, N. *The Comprehensive Guide to Board Wargaming.* New York: Hippocrene, 1977.

_____. *The Best of Board Wargaming.* New York: Hippocrene, 1980.

Palmer, R., and W. Lee. Totopoly [Board Game]. Waddingtons, 1938.

Parks, A., and J. Hawkins. Parthenon: Rise of the Aegean [Board Game]. Z-Man Games, 2005.

Parlett, D. Hare and Tortoise [Board Game]. Intellect Games, 1973.

_____. Hase und Ingel [Board Game]. Ravensburger, 1979.

_____. *The Oxford History of Board Games.* Oxford: Oxford University Press, 1999.

_____. *The Penguin Encyclopedia of Card Games.* London: Penguin, 2000.

Patrick, G. T. W. *The Psychology of Relaxation.* New York: Houghton Mifflin, 1916.

Pauchon, S. Yspahan [Board Game]. Ystari, 2006.

Payne, B. Villa Paletti [Board Game]. Zoch Verlag, 2001.

Pearce, C. "Theory Wars: An Argument Against Arguments in the So-Called Ludology/Narratology Debate." Paper presented at the DiGRA 2005 Conference: Changing Views—Worlds in Play, Vancouver, 2005.

_____. "Communities of Play: The Social Construction of Identity in Persistent Online Game Worlds." In *Second Person: Role-Playing and Story in Games and Playable Media*, edited by N. Wardrip-Fruin and P. Harrigan, 311–318. Cambridge: MIT Press, 2006.

Pedlow, S. "20 Copies of Ravensburger's Wildlife Adventure Found!" Retrieved August 2, 2007, from http://groups.google.com/group/rec. games.board/tree/browse_frm/month/1993-06/ef8a536982cfccbd?rnum=91&_done=%2 Fgroup%2Frec.games.board%2Fbrowse_frm %2Fmonth%2F1993-06%3Ffwc%3D2% 26#doc_99a4027af6eb8ab5, 1993.

Peitz, J., D. Eriksson, and S. Björk. "Augmented Board Games — Enhancing Board Games with Electronics." In Proceedings of the DiGRA 2005 Conference: Changing Views — Worlds in Play, Vancouver, 2005.

Pellis, S. "Keeping in Touch: Play Fighting and Social Knowledge." In *The Cognitive Animal*, edited by M. Bekoff, C. Allen, and G. M. Burghardt, 421–427. Cambridge: MIT Press, 2002.

Pellis, S. M., and V. C. Pellis. "Structure-Function Interface in the Analysis of Play Fighting." In *Animal Play: Evolutionary, Comparative, and Ecological Perspectives*, edited by M. Bekoff and J. A. Byers, 115–140). Cambridge: Cambridge University Press, 1998.

Perla, P. *The Art of Wargaming: A Guide for Professionals and Hobbyists*. Annapolis: Naval Institute Press, 1990.

Perrin, S., R. Turney, S. Henderson, W. James, and G. Stafford. Runequest [Role-Playing Game]. Chaosium, 1978.

Peterschmidt, L., and R. Miller, R. Warhammer 40,000 Collectible Card Game [Card Game]. Sabertooth Games, 2001.

Petersen, C. T. Twilight Imperium 3rd Edition [Board Game]. Fantasy Flight Games, 2005.

Peterson, S. Call of Cthulhu [Role-playing Game]. Chaosium, 1981.

Petty, M. "Destroying Some Common Myths About Game Design." Retrieved February 12, 2008, from http://www.protospiel.org/, 2006.

Pokémon [Card Game]. Wizards of the Coast, 1999.

Pollard, E. J. "Re: The Metagame (Again?)." Retrieved January 2, 2009, from http://www. boardgamegeek.com/article/2952291#29522 91, 2008.

Pondsmith, M. "Traveller." In *Hobby Games: The 100 Best*, edited by J. Lowder, 331–334. Renton: Green Ronin, 2007.

Pope, J. Border Reivers [Board Game]. Reiver Games, 2006.

_____. "Re: Are You a Gamer Who Has Published Since Joining the Geek?" Retrieved January 6, 2010, from http://boardgamegeek. com/article/3078326#3078326, 2009.

Pope, J., and T. Cheatham, T. Carpe Astra [Board Game]. Reiver Games, 2008.

Pratt, A. E. Clue [Board Game]. Waddingtons, 1948.

Pratt, F. *Fletcher Pratt's Naval War Game*. Holland MI, Lake Shore Press, 1943.

Pritchard, D. (ed.). *The Games and Puzzles Book of Modern Board Games*. London: William Luscombe, 1975.

Pulsipher, L. Valley of the Four Winds [Board Game]. Games Workshop, 1980.

_____. Britannia [Board Game]. Gibsons Games, 1986.

_____. "The Essence of Euro-Style Games." *The Games Journal*. Retrieved March 18, 2008, from http://thegamesjournal.com/articles/Ess ence.shtml, 2006.

_____. "Interaction in Games." Retrieved January 4, 2010, from http://pulsiphergamedes ign.blogspot.com/2009/11/interaction-in-gam es_08.html, 2009a.

_____. "The System and the Psychological in Games." Retrieved October 14, 2010, from http://pulsiphergamedesign.blogspot.com/20 09/05/system-and-psychological-in-games. html, 2009b.

Quinto [Board Game]. 3M, 1964.

Randles, P., and D. Stahl. Piratenbucht [Board Game]. Amigo Spiele, 2002.

Randolph, A. Twixt [Board Game]. 3M, 1961.

_____. Oh-Wah-Ree [Board Game]. 3M, 1962.

_____. Breakthru [Board Game]. 3M, 1965.

_____. Mad Mate [Board Game]. 3M, 1972.

_____. Hol's der Geier [Card Game]. Ravensberger, 1988.

_____. Rasende Roboter [Board Game]. Hans im Glück, 1999.

Randolph, A., and M. Matchoss. Sagaland [Board Game]. Ravensburger, 1981.

Rasmussen, M. M. Top Secret [Role-playing Game]. Tactical Studies Rules, 1980.

Ray, D. Sticks and Stones [Board Game]. Metagaming, 1978.

Redhead, S. (ed.). *Rave Off!: Politics and Deviance in Contemporary Youth Culture*. Brookfield: Ashgate Publishing, 1993.

Rein-Hagen, M. Vampire: The Masquerade [Role-Playing Game]. White Wolf, 1991.

_____. Werewolf: The Apocalypse [Role-Playing Game]. White Wolf, 1992.

Rein-Hagen, M., A. Bates, P. Brucato, K. Cliffe, G. Fountain, E. Hall, et al. Hunter: The Reckoning [Role-Playing Game]. White Wolf, 1999.

Rein-Hagen, M., S. Chupp, and J. Hartshorn. Wraith: The Oblivion [Role-Playing Game]. White Wolf, 1994.

Rein-Hagen, M., S. Chupp, I. Lemke, and J. G. Timbrook. Changeling: The Dreaming [Role-Playing Game]. White Wolf, 1995.

Rein-Hagen, M., G. Davis, T. Dowd, C. Cowart, D. Bassingthwaite, S. P. Somtow, et al.

Mind's Eye Theatre: The Masquerade [Live Action Role-Playing Game]. White Wolf, 1993.

Richardson, T. The Dragon and the Pearl [Board Game]. Spirit Games, 2004.

Riedesser, W. Ave Caesar [Board Game]. Ravensberger, 1999.

_____. Q-Jet 21XX [Board Game]. Möbius Games, 2005.

Rieneck, M., and S. Stadler. Die Säulen der Erde [Board Game]. Kosmos, 2006.

Roberts, C. S. Tactics [Board Game]. Avalon Game Company, 1954.

_____. Gettysburg [Board Game]. Avalon Hill, 1958a.

_____. Dispatcher [Board Game]. Avalon Hill, 1958b.

_____. D-Day [Board Game]. Avalon Hill, 1961.

Roberts, C. S., and Nissen Thiem. Verdict [Board Game]. Avalon Hill, 1959a.

Roberts, J. M., M. Arth, and R. Bush. "Games in Culture." *American Anthropologist* 61, no. 4 (1959b): 597–605.

Roberts, K. *Contemporary Society and the Growth of Leisure.* London: Longmans, 1978.

Rodriguez, H. "The Playful and the Serious: An Approximation to Huizinga's Homo Ludens." *Game Studies: The International Journal of Computer Game Research* 6, no. 1 (2006).

Rosen, T. "Tom Rosen: Joe and Bob." Retrieved May 4, 2010, from http://www.boardgame news.com/index.php/boardgamenews/com ments/tom_rosen_joe_and_bob/, 2009.

Rosenberg, U. Bohnanza [Card Game]. Amigo Spiele, 1997.

_____. Mamma Mia [Card Game]. Abacusspiele, 1999.

_____. Agricola [Board Game]. Lookout Games, 2007.

_____. Le Havre [Board Game]. Lookout Games, 2008.

Rösner, H.-R., and W. Kramer, W. El Capitan [Board Game]. Z-Man Games, 2007.

Ross, R. Haithabu [Board Game]. Hexagames, 1975.

Rossney, B. "Re: The Golden Age of Board Games." Retrieved March 4, from http://groups.google.com/group/rec.games.board/m sg/7568055773869cfl, 1993.

_____. "McMulti." *The Games Cabinet.* Retrieved March 8, 2008, from http://www.game cabinet.com/reviews/McMulti.html, 1994.

Rousseau, J. J. *The Social Contract or Principles of Political Right* (2008 edition, translated by G. D. H. Cole). New York: Cosimo, 1762.

Rowland, H., and G. Pinder, G. Days of Decision III [Board Game]. Australian Design Group, 2004.

Roznai, J., and L. Roznai. Nippon Rails [Board Game]. Mayfair Games, 1992.

Roznai, L. Australian Rails [Board Game]. Mayfair Games, 1994.

Russell, S. "Re: The Abject Failure That Is Called 'Gateway.'" Retrieved February 3, 2009, from http://www.boardgamegeek.com/article/2476132#2476132, 2008.

Saari, M. "Making Decisions." *The Games Journal.* Retrieved March 21, 2009, from http://www.thegamesjournal.com/articles/Making Decisions.shtml, 2003.

Sackson, S. Acquire [Board Game]. 3M, 1962.

_____. Focus [Board Game]. Parker Brothers, 1964.

_____. Bazaar [Board Game]. 3M, 1967.

_____. *A Gamut of Games.* London: Random House, 1969.

_____. Executive Decision [Board Game]. 3M, 1971.

Sager, M. Highlander TCG [Card Game]. Thunder Castle Games, 1996.

Salen, K., and E. Zimmerman, E. *Rules of Play: Game Design Fundamentals.* Cambridge: MIT Press, 2004.

St. Laurent, J. J. Crude: The Oil Game [Board Game]. St. Laurent Games, 1974.

Sandercock, C., and R. A. Martin. Maharaja [Board Game]. Avalon Hill, 1994.

Sarrett, P. "Games from Europe." Retrieved May 7, 2007, from http://groups.google.com/gro up/rec.games.board/browse_frm/month/1993 -8?start=500&sa=N, 1993.

Sauer, N. Email Interview, 2008.

Scattergories [Board Game]. Milton Bradley, 1988.

Schacht, M. Kardinal & König [Board Game]. Goldsieber, 2000.

_____. Coloretto [Card Game]. Abacus Spiele, 2003a.

_____. Industria [Board Game]. Queen, 2003b.

_____. Zooloretto [Board Game]. Abacus Spiele, 2007.

_____. Zooloretto [Video Game]. Spinbottle Games, 2009.

Schafer, J. Civilization V [Video Game]. Firaxis Games, 2010.

Schell, J. *The Art of Game Design: A Book of Lenses.* Burlington MA: Morgan Kaufmann, 2008.

Scherer-Hoock, B. "Evolution of German Games." *The Games Journal.* Retrieved June 8, 2007, from http://www.thegamesjournal. com/articles/GermanHistory2.shtml, 2003.

Schiller, F. *On the Aesthetic Education of Man In a Series of Letters* (translated by R. Snell). New Haven: Yale University Press, 1954.

Schlickbernd, J. "Review of Die Macher (LONG)." Retrieved June 7, 2007, from http://groups.google.com/group/rec.games.board/b rowse_thread/thread/e03443f2827dd669, 1989.

Schloesser, G. Email Interview, 2008a.
_____. "International Gamers Awards." Retrieved April 21, 2008, from http://www.in ternationalgamersawards.net/, 2008b.
_____. "The Gamers' Place of Pilgrimage." *Knucklebones* (March 2008c): 30–33.
Schmeil, K.-H. Die Macher [Board Game]. Moskito, 1986.
_____. Tyranno Ex [Board Game]. Moskito, 1990.
_____. Extrablatt [Board Game]. Moskito, 1991.
Schwarz, H. "History of the Nuremberg Toy Trade and Industry." Retrieved May 8, 2008, from http://www.musee-du-jouet.com/eu rope/nurembergang.doc, 2003.
Schwarz, H., and M. Faber. *Games We Play: History of J. W. Spear and Sons*. Nuremberg: Verlag W. Tummels, 1997.
Sciarra, E. Bang! [Card Game]. Abacus Spiele, 2002.
Seay, D., J. Zinser, and D. Williams. Legend of the Five Rings [Card Game]. Alderac Entertainment Group, 1995.
Seldner, D. "Games Owned but Not Played. How Many?" Retrieved January 9, 2010, from http://www.boardgamegeek.com/article/295 9403#2959403, 2009.
Seyfarth, A. Manhattan [Board Game]. Hans im Glück, 1994.
_____. Puerto Rico [Board Game]. Alea, 2002.
_____. San Juan [Card Game]. Alea, 2004.
_____. Giganten der Lüfte [Board Game]. Queen, 2007.
Seyfarth, A., and K. Seyfarth. Thurn and Taxis [Board Game]. Hans im Glück, 2006.
Shapiro, D. "To Boldly Go." *The Games Journal.* Retrieved June 8, 2007, from http://www. thegamesjournal.com/articles/ToBoldlyGo.sh tml, 2003.
Sharpe, R. "The Game of Diplomacy." Retrieved February 14, 2007, from http://www. diplomacy-archive.com/god.htm, 1978.
Shaw, T., and L. Schutz. Waterloo [Board Game]. Avalon Hill, 1962.
Sherry, J. L. "Flow and Media Enjoyment." *Communication Theory* 14, no. 4 (2004): 328–347.
Siggins, M. "Editorial." *Sumo* 0 (1989).
_____. "Inside Pitch." *Sumo* 2 (1990).
_____. "Die Siedler von Catan." *Sumo* 23 (1995).
_____. "Review: The Oxford History of Board Games." Retrieved May 4, 2009, from http:// www.gamecabinet.com/reviews/OxfordHisto ryBoardGames.html, 2000.
Sigman, T. "Pawn Takes Megabyte." *The Escapist.* Retrieved October 4, 2008, from http:// www.escapistmagazine.com/articles/view/is sues/issue_105/783-Pawn-Takes-Megabyte, 2007.
Simonitch, M. Hannibal: Rome vs. Carthage [Board Game]. Avalon Hill, 1996.

Simonsen, R. A. StarForce Alpha Centauri: Interstellar Conflict in the 25th Century [Board Game]. Simulations Publications Inc., 1974.
_____. Battle Fleet Mars [Board Game]. Simulations Publications Inc., 1977.
_____. Star Trader [Board Game]. Simulations Publications Inc., 1982.
Simonsen, R. A., and J. F. Dunnigan. War in the East [Board Game]. Simulations Publications Inc., 1974.
Simonsen, R. A., and B. Hessel. Dragonslayer [Board Game]. Simulations Publications Inc., 1981.
Smith, E. L. The Sword and the Stars [Board Game]. Simulations Publications Inc., 1981.
Smith, J. *New Orleans Beat.* New York: Ivy Books, 1995.
Smith, L. Dragon Dice [Dice Game]. Tactical Studies Rules, 1995b.
Smith, P. K. "Play Fighting and Real Fighting: Perspectives on Their Relationship." In *New Aspects of Human Ethology*, edited by A. Schmitt, K. Atzwanger, K. Grammer, and K. Schäfer, 47–64. New York: Plenum Press, 1997.
Sniderman, S. "Unwritten Rules." *The Life of Games.* Retrieved July 12, 2005, from http:// www.gamepuzzles.com/tlog/tlog2.htm, 1999.
Snyder, M. Dust Devils [Role-Playing Game]. Chimera Creative, 2002.
Soares, J. Russian Rails [Board Game]. Mayfair Games, 2004.
Solitander, N. "Re: I Don't Get Game Publisher Economics. Retrieved February 3, 2009, from http://www.boardgamegeek.com/article/289 2045#2892045, 2008.
Solko, D. "Re: Competitive Gaming." Retrieved January 14, 2010, from http://www.board gamegeek.com/article/581424#581424, 2005.
Solomon, E. Sigma File [Board Game]. Condor, 1973.
_____. Thoughtwave [Board Game]. Intellect Games, 1974.
Speier, M. "The Adult Ideological Viewpoint in Studies of Childhood." In *Rethinking Childhood: Perspectives on Development and Society*, edited by A. Skolnick, 168–186. Boston: Little Brown, 1976.
Spellfire [Card Game]. Tactical Studies Rules, 1994.
Spencer, A. "Why Hobby Gamers Don't Like Monopoly." Retrieved February 10, 2009, from http://www.boardgamegeek.com/arti cle/2527728#2527728, 2008.
Spencer, H. *The Principles of Psychology.* London: Longman, Brown, Green and Longmans, 1855.
"Spiel des Jahres." Retrieved June 8, 2008, from http://www.spiel-des-jahres.com/cms/fro nt_content.php?idcat=33, 2008.

"Spieleautorenzunft e.V." Retrieved May 8, 2008, from http://www.spieleautorenzunft.de/englisch/verein/index.html, 2008.

"Spielefest." Retrieved June 14, 2008, from http://www.spielefest.at/, 2008.

"Spielen in Österreich." Retrieved May 9, 2008, from http://www.spiel-der-spiele.at/, 2008.

"Spielwarenmesse International Toy Fair." Retrieved May 2, 2008, from http://nuremberg toyfair.com, 2008.

Stam, R. *Film Theory.* Oxford: Blackwell, 2000.

Staupe, R. David and Goliath [Card Game]. Pegasus Spiele, 1998.

Stebbins, Robert A. *Amateurs, Professionals, and Serious Leisure.* Montreal: McGill-Queen's University Press, 1992.

Steinkuehler, C. *Cognition and Learning in Massively Multiplayer Online Games: A Critical Approach.* Unpublished Doctoral Dissertation, University of Wisconsin, Madison, 2005.

Stepponat, L. Die Rückkehr der Helden [Board Game]. Pegasus Spiele, 2003.

_____. "Re: Everything I DIDN'T Get from First Reading of the Rules, and the Clarifications I Got Later." Retrieved January 4, 2009, from http://boardgamegeek.com/article/215 6581#2156581, 2008.

Stern, A., and M. Mateas. "Interaction and Narrative." In *The Game Design Reader: A Rules of Play Anthology,* 642–666. Cambridge: MIT Press, 2007.

Stevens, V. *Participatory Simulations: Building Collaborative Understanding Through Immersive Dynamic Modelling.* Unpublished Master's Thesis, Massachusetts Institute of Technology, 1998.

Stewart, I. *Does God Play Dice? The Mathematics of Chaos.* Cambridge, MA: Blackwell, 1989.

Stöckmann, B., and J. Jahnke, J. "Germany — a Ludorado: An Introduction to the German Board Game Market and the Possibilities It Offers." *Homo communicativus* 2, no. 4 (2008a).

_____. "Playing by the Book: Literature and Board Games at the Beginning of the 21st Century." *Homo communicativus* 3, no. 5 (2008b).

Stocks and Bonds [Board Game]. 3M, 1964.

Stolze, G., and A. Tinworth. Demon: The Fallen [Role-Playing Game]. White Wolf, 2002.

Stribula, M. R. Lunar Rails [Board Game]. Mayfair Games, 2003.

"Süddeutsche Spielemesse." Retrieved June 14, 2008, from http://cms.messe-stuttgart.de/cms/spiele-start0.0.html, 2008.

Suits, B. "What Is a Game?" *Philosophy of Science* 34, no. 2 (1967): 148–156.

_____. *The Grasshopper: Games, Life and Utopia.* Toronto: Broadview Press, 1978.

Sutton-Smith, B. *The Ambiguity of Play.* Cambridge, MA: Harvard University Press, 1997.

Sutton-Smith, B., and E. M. Avedon, E. M. "Introduction." In *The Study of Games.* New York: John Wiley, 1971a.

_____. *The Study of Games.* New York: John Wiley, 1971b.

Sutton-Smith, B., and R. E. Herron. *Child's Play.* New York: John Wiley, 1971.

Svitavsky, W. L. "Geek Culture: An Annotated Interdisciplinary Bibliography." *The Bulletin of Bibliography* 58, no. 2 (2001): 101–108.

Sweetster, P., and P. Wyeth. "Game Flow: A Model for Evaluating Player Enjoyment in Games." *Computers in Entertainment* 3, no. 3 (2005): Article 3A.

Szwarce, H. Image [Board Game]. 3M, 1973.

Takahashi, K. Yu-Gi-Oh! [Card Game]. Upper Deck Entertainment, 2002.

Tam, P.-W. "An Old School Board Game Goes Viral Among Silicon Valley's Techie Crowd." Retrieved January 9, 2010, from http://online.wsj.com/article/SB12609228927569282 5.html, 2009.

Taylor, C. B., and J. B. Wood. Machiavelli [Board Game]. Battleline, 1977.

Taylor, R. Rivets [Board Game]. Metagaming, 1977.

_____. Black Hole [Board Game]. Metagaming, 1978.

Taylor, S. C. Wooden Ships and Iron Men [Board Game]. Battleline, 1975.

_____. Platoon [Board Game]. Avalon Hill, 1986.

_____. Gettysburg —125th Anniversary Edition [Board Game]. Avalon Hill, 1988.

Taylor, T. L. *Play Between Worlds: Exploring Online Game Culture.* Cambridge: MIT Press, 2006.

Tepper, S. "SDJ by the Numbers." Retrieved March 9, 2008, from http://www.boardgame news.com/index.php/boardgamenews/com ments/scott_tepper_sdj_by_the_numbers/, 2007.

Teuber, K. Barbarossa [Board Game]. Altenburger und Stralsunder, 1988.

_____. Timberland [Board Game]. HABA, 1989.

_____. Adel Verpflichtet [Board Game]. F.X. Schmidt, 1990a.

_____. By Hook or Crook [Board Game]. Avalon Hill, 1990b.

_____. Fair Means or Foul [Board Game]. Gibsons Games, 1990c.

_____. Drunter and Drüber [Board Game]. Hans im Glück, 1991.

_____. Der Fliegende Holländer [Board Game]. BanDai, 1992.

_____. Die Siedler von Catan [Board Game]. Kosmos, 1995.

_____. Entdecker [Board Game]. Goldsieber, 1996.

_____. Löwenherz [Board Game]. Goldsieber, 1998.

_____. Die Sternenfahrer von Catan [Board Game]. Kosmos, 1999.

_____. The Settlers of Zarahemla [Board Game]. Inspiration Games, 2003.

_____. Hoity Toity [Board Game]. Überplay, 2004.

_____. Catan [Video Game]. Big Huge Games, 2007a.

_____. Die Siedler von Catan: Das Würfelspiel [Board Game], Kosmos, 2007b.

Thai, K. "Board Games Are Back." Retrieved September 4, 2009, from http://money.cnn.com/2009/07/10/news/economy/board_games_resurgence.fortune/, 2009.

Thayer, A., and B. Kolko. "Localization of Digital Games: The Process of Blending for the Global Games Market." *Technical Communication* 51, no. 4 (2004): 477–488.

Thibault, F. Ploy [Board Game]. 3M, 1970.

_____. Contigo [Board Game]. 3M, 1974.

Thompson, H. Chitin: I [Board Game]. Metagaming, 1977a.

_____. Warp War [Board Game]. Metagaming, 1977b.

_____. Starleader: Assault! [Board Game]. Metagaming, 1982.

Tidwell, K. "An Interview with Alan R. Moon." *The Game Cabinet.* Retrieved March 4, 2008, from http://www.gamecabinet.com/news/AlanMoonInterview.html, 1997.

_____. Email Interview, 2008.

Toncar, W. 6-Tage Rennen [Board Game]. Holtmann VIP, 1986.

Tresham, F. 1829 [Board Game]. Hartland Trefoil Ltd., 1974.

_____. Civilization [Board Game]. Hartland Trefoil Ltd., 1980.

_____. (Civilization Expansion Trade Cards Set [Board Game Expansion]. Avalon Hill, 1982.

_____. 1830: The Game of Railroads and Robber Barons [Board Game]. Avalon Hill, 1986.

_____. Civilization Western Expansion Map [Board Game Expansion]. Hartland Trefoil Ltd., 1988.

Tresham, F., and M. Meier-Backl. 1835 [Board Game]. Hans im Glück, 1990.

A Trip Around the World [Board Game]. Otto Maier Publishing Company, 1884.

Tsao, V. Junta [Board Game]. Creative Wargames Workshop, 1978.

Tweet, J., A. Forsythe, R. Baker, P. Barclay, and D. Low. Axis and Allies Miniatures [Collectible Miniatures Game]. Avalon Hill, 2005.

Tweet, J., and M. Rein-Hagen. Ars Magica [Role-playing Game]. Lion Rampant, 1987.

"2008 Sales, Demographic and Usage Data: Essential Facts about the Computer and Video Game Industry." Retrieved January 5, 2009, from http://www.theesa.com/facts/pdfs/ESA_EF_2008.pdf, 2008.

Tychsen, A., K. Newman, T. Brolund, M. Hitchens. "Cross-Format Analysis of the Gaming Experience in Multi-Player Role-Playing Games." In *Proceedings of the DiGRA 2007 Conference—Situated Play*, 49–57. Tokyo, 2007.

Uherske, C. "Things I'm Sick Of!" Retrieved December 14, 2009, from http://boardgamegeek.com/geeklist/10104, 2005.

Urack, D. Traber Derby Spiel [Board Game]. BURK-Verlag, 1989.

"U.S. Census Bureau, Male, 18 or Older, Employed Full-Time Year Round, 2005." Retrieved February 15th, 2009, from http://pubdb3.census.gov/macro/032006/perinc/new02_037.htm, 2006.

Vaccarino, D. X. Dominion [Card Game]. Rio Grande Games, 2008.

Varney, W. "Playing with 'War Fare.'" *Peace Review: A Journal of Social Justice* 12, no. 3 (2000): 385–391.

Van Ness, C. Sorry! Sliders [Board Game]. Parker Brothers, 2008.

Van Ness, C., R. Daviau, and S. Baker. Heroscape [Collectible Miniatures Game]. Hasbro Inc., 2004.

Van Zandt, A. "Re: Monopoly: A Review with Strategic Discussion." Retrieved February 10, 2009, from http://www.boardgamegeek.com/article/3021066#3021066, 2009.

Vasel, T. "Interviews by an Optimist #73—Wolfgang Kramer." Retrieved February 12, 2008, from http://www.boardgamegeek.com/thread/82783, 2005a.

_____. "Interviews by an Optimist #46—Peter Olotka." Retrieved February 14, 2008, from http://www.thedicetower.com/thedicetower/index.php?page=614, 2005b.

_____. "Interviews by an Optimist #14—Mike Siggins." Retrieved March 4, 2008, from http://www.thedicetower.com/thedicetower/index.php?page=582, 2005c.

_____. "Interviews by an Optimist #38—Rob Daviau." Retrieved October 15, 2009, from http://www.thedicetower.com/thedicetower/index.php?page=606, 2005d.

_____. "Interviews by an Optimist #32—Scott Alden." Retrieved April 23, 2009, from http://www.thedicetower.com/interviews/int032.htm, 2005e.

Vasel, T., P. Sauberer, S. Appelcline, J. Little, L. Levy, M. Dontanville, et al. "Musings on Kibitzing." Retrieved August 25, 2008, from http://www.boardgamenews.com/index.php/boardgamenews/comments/musings_on_kibitzing_27/, 2006.

Vasey, C. Chariot Lords [Board Game]. Clash of Arms Games, 1999.

Verbeten, S. "Making the Cut." *Knucklebones* (January 2007): 30–32.

Verenikina, I., P. Harris, and P. Lysaght. "Child's Play: Computer Games, Theories of Play and Children's Development." Paper presented at the Young Children and Learning Technologies. Selected papers from the International Federation for Information Processing Working Group 3.5 Open Conference, Melbourne, 2003.

Vorderer, P. "Interactive Entertainment and Beyond." In *Media Entertainment*, edited by D. Zillman and P. Vorderer, 21–37. Mahwah, NJ: Erlbaum, 2000.

Vorderer, P., T. Hartmann, and C. Klimmt. "Explaining the Enjoyment of Playing Video Games: The Role of Competition." Paper presented at the Second International Conference on Entertainment Computing, Pittsburgh, PA, 2003.

Vygotsky, L. S. *Thought and language, Second Edition*. Cambridge, MA: MIT Press, 1962.

_____. "Play and Its Role in the Mental Development of the Child." In *Play: Its Role in Development and Evolution*, edited by J. S. Bruner, A. Jolly, and K. Sylva, 537–554. Aylesbury: Penguin, 1976.

Walczyk, T. StarSoldier [Board Game]. Simulations Publications Inc., 1977.

Walker, B. "Essen Games Fair." *Games International* 2 (1988).

_____. "Interview with Wolfgang Kramer. *Games International* 13 (1989).

Wallace, M. Way Out West [Board Game]. Warfrog, 2000.

_____. Age of Steam [Board Game]. Warfrog, 2002.

Ward, C., E. B. Bauer, and B. B. Smuts. "Partner Preferences and Asymmetries in Social Play Among Domestic Dog, Canis Lupus Familiaris, Littermates." *Animal Behavior* 76, no. 4 (2008): 1187–1199.

Waskul, D., and M. Lust. "Role-Playing and Playing Roles: The Person, Player, and Persona in Fantasy Role-Playing." *Symbolic Interaction* 27, no. 3 (2004): 333–356.

Watson, D. M., and D. B. Croft. "Age-Related Differences in Playfighting Strategies of Captive Male Red-Necked Wallabies (Macropus Rufogriseus Banksianus)." *Ethology* 102 (1996): 33–346.

Watts, D. G. Railway Rivals [Board Game]. Rostherne Games, 1973.

_____. Dampfross [Board Game]. Schmidt, 1984.

Weber, B. Ido [Board Game]. Goldsieber, 1998.

Weisman, J. "Magic: The Gathering." In *Hobby Games: The 100 Best*, edited by J. Lowder, 192–195. Seattle: Green Ronin, 2007.

Weisman, J., and K. Barrett. Mage Knight [Collectible Miniatures Game]. Wizkids, 2000.

Weisman, J., J. Grubb, J. Leitheusser, S. Johnson, and J. Quick. Heroclix [Collectible Miniatures Game]. Wizkids, 2000.

Weissblum, A., and A. R. Moon. Das Amulett [Board Game]. Goldsieber, 2001.

_____. New England [Board Game]. Goldsieber, 2003.

Wells, H. G. *Little Wars; a Game for Boys from Twelve Years of Age to One Hundred and Fifty and for That More Intelligent Sort of Girl Who Likes Boys' Games and Books*. Frank Palmer, 1913.

Weninger, C. "Social Events and Roles in Magic." In *Gaming as Culture: Essays on Reality, Identity and Experience in Fantasy Games*, edited by J. P. Williams, S. Q. Hendricks, and W. K. Winkler, 57–76. Jefferson NC: McFarland, 2006.

Werneck, T. "The Significance of the Inventor of a Game as a Shaping Factor for the Recent Development of a Culture of Games in German Speaking Countries." Paper presented at the Board Game Studies Colloquia VII, Philadelphia, 2004.

_____. Email interview, 2008.

Wettering, R. Rette Sich Wer Kann [Board Game]. Kosmos, 1993.

Wheaton, B. "Researching Gender, Power and Difference in the Windsurfing Culture." In *Power Games: A Critical Sociology of Sport*, edited by J. P. Sugden & A. Tomlinson, 240–267. New York: Routledge, 2002.

Whitehill, B. *American Boxed Games and Their Makers: 1822–1992*. Radnor: Wallace-Homestead, 1992.

_____. "A Brief History of American Games." *Toy Shop*. Retrieved May 18, 2008, from http://www.thebiggamehunter.com/_mgxroot/page_10768.html, October 1997.

_____. *Americanopoly: America as Seen Through Its Games*. Renens: Musé Suisee de Jeu, 2004.

Wick, J. "Wiz War." In *Hobby Games: The 100 Best*, edited by J. Lowder, 369–371. Renton: Green Ronin, 2007.

Wieck, S., C. Earley, and S. Wieck. Mage: The Ascension [Role-Playing Game]. White Wolf, 1993.

Wiersinga, J., and T. Jannink. Oraklos [Board Game]. Splotter Spellen, 2002.

Wiersma, R. Gheos [Board Game]. Z-Man Games, 2006.

Williams, D. Deadlands: Doomtown [Card Game]. Five Rings Publishing, 1998.

_____. Warlord: Saga of the Storm [Card Game]. Alderac Entertainment Group, 2001.

Williams, D., and R. Lau, R. Legend of the Burning Sands [Card Game]. Publishing, 1998.

Williams, G. Artifact [Board Game]. Metagaming, 1980.

_____. "Poll: How Many Games Do You Buy a

Month?" Retrieved January 10, 2010, from http://www.boardgamegeek.com/article/270 9296#2709296, 2008.

Williams, J. P. "Consumption and Authenticity in the Collectible Games Subculture." In *Gaming as Culture: Essays on Reality, Identity and Experience in Fantasy Games*, edited by J. P. Williams, S. Q. Hendricks, and W. K. Winkler, 77–99. Jefferson NC: McFarland, 2006.

Williams, J. P., S. Q. Hendricks, and W. K. Winkler, W. K. (eds.). *Gaming as Culture: Essays on Reality, Identity and Experience in Fantasy Games.* Jefferson NC: McFarland, 2006.

Willis, L. Olympica [Board Game]. Metagaming, 1978.

_____. Holy War [Board Game]. Metagaming, 1979.

Wilson, K. Arkham Horror [Board Game]. Fantasy Flight Games, 2005.

_____. Sid Meier's Civilization: The Board Game [Board Game]. Fantasy Flight Games, 2010.

Winkler, W. K. "The Business and Culture of Gaming." In *Gaming as Culture: Essays on Reality, Identity and Experience in Fantasy Games*, edited by J. P. Williams, S. Q. Hendricks, and W. K. Winkler, 140–153. Jefferson NC: McFarland, 2006.

Winter, B. James Bond 007 GoldenEye [Card Game]. Heartbreaker, 1997.

_____. "Re: The Abject Failure That Is Called 'Gateway.'" Retrieved February 3, 2009, from http://www.boardgamegeek.com/article/246 6805#2466805, 2008.

Winters, L., and P. Winters. High Bid [Card Game]. 3M, 1962.

Wiselely, C. Loopin' Louie [Board Game]. Milton Bradley, 1992.

Witt, J. "Re: Giving Up on Games Too Quickly." Retrieved March 14, 2008, from http://www.boardgamegeek.com/article/453484#453484, 2005.

Wittig, R. Das Spiel [Board Game]. Edition Perlhuhn, 1980.

_____. Wir Füttern die Kleinen Nilpferde [Board Game]. Edition Perlhuhn, 1983.

_____. Drachenlachen [Board Game]. Hexagames, 1984.

_____. Müller and Sohn [Board Game]. Franckh-Kosmos, 1986.

_____. Kula Kula [Board Game]. Blatz, 1993.

_____. Doctor Faust [Board Game]. Blatz, 1994.

Wolf, K.-M. "A Talk with Alex Randolph." Retrieved May 1, 2009, from http://brettboard.dk/lib/talks/alex1.htm, 1988.

Wolf, M. J. P. "Genre and the Video Game." In *The Medium of the Video Game*, edited by M. J. P. Wolf, 113–134. Austin: University of Texas Press, 2002.

Woods, S. "Playing with an Other: Ethics in the Magic Circle." Retrieved August 21, 2008, from http://cybertext.hum.jyu.fi/articles/90.pdf, 2007.

_____. "Last Man Standing: Risk and Elimination in Social Game Play." *Leonardo Electronic Almanac: Special Issue from perthDAC.* Retrieved August 21, 2009, from http://www.leonardo.info/LEA/PerthDAC/SWoods_LEA 160203.pdf, 2009.

Wrede, K.-J. Carcassonne [Board Game]. Hans im Glück, 2000.

_____. Carcassonne — Wirtshäuser und Kathedralen [Board Game Expansion]. Hans im Glück, 2002.

_____. Carcassonne — Händler and Baumeister [Board Game Expansion]. Hans im Glück, 2003a.

_____. The Ark of the Covenant [Board Game]. Inspiration Games, 2003b.

_____. Carcassonne — Burgfräulein und Drache [Board Game Expansion]. Hans im Glück, 2005.

_____. Carcassonne — Der Turm [Board Game Expansion]. Hans im Glück, 2006.

_____. Carcassonne [Video Game]. Sierra Online, 2007a.

_____. Carcassonne — Abtei und Bürgermeister [Board Game Expansion]. Hans im Glück, 2007b.

_____. Carcassonne — Graf, König und Konsorten [Board Game Expansion]. Hans im Glück, 2008.

Wrede, K.-J., and L. Colovini. Carcassonne: Neues Land [Board Game]. Hans im Glück, 2005.

Wrede, K.-J., and R. Knizia. Carcassonne: Die Burg [Board Game]. Hans im Glück, 2003.

Wu, J. Carcassonne: Fruit Trader [Board Game Expansion]. Web Published, 2005.

_____. Carcassonne: Treasure Hunt [Board Game Expansion]. Web Published, 2008.

Wujcik, E. Amber Diceless Role-Playing Game [Role-playing Game]. Phage Press, 1991.

Wundt, W. *Outlines of Psychology* (translated by C. H. Judd). Leipzig: Engelmann, 1902.

Xena: Warrior Princess CCG [Card Game]. Wizards of the Coast, 1998.

Yao, A. "Re: It Finally Happened. Someone Made Fun of Me for Playing Games." Retrieved May 9, 2009, from http://www.board gamegeek.com/article/2237594#2237594, 2008.

Young, C. "Return of the Heroes Rules Rewrite v1.0." Retrieved January 31, 2009, from http://boardgamegeek.com/file/info/28176, 2007.

Yu, B. Voltage [Card Game]. Mattel, 2006a.

_____. Desert Bazaar [Board Game]. Mattel, 2006b.

Yu, D. "2009 Interview with Tom Werneck." Retrieved August 3, 2011, from http://opinion

atedgamers.com/2011/06/20/dale-yu-2009-interview-with-tom-werneck-spiel-des-jah res-jury-member-part-1-of-3/, 2011a.

_____. "The Art of Design: Interviews with Game Designers #7 — Wolfgang Kramer." Retrieved August 3, 2011, from http://opinio natedgamers.com/2011/06/10/the-art-of-desi gn-interviews-to-game-designers-7-wolfga ng-kramer/, 2011b.

Zagal, J. P. "A Model to Support the Design of Multiplayer Games." *Presence* (2000): 448–462.

Zagal, J. P., J. Rick, J., and I. His. "Collaborative Games: Lessons Learned from Board Games."

*Simulation and Gaming* 37, no. 1 (2006): 24–40.

Zamborsky, S. "Re: The Caboose — a Couple of Questions," email to author, 2009.

_____. Cleopatra's Caboose [Board Game]. Z-Man Games, 2010.

Zappa, L. "Re: Mechanism Based Game Genres?" Retrieved February 9, 2009, from http://www.boardgamegeek.com/article/1491456#14 91456, 2007.

Zoch, K. Bausack [Board Game]. Zoch Verlag, 1987.

_____. Zicke Zacke Hühnerkacke [Board Game]. Zoch Verlag, 1998.

# Index